T0351559

Selected Letters

~ *of* ~

EDITH SITWELL

Edited by Richard Greene

VIRAGO

First published in Great Britain in 1997 by Virago Press
Published in paperback in 1998 by Virago Press
A print-on-demand edition published by Virago Press

A CIP catalogue record for this book
is available from the British Library.

ISBN 978-1-84408-508-8

Typeset in Goudy by M Rules
Printed and bound in Great Britain

Virago Press
An Imprint of
Little, Brown Book Group
100 Victoria Embankment
London EC4Y 0DY

A Member of the Hachette Livre Group of Companies

www.virago.co.uk

CONTENTS

INTRODUCTION

William Butler Yeats wrote in 1930 that when he had read Edith
Sitwell's *Gold Coast Customs*, he had felt that 'something absent from
all literature for a generation was back again, and in a form rare in the
literature of all generations, passion ennobled by intensity, by
endurance, by wisdom. We had it in one man once. He lies in St
Patrick's now under the greatest epitaph in history.'[1] Yeats's view of
Sitwell was by no means unique. In 1946, Stephen Spender characterised her later work as 'ripe and magnificent'.[2] In 1949, Katherine
Anne Porter found in her work 'the true flowering branch springing
fresh from the old, unkillable roots of English poetry, with the range,
variety, depth, fearlessness, the passion and elegance of great art'.[3] In
1957, Cyril Connolly wrote: 'When we come to compare the collected
poems of Dame Edith Sitwell with those of Yeats, or Mr. Eliot or
Professor Auden, it will be found that hers have the purest poetical
content of them all.'[4] In 1959, Marianne Moore wrote: 'Great in far
greater ways, Dame Edith Sitwell is a virtuoso of rhythm and accent.'[5]
At the time of Sitwell's death in 1964, Denise Levertov remarked:
'Perhaps no one has ever lived who had a more highly developed
understanding of the relation in poetry of meaning and aural values.'
And Allen Tate described her as 'one of the great poets of the twentieth century'.[6]

In 1995–96, an exhibition at the National Portrait Gallery of works
related to the Sitwell family was attended by over 30,000 people,
demonstrating that Edith and her brothers Osbert and Sacheverell
maintain a remarkable grasp on the public imagination. However, her
reputation as a poet has been subject to shifts in taste. Especially in the
1960s, some critics dismissed her work, yet, a generation later, her

poetry remains in print and is extensively represented in major anthologies. Her prose works are widely available and have been translated into many languages. She has been the subject of several biographies, and a substantial body of criticism of her writings now exists. It seems likely that she will continue to be seen as a major poet and one of the outstanding literary figures of her time.

Her letters occupy an important place in the canon of her writings. Whereas her finest poems deal with large ethical issues and achieve a remarkable breadth of vision, her letters are characterised by immediacy and particularity of concern. Her personal letters uncover the struggles of a sometimes agonised life, yet they are also the repository of an extraordinary comic sense and a trenchant wit, exercised upon hundreds of subjects, ranging from the vanities of a bemedalled Fascist general to the swooning of a lovesick macaw. In other respects, her letters communicate a solicitude for the griefs and privations of her friends, as well as a capacity for rage. Her letters to newspapers and journals, likewise, cover an array of topics, from the barking of dogs in Bayswater to disputes with reviewers such as Geoffrey Grigson. Her combativeness as a letter-writer found perhaps its most fitting application in the early days of the Second World War, when she was drawn into a propaganda exchange with Goebbels. Towards the end of her life, her letters provide an unsanitised but deeply poignant account of increasing disability and serious illness.

In 1970, John Lehmann and Derek Parker edited a volume of her selected letters.[7] Unfortunately, her younger brother, Sacheverell, forbade the inclusion of any family letters in the book. Since her career was inextricably bound up with those of her brothers, such a loss meant that the edition could not represent either her personal or professional lives in a satisfactory manner. Permission has now been granted by her literary estate for those letters to be published. While biographers have been allowed to refer to this material, it is brought forward in bulk for the first time in this volume.

Lehmann and Parker were further constrained by the necessity of making their selection from a very limited body of material. Derek Parker reports that with the exception of very short or repetitive letters, the whole correspondence available for their 70,000-word selection was perhaps '110,000 but not over 150,000 words'.[8] This difficulty was exacerbated by the need to cut letters that would have caused offence to persons then living. Letters now available in British, American, and Canadian libraries, as well as those in private hands, total not less than several million words. Hence it has been possible to assemble not only a more substantial selection, but one that is much more representative of her long career, her wide range of personal and professional connections, and of the complexity of her thoughts and personality. The passage of twenty-six years has also made it possible to publish her angrier letters without fear of litigation.

The Lehmann–Parker volume contains no letters before March 1919, by which time she was already thirty-one years old, and barely a tenth of the book is devoted to the years before 1930. This new selection opens in 1903, and gives consistent coverage from 1910. These early letters, most of which were unknown to her biographers, allow the reader to see her attempting to establish a personal life apart from her difficult and erratic parents, Sir George and Lady Ida Sitwell, to observe her reactions to her mother's conviction for fraud in 1915, and to follow her evolving alliances with her brothers as they entered the staid world of Georgian letters as flamboyant pioneers of modernism. Through the 1920s, it is possible to see her established as a poet and as a literary controversialist, seeking 'converts' to the writing of T. S. Eliot and Gertrude Stein, and, of course, seeking converts to her own writing and that of her brothers.

Lehmann and Parker were able to bring forward relatively few letters that Edith Sitwell wrote to other women. The material now available makes it possible to understand her relationships with artists, poets and writers such as Gertrude Stein, Virginia Woolf, Stella Bowen, Charlotte Franken Haldane, Hilda Doolittle ('H.D.'), Bryher (Winifred Ellermann), Rosamond Lehmann, Carson McCullers, Katherine Anne Porter, Marianne Moore, and Pamela Hansford Johnson. Sitwell occasionally expressed a general irritation with women, and was certainly jealous of her position as the leading woman poet in England. However, her letters show her to have been capable of great sympathy for other women writers and of enthusiasm for their work. In a number of letters she presses the formalist case for a poetry that is technically sound and concentrated; she maintains that women should avoid self-indulgence and write in 'as hard and glittering a manner as possible'

(Letter 214). While she cannot be described as an essentially feminist writer, her letters reveal a continuing concern about the role of the woman poet, particularly her own struggle to overcome 'timidity' and to speak with competence and authority.

It is generally assumed that collections of letters are what P. D. James calls 'epistolary autobiography'.[9] Sitwell's letters can be approached in this way, but only with caution. They do unfold the story of her life in her own words and have great documentary value, but her accounts of matters of fact cannot always be relied on, and sometimes are not meant to be. Her letters are replete with hilarious stories of bores and lunatics, such as the leper's mother whose daily communications supposedly prevented her from working for eight months (Letter 358). She assembles a huge cast of characters, including her parents, her maid Ethel, Gertie Waddyer (wife of the Parsee millionaire), Lady Fitzherbert, Caitlin Thomas, F. R. and Queenie Leavis, Billy McCann, Walter Reisch, Alice Hunt, and the old ladies at the Sesame Club. Stories about them often begin with some actual occurrence, but soon take on an outlandish life of their own. Although she wrote only one novel, her letters can be approached as a significant body of light fiction intended for an intimate readership. This aspect of her letters would be obscured if they were too readily assimilated to the genre of autobiography.

Her biographers have, of course, rightly observed her tendency to fantasise about the past, to exaggerate, embroider, and even invent episodes to support a view of herself which she believed to be the truth. She claims, for example, that when she was seventeen, her mother, craving whisky, sent her to pawn false teeth (Letter 232). She makes another claim, reiterated in her memoir *Taken Care Of*, that the painter Pavel Tchelitchew was once intent on killing her, but was interrupted by the arrival of Cecil Beaton at his studio and settled down instead to tea (Letter 382). Examples could be multiplied. She wished her correspondents to understand her as having been ill-used by her mother, little regarded by her father, and misunderstood by malicious critics. She wanted her loyalty and generosity recognised, her ill-health and poverty sympathised with, and her artistic accomplishments honoured.

At the centre of her epistolary narratives is a project of self-fashioning. Her letters illustrate, overwhelmingly, her lifelong battle to achieve a personal and literary identity in the face of misfortune, actual betrayal, and her own psychological fragility. Her studied eccentricities and her assumption of a haughty public persona were aspects of a struggle to define a meaningful life against the conventional standards of conduct for a woman born under the reign of Queen Victoria. For example, her adoption of Plantagenet garb can be seen as a direct riposte to prevailing notions of feminine beauty. She saw her appearance very much as a conscious creation: 'My face – awful though it may be – is the only one I have got, and is my copyright, as is Façade . . .' (Letter 320). She refused to study the arts of pleasing and saw the price of her freedom as permanent resistance. A reader cannot, however, avoid the judgement that she was often self-deceived and irrationally defensive. Yet a more submissive response to the personal and cultural pressures that bore upon her would probably have resulted in a life of greater anguish and less distinction.

She speaks of great art creating 'a perfect world, in which there is no sin, and in which sorrow is holy and not ugly' (Letter 136). Taken together, her letters, like her poetry, record a longing for a better self in a richer world, and this is probably the unifying theme among them. For all the bitterness expressed in her most unguarded letters, she maintains a constant desire for imaginative and spiritual transformation. Even in her worst moments she is never far from a belief in the possibilities of justice. At the core of her thinking, as expressed in Letter 204, is hope for ultimate renewal: 'I see the spring like that, – like Christ covered with the scarlet coloured blood of all the martyrs. What splendour. Nothing is lost.'

Texts and editorial procedures

Two collections have not been available for inclusion in this selection. Sitwell's letters to the painter Pavel Tchelitchew are embargoed at Yale University and those to Graham Greene are embargoed at Georgetown University. Nonetheless, both correspondences are represented in this book by letters that have been deposited in other libraries, or have already been published.

The letters in this volume are presented in chronological order. The original punctuation has been retained as far as possible, but adjusted where necessary. Except in a few instances where she herself queries a word, corrections of spelling have been made silently. Since she often begins new sentences at the margin, and indentations seem not always to be meaningful, it has been necessary to regularise paragraph division. Abridgements within letters are signalled by ellipses; postscripts have been omitted silently; and some addresses have been shortened. In some cases, words have remained indecipherable owing to Sitwell's use of what can best be described as the horizontal minim.

BIOGRAPHICAL NOTE

Edith Louisa Sitwell was born on 7 September 1887, daughter of the scholarly and eccentric Sir George Sitwell, who would have preferred a son. Her mother was the eighteen-year-old Lady Ida, daughter of the Earl of Londesborough and granddaughter of the Duke of Beaufort, a woman not ready for the task of bringing up a clever and provoking child.

Osbert, born in 1892, was the child his parents had really wanted, and he enjoyed the affection denied his sister. For Sir George, whose remarkable intelligence was, to a degree, squandered in the study of genealogy and antique curiosities, Osbert represented male issue and Edith a dynastic dead-end. Lady Ida was certainly more enthusiastic about her second child, possibly because his birth had brought her closer to the husband from whom she had fled on the second day of her marriage.

Sacheverell Sitwell, born in 1897, recalled his childhood with fondness, and it seems that the passage of ten years made both Sir George and Lady Ida more sympathetic parents, especially for a boy. Nonetheless, Lady Ida, apparently a heavy drinker, still devoted her days to socialising, while her husband gradually withdrew into scholarship, landscaping projects, and hypochondria.

Edith's early years were divided mainly between Renishaw Hall in Derbyshire and Scarborough, where Sir George's mother, Louisa Sitwell, widowed since 1862, made her home, as did the Londesboroughs. The family often travelled on the Continent, especially in Italy, and in 1909 Sir George purchased the dilapidated Castello di Montegufoni near Florence, where he spent most of the rest of his life engaged in an expensive restoration.

As a child, Edith read extensively and became an accomplished pianist, but she would later resent having been deprived of a classical education (see Letter 209). Helen Rootham, a translator and musician employed as her governess from 1903, introduced her to developments in contemporary music and to the poetry of the French symbolists, who would exercise a powerful influence on her own writing. Rootham became her closest friend and companion for the next thirty-five years.

Edith did not marry, and remained in a constricting relationship with her parents until she was in her mid-twenties. Despite her acquired skill of publicly slapping down reporters and reviewers, it seems that she had great difficulty managing conflict in her private life. Her surviving letters to her parents are unfailingly civil, so it is not clear that they were aware of the depth of the disaffection she expressed to Osbert: 'We are bound up as brother and sister much more than most brothers and sisters, on account of having had such a terrible childhood, and such an appalling home. I don't believe there is another family in England who have had parents like ours' (Letter 17).

In 1914, she made her escape. With Rootham, she took a shabby flat at Pembridge Mansions, Moscow Road, in Bayswater. Though she might have separated herself from her parents, family trouble was inescapable and no longer private. Lady Ida's personal extravagance and her generosity to friends had by 1911 left her about £2,000 in debt, a fact she concealed from her husband. She turned to Julian Field, a supposed financial expert but in fact a swindler and blackmailer; he arranged for promissory notes of hers to be discounted by money-lenders and kept almost all the money. Her liability would shortly balloon to over £12,000. From autumn 1913 she was embroiled in lawsuits, but Sir George decided not to settle out of court in the belief that Field, who was actually bankrupt, should bear responsibility. In March 1915, Lady Ida was convicted, with Field, of fraud against a woman who had backed some of the notes, and then served a brief sentence at Holloway prison.

By this time, Edith had already begun to publish poetry, and was establishing herself as a literary figure. Having learned the benefits of mutiny in her private life, she rebelled against literary fashion. She became the sworn enemy of late Georgianism and its chief proponent, the poet and critic John Squire. From 1916–21 she edited the controversial anthology *Wheels*, which carried works by the three Sitwells and other modernists such as Wilfred Owen, Aldous Huxley, and Wyndham Lewis.

Early in their careers, the Sitwell siblings presented a unified front to the literary world. Having formed a common cause against difficult parents, their reliance on one another was intense, and often obsessive. It can be claimed reasonably that Edith's encouragement made a poet of Sacheverell when he was still in his teens, and that in turn the grand style which he achieved in the 1930s was one of the decisive influences on the poetry which she wrote during the Second World War. Their collaboration, however, was at its closest in the early 1920s, when the composer William Walton, effectively a fourth sibling, undertook, at Osbert's and Sacheverell's suggestion, the project which became *Façade*, a jazz setting of rhythmic nonsense poems by Edith. Osbert and Sacheverell organised the first performances and came up with the memorable flourish of having Edith recite the poems through a megaphone from behind a painted curtain.

The marriage of Sacheverell to the Canadian Georgia Doble in 1925 marked, in a sense, the dissolution of the family firm. He left the house he had shared with Osbert in Carlyle Square, and by 1927 he was permanently settled at Weston Hall in Northamptonshire. Osbert, a homosexual, quietly resented his brother's defection to married life. He also came to dislike and distrust his sister-in-law. The brothers continued to support each other in literary matters and in their regular rows with Sir George, but their relations grew more distant.

In the late 1920s, Edith's own life came to focus on Paris. In 1927, Gertrude Stein introduced her to the Russian painter Pavel Tchelitchew, with whom she fell in love. Tchelitchew was a homosexual, and their relationship, though clearly passionate, remained, apparently, unconsummated. Through the 1930s she devoted an enormous effort to promoting his work and to the general welfare of his *ménage*. She had to compete for attention with his various lovers, especially Allen Tanner and Charles Henri Ford. Her services to Tchelitchew often met with ingratitude, though she stood by him with stubborn loyalty.

Edith's own poetry dried up in the 1930s. Of her earliest work, she had said 'I am going in for writing horrors' (Letter 15), but the Gothic element in her apprenticeship poems soon gave way to the surreal playfulness typified by *Façade*. There was also in her work of the 1920s another strain, which explores the isolation of a feminine consciousness, as in the sequence *The Sleeping Beauty* or one of her best-known pieces, 'Colonel Fantock', a fantasy based on her childhood at Renishaw. By the late 1920s, perhaps nudged by Sir Edmund Gosse, who urged her to be 'less funny and more human' (see Letters 83, 85, and notes), she was examining social and moral issues. In her *Gold Coast Customs*, she wrote of the upper classes in London cannibalising the poor, but beyond this stern satire she would reach an impasse, as she sought a more explicit approach in poetry to problems of pain, violence, poverty, and desire. Through the 1930s, she published almost no new poetry and saw her reputation decline, as fashion favoured W. H. Auden, Stephen Spender, and other poets of the political left, whom she then regarded with suspicion and contempt.

The 1930s were, generally, a difficult period for her. Her dealings with Tchelitchew remained frustrating and costly. Helen Rootham underwent various operations for cancer from 1928, and required constant nursing. In 1932, they gave up the Bayswater flat and moved to Paris, where they lived with Rootham's sister, Evelyn Wiel, who promptly became, like her ailing sister, a dependent of Edith's. Since she received little money from her father, Edith supported herself and her friends at this time by writing the successful popular biographies *Alexander Pope* (1930) and *Victoria of England* (1936), as well as *English Eccentrics* (1933), a comic masterpiece and probably her most enduring prose work. In 1934, she found herself in the midst of controversy, as her *Aspects of Modern Poetry* was judged by some reviewers to have plagiarised, among others, F. R. Leavis, whose opinions she always ridiculed. In 1937, she published her only novel, *I Live Under a Black Sun*, which combined a fantasy on the life of Jonathan Swift with a symbolic account of her relations with Tchelitchew. This unusual and haunting work found some admirers, but was not a commercial success.

Lady Ida Sitwell died in 1937. Edith did not attend the funeral, and appears to have been incapable of further grief on her account. At the same time, Helen Rootham was declining rapidly. Her death from spinal cancer in 1938 was one of the most harrowing events of Edith's life.

At the beginning of the Second World War, Edith returned to Britain reinvigorated as a poet. She had developed a more expansive rhetoric, and the playfulness of her early work had been succeeded by a moral and religious intensity. She spoke now in the persona of an aged maternal seer, acquainted with all the world's grief. Her best-known poem, 'Still Falls the Rain', represented the bombing raids as an assault on the body of Christ. The moral extremities of wartime, combined with the still raw experience of Rootham's death, had led her to redefine the centre of her poetry as the Christian mystery of redemption. From the early 1940s, many critics celebrated her as one of the leading poets of the time.

For most of the rest of her life, she lived with Osbert and his lover David Horner at Renishaw. She used the Sesame Club on Grosvenor Street as her London residence, regularly entertaining writers and artists there. She became close friends in 1940 with the historical novelist and shipping heiress Bryher (Winifred Ellerman), the lover of the imagist poet Hilda Doolittle ('H.D.'). Bryher was a fervent admirer of Edith's work, and gave her a house in Bath, as well as providing the money for projects and causes she espoused. Edith formed other important friendships at this time with Stephen Spender, John Lehmann, and Denton Welch.

In 1943, Sir George Sitwell died in Switzerland. He had taken refuge there with a cousin and her husband, who was a banker. His estate was discovered to be greatly depleted, and there was evidence that the banker, Bernard Woog, had swindled the old man. Edith even entertained the unfounded suspicion that Sir George had been murdered (see Letter 215). The episode drove a wedge between Osbert and Sacheverell, both of whom felt injured by the eventual settlement. Edith, who received little from the estate, was often caught between them, as they argued over money and Osbert's supposed failure to support Sacheverell's career (see, for example, Letters 270 and 282). By the 1960s, the brothers were nearly estranged.

The late 1940s brought Edith commercial success with *Fanfare for Elizabeth*, a biography, in 1946, and critical success with a group of poems on the atomic bomb, among them 'The Shadow of Cain', arguably her finest poem. In October 1948, she and Osbert set out on the first of a series of lecture and reading tours in the United States, where they were greeted by large and enthusiastic audiences. Privately, however, this journey caused her great pain. A reunion with Tchelitchew, whom she had not seen since before the war, went badly. He resented her celebrity, and by March it was clear that the intimacy between them was over (see Letters 264, 265, and 266). Although they resumed communication, the breach between them was never healed.

Another cause of grief entered her life in the summer of 1950, when a tremor in Osbert's arm was diagnosed as Parkinson's disease. He was then at the height of his own career, having completed *Left Hand, Right Hand!*, the five-volume autobiography that is his masterpiece. His condition, despite various treatments, continued to deteriorate. Within a few years, walking and even dressing became excruciating labours. Not only was Edith burdened by her brother's condition, she was permanently enraged by the attitude of David Horner, who seemed bored by Osbert's illness.

In 1951, Edith was engaged by Columbia Pictures to write a screenplay of *Fanfare for Elizabeth*. She worked on the project both at Renishaw and in Hollywood, but by spring 1954 it was clear that a script acceptable both to her and the studio could not be written, so the project was abandoned.

Through the 1950s, she continued to enjoy public acclaim. As honorary doctorates accumulated, she referred to herself for a time as 'Dr. Edith Sitwell, D.Litt., Litt.D, D.Litt.'. In 1954 she became Dame Edith Sitwell, a development that provided her with excellent ammunition against the 'pipsqueakery' – all the hostile reviewers with whom she had conducted a perpetual war. Throughout her career, she was extremely sensitive to negative criticism. Whereas Sacheverell, a remarkable but now neglected poet, retreated in the face of mixed reviews and published little poetry after 1936, she almost always chose to joust with her critics. In 1941, she, Osbert and the reluctant Sachie had even won a libel case against *Reynolds News* over an article that portrayed their work as *passé*. In the 1950s, however, the fashion that had favoured her work ebbed. Critics associated with 'The Movement' found fault with her grand rhetoric and recurrent imagery. In her last years, she fought her literary battles with desperate energy, unwittingly creating the conditions for a violent backlash against her work as soon as she was dead and could no longer defend it.

In 1955 she was received into the Roman Catholic Church. She had been an orthodox Christian throughout her life and remained so to the end, though she lost interest in liturgical matters. She was not a mystic, and her most intense religious perceptions were bound up with artistic or literary ones (see, for example, Letter 314). She understood theology in terms of artistic form, and discovered in the thought of St. Thomas Aquinas, with its emphasis on the religious intelligibility of the forms of the physical universe, a God who resembled a poet (see Letter 317).

Her last years were only a little comforted by her new religious commitment. Tchelitchew's death in April 1957 was followed in July by what she judged a disappointing response to her *Collected Poems*. Osbert was growing ever more enfeebled, and her domestic relations with David Horner were altogether poisonous. From 1959 to 1961 she suffered grave injuries from a series of falls, probably owing to excessive drinking, and was confined to a wheelchair. During this period she was able, nonetheless, to break new ground as a poet. *The Outcasts*, published in 1962, marked a recovery of the lightness of touch of her work from the 1920s without loss of the moral seriousness of her subsequent poetry. The same year also saw *The Queens and the Hive*, a biography of Elizabeth I and Mary Queen of Scots, become a best-seller.

In March 1963, she undertook a round-the-world voyage with her Australian secretary Elizabeth Salter, which ended in her suffering a haemorrhage and being flown home from Bermuda. She contracted pneumonia and nearly died during that summer. Her last literary project, the vigorous but embittered memoir, *Taken Care Of*, was completed in late 1964. She suffered a cerebral haemorrhage and died at St. Thomas's Hospital on 9 December 1964.

Selected Letters
~ *of* ~
# EDITH SITWELL

1903

In childhood, Edith Sitwell (ES) and her brothers often visited their paternal grandmother Louisa Lucy, Lady Sitwell, at Scarborough and at her country house in Surrey. One of five daughters of Colonel The Honorable Henry Hely-Hutchison of Weston, she had married Sir Reresby Sitwell, 3rd Baronet, but was widowed in 1862. She was left to raise two children, Florence Alice (1858–1930), known as 'Floss', and George Reresby (1860–1943), who succeeded as 4th Baronet at the age of two. A woman of enterprising piety, always concerned for the spiritual recovery of fallen women, she was otherwise shrewd and practical, especially about money. Although they would come to find amusement in her religiosity, she treated her grandchildren with respect and affection.

This letter alone has come to light from the period before 1910, and is one of the few to Lady Ida that have survived. It reflects apparently pleasant relations between the fifteen-year-old ES and her mother, although later she would describe her childhood as 'hell'.

1. To Lady Ida Sitwell

Gosden House
Bramley
Guildford

18 February 1903

Darling Mother,

I am afraid I haven't written to you for a couple of days, but I think Maum[1] gave you our messages. I wonder if you have heard from Father, and how he is. Grannie had a letter from Boysie[2] this morning, thanking her for the hamper. Maum has seen it, and says it is very funny. I daresay Grannie will show it to me later. We had such a lovely day yesterday, quite the loveliest we have had. Sachie came for a walk with us in the morning, and enjoyed it immensely, talking the whole time. He does love

going out with us. In the afternoon, I went for a drive with
Grannie and Auntie Floss; they were calling in Guildford.
Grannie is expecting some new Angelus music to-day. For the
last couple of evenings the music out of the drawer has been
played.

Sachie wants me to give you his very best love, and hopes
you are quite well, and says that we have been finding several
primroses. He also hopes that 'Mr. and Mrs. Audey Worgle' are
quite well.

With very best love,
ever your loving
'Dish'

1910

*As late as 1908, ES had prepared for a career as a concert pianist. Letters
2 and 4 to Roger Quilter (1877–1953), a then popular composer of songs
and stage musicals, reflect the convergence of her interests in music and
poetry. She offers him advice on his opera, apparently never performed,
based on a Chinese story in which the emperor Ming Huang was obliged to
have the Lady T'ai Chen strangled to prevent an uprising among his troops.*

2. To Roger Quilter

Ingleborough
Yorkshire

16 September 1910

Dear Mr. Quilter,

I don't know whether you will be horribly bored – but I have
been getting some information out of a cousin of mine who
knows a tremendous lot about everything Chinese, and I wondered whether it would be of any interest to you.

We have been talking a lot about *The Lute of Jade*,[1] and also about Lafcadio Hearn's[2] writings; and I got him onto the subject of the story of Ming-Y. He pointed out to me that the tragic event sung of in 'The Never-Ending Wrong', by Po Chü-I, took place in the lifetime of Sie-Tao. So do you think it possible that Sie-Tao and Ming-Y have sung about the Emperor Ming-Huang and the Lady T'ai Chên? The poets Tu-Fu and Li Po were also contemporaries of Sie-Tao, and perhaps loved her. Probably you know all this already.

When I get to London, I shall go and look at the early Chinese paintings at the British Museum; I am told they are very interesting. . . .

---

3. *To Sacheverell Sitwell*

Wood End
Scarborough

[*c.* 15 November 1910]

My darling Sachie,

Very many happy returns of your birthday, and bless you. I hope you will have a very happy day. Darling thing, it seems so strange that you are 13: it was such a little while ago that you were a fat, pink baby. You are nearly grown-up, my goodness. I am sending you a book of Dickens, which I hope will arrive in time.

I do wish Osbert wouldn't write Mother cross letters. At least, I think it would be better not. I am so terrified of Father turning round, and saying we are not to go to London at all. And after all, he *is* extravagant. I wouldn't say so for worlds, for you know I'm devoted to him, but he *is*. And we are all being punished for it more than he is, for I at any rate, will have to be here for two months! It is hard. . . .

1911

4. *To Roger Quilter*

Hinton Wood House
East Cliff
Bournemouth

16 May 1911

Dear Mr. Quilter,

Thank you so much for your letter. I was so delighted to hear about your opera; it is nice of you to tell me about it, and I am so glad you have started it. I think it will be such an effective beginning, the song which one will hear in semi-darkness, before the curtain is raised; and I love your idea of the crane flying homeward across the sunset; it is so Chinese, and quite charming.

About the introduction of Sie-Tao's name. If I were you, I would leave the beginning just as you have written it, I mean the part about Ming-Y not having long to live, and being friendless. But I should make it understood that he has come into the forest, with the idea of finding either Sie-Tao herself, or her tomb. I think it would give an excuse for explaining her, if you make Ming-Y lament that he should die before finding the tomb. Then, if I may really say what I think, I believe you would find it worked more easily if, after you have spoken of the golden city that stood where the forest now grows, you turned as much of the explanation as possible into a direct appeal to Sie-Tao, saying: 'Now, when all else has passed away, the fame of *your* beauty still lingers,' etc. I think it is a good way of letting the audience know about her, without making it obvious that that is what you are doing. And it would, I imagine, only mean changing a few words.

I am afraid these suggestions may not be of any help to you, but my reason is becoming unhinged. An invalid cousin of mine is staying here, and her one comfort is a concertina! She plays hymns on it all day, poor lamb, and sings in a weak voice, very out of tune, and I don't find it inspires me.

I have just been seized with an expression to describe the peach-blossoms; it is rather unmeaning, but I have never, from being a child, seen very delicate flowers, without thinking of it: 'like blown spray from the fountain of dreams'. I suppose peach-blossoms would be very faint-coloured by moon-light. What a bore it is that everyone reads Sappho, for how lovely it would be if you could use 'And round about, the breeze murmurs cool through apple-branches, and sleep flows down upon us in the rustling leaves.' One of the most divinely beautiful things in the world, and I think the feeling would be just right for your opera.

It must be very hard for you to keep the word-part subdued enough for music; it is a great temptation to over-elaborate. I envy you, having it to write, for it is a subject of endless possibilities.

If there is anything I can do, in the way of looking out things for you, please let me know, as I should be delighted. . . .

---

5. *To Osbert Sitwell*

Hinton Wood House
East Cliff
Bournemouth

[6 August 1911]

Darling old boy,

Thanks so much for your letter; I was glad to get it. Funnily enough, I was just sitting down to write to you, and say how delighted I am about the exam. I only heard you had passed last night. I didn't dare write and enquire, in case you hadn't passed, and it made things worse, asking. I *am* glad: it is splendid. You must have worked hard.

Auntie Puss[1] died suddenly early yesterday morning. It was a shock to Grannie and Auntie Georgie.[2] Father is being pompous, and coming home for the funeral. Poor Auntie Puss! But still, she was 84, which after all, is a great age. Of course, as you can well imagine, Auntie Floss had a field-day yesterday, with prayers, and tracts, and Bible readings. . . .

1912

6. *To Osbert Sitwell*

18 Langham Street
W.

13 February 1912

Darling Osbert,

Do you suppose I have been allowed to go in peace to Miss Rootham's?[1] – No, bless you! I was just standing at the door in my hat and new sealskin-rabbit coat of ravishing beauty, when a telegram was thrust into my hand: 'Father wants you to stay in home till Thursday, then come to Curzon.' I suppose that means Scarborough. I wish someone would heave half a brickbat at both of them. I *wish* I had given them measles.

Thank you so much for your letter, which cheered me up and made me laugh. I cried the whole of yesterday and all last night, and they had to give me things to soothe me. I love your quotation from Herbert-Spencer. I laughed till I nearly cried. I shall keep the letter, as it will make you a splendid story.

Do give me your advice. Shall I 'grow' some more hair?
Have you written and given Mr. King[2] my ultimatum?
Best love, my dear old boy,

Ever your loving sister
Edith

I haven't read all the Yeats plays you mention – only *Shadowy Waters*. I understand it and will try to explain it when we meet.

7. *To Sacheverell Sitwell*

Friday [1912]

My darling Sachie,

Thank you so much for your post-card: it is splendid, isn't it? I hope we shall have a good time. Do you know whether Osbert is in Italy³ or at his crammer's?⁴ Could you let me know? I should like to write to him.

Did I tell you that I sent Cox a telegram saying: 'Fly at once, the Bishop knows all.'⁵ But Auntie Floss discovered the plot, and warned the brute, and the telegram was prevented. I could have sworn. Auntie Floss has developed a sense of humour: it is such a blessing. She wasn't at all shocked about the telegram, but laughed like anything, and it was only that she was afraid Cox would go and worry Grannie, that made her prevent it.

Life is a Bore. It has rained unceasingly for four days. Auntie Georgie and Cousin Edda⁶ have arrived. Cousin Edda is the fine flower of Churchiness. Her smile is sadder and sweeter than ever, and the toe-caps of her elastic-sided boots simply flash in the sunlight. . . .

---

8. *To Sacheverell Sitwell*

60 Pont Street

Monday [n.d.]

My own darling Sachie,

I believe I shall get this off by 5.30 after all. I miss you most dreadfully. You don't know what a difference it makes to me when you are with me. You are always kind to me, and always loving, never cross, and always sympathetic, and it makes me happy being with you. I am telling you this because it is nice to know that people love one. Don't make yourself unhappy, darling. Better times will be coming, and all the plans may be

changed. One never knows. I shall think of you a lot. Try to
bear up, and remember we all miss you. Father will miss you too.
I will see that Mother gets the bit of paper. . . .

---

*Joan Wake (1884–1974), daughter of Sir Hereward Wake, 12th Baronet,
and a cousin of the Sitwells, claimed that ES had written her first complete
poem in January 1913 at her family's home, Courteenhall, in Northamptonshire. Although ES sent her her early work for criticism, they had little
contact in later life, when Wake distinguished herself as a local historian.*

9. *To Joan Wake*

14 Pitt Street
Kensington
W.

Thursday [n.d.]

My dear Joan,

I have been working at my ballad-thing, and think it is about
finished, so am sending it to you. I am in two minds about it.
Sometimes I think it absolutely contradictory, and awful dog-
gerel. At other moments it seems to me really rather good of its
kind, and for someone who has had only eighteen months experience of writing. But oh, I *do* hope it isn't ladylike. I wish you
would criticise it. There is a lot I want to ask you about it.
Could you come to tea on Tuesday. Come any time that suits
you, but the earlier the better. I am writing to ask Miss Fox.[7]
Will you be at Aunt Blanche's[8] on Sunday? I am going. Did you
get the other thing I sent you?

Best love,
Yours affectionately,
Edith

1913

10. *To Sir George Sitwell* (incomplete draft)

[1913]

Darling Father,

I am writing to you as you asked. You understand I was only able to be at Miss Fussell's for nine months in the year, at the price arranged. So the whole year would have worked out at £120 – plus extra food which we had to get in, and of course we only had one sitting room, with which one really cannot manage. We were led to understand beforehand that we could have the use of another sitting room when necessary, but that turned out to be a myth. There were several extras which now go into the housekeeping accounts, and these Helen will show you when we see you. We should have had to pay more if we had stayed the 2nd year, even if that had been possible. When Helen is able to pay exactly half of the entire expenditure, you will be paying about £20 a year more for me than you were doing at Miss Fussell's, and that is probably what we should have had to pay her if we had stopped. At present, as Helen has already told you, she is only able to pay for herself, to the exclusion of the servant. I don't think you will find that a heavy drain. We will see if we can find someone else like Miss Fussell, but if not, a flat is undoubtedly cheaper than rooms.

1914

Through 1913–14, ES and Helen Rootham were seeking to establish a res-idence in London more permanent than the boarding house run by Miss Fussell where they had been staying. ES decided to sell an inherited diamond pendant to pay for furnishings, but Coutts bank would not release it to her without her father's permission, which was slow in coming. By July 1914, nonetheless, they were settled in the Moscow Road flat that became their home for eighteen years.

11. *To Osbert Sitwell*

22 Pembridge Mansions
Moscow Road
Bayswater
W.

Thursday [*c*. May 1914]

Darling Osbert,

I forgot to say – *don't* tell the wife of the Red Death *or* the Red Death itself,[1] about the pendant, what I told you today. I don't want them to know. This *is* not the moment, this *is* not the atmosphere. Don't on any account let on, or I am lost.

Burn this letter.

The vases look heavenly; you were a darling to give them to me.

Today was great fun.

Very best love,
ever your loving
Edith

12. *To Lady Ida Sitwell* (fragment)

30 St. Petersburg Place
Bayswater
W.

20 May 1914

My darling Mother,

Thank you so much for your letter; you were a saint to do all this so quickly, and thank you ever so much. I shall be ever so glad if you will help me, as I want some money at once, and if Father will lend me some money, as soon as I get hold of the diamonds and sell them, I will pay him back. If you could get him to send me a cheque by return, it would be a blessing. You see I want to get some stuff for curtains, which Helen is going to make, so as to save expense. Do you think you could get him to lend me the money? Because you see, I can pay him back at once, the minute I get my diamonds. You were a darling to write me such a nice letter. I will be careful, as you say. I am writing to Father tonight.

---

13. *To Sir George Sitwell* (incomplete draft)

30 St. Petersburg Place

20 May [1914]

Darling Father,

I am so glad you are better, and able to come up to London on Monday. If you will very kindly lend me some money towards the furnishing, I will pay you back directly I have sold my diamond pendant, and I want to sell it as soon as possible. I shall be ever so grateful if you will lend me the money, as we want to get into the flat, and can't till we have got some furniture in. I am dodging the academy with great skill; I hear it is more awful than ever, and the only thing to excite one is when a suffragette gets loose.

14. *To Lady Ida Sitwell* (draft)

[*c*. May 1914]

My darling Mother,

Would you be a perfect angel and buck Father up to give me
that letter to take to Coutts bank to say I can have my diamond
pendant. After all, it won't really be any trouble for him. You
see I simply must have the money, and as he put it in under his
name without asking me, I am obliged to have a letter from
him, telling them they can open the parcel. Do be a saint and
let me know at once, because I am getting rather fussed. . . .

---

15. *To Joan Wake*

22 Pembridge Mansions
Moscow Road
Bayswater

Wednesday [n.d.]

My dear Joan,

I don't know where this will find you, so am sending it to
Emperor's Gate. I couldn't write yesterday, for your letter only
reached me last night when I was in bed. I will meet you on
Friday at 4.30 outside the Griffin, Temple Bar; it will be fun. I
am looking forward to it hugely.

Now for a good wrangle, and I will try and criticise the things
as though they were the work of someone else. I think you are
mostly right in theory, but I don't agree with you in one respect.
I think everything is permissible as long as one succeeds in
getting the effect one is out for. The reason why I curse at
Masefield[2] is because he doesn't always. Sometimes he does, and
then I like him. Gibson[3] invariably does; that makes him a poet.
I don't care what people write about, as long as they write
properly.

Now in 'The Drunkard', I simply set out to give an impression of horror; I think I have done that. It is also an experiment in rhythm; I have tried to get the beat of a terrified heart; also the drunken reel of the murderer. In judging it, remember, the man is dazed and stupid. Since sending it to you, I have added some more verses. I want you to like it, because I believe it is one of the best things I have done. 'The Fair' is rather bosh, on the whole, and in *that* I was *not* possessed by my subject. It is merely a study. I am going in for writing horrors, as it is obvious I do that better than anything else.

Best love, and I am so much looking forward to Friday,
ever your affectionate
Edith

P.S. I hope you will always say *just* what you think; I should hate it if you didn't.

---

16. *To Elkin Mathews*[4]

22 Pembridge Mansions
Moscow Road
Bayswater

6 July 1914

Sir,

I am intending at some time to have a small volume of verse published. I shall probably have it done in paper cover form, like Mr. Gibson's *Fires*. There will be about thirty pages. Would you kindly let me know about what the cost would be?

Yrs. faithfully
Edith Sitwell

ES's accomplice in the escape from her 'appalling home' to the independence of her own flat was, of course, Helen Rootham. ES, in time, assumed complete financial responsibility for her and her sister Evelyn Wiel as 'charges of honour and gratitude' (Letter 232). Nothing better illustrates ES's unusual sense of loyalty and obligation. After a lifetime of payments she became resentful (see Letter 345), but continued to meet the demands until the death of Wiel in 1963 (see Letter 386).

17. *To Osbert Sitwell*

[Envelope marked: '*To My brother Osbert Sitwell.* To be opened in the event of my decease *before 15th November 1918*.']

22 Pembridge Mansions
Moscow Road
Bayswater

28 July 1914

Darling Osbert,

This letter is being placed with my will, for you to read when I die. There are some things I should like to happen, and I think you will do them for my sake, if I should die before you. Do you remember the letter in *The Way of All Flesh* – well, this isn't that kind of letter.[5] It is because we are bound up as brother and sister much more than most brothers and sisters, on account of having had such a terrible childhood, and such an appalling home. I don't believe there is another family in England who have had parents like ours.

Well, if I should die, I leave Helen Rootham to your care; I know you will do what you can for her – because she has been so good to me – such a good friend to me, as you know. The £5000 which will one day be mine if I live till Sachie is of age (twenty-one) I have left to her. But if I die before that sum becomes mine – then Osbert, for my sake, I implore you to make her an allowance, that allowance that would have been mine. For my sake, give her, or see that she gets £200 a year. Otherwise, she is quite unprovided for, and it is too dreadful to contemplate. I think I shouldn't be able to rest in my grave. I know that if you have no money of your own, you cannot personally do this, but you are the eldest son, and the heir, and you *will* see that this is done. Of course, if I die when Sachie has attained his majority, the money is legally Helen's, with the exception of one small temporary legacy. All this will be found in my will.

To less important things. Please see to it that I am cremated. The other thing would be too like living with Father. And I think Father ought to defray the cost of my cremation.

This letter is for you only.

> Your loving sister
> Edith Louisa Sitwell

From 1913 to 1915 Lady Ida was embroiled in a series of lawsuits arising from her connection with Julian Field, a money-lender and blackmailer. She was convicted of fraud on 13 March 1915 for having induced a woman to guarantee a loan of £6,000, and was sentenced to three months in Holloway Prison. The events were humiliating to SS, who was still at Eton, and even more so to OS, as the evidence at the criminal trial included letters from Lady Ida to Field claiming that OS would assist them in getting fellow officers to back her notes.

18. *To Osbert Sitwell*

> Park House
> 21 Park Parade
> Harrogate

Thursday [1914]

My darling Osbert,

Just a line to ask how you are getting on. Please do write to me and tell me what you are doing. I do think things seem more cheerful, don't you, though we must have bad news. If only one thought those foul swine would get the worst of it. But they will, eventually, to a certainty.

Dear old boy, how I hope and pray you won't have to go.[6] I think I shall go mad if you do. Please write and tell me if you know when you will have to.

I am staying with Inez[7] once more.

Did you have an odious letter from Mother? She is drunk all the time now, and I think has really come to imagine that she has done the right thing and covered herself with glory. She says only middle-class people look down on her! I wish you would tell me what really has happened about Aunt G.[8] and Sir George S. as Mother is more than incoherent with 'emotion' and whisky. Oh, it's been a *lovely* summer.

Have you been having a splendid time with the Red Peril?

I have read *The Inferno*.[9] It is wonderful, the most awful study of on-coming madness one could think of, and the strange thing is, it is entirely a writer's madness. I mean no one but a writer or artist of some sort would find significance in such small things.

Do write to me, darling old boy. I want to know what you are doing. Write to me here.

Very best love,
ever your loving
Edith

---

19. *To Constance Lane*[10]

22 Pembridge Mansions
Moscow Road
Bayswater

[2 December 1914]

Dearest Constance,

Here is the poem I told you about, and I have also sent you a few small lyrics. I want badly to know what you think of 'The Mother'. I think it is horribly true – I am quite sure it is. Anyhow, it makes me quite ill, and if I try to read it aloud, I always cry, and so does everyone else.

I was so glad you came yesterday. Don't forget next Wednesday. I was so glad to see you, my dear.

Let's try and have some music together.

Best love,
ever your affectionate
Edith

1915

20. *To Sacheverell Sitwell*

22 Pembridge Mansions
Moscow Road
Bayswater

[12 March 1915]

My darling Sachie,

I know how painful all this is for you, but try not to worry too much about it, my poor old darling. A notice will be put in the paper after the case is over, that Osbert *never* did any of these foul things. I saw Osbert today, and he was quite calm, though naturally *awfully* upset, as I am, and as you must be. She is a *monster*. There is no other word for it. It is very sordid. My poor darling, I feel for you *very* much. Don't [worry] too much, my sweet old thing. Anything of this sort is so dreadful for anyone young like you. It is horrible that anyone young should have to bear what you have to bear.

Osbert is well again, and goes back to the front, I am afraid, on Sunday.

Best love, my precious,
ever your loving
Edith

I have ordered those 'poems' for you.

21. *To Sacheverell Sitwell*

22 Pembridge Mansions
Moscow Road
Bayswater

[19 May 1915]

My darling Sachie,

. . . Mother came out yesterday, and I went to see her at Aunt Millie's.[1] She seems absolutely unchanged; rather nervous, it is true, but she actually made jokes about the life in there. Of course, she is hardly believable, is she? However, Osbert says she is amiably disposed. Isn't it *heavenly*? Osbert has another *month* at Chelsea Barracks. It is such a load off one's mind.

Your beautiful Aunt Sybil[2] was at Aunt Millie's. I like her, though. Grannie[3] has left *everything*, money and emeralds, to Aunt Millie. No one else has got anything at all. Her ladyship hasn't got anything, no one has.

I must end; no more news. Do send me the poem, and criticism.

Very best love
ever your loving
Edith

22. *To Sacheverell Sitwell*

22 Pembridge Mansions
Moscow Road
W.

[9 December 1915]

My darling,

It seems I have properly 'got off' with the *Times Literary Supplement*, for they have returned to the charge (today), and have given me a long, and, it seems, extraordinarily enthusiastic notice.[4] Helen says she doesn't see how I could possibly have got a better one. I enclose it, (in separate envelope enclosed in this). I hope you got 'The Song of David',[5] also Gordon Bottomley's 2 volumes of *Chambers of Imagery*.[6] I think they contain very fine poems: 'Babel, the Gate of the God', and a good many others, are superb. Do let me know what you think of them.

I had a letter from Osbert yesterday, dated Sunday

Very best love, my darling
ever your loving
Edith

Helen's best love, too.

1916

23. *To Sacheverell Sitwell*

22 Pembridge Mansions
Moscow Road
W.

[6 January 1916]

My darling,

Thank you so much for your letter. I do *hope* you will come up to London on Monday. I do hope you will. Do write to me again. I am tremendously interested, hearing about your essay, and the idea of the origin of tragedy is certainly original. Have you ever read Nietzsche's book *The Birth of Tragedy*? It is marvellous. I think the phrase about the table and chair comedies of Bernard Shaw is excellent, and should certainly use it.

I hope the books have arrived.

Do either read to me or send me your essay when it is written; I shall insist.

I spent the morning with the Young-and-Pretty-Married-

Woman, with a skin-like-a-magnolia-flower-and-ah-such-an-
arrogant-mouse![1] So if this letter should prove dull, well, you
will understand why; for she has sucked my brains as your grandmother was taught to suck eggs, and the result is that vacuum
abhorred by nature. If the Y. and P.M.W. would only profit by
her powers of suction, I shouldn't mind, but she doesn't, all
being as it was in the beginning, with the exception of my
mind. And she has now taken to reading poetry, partly to dazzle
the Aged Peer,[2] and partly so as to lay down the law to me on
my own subject. She is always making discoveries; she has just
discovered quite a good new man called John Keats. No, Ediss,
you really should read him. . . .

I haven't heard from Osbert.

You don't tell me if Major Brockwell[3] is still with you. I do
hope you'll come up on Monday, my darling.

> Very best love
> ever your loving
> Edith

Helen's best love.

---

24. *To Sacheverell Sitwell*

> 22 Pembridge Mansions
> Moscow Road
> W.

[9 February 1916]

My darling old pet,

Thank you so much for your letter. I am so sorry you are so
sad, my poor darling thing. One can't really say anything; only
try not to be more sad than you can help. You will let us know
when your first whole holiday is, won't you, darling; so that
Helen and I can come down and see you. Won't it be lovely if
you come and live with us? We are longing for it to happen.

I heard from Osbert, two days ago, but he told me nothing – The enclosed ought to get Ginger in the eye; it is a very good notice, and I am delighted with it. Do you think Ginger will try and hire a bravado to knife the reviewer? . . .

---

25. *To Sacheverell Sitwell*

Please burn

22 Pembridge Mansions
Moscow Road
Bayswater

[3 March 1916]

My darling,

How are you? Do write; I haven't heard from you for ages. And tell me when you come up. I do hope they won't drag you down to Renishaw, but I bet they will.

My pet, I am so *very* sorry, I am afraid I shan't be able to come down to Renishaw this time. Because Helen can't get away; and both she and I realise that Ginger is in the sort of state that it would be most dangerous for me to go down alone. I don't see how I would ever get away again.

My darling, it *isn't* a lack of love for you. Only I *have* to think of the future, when you get away for good. It would be fatal if I once let them get a grip on me again. You *know* I love you.

For heaven's sake, burn this as soon as read.

I shall let you have books, so as to try and make the time as little awful for you as possible. Would you like Baudelaire's *Fleurs du Mal*? Let me know.

Very best love, my darling,
ever your loving
Edith

26. *To Richard Jennings*[4]

22 Pembridge Mansions
Moscow Road
W.

[June 1916]

Dear Mr. Jennings,

We are so disappointed that you will not be able to come tomorrow; I hope it will rain, and then perhaps you will not be able to go into the country, but will come here instead, and read Swinburne.

I am sending you our small book,[5] which has just arrived. Looking at the cover, I feel it is the sort of thing that would happen in our family. I do hope you'll like the book. If ever you have a moment, do tell me what you think of it. I am trembling with fright; I am sure that the poem called 'The Spider' will infuriate everyone. When I brought out my last book, an old lady said to me: she hoped I wouldn't mind, but would I tell her, was it *meant* to be *Poetry*?

I hardly dare ask you if you will once more save all our lives and avert the righteous fury of *The Times*. You have been so very kind to us, that it seems abominable to ask you. But if you can, and will, be so very kind again, I have a copy in reserve, if you would let me know.

Yours sincerely
Edith Sitwell

1917

27. *To Elkin Mathews*

22 Pembridge Mansions
Moscow Road
Bayswater W.2

7 January 1917

Dear Sir,

Thank you for your letter of the 3rd inst., but I do not want to pay for my book. I should be obliged if you would kindly return my manuscripts to me as soon as possible, as I have found a publisher for them;[1] and though he *has* accepted them, he naturally would like to see them at the earliest opportunity.

Believe me,
Yours faithfully
Edith Sitwell

I believe the copy of *Wheels*[2] belongs to Mr. Jennings.

---

28. *To Richard Jennings*

22 Pembridge Mansions
Moscow Road
W.2

Saturday [1917]

Dear Mr. Jennings,

Here is my little book, with my best wishes. I do hope you'll like it. If you are not too busy, do please write and criticise it. I am most awfully grateful to you for having tried to get Elkin Mathews to take it. I eventually, as you may have heard, scored off the gentleman, leaving him breathless with surprise.

I hope you had a nice time in the country, which I know some people enjoy, though personally I think it is a depraved taste. My parents, for instance, are perfectly happy posturing as lords of creation to an audience of cows. I am not.

Yours sincerely
Edith Sitwell

The new kitten has really written this letter – not me. At least she has guided the pen, which accounts for the curious calligraphy.

Siegfried Sassoon (1886–1967), poet and holder of the Military Cross, had protested against the continuation of the war in a letter that was eventually read out in the House of Commons. At the instigation of Robert Graves, who wished to protect him from military discipline, he was incarcerated at Craiglockhart War Hospital through the summer and autumn of 1917 for the treatment of shell-shock. He and ES developed a close friendship, punctuated by sharp disagreements, through the 1920s and early 1930s.

29. *To Siegfried Sassoon*

22 Mulberry Walk
King's Road
Chelsea
London, S.W.

30 August 1917

Dear Mr. Sassoon,

We have got your address from Mr. Ross,[3] as we wish to write and tell you with what great sympathy – and envy – we regard your courage. It is very difficult to write a letter like this without appearing very stilted and lacking in a sense of humour. I wonder if you see the papers and if you have seen Mr. Wells' correspondence, which seems also admirable?[4]

I expect all the old gentlemen are ever so pleased that you are a poet; it gives them the opportunity of jumping on two vices at the same time.

This is a round robin from myself and my two brothers, Osbert and Sacheverell. We send you our book[5] as a tribute.

Yours sincerely,
Edith Sitwell

30. *To Robert Baldwin Ross*

22 Pembridge Mansions
Moscow Road
W.2

[*c.* December 1917]

Dear Mr. Ross,

I am sending you *Wheels* in its 2nd. edition, from us all, and we are all most grateful for your kindness and encouragement. For really, we have had an awful time, especially Miss Tree[6] and myself. At the same time, we have had a lot of fun, and the 2nd. edition is working wonders; even the *Weekly Despatch* has climbed down – very inelegantly, as I think. We are hoping for another *Wheels* in October, and are working hard for this. I am very proud indeed of Sacheverell's new work, which seems quite extraordinary for a boy of nineteen. He has developed strangely in the last few months.

Yours sincerely
Edith Sitwell

1919

31. *To Robert Nichols*[1]

22 Pembridge Mansions
Moscow Road
London, W.2

26 February 1919

Dear Robert,

I was so delighted to get your letter, which arrived a couple of days ago, after an interminable Odyssey. I shall always like the Americans now, because they have taken you to their hearts – but then I knew you would take them by storm, for with all their faults they do recognise real vitality when they see it. You have probably done more to them than either you or they can guess yet, and this will bear fruit presently. Why, in heaven's name why, haven't they got a poetry of their own? Of the poets you mention (those among them whose work I know, at any rate), Lindsay[2] and Eliot[3] seem to me to be the only live writers. Perhaps you will galvanise the others; if any man could, it would be you.

As for the kind of women you mention – they should have been allowed to remain an organism with as much life as a sea-anemone. The trouble is, that these creatures realise that it is fashionable to be smeared with brain, and in consequence they lose their one point of usefulness. I have written a poem about this – vaguely about it, which I send you together with two more. I have destroyed all the poems I have written in the last three months except these three, as they were the product of anaemia.

The horror of Scarborough has, however, acted like electricity upon me. What a strange place – partly a clownish bright-coloured tragic hell, partly a flatness where streets crawl sluggishly, and one drop of rain (no more) drops on one's face half way down the street, and there are no inhabitants, or so it seems, but boys so indistinguishable in their worm-white faces that they have to wear coloured caps with initials that one may be known from another. Osbert didn't 'get in'. I suppose they found out he is a poet.[4]

Talking of poets, I went to a depressing evening where all the guests were female poets. Miss Klemantaski,[5] who is a very nice girl, got this up so that I might meet Charlotte Mew.[6] What a grey tragic woman – about sixty in point of age, and sucked dry of blood (though not of spirit) by poverty and an arachnoid mother. I tried to get her to come and see me, but she is a hermit, inhabited by a terrible bitterness, and though she was very nice to me, she wouldn't come. Besides her, I met an appalling woman called Madeleine Caron Rock,[7] extremely fat and exuding a glutinous hysteria from every pore. I sat beside her on the sofa, and became (much against both our wills) embedded in her exuberance like a very sharp battle-axe. Whenever anyone mentioned living, dying, eating, sleeping, or any other of the occurrences which beset us, Miss Rock would allow a gelatinous cube-like tear, still warm from her humanity, to fall upon my person, and would then leave the room in a marked manner. A moment afterwards, the flat would be shaken by a canine species of howling, and after an interval, Miss Rock would return and beg all our pardons with great insistency. She is rather a good poet, all the same . . .

In 1919 ES formed an alliance with Marguerite Bennett (1873–1960), a poetry reciter and wife of the novelist Arnold Bennett (1867–1931), to conduct readings and lectures in London. In 1920, she, ES and Rootham formally established the Anglo-French Poetry Society. After a period of pleasant collaboration, the organisation dissolved amid recriminations in 1922.

32. To Marguerite Bennett

Wednesday [1919]

My dear Mrs. Arnold Bennett,

Yesterday I got a letter asking me to give a lecture to a guild called the 'Lend a Hand Guild', at Lady Baring's house, 29 Cadogan Square on Thursday, March 17th at 3. I spent an exciting day hunting the young woman who had asked me, both on the telephone and at her club haunts, and did not find her, but this morning I succeeded in getting her on the telephone. I said I proposed to lecture on modern English poetry and the influence on it of modern French poetry, and that I was going to ask you if you would *most* kindly recite some French poems in illustration of the lecture. She was absolutely *thrilled*. *Please* do recite for me. It will make all the difference in the world; and not only that; I intend to speak about your club at the end of the lecture, and to take down the names and addresses of people interested. They are just the sort of people we want, they adore the idea of recitations; and it may mean another drawing room to make use of. Oh, I really am pleased about it. I don't see why we shouldn't get hold of several drawing rooms though it. . . .

33. *To Robert Nichols*

22 Pembridge Mansions
Moscow Road
London, W.2

Monday [October 1919]

Dear Robert,

Your letter and post-card have arrived, and I at once set to work to see about your being put up at Swan Walk.[8] That is alright, so all you have to do is to turn up there. All you have to do! Good heavens! Whether you can get up is another matter. One can only hope for the best.

I am awfully distressed about your going to Wales; but if it is going to produce another *Ardours and Endurances*,[9] it is worth it. You say you will not be patronised. But who short of an imbecile would dare patronise you? It is all very well, but let these young gentlemen turn out work on your level before they can even attempt to criticise you. *Of course* I know that it is pride and not conceit on your part. How can you help knowing your work is magnificent? It is too contemptible of people, and only jealousy of the basest kind, to cast such ridiculous aspersions. I have never heard you say a conceited thing. . . .

---

34. *To Susan Owen*[10]

Pembridge Mansions

3 November 1919

My dear Mrs. Owen,

All my thoughts are with you today, and will be tomorrow, unceasingly. If only one could express what one feels, ever. My heart aches for you. I am dumb when I think what not only you, his mother, but we all, have lost. I shall keep the 4th of November always, as long as I live, as a day of mourning.

I know you are broken-hearted, but oh, you are just the mother for such a son.

Tomorrow, his first poems in book form[11] will be with you – the immortality of his great soul. What a wonderful moment it will be for you, though an agony, too.

I cannot write more, because words are so little before the face of your loss and your grief. They sound too cold.

I shall write in a few days' time. God bless you.

All my reverence and all my thoughts,

Yours ever,
Edith Sitwell

1920

35. *To Arnold Bennett*

22 Pembridge Mansions
Moscow Road
W.2

[29 January 1920]

My dear Mr. Bennett,

I can't express how grateful I am to you for sending me the cutting from the *Manchester Guardian*. You really are too kind – and the kindness is all the greater because you are necessarily so busy. Nobody else would have thought of doing such a thing.

I am feeling rather happy, because my part of the debate has had really marvellous notices – we had a column report and a leading article in the *Morning Post* for instance – but none has pleased me so much as the cutting you sent me.

We did enjoy your coming here the other evening, and both hope very much that you are feeling better.

Again thank you very much.

Yours ever
Edith Sitwell

36. *To Marguerite Bennett*

22 Pembridge Mansions
Moscow Road
W.2

Tuesday [May 1920]

My dear Mrs. Bennett,

I do hope you will see your way clear to joining Helen
Rootham and me in this plan. It would be such a great thing
if you would. Please do, if you can possibly. I am longing to
hear you recite again. If you do give this recital, *please* do
recite 'La Vie Antérieure'. I shall never forget hearing you
recite it. (But then, there is so much one longs to ask for.) I
think that nobody who has not heard you recite, can know
how great a poet Baudelaire is. I do hope your cold was better
before you went to Nottingham, and that you are quite well
again now.

With kindest regards, and my homage,

Yours very sincerely
Edith Sitwell

37. *To William Kean Seymour*[1]

Wood End
Scarborough

22 December 1920

Dear Mr. Kean Seymour,

I was so disappointed I was unable to come to the 'Voices'
meeting; it would have interested me enormously, and I should
have been particularly interested in hearing you read your satire;
but alas, as you will see from the address, it was impossible. Do
ask me to another one, will you? I shall be returning to London
in about three weeks from now.

I hope you and Mrs. Kean Seymour will have a happy

Christmas. I believe, if only people would drop Christmas
for a year or two, one might start a new idea of it (rather
Botticellian, or Palestrina-ish), which would make it tolerable.
If *only* the Church hadn't turned holly into a kind of red face!
When you think how Keats wrote about it, it does seem such a
shame . . .

My brother Sacheverell is very ill with influenza; the last five
days have been a nightmare. But he is better now, and going on
well, so we are beginning to breathe again.

Before this worry, I had just started discovering, indeed *had*
discovered, a new field in poetry; and was developing it hard.

With all good wishes to you both, believe me,

Yours very sincerely
Edith Sitwell

I have become a member of the Tomorrow Club.

1921

38. *To (Leonard?) Moore*[1]

Private

Renishaw Hall

3 August 1921

Dear Mr. Moore,

I received the enclosed letter from Messrs. Parsons today. I
don't quite understand the remark about their readers. I rather
understood at the time of signing the contract, that we were
bound on both sides for *two* years publication of *Wheels*. Of
course, the reference to their readers may be a pure matter of form
(I can't remember if they did the same last year); but I should be
glad if you would, *without* mentioning the matter to Messrs.
Parsons, refer to the contract and see how the matter stands.

If they are *not* bound to us for this year, I do not wish the book to be refused, so its withdrawal must come from our side, and in *that* case perhaps you would kindly find us another publisher.[2]

Yours sincerely
Edith Sitwell

This is my address for the next few weeks.

---

39. *To Marguerite Bennett*

Renishaw Hall

13 August 1921

My dear Marguerite,

We are staying here at our home till the 2nd of September, and we should so love it if you and Mr. Bennett would come and stay with us – any date till the 2nd that suits you. Please do try and come. You don't know what a pleasure it would be to us. This is a lovely house (and what a perfect place to hear you recite in: it is absolutely made for Samain's 'Silence'); we have got rid of the ghosts; since Helen's encounter with them, we've not heard a sound or seen anything of them. *Do* come. . . .

By the by, do you know Lady Rothermere?[3] I have just met her, and have been to her house. She is the kind of woman who will be too useful for words. I'll ask her to our first meeting. She has an enormous studio, too. I feel very excited about it all.

I'm *longing* to hear you recite again. If only you can come here, it will be too lovely. . . .

1922

40. *To Marguerite Bennett*

22 Pembridge Mansions
Moscow Road
W.2

Monday 23rd January [1922]

Dear Marguerite,

As it was you who first suggested that Mademoiselle Gabain[1] should recite, I took it for granted that you had explained to her that the poems for recitation were chosen by the Managing Committee, and that in case of any difference of opinion between the Members of the Committee, it was *I*, as the poet on the Committee, who had the casting vote. If you remember, that was one of the first rules of the Society. Consequently, when Mademoiselle Gabain, instead of merely stating that she did not feel equal to doing the poems chosen, wrote a long letter criticising the merits of the poems in question (of which it is impossible that she should be such a good judge as I am) – and in a very impertinent way set her extremely amateur opinion against my expert one, and suggested that she could choose a better programme. I was naturally extremely angry, and she was very properly put in her place. When she started criticising the merits of the Rimbaud poems, she made herself doubly ridiculous, as it so happens that Helen is extremely well known in the literary world both in France and England, as the finest translator of Rimbaud there has yet been. Therefore the patronising letter Mademoiselle Gabain complains about was called down by her own impertinence and presumption. Mademoiselle Gabain has still got to make a name for herself, and she must wait until she has done so, before she is in a position to set her opinion up against that of experts. . . .

41. *To Marguerite Bennett*

> 22 Pembridge Mansions
> Moscow Road
> W.2

26 January 1922

Dear Marguerite,

I don't know why you thought you dared write such a letter about Helen to me. Your spiteful impertinence merely throws a most unpleasant light upon yourself. Conceit about any form of art is really the last thing that Helen can be accused of! As for her art, I do not choose to discuss Helen's art with you.

> Yours
> Edith Sitwell

In 1919, SS had gone up to Oxford briefly. There he met the young composer William Walton (1902–83), whom he persuaded to leave the university. Walton lived with SS and OS at Carlyle Square, at their expense, and worked on various projects, including, in 1921, Façade, a sequence of Edith's poems set to jazz music. The following letter to Brian Howard (1905–58), the pseudonymous Charles Orange, a poet and aesthete now best remembered as the model for Anthony Blanche in Brideshead Revisited, *describes the second public performance of* Façade, *which occurred at the house of Mrs. Robert Mathias, a patron of the Ballets Russes, on 7 February 1922.*

42. *To Brian Howard*

> 22 Pembridge Mansions
> Moscow Road
> W.2

[February 1922]

Dear Charles Orange,

The blame, let me tell you, is *yours* that I haven't answered sooner; you sent your letter to no. 17, whereas mine is no. 22! and moreover, no. 17 is inhabited by a woman who has gone insane, and who will have to leave the flats; but meanwhile she is being a great nuisance to me, keeps me awake all night, sometimes, and accuses [me] of burgling her flat. So please don't address a letter to me there again, as it makes her much worse. . . .

I wish you every success for *The Eton Candle*.[2] Will you let me know about subscribing? How splendid about the Swinburne.

It was not songs which were done at Mrs. Matthias', but I recited a great many of these and other of my own poems down a sort of megaphone, to the accompaniment of music by W. T. Walton (who will probably be the best composer we've ever had in England). Flute, trumpet, clarinet, cello, and drum. All done behind a huge curtain painted for me by Frank Dobson.[3] The audience was stunned.

All best wishes for your success.

Yours
Edith Sitwell

I'm writing to Mr. Acton,[4] the moment I have a second to do anything in. Will you hang up the enclosed notice in your room? As I want to sell these books quickly, before I produce my 'Bucolic Poems'. Come and see me when you are in London; and bring Mr. Acton. I lecture at Oxford on Wednesday, that is why I'm so rushed for time. I'll send Mr. Acton a book.

43. *To Marguerite Bennett*

22 Pembridge Mansions
Moscow Road
W.2

[21 April 1922]

Dear Marguerite,

I should like to choose the poet who is asked to read for the May meeting. So long as my name is on the Committee, I can't run the risk of the repetition of what happened in March.

For the meeting on the 28th, would you very kindly recite in the first half of the meeting, so that the second half is devoted to the poets' reading. Several members have asked if there could be this rearrangement of the usual procedure, for this particular meeting.

Yours
Edith Sitwell

---

44. *To Marie Adelaide Belloc Lowndes*[5]

22 Pembridge Mansions
Moscow Road
W.2

Tuesday [1922]

Dear Mrs. Belloc Lowndes,

Thank you so much for your kind letter. It is a great pleasure to me to think that you are going to have *Façade*. I enclose the two copies in different covers, as I have not an envelope large enough to contain the two.

I am so very sorry to hear you have been so unwell, and hope that you are really better now. I should love to come and have tea with you, and will ring you up and suggest a day when I return from Oxford, where I am going to lecture tomorrow.

Yours very sincerely
Edith Sitwell

---

45. *To Arnold Bennett*

22 Pembridge Mansions
Moscow Road
W.2

22 May 1922

Dear Mr. Arnold Bennett,

Mr. Hamar, the author of the enclosed play, has asked me to send it to you with the entreaty that if you have time, you will read it. He would be so very grateful; and so grateful too if you were kind enough to suggest something with regard to its future.[6]

I am sending this with considerable trepidation, so if you feel inclined to curse me, please don't!

Yours very sincerely
Edith Sitwell

---

46. *To Arnold Bennett*

Pembridge Mansions

14 November 1922

Dear Mr. Bennett,

I am about to send up a new collection of poems to any publisher who will be idiot enough to publish them. The collection consists of a good many new poems, as well as the whole of *Façade*, and all my poems which appeared in the 1920 and 1921 *Wheels*. I wonder whether you would do me the great honour of allowing me to dedicate this book to you? It would give me such great pleasure that I feel you will. I want to do it as an act of homage to your work, and in proof of my gratitude for your great kindness and encouragement. Please do let me.[7]

Helen and I both send our love.

> Yours very sincerely.
> Edith Sitwell

1923

ES's correspondence with John Freeman (1880–1929), a poet and winner of the Hawthornden Prize in 1920, illustrates her struggle to assert modernist poetics against the prevailing taste for bucolics. Freeman was a 'Georgian' poet and member of what the Sitwells called the 'Squirearchy', the literary circle of John Squire (1884–1958), whose outspoken antimodernism made him a favourite and not undeserving target of ES's harshest criticism. Freeman, a less abrasive figure, represented, on the other hand, a strain of civility and competence among more traditional poets. She was obliged in her letters to treat with respect what she saw as his genuine accomplishments, but still to make a case for Eliot and the modernist movement. At the same time as she was engaging widely in public debate, she is curiously diffident in these letters about her views on the nature and direction of literature.

47. *To John Freeman*

> 22 Pembridge Mansions
> Moscow Road
> W.2

26 April 1923

Dear Mr. Freeman,

Thank you so much for your letter. Miss Rootham and I are delighted that you will be able to come on the 8th of May.

I feel really distressed that you should feel incredulity when I speak of my great admiration for 'The Caliphs' . . . The proof of my admiration is that when it appeared in the *Spectator* I wrote Mrs. Williams Ellis[1] a letter praising its great beauty, and, when I dined with her about a fortnight later, I returned to the subject again.

My position is this: I have a very catholic taste in poetry, and can and do admire poems for very many different qualities. Sometimes, when I first see a poet's work I dislike it; this has happened with many poets for whose work I now feel a great respect; but in the long run, I am always won over by its qualities of music, beauty, and sincerity. When I first saw your work I distrusted it because you were in the company of people whose work I despise – Mr. Squire and Mr. Shanks[2] – but this distrust has now been displaced by a very real admiration and respect, and you rank in my mind among the very few modern poets whose work gives me unalloyed pleasure.

I write the kind of verse which I happen to write best, but I read and love many kinds of poetry. May I hope that you will give way to your impulse of kindness, the one you speak of in your letter? I, in my turn, will send you as hostage my new book, though I am afraid it may not give you pleasure. Yet it will give me pleasure to send it, because of my admiration for your poems. So I shall be egoistic in the matter.

Yours sincerely
Edith Sitwell

P.S. The fight between Mr. Noyes[3] and myself takes place on the same day as the party, May 8th, at 5.30, at the London School of Economics, Houghton Street, Aldwich, W.C. and tickets can be obtained from the Secretary at that address.

48. *To Louis Untermeyer*[4]

22 Pembridge Mansions
Moscow Road
W.2

[1 July 1923?]

Dear Mr. Untermeyer,

Your letter reached me too late for me to reply to your address in Paris. That was because it went to my brothers' house in Chelsea. It will be such a pleasure to meet you and Mrs. Untermeyer,[5] and to talk about poetry, and I am looking forward to it very much.

I should be delighted if you could both come and have tea with me here on Thursday, at 4.30, and I do so hope you will be able to come. Moscow Road is quite close to the Queen's Road (Bayswater) Underground and Tube stations, and this is on the even number staircase. I warn you of that fact, because otherwise people go right to the top of the wrong staircase – and there is no lift.

Hoping to see you and Mrs. Untermeyer on Thursday,

Cordially
Edith Sitwell

If not Thursday, would Saturday suit you?

---

49. *To Gerald Cumberland*[6]

22 Pembridge Mansions
Moscow Road
W.2

8 July 1923

Dear Mr. Cumberland,

I want to tell you how very grateful I am for your kind notice of *Façade* in *Vogue*. It gave me enormous pleasure to know that you liked it because I owe your poetry a great debt of gratitude. Your poem 'The Bathers' opened my eyes, when I was first trying to write, to every kind of new possibility. What a lovely poem! and how glad I am, after all these years, of the opportunity of expressing my gratitude to you for having written it.

You can understand why, having learnt so much from a poem of yours, I was particularly delighted to know that you liked *Façade*.

With many thanks,

Yours sincerely
Edith Sitwell

50. *To John Freeman*

22 Pembridge Mansions
Moscow Road
W.2

Friday [summer 1923]

Dear Mr. Freeman,

Thank you so much for your letter; I was very glad to get it.

Yes, Osbert and I were at the giving of the Hawthornden Prize; we got involved with Mr. Marsh[7] at a lunch party, and eventually found ourselves rushing off to the Aeolian Hall with him. But we were only there for ten minutes, as we found Mr. Chesterton[8] a little too heavy for this weather. Personally, I was rather disappointed at Mr. Garnett[9] getting the prize, as I do not like *Lady into Fox* (a book which I have not read!). That means that I do not like the name, or the people who *do* like it and recommend it. Also I had hoped that Bob Nichols would be the prize winner, for many reasons. Whatever anyone can say about *Fantastica*, nobody could justly deny Bob's great gifts, and that he does work hard. At least, I feel that.

Nothing much has been happening within my knowledge, excepting a little music, and the fact that some pigeons have decided to live in our coal-cellar, instead of in the nice cool stupid trees in Kensington Gardens. In this heat, I can read nothing, think of nothing, do nothing. Are you reduced to that state, also? Perhaps if one had an anthology of poems for the hot weather, one would be happier. If such an anthology existed, 'The Caliphs' would be one of the loveliest poems in the book. It would be a very small anthology, but 'Kubla Khan' would be in it, and 'The Eve of St. Agnes'. . . .

---

51. *To John Freeman*

Chez Madame Weil
129 Rue Saint-Dominique
Paris VIIe
Tuesday [n.d.]

Dear Mr. Freeman

I cannot thank you enough for sending me such a beautiful poem, one as lovely as 'The Caliphs', and with as exquisite and subtle a music. May I read it aloud next time I read poems anywhere? First, I shall learn it by heart, for one does not know a poem really until one has it clearly in the memory. Don't you find that, also? I want to give a reading soon.

Your description of the pantomime, and the book of the words, delighted me. I'm so glad you like pantomimes: so do I, and I can't forgive myself that I did not see Nellie Wallace[10] as the Widow Twankey in the Lyceum Pantomime two years ago. Have you ever seen Nellie Wallace? In her own way she is an extremely fine artist – one of the only fine artists on the English stage. She is an extraordinary mime, has great personality, and has the most significant appearance I've seen in an English actress. Everything acts: her cheeks (which she flaps as though they were being blown by a wind, when she cries), her hands, her feet, her body. She is very tragic, though she is a low-comedy actress: the epitome of starvation.

I've just seen the most marvellous clowns in the world, the

brothers Fratellini;[11] perhaps you saw them when they came to England, once. They weren't appreciated, though. If you remember, they are the clowns whom Cocteau engaged to play in Shakespeare, and great French painters are always painting and drawing them. One is very beautiful to look at, like a Watteau clown, and with the most marvellous clothes; one is like Mr. Trevor Bigham, (one of the chiefs at Scotland Yard) and has the same sober rather sad dignity; the third is like a very fantastic fish. They are extraordinary, and I saw them in a lovely shooting scene like something out of Stravinsky's 'Chansons Plaisantes'. There was a twittering of birds, the clowns shot into the air, and down tumbled showers of carrots and turnips and onions, and one very large fish – in fact everything countrified excepting a bird. But one can't describe it; it has to be seen. I hope and believe you would like them as much as I did. For I, also, never go the theatre, excepting to a Mozart opera, or certain Russian operas, or the Russian ballet. But music-halls delight me, and circuses still more. . . .

---

52. *To John Freeman*

22 Pembridge Mansions
Moscow Road
W.2

Friday [n.d.]

Dear Mr. Freeman,

. . . Thank you so much for your letter; only a bad headache prevented me from answering it before. I am glad you like the first poems in Sachie's book. I am very proud of them. He is a young creature still. What you say about the technical side of the longer poems interests me enormously. Unrhymed verse is so horribly difficult to write, with regard to the endings. I am nearly going mad myself at the moment, puzzling it all out, and I feel your remarks may help me a little, if anything can. But it is all very difficult. Perhaps unrhymed verse should not be written by women. But if so, it limits one very much. I do not and cannot agree with you about one thing; I do not see the slightest resemblance between Sachie's work and that of Mr. Conrad Aiken.[12] Sachie is so tremendously alive always, even at his quietest; and I do not feel even that Mr. Aiken's work is dead – in my belief it cannot be dead, because there was never any life there to die. . . .

1924

53. *To John Freeman*

Chez Madame Wiel
129 Rue Saint-Dominique
Paris

15 January 1924

Dear Mr. Freeman,

. . . It is such a disappointment to me that you do not like *The Waste Land*. In the first place, though I agree with you that a poem cannot exist without form, I find form in this poem. Is it not true, this passage from one of Coleridge's Lectures: 'The true ground of the mistake lies in the confounding mechanical regularity with organic form. The form is mechanic, when on any given material we impress a pre-determined form, not necessarily arising out of the properties of the material; – as when to a mass of wet clay we give whatever shape we wish it to retain when hardened. The organic form, on the other hand, is innate: it shapes, as it develops, itself from within, and the fullness of its development is one and the same with the perfection of its outward form. Such as the life is, such is the form.'[1] I find that organic form in all Tom Eliot's poems. But why should I say that, or quote that, to you, whose form is never mechanic, but always living. And anyhow, I can't argue.

Robert Graves[2] must meet you. He *must*. Because, apart from his pleasure at the meeting, he can argue, and I can't. And I do so want you to be converted to liking poems which at the present time you find antipathetic. Robert is obviously the person to do this, for he has enthusiasm and learning, and, I think (but I am not sure, for I did not know him then) was at one time unconverted himself. The meeting must be arranged, though at the moment the Graves family is invisible, as there is a new small son. They are both most charming people. . . .

---

54. *To Sydney Schiff* [3]

2 Carlyle Square
Chelsea S.W.3

12 March 1924

Dear Mr. Schiff,

I have just read *Prince Hempseed* [4] for the first time. I do hope you don't mind my writing to you about it, because I think it is such a fine book and I was deeply moved by it. It seems to me to be more alive psychologically than any novel by a living English writer that I have read, and one would have thought that even the impenetrable stupidity of the British public would have been pierced by the terrible sincerity and truth of this book. But I suppose you've had the usual kind of abuse.

I couldn't have believed, until I read *Prince Hempseed*, that any book about a child could be so interesting; but this goes beyond interest, and all I can say is, if the English people would read this book properly, they might become less brutish. It's an awful thing to think of poor sensitive bewildered children being driven into life like this, amidst such hopeless loneliness. I hope you don't mind my saying all this; but, you see, I do think the book is such a fine achievement that I can't help telling you so.

I wonder if Dr. Henry Head [5] has read it. He's always saying he wishes someone would write a really fine book about a child's psychology. . . . At least he said so on the few occasions when I have met him.

Please give Mrs. Schiff[6] my love,

and believe me
yours very sincerely
Edith Sitwell

---

55. *To Virginia Woolf*[7]

22 Pembridge Mansions
Moscow Road
W.2

Wednesday [1924?]

Dear Virginia,

I am so disappointed you can't come tomorrow. Of course I shall love to come to tea with you. May it be one day the week *after* next? It sounds ages off – but next week will be a dispiriting one, devoted to a bad but persistent sculptor, a niece of a friend of my mother's, and a reading at the Poetry Bookshop. Any day the week after would suit me beautifully.

I'm having such trouble with the lady who will write me letters about her chef. However, I've written her pages, with quotations, about the destructive qualities of the Wombat – one of the species has, apparently, prevented Melbourne from getting a drop of water for six weeks, and has also caused a landslide, by persisting in burrowing. I have said that will she let me have *at once* any information she may possess about the Wombat, and will she tell me also if an *ordinary* bat could or would do such a thing.

Yours ever
Edith Sitwell

56. *To John Freeman*

Grand Hotel des Bains
Locquirec
par Morlaix
Finistère
France

16 September 1924

Dear Mr. Freeman,

I should have written ages ago, but was not sure of the address in Finistère, so thought I would wait till I got here.

We were all so extremely disappointed you could not come and stay at Weston.[8] But at least you were spared the vilest weather in the world – rain every single day excepting one.

Thank you *ever* so much for your kind promise of *The Grove and Other Poems*. I need not tell you with what excitement I am looking forward to the arrival of the book. When will it be out? Very soon, I hope. Will it [be] out before my return from Paris in November? . . .

This is a delightful, fresh, bright-coloured, clear seaside country place, where everything tastes of the sea. Thank goodness, the weather is good, at last. Did you enjoy your stay in the country?

I have no news of any kind, excepting news of books. Robert Graves is bringing out a new book about poetry in the early spring,[9] and Sacheverell's new book of poems is almost ready.[10] I do believe and hope you will like those poems. It *isn't* sisterly pride, but that they are perfectly marvellous.

Such lovely books as we found in the library at Weston; we did wish you had been there! Wonderful books of travel, illustrated, of the 17th and 18th centuries – incredibly fantastic. Also lovely editions of Pope and Dryden (Dryden's family place is quite near Weston, by the way, within three miles), and there was also an extraordinary book about witches, *Sadducismus Triumphatus*[11] written by the chaplain to Charles the Second, Joseph Glanvill. Some of the stories had a queer mad sort of beauty, and I've been turning them into poems. There was also a vast collection of State Trials – including the trial of Guy Fawkes and also of Lady Essex for murdering Sir Thomas Overbury. Sachie is lucky to have had all this left him. All the time, we kept on wishing you were there. Apart from everything else, we should all have had such fun hunting for treasures in the library, for there are heaps of books put away, and we keep on finding fresh things.

We also had great fun with the country neighbours, who think we are raving mad. I caused a scandal by having no visiting cards!

With kindest regards
Yours very sincerely
Edith Sitwell

1925

57. *To John Freeman*

Chez Madame Wiel
129 Rue Saint-Dominique
Paris VIIe

17? January 1925

Dear Mr. Freeman,

I was so delighted to get your letter, and so delighted, too, to hear that *The Grove* will be out on the 25th. It is so very good of you to say you will send me a copy, and I am looking forward happily to reading the beautiful poems I have admired so much, in a more suitable setting than that in which they first appeared. And that reminds me, how strange it was to see that lovely poem 'The Dancers' in the midst of the limping pedestrian poems of which Mr. L. A. G. Strong's anthology is composed. It seemed to belong to a different dimension altogether; it does

live in a different dimension. I have been having a sharp battle
with Mr. Strong because he included such a gross attack on Tom
Eliot's *The Waste Land*.[1] I confess I was absolutely furious, and
charged Mr. Strong, head down, like a bull. But he is going to
behave well, and, I hope, apologise.

My own new book, *Troy Park*, has just gone to the printers.
That is why I have not written a letter; and I hope you will for-
give me. I do hope you will like at any rate some of the poems.
One of the very first copies shall be sent you.

It was very kind of you to praise Sachie's garden poems to a
reviewer. Do be converted to 'Actor Rehearsing'. I think it is
such a wonderful poem.

There was a very small party here the other evening, and I
have scarcely recovered from the horrors of it yet. The people
were all of different shapes mentally. In truth, some were of no
shape at all. There were several unfortunate Russian refugees
who have got the Bolsheviks well on their nerves and can't talk
about anything else, an American who thinks it chic to admire
the Bolsheviks, and did! Whilst the people from the Paris version of the Poetry Bookshop brought with them the young
pianist and composer George Antheil,[2] so much admired by Mr.
Ezra Pound[3] (who knows nothing about music). Mr. Antheil is
tiny and round and flat, and talking to him, as I remarked to
somebody else, is very much like talking to a shut oyster that is
being irritated by a pearl (probably a Tecla). I was assured by his
admirers that he plays so loudly and so fast, and his own music is
so difficult, that between the pieces he has to be carried out and
slapped with wet towels like a boxer, and rubbed, and given
smelling salts. I longed to ask if he wore boxing gloves, but
didn't dare.

I was so disappointed not to see you before I went away, but
am looking forward to seeing you in March; I shall be home
again then.

Yours very sincerely,
Edith Sitwell

This abrupt end to the letter is because the light has now faded, and the oil has not made its appearance for the lamps, so I can't see properly.

ES met the subject of this letter, the writer and patron of the arts Gertrude Stein (1974–1946), and her companion Alice B. Toklas (1877–1967) in Paris in 1924. Having written very cautiously of Stein's Geography and Plays in the Athenaeum and Nation in July 1923, she soon revised her opinion and undertook 'propaganda' work on Stein's behalf. ES attempted, unsuccessfully, to find a publisher for a bulky collection of Stein's short pieces, entitled Portraits and Prayers, and in 1926 she persuaded her to come to England for a lecture tour.

58. *To Violet Schiff*

Chez Madame Wiel
129 Rue Saint-Dominique
Paris VIIe

25 March 1925

My dear Violet,

I did appreciate your letter so much. It is so nice when one is ill – or indeed at all times – to know that people one likes are thinking of one. I am glad you miss me; I miss you very much too, and am looking forward tremendously to the end of April, when I shall be in London again, and shall see you, and we shall have long talks, I hope.

It was an unpleasant operation, but *not* internal, thank heavens; and now I am just beginning to wake up again, though I am incapable of any effort whatsoever. You said nothing in your letter of how you are. I do hope you are very well.

Just before I was taken ill, I saw a lot of Gertrude Stein, whose work I admire more and more. She tells me her novel *The Making of Americans* which is considerably longer than *Ulysses* will be published in September. Now I am trying to find a publisher for another book of hers, and think I have succeeded. She is an impressive oldish woman; her figure looks like that of a German haus-frau, or perhaps a head-mistress; but she has a superb face, with sensitive modelling. And she seems full of rich, earthy, Schumann-esque life, if you know what I mean. Yet in some ways she is very limited in her understanding. For instance about the war. Her attitude towards the war horrified me. She can't understand suffering; she is infinitely interested in subtleties of character. She is very dictatorial, and never listens to anything anybody else may say; she merely interrupts them in the middle of a sentence, says 'It isn't so, at all', or, 'It certainly is not for that reason', and takes matters into her own hands. But I like her. She lives surrounded by some of the most wonderful modern pictures I have ever seen – superb Picassos, as well as many pictures by Juan Gris, Matisse, etc. I think it was she and her brother who first found and helped Picasso. She is a most remarkable woman.

It is a horrible brown day like a railway terminus; I am so tired of it.

Do you remember a young man called Raymond Mortimer?[4] I hear he has got a new flat, the dining room of which is papered with old newspapers, the drawing room of which is decorated by Duncan Grant.[5] I have no patience, have you? Any amount of silliness leaves one undisturbed, but this craving for originality when coupled with such vacuity, is too much. . . .

---

59. *To Gertrude Stein*

as from Hotel Reina Victoria
Madrid

24 April 1925

Dear Miss Stein,

Thank you so much for your letter and the wonderful portrait,[6] which have followed me through Spain, and only reached me last night, on my return from Toledo. I read the portrait aloud at dinner to an audience of my two brothers, a young composer called William Walton, and a young painter called Richard Wyndham,[7] and, tired as we were, it exhilarated, stimulated, at the same time calmed our nerves to the extraordinary degree. The sound and rhythm seem to me, if I may say so, inevitability itself – but nobody but you would have found this inevitability. You can have no idea what a delight it is to me that you are going to include this in the book. I am waiting for the appearance of that book with the greatest impatience, and I do hope Duckworth's will take it, because it is a nice firm, and it will be such a feather in their cap.

We spent a fortnight drowsily at Granada. The gypsies made me think of your 'Sweet Tail'.[8] They are such beautiful people, and they made the pretty, frizzy young women at the hotel look so silly. Among the minor beauties, I loved the pink and white barracks, like a battle piece by Handel. You must, of course, know this well.

I am feeling sad, because, as plans are at present, I see no prospect of staying in Paris on my way back to London, and I did want to see you and Miss Toklas[9] again before the Autumn, when I am determined to be in Paris again. How I wish you were coming to London this summer; that is selfishness on my part; I wish it firstly because I should like to see you both and talk to you, and secondly because I have a longing to give an immense party in your honour.

This is a remarkably dull and stupid letter, but I am lying down, gasping for breath like a fish out of water. I don't feel quite strong yet, and, though I love my days, motoring and seeing everything reduces me to this state every evening.

Osbert and Sacheverell ask me to convey their homage; I send the same, and a thousand delighted thanks for the portrait.

With all best wishes to you and Miss Toklas.

Yours ever
Edith Sitwell

Georgia Doble (1905–80) was the daughter of the Canadian banker Arthur Doble. An elegant and fashionable young woman, she met SS in April 1924, and they were married in Paris on 12 October 1925. ES welcomed her to the family with great warmth, but their relations in later years were complicated by the disputes between OS and SS and what ES felt was Georgia's tendency to meddle.

60. *To Georgia (Doble) Sitwell*

22 Pembridge Mansions
Moscow Road
W.2

[24 July 1925]

Darling Georgia,

Come early tomorrow, won't you. I am *so* glad, dear, about this. It is lovely to think somebody is coming into the family whom one can care for, instead of somebody whom, quite possibly, one couldn't bear – which is what so often happens. Congratulations sound such cold things. 'I hope you will be very happy' is formal and silly. But we understand each other, you and I.

Best love, dear,
Always your most affectionate
Edith

61. *To Gertrude Stein*

22 Pembridge Mansions
Moscow Road
W.2

[September? 1925]

Dear Miss Stein,

I have been too crushed to write to you before – and too furious. I can't apologise to you sufficiently for my publisher being

such a fool. He wrote to me in a light-hearted, airy way, simply
saying that he had sent your book back !! *I had written him two
letters* about it, so I wash my hands of him. But all the same, I do
apologise. What can we do next? I shall be meeting Mrs. Woolf
tomorrow night, and will see if *she* shows signs of being of the
faintest use. I can't tell you what I feel about this. All I can say
is, I have had it myself for years, and the insults I have had to put
up with are getting worse and worse. But we will *not* give in.
Meanwhile I have got a long article about you coming out in
Vogue.[10] I have just finished it; I didn't want to do it while I was
ill, for fear of bungling it. Lecturing at Cambridge the other
evening, a man tried to 'take me on' about your work. 'What use
is it, if it takes so long to understand?' he enquired. 'It is of no use
at all,' I replied. 'Literature of great worth is never "of any use".'

I do wish you and Miss Toklas were coming over here this
summer. It would be so nice to have you in London.

I am sure I shall kill somebody soon – a reviewer, or possibly a
publisher. I am going to consult with Dorothy Todd,[11] who is
very sensible, about a publisher for you. Meanwhile, I should like
to do something drastic to the idiot who sent your book back.

With all best wishes to you and Miss Toklas.

Yours ever
Edith Sitwell

---

62. *To Sacheverell Sitwell*

22 Pembridge Mansions
Moscow Road
W.2

[10 September? 1925]

My darling,
Thank you ever so much for your letter. I *do* hope you will be
very happy, my darling boy and best and most lovely of poets.
You know how much I love you. And how deeply proud I am of
being your sister.

My darling, I am *so* miserable, but there is absolutely no possibility of my coming to your wedding. You know I would strain every nerve to do it, if it were possible. But it is utterly out of the question. On my birthday night, when I got back from dinner at Roderick's, I found a letter waiting for me from Coutts. They said I am £68 overdrawn, *beyond* the amount that has been *so* generously guaranteed; and would I please make arrangements to repay them this £68. I nearly had a fit, and scarcely slept at all for 2 nights. Now I have made arrangements with them, whereby they keep 3/4 of my dress allowance for six months, and allow me to repay the rest by my rebate next year. That means I can afford *no* railway journeys, no books, no new clothes, no taxis. I am in the worst financial crisis I've been in. . . .

Even if Father paid my fare (which he won't) and I stayed at the Castle, it would still be impossible, as I've got no clothes to come to your wedding in, and should have to buy at least two new pairs of shoes, and a new dressing gown – all of which is impossible. I shall think of you and Georgia every instant of the day, with the utmost love.

I am giving you and Georgia a really lovely gramophone as a wedding present when you return to England. Don't worry about that, my darling, because by that time my financial situation will have cleared itself up, and I shall be able to go on as usual. *Will you please tell Georgia about the gramophone* with my best love. Please don't forget, because I want her to know.

Very best love, my darling, and bless you.

Ever your loving
Edith

Poor Helen, I am delighted to say, has got two pupils, but every penny of that will have to go into the housekeeping. She has not got a winter coat; so that you can see that we are absolutely *obliged* to economise. I have let her in for this, and *can't*, out of decency, go and leave her to it, even if I had it. But *don't* worry, for we shall get through all right.

63. *To Georgia Sitwell*

Montegufoni

[16 October 1925]

Darling Georgia,

I think of you all the time, and love you. Darling, I do hope you will be happy with us. I know Sachie, who has an angelic character, will make you happy. I do hope we shall too. At least if affection goes for anything, you will be. For I really do care for you. As I said in my letter to Sachie, your nature is just as lovely as your appearance, and it would be beyond words if one didn't value you at your real worth. Trust me implicitly. You can, you know.

I am longing for the time when we shall be together again. Meanwhile, darling, I think of you all the time.

My very best love
Your loving sister
Edith

64. *To Sydney Schiff*

Montegufoni

19 October 1925

Dear Sydney,

(We were going to call each other by our Christian names, weren't we?) I am really writing to tell you that I sent a poem to *The Calendar*, as you asked me to (a long time ago, but this was the first poem I had), and they have refused it, and returned it to me with a correction in my spelling. I need hardly tell you what impertinence this treatment is to a writer of any standing, but I shall not write to the editor myself; I shall leave any necessary protest to you. Indeed, I only tell you this because I know you will be so vexed, and also because I think it is better to warn you in case you should ask other poets to contribute.

Sachie's wedding went off very well, and everybody seems happy. She is a charming girl. I think you and Violet met her for two minutes at my teaparty in the summer. But she arrived very late, so that she was not able to talk to anybody for long.

I am here with Osbert for another week, and then return to London, where I shall remain for the whole winter. It is so delightful to think I shall be seeing you both so soon.

This is a most lovely and romantic place, at once grandiose and peaceful, in spite of a warlike history, with huge walls, plants growing in them, gigantic coats of arms, and a 13th century tower. The only disadvantage is a constant incursion of tarantulas, scorpions, Mrs. Hwfa Williams, and Mrs. George Keppel,[12] these ancient and malevolent women are always here.

Please give my love to Violet. I wish you were both here.

> Yours very sincerely,
> Edith Sitwell

---

65. *To Sacheverell and Georgia Sitwell*

Montegufoni

[19 October 1925]

My darling Sachie and Georgia,

An awful thought has struck me – have you got any of my letters? I've written hundreds to you, but I thought Holland in Italian was 'Hollandia' and wrote this on the envelopes, and now find they drop their H's and it is 'Ollandia'.

Yesterday Mother told me (apropos of Julia leaving when it suits her) – that 'In future I shall think of myself. I shall be *selfish* in future. And see how people like that.' Today Mrs. Keppel is coming over to lunch with a party of monsters, and everybody is behaving as though she were Queen Alexandra. What muddled minds! I should think it will be intolerable.

One cutting (in a Canadian paper) about the wedding, says: 'The witty and beautiful daughter of the Earl of Londesborough

. . . from whom her children inherit their brains, has been the sensation of London more than once. She is a most keen ornithologist, and her collection of birds' eggs is one of the most famous in Europe! . . . Sir George Sitwell, besides being a soldier, is the author of that amusing brochure *Who Killed Cock Robin*.'[13]

Anyhow, it is most lovely weather, and I do wish you were both here – for my sake, not yours. I do think of you both so much, darlings, and long for the time we shall see each other again. I do *hope* you've got my letters.

Very best love
ever your loving
Edith

---

66. *To Gertrude Stein*

22 Pembridge Mansions
Moscow Road
W.2

1 November 1925

Dear Miss Stein,

You can imagine my delight on returning from Italy, to find *The Making of Americans* and your letter awaiting me. I cannot thank you enough; I feel it is the greatest privilege to have received this book from you yourself, and inscribed in your handwriting. It is one of my most valued possessions. Though I only arrived late last week, and have consequently only just begun the book, one feels its greatness and its rich life even in the first sentences. It will be monstrous if the book isn't treated properly. Of course it won't be. No work of this quality ever is.

I'm so glad you liked the article in *Vogue*. It ought to have been much better, but one is at a disadvantage in dealing with people who prefer to be treated as half-wits, which is, alas, the case with every English audience.

We are hoping to come to Paris again some time soon, but do not quite know when. I was there for two days only at the beginning of last month, marrying Sacheverell to a nice Canadian girl, and we wanted so *very* much to come and see you, but it was a Sunday, and the hotel people said a *petit bleu* was impossible, and, as there were several of us, and Sacheverell wouldn't let me out of his sight (it being the day before his wedding) we didn't like to come and take you by surprise. The following afternoon, Osbert and I left for Italy.

I wish there was some chance of you and Miss Toklas coming to England. Is there no hope of this?

I hope something will be done with the Hogarth Press and Virginia Woolf. I hear she is very ill, poor woman. I met her this summer, and liked her very much indeed.

Helen and I both send our very best wishes to you and Miss Toklas, and I send, also, most grateful and delighted thanks.

> Believe me
> yours ever
> Edith Sitwell

---

67. *To Georgia Sitwell*

> 22 Pembridge Mansions
> Moscow Road
> W.2

[16 December 1925]

My darling Georgia,

. . . Snow is on the ground. The air cuts the inside of one's nose and throat to atoms, Inez is in London (my principal bore), some kind of a Harmsworth[14] sneezed (very respectfully, it is true) in my face. Miss Ruby M. Ayres[15] says I am a Highbrow. Mr. de Vere Stacpoole[16] says (in a public speech) that I am an example of Sexual Unrest. Helen went away to lecture and came back suffering from diarrhoea and Sacred Glyphs and

Metaphysics. The *Sunday Express* has got hold of a photograph of me that I have never seen, and has published it. Judge Atherly Jones[17] says did I know William Morris, who died in 1881.

Enough of this.

Do write to me.

Very best love, darling, and all best wishes for Christmas
and the New Year,
ever your loving
Edith

---

68. *To Allanah Harper*[18]

22 Pembridge Mansions
Moscow Road
W.2

31 December 1925

Dear Miss Harper,

I am absolutely delighted with the article dealing with the three Sitwells. It is quite evident to me that you get every single implication contained in our work, and I'm more pleased with it than I can say. I don't think there is anything to question at all. You have presented the whole thing so clearly. How nice it is to have people understand one's work like this. If I may say so, I regret that you are mentioning Nancy Cunard,[19] because I think she can hardly be regarded as a serious poet. Her work at its best is a bad parody of Mr. Eliot, and at its worst is without shape and without meaning. It is rather a shame that a great poet like Mr. Eliot should have his work dogged by this kind of thing. But that doesn't take away my pleasure that you have understood our work so well, and cared for it so much. . . .

1926

69. *To Gertrude Stein*

22 Pembridge Mansions
Moscow Road
W.2

1 January 1926

Dear Miss Stein,

I should have written ages ago to thank you for your kind letter, but was laid up with a wretched form of influenza. First of all, I must tell you how bitterly disappointed I am – and the Cambridge people will be – that you are not able to accept this invitation. I wish very deeply that you had been able to do so, because I do feel that your actual presence in England would help the cause. It is quite undoubted that a personality does help to convince half-intelligent people. Would it not be possible for you to come over in the summer for a stay? I only wish this flat had more bedrooms in it, so that we could ask you to stay with us, but it is a small flat, with only the bedrooms into which we fit ourselves. I still live in hopes of giving a large party in your honour. If I work up Oxford, and University College, London, as well as Cambridge, to invite you to lecture, wouldn't you then reconsider your decision, and, perhaps, come to London sometime in the summer?

I am still working hard at propaganda. It is miserably disappointing, Virginia Woolf not taking the book . . . However . . . A great writer like yourself is absolutely bound to win through. There can't be any question about it. Meanwhile, of course one does hate the insults. People have now taken to insulting me publicly. A gentleman who writes bad novels, at a public dinner at which I was a guest, said in his speech, 'Modern literature suffers from sexual unrest, and Miss Edith Sitwell is a notable example of this!' So courteous! But it shows what one has to put up with.

I hope you are not allowing the trials, to which every pioneer is subjected, to prevent your doing a tremendous amount of work. And by the way, has Tom Eliot put your portrait of him in the *Criterion* yet?[1]

Alas, I don't see much chance at the moment of coming to Paris, because work, for one thing, keeps us here. We had been hoping to come, but apart from everything else, I have got a good many lectures coming on. In which, as you may imagine, I shall lose no chance of doing propaganda work for you. It is very disappointing about Paris; I had been hoping for long talks with you. And for this reason, I shall take the first opportunity I have for coming. But I don't know, quite, when that will be.

Do, if you can, reconsider this question of coming over here and helping in the invaluable way that only you can, with the propaganda.

Helen and I send you and Miss Toklas all our heartiest best wishes for the New Year. And may we soon meet again.

> Yours always
> Edith Sitwell

There are *many* fresh admirers.

---

70. *To Gertrude Stein*

> 22 Pembridge Mansions
> Moscow Road
> W.2

Wednesday [c. April 1926]

Dear Miss Stein,

I was so perfectly delighted to get your letter yesterday, and to know that everything is arranged. I hope you will have all the success you deserve – in fact, I know you will! There is great excitement in *all* quarters about your visit. I saw Mr. Elton from Cambridge a few days ago, and he was full of enthusiasm. Your reputation grows *every day* in England, and more and more converts are made. Of course, on some sides there is anger and rudeness, but that is only to be expected, but also to be enjoyed. After all, people don't break into furies about something which is dull [?], only about work which is full of real fire and contains elements of what appears as danger to safe comfortable people. Anyhow, your work is being discussed *everywhere*. I am looking forward to your visit more than I can say, and to the party. We suggest the date for that might be either the 1st or the 2nd of June. Will you tell me which suits you best?[2]

Helen Rootham and I do wish we were coming over to Paris for Easter, but alas it isn't possible. She is going away lecturing at that time, and I have to rehearse a young man who is doing a lot of poems of mine to orchestral accompaniment on April the 27th. I wish you and Miss Toklas were coming for more than a week or ten days; but that is better than nothing. I think your plan about the lectures is splendid, and it is far best for you to illustrate it at the end. *If* the Oxford lecture is in the afternoon, I shall come down with you, and return the same evening. I'm so glad you are going to read the portrait of me.

Reading over this letter, I can see I haven't given you any proper idea of the way in which things are progressing here. I really am astonished at the quickness, and feel most happy about it. I do hope you will feel contented with the progress that has been made.

Did I tell you that Tom Eliot has let me review *The Making of Americans* for the April *New Criterion*? It is not a long review, because the space doesn't permit of it, but as everything in the *New Criterion* is regarded as a newer and more important Apocalypse, I hope it will help. I needn't tell you the review is a most enthusiastic one. I'm doing a variation on part of 'Accents of Alsace'.[3] I hope you don't mind.

All best wishes from Helen Rootham and me to you and Miss Toklas, and we are looking forward with the greatest enthusiasm to June.

Yours ever
Edith Sitwell

I suggest the 1st or 2nd of June, because we do want to have the honour of introducing you before you go to Cambridge.

---

71. *To J. R. Ackerley*[4]

22 Pembridge Mansions
Moscow Road
W.2

26 May 1926

Dear Mr. Ackerley,

I hope you have not forgotten you are coming to a party here next Tuesday (the 1st) at 9 o'clock. Any 27, 127, 27A, or 27C bus would put you out at the Royal Oak, Westbourne Grove; and half way up Queen's Road, on the right hand side, you will find Moscow Road. This is *not* the rich Jewish red-brick block of flats, but the untidy, dingy, badly lighted block of flats just past the garage clock; and my name is on the board in the hall.

It will be nice to see you.

Yours sincerely
Edith Sitwell

Or the Queen's Road Underground and Tube stations are just round the corner.

---

72. *To Gertrude Stein*

22 Pembridge Mansions
Moscow Road
W.2

2nd July 1926

Dear Miss Stein,

Thank you so much for your very kind letter. Your visit here made us all very happy, for we did feel that you had a very real triumph, and this fresh piece of news about the Hogarth Press[5] seems to clinch it. How delighted I am about that. I must tell you (because it is so vastly to his credit) that a young man called Thomas Driberg,[6] whom you met at the party, a young man at Oxford, has been writing to Virginia Woolf ever since your lecture, clamouring that she should print it. Apparently there have been most enthusiastic notices in the Oxford press, but I have not seem them. Sachie, who is usually a most taciturn creature, still keeps breaking into delighted howls of laughter, apparently apropos of nothing; it always turns out that he is remembering what you did to the hecklers at Oxford. You won Sachie's and Osbert's hearts completely, but then you've won all our hearts. We are so glad you like us, because we like you with such enthusiasm, there is no other word for it. . . .

---

73. *To Violet Schiff*

Renishaw Hall

Bank Holiday [1926?]

Dear Violet,

I wanted to write to you such ages ago, but having been ill, I was sent down to the country (not this countryside, but Sachie's small house in Northamptonshire), and left your letter behind, like an idiot. So I couldn't write, because I didn't know the address. It was such a delight to hear from you. I hate this houseless condition of yours, because I feel it may keep you both abroad longer than is necessary, and deprive me of you. I miss you and our talks very much indeed, and shall hate the winter more than ever if you are not there. I do hope you are better, because if you are, it is worth while your being abroad.

I've been ill with heart trouble – why, I can't imagine, as it has always been quite strong, and so Sachie lent me his country house for a fortnight. I sat out on the verandah all day, reading and sleeping. I read a lot of Dryden, in a lovely first edition (Dryden was by birth a county neighbour, which accounts for

the library being full of his work) – Pope, the life of Alexander
the Great, of whom there is a portrait wearing a periwig, and
delightful eighteenth-century books about the moral worth of
animals, praising the industry of the Bee, reproving the Ostrich
for being a Bad Parent. There are a few lovely pictures in the
house – a Van Dyck portrait of Henrietta Maria, a Lely portrait
of Nell Gwynne, dressed as a shepherdess, in brown satin.

Here it is very different, and strange and beautiful, everything
has a remote air, like something in a legend. There are not such
beautiful pictures in the house, but there is the most lovely
tapestry I have ever seen, representing palaces with gardens full
of pools and fountains, with 1690 nymphs and queens and god-
desses wreathed with pearls and crowned with feathers walking,
sitting, and being mirrored in the water.

Do write to me soon.

With love to you both
always yours affectionately
Edith

74. *To Sacheverell Sitwell*

22 Pembridge Mansions
Moscow Road
W.2

[16 September 1926]

My darling Sachie,

Exalt the Eglantine has arrived, and is really too heavenly for
anything.[7] *What* a lovely book it is. It arrived late on Tuesday
night and I've done nothing but read it ever since, I need
scarcely say. The more one reads the poems, the lovelier they
become. I simply wouldn't know which to sáy I think are the
most heavenly of the lot. The variations of beauty are so keen,
and all the changes of sunlight and shade. They seem to me, as
usual, to be quite unlike anything else, excepting the actual

subject of the poems. The Hardwick ones are so strange and wild-wood, and haunted, and they are like nothing on this earth excepting Hardwick. Another poem which drives one wild is 'Black Shepherdess', and the lovely poem which begins 'Black ladies by the crystal water born', is another one of my special loves. But the whole book is intoxicating in its beauty and newness and strangeness. What a very great poet you are, my darling. I feel I shall never be able to tell you how violently proud I am of you, and how wonderful it is for me to be your sister. Just think of what fortune it is for me. 'Change in the Mirror', again, is a poem which drives me quite mad. The way it slips away at the end is so strange and beautiful.

But you know when I start talking about your poems, I become so garrulous. The book arrived just when I was feeling very depressed, and made all the difference in the world. After all, what does anything matter when one comes of a family which can produce poetry like that?

I'm sending this to Carlyle Square, because I don't know where you are, or rather will be, and if I send it to the Alexandra Hotel, they'd be sure to forget to give it to Georgia.

The whole book is a real triumph.

Meanwhile, I've just got your postcard. What is happening? Is Diaghileff being tiresome as well as some other people?[8] I'm longing to know what has happened? And I'm longing for you to get back to England. You're probably frightfully tired. Osbert has had a marvellous victory over the whole of the theatrical profession.[9]

> Very best love and congratulations, my darling,
>   Ever your loving
>   Edith

I've just heard you and Georgia are at Dieppe. Give her my very best love.

75. *To Sacheverell Sitwell*

22 Pembridge Mansions
Moscow Road
W.2

[26 October 1926]

My darling Sach

The more I read the book,[10] the more wonderful it seems to me. It is really a *great* book. Arthur[11] says, and I more than agree with him, that the passage about Pyramus and Thisbe will, in the future, be regarded as one of the greatest passages in English literature. As I say, I agree, but the whole book in its entirety is to me like some wonderful and unspeakably moving music. It excites one, moves one, intoxicates one, to an incredible degree. The worst is, it unfits one for daily life. To have to eat one's lunch in the middle of reading it is practically impossible. And I got, literally, *no* sleep after reading it, on Friday night. I *couldn't* sleep after it. This isn't talent – not even great talent – not even a great gift – it is genius. You know what my pride in you is. I am most terribly proud to be your sister.

Poor little Miss Lloyd; was there ever a delicate little ephemeral fly entombed in such amber as this![12] If she could know it, it might seem to her after all as though her hard life had been worth living. Indeed, it seems to make our childhood worth while; and it needed something fairly powerful to do that. The beauty of the book is something indescribable.

It is as important that you should write this prose as it is that you should write poetry. And you know what that means from me! I *couldn't* say anything more convincing.

Very best love to you both, and deepest pride in the book,
Ever your loving
Edith

Please tell darling Georgia how sweet I think it was of her to be so generous and lend Osbert and me her car. Not many people would be so kind.

The actor and playwright Noël Coward (1899–1973) had satirised the Sitwells in his play London Calling, *and after making peace with OS sent an apology to ES. For many years, she continued to regard him as an enemy and a buffoon. The two were, at last, reconciled in 1962 (see Letter 381).*

76. *To Noël Coward*

Pembridge Mansions

6 December 1926

Dear Mr. Coward,

I accept your apology.

Yours sincerely,
Edith Sitwell

---

77. *To Sacheverell Sitwell*

22 Pembridge Mansions
Moscow Road
W.2

[c. December 1926]

My darling Sachie,

I think the new Canto of *Doctor Donne and Gargantua*[13] too wonderful for words. There can be absolutely no doubt that it is one of your greatest poems – The huge scale, the amazing beauty, the strangeness of it all.

> 'Pompey is an arrogant high hollow fateful
> rider.'

Now *why* is that such a great and terrible line? It is one of those great lines of poetry whose greatness and beauty can't be defined, it comes from such mysterious distances. 'Stabbed Caesar and dead Pompey are ghosts in hollow porches' is another. But that is only to choose two lines out of a supreme and miraculous poem, a poem which ranks with the greatest poems in the English language. It is absolutely terrific, the whole poem. Who among these little poets is there even to crawl round your boot-buttons? There is nobody else to make a world like your world. . . .

Cecil Beaton (1904–80), the photographer and designer, achieved his early success largely on the strength of photographs of the Sitwells. ES, a lifelong friend, had her first sitting on 7 December 1926, and remained one of his favourite subjects.

78. *To Cecil Beaton*

22 Pembridge Mansions
Moscow Road
W.2

Thursday [n.d.]

Dear Mr. Beaton,

Thank you ever so much for the photographs; I am absolutely enchanted with them. What an extraordinary gift you have; really it is quite unbelievable. I'm most grateful to you for having given me these.

I do hope your influenza is better; I am so very sorry to hear how ill you have been. Are you coming to tea on Saturday? If so, I must tell you – otherwise you would never come to see me again – that this tea-party is designed to terrify Somebody who *will not leave me alone*. And if I design to terrify, I do terrify. It won't be me – the source of the terror, I mean. But the Mad Hatter's Teaparty simply won't be in it! I thought I'd warn you, otherwise you might not know it was only my fun!

Thank you ever so much again,
Yours sincerely
Edith Sitwell

1927

Stein introduced ES to one of her protégés, the Russian painter Pavel
Tchelitchew (1898–1957), in 1927. The two fell in love and embarked on
what Toklas called a 'long and violent affair', which, nonetheless, appears to
have been unconsummated. 'Pavlik' was homosexual and had various lovers,
notably the pianist Allen Tanner and, subsequently, the poet and novelist
Charles Henri Ford. ES, making the best of her disappointment, assumed the
role of patroness to the painter, and 'sybil' within the symbolic system of his art.

79. To Gertrude Stein

Chez Madame Wiel
129 Rue Saint-Dominique
Paris VIIe

Friday [1927]

My dear Gertrude,

By this time you will have received Helen's *petit bleu*, saying
how delighted I shall be to lunch with you and Alice on
Monday, and how disappointed she is that she cannot.

I rushed off to an early sitting this morning, after an entirely
sleepless night, so the *petit bleu* was a rather huddled and hurried
one. I am enjoying the sittings enormously. What a really
extraordinary artist! How right it is that it is always you who find
the artists who make a new world for one.

With love to you and Alice
Yours ever
Edith

I shall miss our talks so dreadfully, in England. I am going to
study forging your signature, so that I can forge it to a document
promising that you lecture in England for months at a time.

80. *To Cecil Beaton*

22 Pembridge Mansions
Moscow Road
W.2

[late February 1927]

Dear Mr. Beaton,

Thank you so much for your letter. Not a word have I heard from the elusive Widgey.[1] I'll pull myself together and write to him. I'm certainly not going to do it, unless you do the photographing part of it. Also, I *must* hear what the voice sounds like, because I hear a rumour that the sound is particularly unpleasant; and I don't want to go down to posterity as the owner of a voice like a steam-whistle.

If you aren't too busy, do come and have tea on Saturday. Madge Garland[2] and Dorothy Todd are coming, also Baba[3] and a few others, and, I hope and expect, Sacheverell, who wants to meet you very much.

I'm so glad you like the 'Heart and Hambone' so much. It will be appearing in a book in a fortnight's time,[4] and of course I shall send you a copy.

Yours sincerely
Edith Sitwell

We must do the film if it is at [all] possible.

---

81. *To Cecil Beaton*

22 Pembridge Mansions
Moscow Road
W.2

[March? 1927]

Dear Mr. Beaton,

I've just had a really strong silent letter from Mr. Widgey, saying he intends to fetch me in 'the motor' on *Monday* morning at 10.30! It is evidently going to be a real Wild West drama. I do *implore* you to be there, as I shall go mad if he films me without you, and, having resisted so far, I don't see how I am to resist again. So I do beg of you to come.

Mr. Widgey has now rescued a gentleman who was being eaten by a bear in the studio – and this gives him such an unfair advantage! I long to ask him about it, and if one does, one will be lost, as one would be forced to commend him for bravery, and he would then be in such a position of vantage. *Do* come on Monday.

I do hope your mother is better.

> Yours very sincerely
> Edith Sitwell

---

82. *To Arthur Waugh*[5]

> 22 Pembridge Mansions
> Moscow Road
> W.2

21 March 1927

Dear Mr. Waugh,

I am most grateful to you for your exceedingly kind notice of my new poems,[6] and for your most valuable elucidation, which will help me a great deal with the public, coming from a critic of your eminence. What you say about my method exactly explains the reasons for that method, and I cannot thank you enough for grasping those reasons, and for making my readers grasp them.

I always remember with great pleasure one of the most delightful evenings I have ever spent, talking to you at Sir Edmund[7] and Lady Gosse's house.

Believe me, with most grateful thanks,

> Yours sincerely
> Edith Sitwell

You ask, not without reason, if a certain embarrassment was caused by the investigations into our family history. We never stop blushing!

---

83. *To Sir Edmund Gosse*

22 Pembridge Mansions
Moscow Road
W.2

28 March 1927

Dear Sir Edmund,

If I were to try to express my sense of what your review means to my career, I should have to write a letter of such a length that it would really be an intrusion on your time. I have given years of hard work and study to my art, and I think that my greatest reward came when I read your most beautiful, kindly, and wise appreciation of that fact in the *Sunday Times* yesterday. It has raised a real bulwark of defence for me against foolish detractors and malicious enemies; and what is equally valuable to me as an artist is your counsel at the end.

My very great gratitude to you can best be expressed by working, and working hard, at eradicating those faults which you have most wisely pointed out.

This is a most inadequate letter of gratitude, but perhaps in my next book you will see the fruit of your counsels, which is perhaps the best sign of gratitude.

I do thank you most gratefully

Yours very sincerely
Edith Sitwell

84. *To Gertrude Stein*

22 Pembridge Mansions
Moscow Road
W.2

25 April 1927

My dear Gertrude,

You can imagine my delight at receiving *An Elucidation* in print. As you know, I have it in typescript, and it has been *most* valuable to me in lecturing, etc. And now I am so happy to have it in printed form. Thank you so much for sending it to me. Your reputation grows every day, it seems to me. It is such a happiness to me to see this happening, under our eyes, as it were.

By the way, I'm having my own new book sent to you from the publishers. It contains a Variation on a theme from 'Accents in Alsace'. I do *hope* you will like it.

One of my greatest friends, Alvaro Guevara, has come with his mother, to live in Paris. He is a painter, and also writer, of real genius, not one of these dear little intellectuals. It would be a great kindness to me, and a great kindness to him, if you would allow him to go and see you and Alice. And yours is such a fine atmosphere. It would be an awful thing if a man with a mind like his had to have it fretted away by the vulgar little clothes-moths that sit drinking and pretending to be geniuses in the cafés. His address is Hotel Windsor Étoile, 14 Rue Beaujon.

I shall see you, I hope, at the end of May, when I *trust* I shall be in Paris, though only for a day or two, to see Sachie's ballet.[8] Sachie now has a son, born on Good Friday.[9] He is too sweet for words, and just like Osbert to look at.

I do hope you and Alice are very well. I am longing to see you again. On Wednesday I go to Florence, travelling straight through. My address will be: Castello di Montegufoni, Montagnana, Val di Pesa, Firenze. Helen and I send you both our love.

Yours ever
Edith

85. *To Sir Edmund Gosse*

Chez Madame Wiel
129 Rue Saint-Dominique
Paris VIIe

11 October 1927

Dear Sir Edmund,

I have just been told that you have, with very great kindness, sent me a copy of *Leaves and Fruit*. My maid has not forwarded it (she believes that books are always lost in the post between London and Paris), but I have another copy, and I cannot thank you enough, both for your graciousness in sending me the book, which I shall value more than I can express, and for the very great honour you have done me in including your essay on my poetry.[10] It has helped me in every way, more than you can know. It has spurred me on to work hard, to eradicate certain faults, to greater courage, to stronger development. And it has helped me inexpressibly in stopping the persecutions which I have had to endure. I can never be grateful enough.

I am so delighted to hear from Osbert that you have now recovered from your serious illness. We all hope very much that you will take great care, and not catch influenza (which has started here already). I hope Lady Gosse received the letter I wrote from the country when you were ill. I wrote for Osbert as well as myself, because Osbert had cut his right hand most terribly, and isn't able to use it even now.

With very great gratitude
Yours very sincerely
Edith Sitwell

Please give my kindest regards to Lady Gosse. I hope you and she will allow me to come and call when I return, in a fortnight's time.

86. *To Cecil Beaton*

Chez Madame Wiel
129 Rue Saint-Dominique
Paris VIIe

[c. October 1927]

Dear Cecil,

Business first, and friendliness afterwards. Please will you send one of the photographs of myself lying in my tomb (*the one with the best hands*, as I'm always fussy on that point) to

Captain Siegfried Sassoon, M.C.
23 Campden Hill Square
W.8

and another ditto to

Miss Gertrude Stein
27 Rue de Fleurus
Paris

and send the lovely account to me. I haven't seen one of your lovely accounts yet, so please let me have it soon. And please do let them have the photographs soon.

How are you? I'm looking forward ever so much to seeing you as soon as I return on the 25th. Here (in France generally, I mean) life has been a mixture of ptomaine poisoning, writing poems, meeting Picasso, and rows with the natives on the subject of whether it is better to have legs like the trunk of an oak (like theirs), or the greyhound, race-horse touch which I prefer. Their rudeness was such that eventually I bought a toy camera and pretended to photograph their legs and feet. They fled for their lives, and I remained in possession of the field of battle.

I stayed near Royon, which is near Bordeaux. It is so hideous that it is beautiful. Very flat sands and sea; hotels full, I am sure, of travelling actors and out-of-work actor managers; villas made of children's toy-bricks (the Swiss kind) and called 'Mon Gout', and 'Mon Trésor', 'La Madeleine'; booths on the seashore with imitation mermaids, lovely shell-boxes, and wheezing marine music, and shooting galleries as bright as stars. And a garden, very small, a public garden, the kind of garden that ought to belong to and lead out of gas works; with large round beds full of yellow calceolarias, surrounded by meat-coloured and corpse-coloured begonias, fringed with pale sea-green, faded, dining room-ish leaves, and a plant like beetroot. And nobody in the garden but widows. Just flocks and flocks of widows. . . .

What a change of scene to meet Picasso. I met him at Gertrude Stein's, and as she is about his greatest friend the evening was a charming one. He is a delightful, kindly, friendly, simple, little man, and one would know him for a great man anywhere. At the moment, he was extremely excited and over-joyed because his mother-in-law had just died. Also he was looking forward to the funeral, because, according to Gertrude, all Spaniards prefer funerals to circuses any day. Gertrude is in fine form at the moment, and told me that the Bloomsburys are like the Young Men's Christian Association. 'Oh but Anti-Christian, surely,' I said to her, 'and anti-moral.' 'That's just it!' she replied. 'In America the Young Men's Christian Association is *always up to something!*'

Yours ever
Edith (S.)

---

87. *To Cecil Beaton*

22 Pembridge Mansions
Moscow Road
W.2

Saturday [n.d.]

My dear Cecil,

I really can't thank you enough for your *most* kind present of the absolutely superb photograph. It really is so extraordinarily kind of you – but then you always are so extraordinarily

nice to me. You are a wonderful artist, and I think this photograph is one of your masterpieces (though it *does* represent
me).

I returned home on Thursday, more dead than alive, after a
ghastly journey and crossing, and was in bed all day yesterday.
That is why I did not write yesterday. What day will you and
your sister come and have tea with me? Should it be next
Saturday, you would find Yeats, the Eliots perhaps, E. M.
Forster[11] perhaps. Anyway I am asking them, and Yeats says he
is coming.

Oh bother, he wants me to be a Rosicrucian. Such a strain,
and so bad for the clothes, as it seems to lead to sandals and
blue veils.

Ever so many thanks again
Yours ever
Edith

---

88. *To Lancelot Sieveking*[12]

22 Pembridge Mansions
Moscow Road
W.2

16 December 1927

Dear Mr. Sieveking,

I have seen the publisher's announcement of your book,
The Brighter Side of Birth Control; and I may tell you that I am
astounded that you have dared to try and put any representation
of me upon the cover of a book dealing with such a subject.[13]
It is indeed lucky that in its very nature, the grossly offensive
drawing precluded all possibility of its publication, otherwise, in
my ignorance of the subject matter of your book, I should have
been trapped into connection with this subject.

I have never heard of such a gross and filthy insult being
offered to any decent woman. And the fact that I am also a

distinguished artist only makes it worse of you and the other person who tried to perpetrate such an insult.

I have no more to say to you; you have no apology which you can make. Understand that from this moment I forget that you have ever been introduced to me.

Yours faithfully
Edith Sitwell

1928

89. *To the Editor of the* Daily Mail

22 Pembridge Mansions
Moscow Road
W.2

[published 17 February 1928]

Sir,

If something is not done soon to stop the unceasing barking of dogs in London several new pauper lunatics – myself and this entire household – will become chargeable to the rates.

I do not know what it is like in other districts, but Princes Square, Bayswater (on which my windows open) is under a reign of terror caused by a yapping dog which barks without ceasing, excepting for the purpose of snatching a hasty meal, all day and sometimes well into the night.

Apparently we have to stand anything, and any nuisance from any insignificant person who has no means of attracting attention, excepting by allowing his dog to make other people's work and rest impossible. We cannot even complain if a dog bites us, unless it has bitten us twice. 'How long, O Lord, Thy slaughtered saints . . .'[*sic*]

I know the dog is the friend of man (alas!). But do we want

other people's friends to sing outside our windows all day, especially if they have maddening and querulous voices?

Edith Sitwell

---

90. *To Georgia Sitwell*

22 Pembridge Mansions
Moscow Road
W.2

[*c*. February 1928]

My darling Georgia,

I am so delighted you and Sachie are coming up on Monday. Do both come and have tea either Monday or Tuesday. Longing to see you both, also to show you my portrait. Life has been perfectly impossible lately. The only amusing news is A that Aunt Albertina[1] says she is going to send me her poems – 'too personal for publication, *deeply* sarcastic' (I am sure they will be divine) and B a charming episode I had with a sergeant of police, who came to interview me Re my great Dog War. After about half an hour or so, he thawed, and began telling me interminable stories about dogs. I turned to Helen and said, 'You know Hardy's dog bit Galsworthy.' 'Ah,' said the sergeant, 'and I bet he bit him back! a sporting lot! Well, if neither bit the other twice, it didn't come within our province. The law takes no cognisance of it!'

Very best love to both
ever your loving
Edith

Helen's best love too.

---

91. *To Sacheverell Sitwell*

22 Pembridge Mansions
Moscow Road
W.2

[c. February 1928?]

My darling old boy,

I went to have a peep at Mrs. Powell,[2] and found her really wonderful, considering. Poor darling, of course she had had a terribly restless night, and the operation had been a great shock to her, but oh, what a comfort it is that it is over. I hope Dr. Child's[3] telegram arrived all right. I arranged with him that it should be *he* who telegraphed, because he would know what to say. No wonder I couldn't get on to anyone on the telephone on Monday afternoon. I had been told the operation was at 2, but it wasn't till five, and lasted till seven. Mrs Powell, who was talking, in spite of weakness, told me everyone had been angels to her, that Dr. Child was too kind for words, and that the sister is an angel. She has been so good and wonderful and so brave, really I can't tell you how brave she has been.

I am feeling so miserable because from my first letter you must have thought me heartlessness itself. But I *swear* that till I got on to Dr. Child I had not the remotest idea that the operation was anything but precautionary. I was told it had to be done because her size might lead the thing into becoming something else, and that it had to be done *in case* it should turn into anything. I don't know why I was told that, but I suppose for fear that I should show *her* any sign of knowing that it was that. Anyhow, thank God, it *can* be cured in that particular case. I have heard more cases than I can tell you, of people who have been absolutely cured. . . .

*In early 1928 Helen Rootham was diagnosed with cancer. A series of oper-
ations allowed her to survive another ten years, but her life and that of ES
were changed by the illness. She became a heavier financial burden and
often required extensive physical care. Always haughty and high-strung, she
became increasingly vituperative against her friend, whose success as a writer
she envied. ES found her agonies altogether pitiable, and complained little
about what she herself suffered on Rootham's account.*

92. *To Gertrude Stein*

22 Pembridge Mansions
Moscow Road
W.2

Thursday [c. February 1928]

My dear Gertrude,

I do hope that you and Alice are keeping well, and that you
are working hard. I am writing this partly to tell you that poor
Helen has had the operation I feared she might have (last
Friday, but with a local anaesthetic. She is laid up here, at the
flat) and that she *may* have to have another very serious operation. I hope to heaven it may be avoided, but I don't know. She
seems to me to be a very ill woman; but then, she never had any
stamina. About a week ago, I was really very shocked at her
weakness . . . Of course, it may be partly her natural state of
health. She doesn't like having the serious operation mentioned
to her. Of course, poor creature, she has had worry after worry,
shock after shock, during these last three or four years, so I am
not surprised she is ill. We have not told her sister in Paris, as it
would worry her so terribly.

Having told you the bad news, I will now change to happier
news. I have been having a lot of fun at lectures lately, and
think we have really got our feet on the neck of the British
Public at last. And having got our feet there, I do not hesitate
to kick. I gave a very successful lecture to the English
Association the other day, a large part of which was devoted to
your work – I say successful, because it, and other lectures, are

always followed by successful wrangles, in which I am developing a fiendish technique.

As for writing poetry, it is a little difficult, as half the time is spent in rushing up a narrow flight of stairs with a heavy tray, and the rest of the time is spent in careering madly to the Royal Free Hospital (it takes 1 hour and 30 minutes to get there and back) to see Osbert's housekeeper, a dear creature who has been with us all since we were children, and who has just had a terrible operation for cancer in the breast. To say that life is impossible at this moment would almost be paying it a compliment. . . .

I have discovered a new young poet with very great promise, Thomas Driberg. (He is an enormous admirer of yours, and met you at our party for you.) He hasn't yet learned to delete, or to be critical, but when he does, I have greater hopes for him than for any other young man of his age. (He is twenty-two.) Some of his lines seem to be the highest poetry, though his work is still very uneven. He has got so much more fire and originality than any other of these boys; if only he works, we really shall have something this time.

Just lately, we have been having the usual attacks, but of a character even vulgarer than before. One gentleman wrote in a newspaper that I appear at dinner parties at home dressed in pyjamas, and that I always look at the world through a monocle!!!! I must say that Father, who is not easily roused, was so infuriated by the pyjamas story that he flew off to a lawyer, but we were advised not to have the paper up for libel, as it would only give all the other papers an excuse to insult me.

Do forgive a rather muddled and very helter-skelter letter, but I am writing at three in the morning, that being the only time now that I can write letters without interruption. Do please, dear Gertrude, when it does not interrupt your work, write and tell me news of yourself and Alice.

> With love to you both from Helen and me,
> yours ever
> Edith

93. *To Gertrude Stein*

22 Pembridge Mansions
Moscow Road
W.2

Monday [*c.* February 1928]

Dearest Gertrude,

Only a very small line to tell you that the pathologist's report has come through about the gland that was taken away under Helen's arm. He says a change has taken place, and that there are signs of *malignant* trouble. So she is going to Paris one day this week to have the other lump taken out by Professor Hartmann. She is longing to see you and Alice, and it would comfort me more than I can say to know that you both have seen her. (As she will *not* allow me to go to Paris, because she says I fuss, and she *must* be quiet.) She will be writing to ask you both to come and see her, and tell you her address, when she gets there.

I am feeling too upset to write more, as you will understand.

Best love to you both
Yours ever
Edith

---

94. *To Gertrude Stein*

22 Pembridge Mansions
Moscow Road
W.2

Thursday [*c.* February 1928]

My dear Gertrude,

I was so grateful to you for your very kind letter, and so sad to hear of your loss. It has been a very sad year for you, and these bereavements cloud one for ever.[4] I feel for you and Alice so much.

I should have written before, but have been too harassed to do anything. Poor Helen had this dreadful operation last Saturday. When I heard last, she was going on well, but I have not heard for two days. Poor thing, she was really so wonderfully brave, and behaved as though it were nothing.

I do wish you and Alice were here, or I were where you are. It is four months since I saw you both, but I feel it is much longer. Our peaceful conversations seem a very long time ago now. . . .

---

95. *To Arthur Waugh*

22 Pembridge Mansions
Moscow Road
W.2

9 March 1928

Dear Mr. Waugh,

I do want to thank you again, however inadequately, for your great kindness in being my chairman yesterday. It made *such* a difference to me, having, as chairman, a critic for whose judgement I have so much respect, and one who has, as I remarked in my lecture, taught me so much. Thank you, too, for the charming things you said about my work, in your delightful speech.

I am writing to you under great difficulties, as my lovely Persian cat, who is almost as large as a sheep, has decided to sit on my lap.

I did enjoy lecturing last night; though I was terrified, yet your presence on the platform gave me confidence. I was so grateful to you for this, as well as for all the rest.

With my kindest remembrances to Mrs. Waugh and yourself.

Yours sincerely,
Edith Sitwell

96. *To E. M. Forster*

22 Pembridge Mansions
Moscow Road
W.2

30 March 1928

Dear Mr. Forster,

I can't tell you what a delight and happiness *The Eternal Moment* has been to me, and I can't ever thank you enough for your very great kindness in sending it to me. Even though I was undergoing the horrors of a bad attack of influenza, I realised what a wonderful book it is. Well, all I know is that 'The Machine Stops' made me feel as though I had come out of a dark tunnel in which I had always lived, into an immense open space, and were seeing things living for the first time. I believe it is the most tremendous short story of our generation. But then the whole book has got every quality of beauty and truth and illumination. I do think 'The Point of It' is such a wonderful story too, and 'The Eternal Moment' is enough to frighten one out of one's wits – but not to frighten one only. It is in a way, the most terrifying ghost story I have ever read.

The strange thing about all these stories is that every time one reads them, and I've read them all several times already, one finds fresh beauties in them. They seem to have an inexhaustible store.

How delightful it would be to see you again, when your are not too busy. Do suggest coming some time. I am always here, though I shall be taking poor Helen Rootham, who has just had to have a most terrible operation, into the country, for a week or two soon after Easter.

Yesterday, I underwent one of the greatest experiences in my life – at a 'Poets Reading' in aid of charity. The whole thing made one feel like a bird that has blundered into a room and is bumping its head against the ceiling in trying to get out. Bob Nichols read a whole Act (I suppose it was a whole Act, it certainly lasted for forty minutes) of his unpublished poetic drama

'Don Juan' with appropriate face and gesture, but not, thank heavens, appropriate action. At moments one did not know if one was in Church or in a Music-hall. But I expect Bob's 'Don Juan' will do a lot of good, morally speaking, for if those who lead harum-scarum lives have got to be such a bore as that, nobody is going to risk it. But I came home, and read 'The Point of It' again, and recovered my temper.

With so many very grateful thanks,
Yours sincerely
Edith Sitwell

ES, who had been contributing columns to the Daily Mail, *had been denounced in a letter to the editor (23 June 1928) as having 'an acid disposition and disagreeable mind'. ES responded in a column two days later that the letter-writer 'has taught me the value of birth control for the masses'. The newspaper was then inundated with letters, and the opinion of the playwright George Bernard Shaw (1856–1950) was sought. He observed that 'if a man hits Gene Tunney in the street he must put up with what he gets in return . . .' (30 June 1928).*

97. *To George Bernard Shaw*

22 Pembridge Mansions
Moscow Road
W.2

1 July 1928

Dear Mr. Shaw,

We telegraphed to you yesterday to express our gratitude for your most generous defence of us. But as I was the immediate cause of your having this most impertinent intrusion on your time, I feel I cannot let the occasion pass without writing to thank you as well as telegraphing. I think most people would have acted on their first impulse, and would have refused to tolerate that intrusion for even one moment; and your generosity and kindness in allowing this, so as to help us, is so great that it is difficult to express one's sense of these in properly measured terms.

I have suffered a good deal of persecution; but your action with the *Daily Mail* will quite undoubtedly change my position in the eyes of a very malicious section of the public. I should never trouble to answer these people, were it not that they render my life intolerable, and prevent me from earning money that I need, if I do not teach them their manners from time to time.

> With homage and most grateful thanks,
> Yours sincerely
> Edith Sitwell

---

98. *To Georgia Sitwell*

> 22 Pembridge Mansions
> Moscow Road
> London, W.2

Friday [n.d.]

My darling Georgia,

. . . I can't tell you what I am going through. 'They' are putting fresh tiles into the flat beneath, and doing it up. So they say. But I don't think it is that. I think they are doing a sound-film of the Battle of Verdun, accompanied by racing contests between traction engines and elephants. Massed choirs are singing the 'March of the Men of Harlech', and a whole nation of mice seems just to be nibbling through the wood work.

Avenge, O Lord, Thy slaughtered saints. What a life! What a *Life*! Also, every now and then, a Face is pressed against the window. Talk about Susanna and the Elders! It is usually the bathroom window.

I went to the Herbalists Association and had a long consulta-
tion, the other day. The shop was crowded with people, but I
got in first. 'I want a message of hope for my dewlaps,' I said.
'Yis, Modom.' So we had a long and helpful talk about my
dewlaps. Then I said to my assistant, suddenly, 'Do you realise
that God has only relented about my hands and my ankles, and
that if the joints in *them* enlarge, it will be the *River* for me?'
'Yis, Modom.' Then, after a pause, 'For *Craggy* joints, use . . .'
Craggy joints . . . Now *have* I craggy joints? . . .

----

99. *To Sacheverell Sitwell*

22 Pembridge Mansions
[*c.* 15 November 1928]

My darling Sachie,

Ever so many happy returns of your birthday, my darling. I do
hope you will get this in time, and so I am posting it directly
after lunch, in hopes.

How was Arthur, over the week-end? I am hoping to see him
on Saturday.

I now belong to the London Library, who are going to ask you
to give me a character, in writing (as one has to be nominated
by a subscriber). I went in there (speechless, as Inez bored my
voice away again last Tuesday, and I haven't been able to do
more than whisper since, sometimes not even that) and it was
like a family party. The old boys simply gambolled round me
when I said I was your sister. I wish you would tell me of some
things to read, as I am practically illiterate. . . .

Stella Bowen (1893–1947), an Australian artist, was for several years one of ES's closest confidantes. She lived with the novelist Ford Madox Ford from 1919 to 1928, and had one child by him. As a generous and trusted friend of Pavel Tchelitchew's, she became an ally in ES's relations with the painter, his family, and his lovers.

100. *To Stella Bowen*

22 Pembridge Mansions
Moscow Road
London, W.2

[5 December 1928]

Dear Stella Bowen,

I can't tell you how touched I was by your letter, or how happy it makes me to feel, at least, that you don't have that awful feeling of unsafety with me. A good deal of the sympathy that is forced on us when we are most unhappy, most raw, is merely a mask for impertinent curiosity. I suppose the same sort of people would have been present at all the public executions when they were a national spectacle. My sympathy for you is sympathy in the original meaning of the word; because, as a matter of fact, I think I do understand completely what you have been through and are going through. You will never find that I ask you impertinent questions, or that I pry, or speak when you want me to be silent. On the other hand, you can say anything to me without it hurting you. Because I see grief on a large scale, and not on a small scale, it can never mean any loss of pride on your part, if you show me that you are suffering. I only see you finer. . . .

I haven't got a shred of voice yet, and frankly am feeling wretchedly ill. It sounds odd, but that is why I want you to be so careful of yourself. You see, during the last 18 months, I've found out too many people in whom I believed. And that, together with overwork, sick-nursing, and being constantly insulted, has had this result. That is why *you* must be careful. You are a very brave woman, but that is just where your danger lies. As a matter of fact, lack of bravery is not one of my faults, either. So be careful. Bravery is a great trap, as well as asset.

Next week (on Tuesday) I have got to have strychnine (?) injected so as to bring back my voice for one day, dash to Edinburgh, lecture the same night, be the guest of the principal club there at lunch next day, return to London, and, two days after, open an immense Fair for the No-More-War Society – Then, I should think, die. The doctor is furious.

Remember, dear, you have not lost the battle. Because you really *have* got something out of life; and you have created yourself. You have your child, you have your beautiful nature, and your understanding – the last two are largely, though not entirely, brought to their perfection by what you have suffered. It has not been in vain.

My love to you,
yours always
Edith Sitwell

This is such a stupid letter. I will write you a less idiotic one in a few days.

---

101. *To Allanah Harper*

22 Pembridge Mansions
Moscow Road
W.2

Wednesday [c. 1928]

Dear Allanah,

. . . I'm in the middle of writing a lecture and thought perhaps these notes from it might interest you. This is what I've said:

'A great many of the poems by the most advanced school – those poems which appear strangest to us – deal with the growth of consciousness, or with consciousness awakening from sleep. Almost all my own poems are about this, or a great many, at any rate. Sometimes you find a consciousness that has been like that of a blind person, becoming aware – intensely aware – of the nature of a tree, or of a flower, or of the way in which rain hangs or falls from certain objects, for the first time, and, through that nature, guessing that there is a reason, a design, somewhere outside this present state of consciousness. This is what I've written about in the "Aubade". Sometimes you find a terrible groping animal consciousness, a consciousness which knows only the flowering and urge of its own hot blood and desires, and, through this, its relationship to other material aspects of the world. You find this in a poem called 'Dark Song' (*Bucolic Comedies*) where the dissonances which end the lines in the place of rhymes give the discontent of the subject – the groping for something without finding it. Sometimes again you get this animal consciousness knowing its own utter segregation and loneliness, cut off from the outer world by the lack of that higher consciousness which alone can bring us to those corre-spondences, as Swedenborg[5] has said, whereby man may speak with angels. You find this in 'The Bear' (*Troy Park*). This heavy lumbering rhythm, this queer half amusing outline and design and the laughable nature of the images, are full of purpose. The animal appears to man, not as a struggling half-awakened nature like his own, but as a blot of thick black darkness, as something whose queer antics raise his laughter, and at the same time, fear.'

. . . I've been having a lot of trouble with silly little Bloomsburys lately. They will think that it matters to me if they, and people like Desmond MacCarthy,[6] like my poetry. It doesn't. I don't *expect* them to. They've civilised all their instincts away. They don't any longer know the difference between one object and another, or one emotion and another. They've civilised their senses away, too. People who are purely 'intellec-tual' are an awful pest to artists. Gertrude Stein was telling me about Picasso, when he was a boy, nearly screaming with rage when the French version of the Bloomsburys were 'superior' to him. 'Yes, yes,' he said, 'your taste and intellect is so wonderful. *But who does the work*? Stupid, tasteless people like me!'

How irritating it is, though. In the 1890s 'superior' people discovered that ugliness is beauty. But the modern intellectual is a bigger fool than that, He has discovered that everything is ugly – including beauty.

Till tomorrow.

Love from
Edith

1929

102. *To Allanah Harper*

22 Pembridge Mansions
Moscow Road
W.2

[16 January 1929]

My dear Allanah,

. . . I can't tell you how grateful I am to you for what you are doing for my poetry on the continent. You have worked *so* hard for me, and with such sensitive understanding of what I am doing, and why. It is almost impossible for me to tell you with what gratitude I regard your work for me, and for poetry in general. I think I have never known anyone excepting the few poets who *are* poets, who has such an extraordinary love for and understanding of poetry as yourself. It is, really, quite extraordinary – not only very unusual, but extraordinary.

I am sending you a *proper* copy of my *Gold Coast Customs next week*, when the book appears. Meanwhile, I am sending you the *proofs* (which have been put into this awful cover by Siegfried Sassoon) – in case they are any use to you in the essay you are writing.

In the *Gold Coast Customs* poem itself, there are all sorts of queer technical devices that I have tried to get (though I do not need to point them out to *you*, I can't resist discussing them with you). For instance, on page 9, the 1¼ syllabled words 'rear' and 'tier' make you feel that the houses are toppling over. Then, on the same page, there is the difference between the deadness of the 'n' sound in 'grin' and 'skin' and the acerbity of the word 'strings' (of nerves)

> *'only the grin*
> *Is left, strings of nerves, and the drum-taut skin.'*

Of course, there are double rhymes over and over again, giving extra emphasis. On page 11 with the 'black gaps' and the 'ape' there is an empty separation between the 'black' and the 'gaps' owing to the assonance, and the 'ape' tightens the thing into a higher key because of the 'a' sound – hurriedly followed by the fresh tightening in 'chasing'. And on page 16 there is the complicated pattern of

> *'dead*
> *Grass creaks like a carrion-birds voice, rattles,*
> *Squeaks like a wooden shuttle, battles, etc.'*

The shuttle battle performance makes it tuneless, as I had meant it should be.

And on page 20 the last verse has got a sort of worm-like turning movement because of the assonances:

> *'The calico dummies*
> *Flap and meet:*
> *Calculate: 'Sally go*
> *Pick up a sailor.'*

And occasionally the lines lengthen themselves out, rear up, and come down with a crash on one's head, as in the first two verses on page 27, where the rhythm gets, imperceptibly, slower and more forceful.

The whole thing has been awfully interesting to do. . . .

Goodness, I had such a time yesterday. There has been a vulgar sordid murder of a man called Messiter, of whom I have never heard in my life. But the *Daily Express* had a huge front-page double-column, with the headlines 'Mystery Solved. Related to Sitwell family of poets'. They had routed out the fact

that my *fourth cousin* (whom I have seen twice in my life) married as his second wife a woman who is sister to the murdered
man's wife – from whom he had been separated for twenty years!
!!!!
They dragged out the whole of our family history – excepting
our scandal. I must say they omitted that. Really, I *do* think it is
an outrage. Reporters were on my doorstep all day, from the
Daily Express (which has had orders from its proprietor never to
mention us as artists, because of course, we are not artists, we
only write poetry to gain publicity!) I gave the reporter absolute
hell! I said: 'How *dare* you come here and interrupt my work to
ask me about this cock and bull story. You behave as though we
were trapeze artists, not serious artists. Go and ask Yeats, or
Shaw, or Davies, or Wells, or Bennett, the sort of artists we are!
But you won't do that! All you want to know is, if I've seen the
victim of some squalid murder.' They said: 'Have you got a photograph of Mr. Messiter, Miss Sitwell?' I enquired: 'Has your
editor got a photograph of *Cain?*' The reporter said: 'I don't
quite understand.' 'Don't you?' I asked. 'Then you shall! I am
the same relation to Mr. Messiter as your editor is to Cain, from
whom I understood he is descended, unless the Bible is wrong
and Darwin right, in which case he is descended from a
monkey!'

That shut them up. Then I said: 'You have come here to ask
me about something ugly; but I will show you something beautiful' (and I showed them Pavlik Tchelitchew's pictures). I
said, to the *Express* representative: 'You have dragged me into
this ugly scandal. In return, you shall please me by photographing these beautiful pictures, and speaking respectfully
of the great artist who painted them, in your paper.' And they
have sent round a photographer, so I am hoping they will do
what I ask.

Much love, dear Allanah (and the proper edition of *Gold Coast
Customs* will come in a few days) and *so* much gratitude from

Edith

103. *To Stella Bowen*

22 Pembridge Mansions
Moscow Road
W.2

[March? 1929]

My dear Stella,

I was so happy to hear from you this morning; for your letters do give me a real feeling of happiness, and security – a feeling of safety.

I am so very glad that you and Julie have escaped having influenza, so far. Please be very careful. I am always having to allow influenza patients to put their heads inside my mouth, and breathe. But this is to be avoided, if possible. So far, during the last fortnight, I've been nursing – or helping to nurse – my mother who was ill in Curzon Street, whilst spending much time at the house of my darling great aunt[1] who was dying in South Kensington, [and] at my brother's house where his soldier servant[2] is ill with pneumonia.

My great aunt, who was the one older member of my family whom I loved, has died. She was 86, nearly blind, and stone deaf. She was the most gallant old woman I ever knew, with dancing blue eyes, and upright figure and an extraordinary, brave voice. All young people were mad about her. And all young men used to regret openly that they did not know her when she was young, for they could not help being in love with her. She spent her life in tilting at windmills, rescuing the downtrodden, championing the oppressed, and fighting the battles of the young. Among other fights, she battled A. against war, B. for the freedom of the Irish, C. in aid of prisoners, and for penal reform. She also trod with a light fantastic toe on the face of the Archbishop of Canterbury, her cousin, and he was terrified to death of her. She also fought my battles with my father, and, preferring me to him, has not spoken to him for ten years. She told him to go to hell.

She has left me a third of her money.[3] It will bring me in (*when* I have paid for everything I mean to buy) about £50 a year more, which is a great deal to me. And, as I say, that will be *after* I've bought things. I tell you this so as to show that there is one less reason for us to worry, at this moment. You know what the first thing I shall do is, naturally? I shall buy a *most* imposing picture of Pavlik's for myself, and I shall give Osbert one, too. I do *hope* I shall get the money soon.

Now for business. Stella dear, I've got a horrible feeling at the back of my mind, that Pavlik is pinching himself and scraping so as to avoid touching that money. Stella, if he is in a bad way at this moment, will you not convey to him that he is to use that £25 of mine (and regard it as part payment of the first picture I am going to buy) for *himself*? And that I can and will lend him another £25 for Schoura[4] as soon as I get this money? – I fail in tact, and my French is bad, so I don't dare approach the subject, direct to him. But if there is any trouble, won't you tell him?

As soon as I get the money, too, Schoura shall have a really lovely present. Meanwhile, is there any flippant thing – a bottle of scent, or something useless and amusing like that, some little thing, which you think would amuse her? If so, will you tell me what you think she would like, and perhaps get it for me and send it to her, so that there was not the trouble of 'duty', and I will send you a pound note or so enclosed in an ordinary letter. Is that a trouble for you, dear Stella? But I know you are goodness to that family, and what an angel you are to them, and I believe no trouble is too much. And afterwards, we can plot together a *really* nice present for her, when the will is proved, and the property handed over.

A boom is going on in England at the moment over Modigliani's pictures. So a friend of mine, who works on the *Daily Express*, has remarked, in that paper, that people who would not invest a few pounds in Modigliani's pictures during his lifetime, are now paying hundreds for them. That there is a great painter called Pavel Tchelitchew now working under much the same conditions, and that collectors would find his works 'a good investment'. . . .

104. *To Stella Bowen*

22 Pembridge Mansions
Moscow Road
W.2

[12 April 1929]

My dear Stella,

. . . Thank you so much for your letter, which I was very glad
to get, though it made me very sad too. *Poor* little Schoura, and
poor poor Pavlik. What *can* be done to help them? My brain
seems numb. I had a telegram from Schoura saying her operation had been successful, and I have telegraphed and written
(needless to say) – but feel completely helpless. What a life!
When my book on Pope[5] is finished, I shall be able to send
Schoura some pretty things to amuse her, but my God, what
does that help, really, in the long run. And I shall be able to
find something to help Pavlik, *of course*. But everything is a
bigger problem than that; and now I know that he is being worried half off his head about his parents, and I know poor Allen[6]
is being worried too. What would they do without you, I should
like to know? What, indeed!

Stella, dear, how can you disbelieve in yourself like that.
Don't you know what you are like? Why, even talking to you for
a few moments makes one feel braver, and more able to face
things. You are one of the bravest and the most reliable people I
have ever met with; your instinct is invariably right, when you
are going to help people. You *couldn't* make a mistake in delicacy – it is quite impossible. As for your saying you do nothing
but dispense easy sympathy, what an absolute distortion of the
truth. Why, you arranged everything, saw to everything, if it
had not been for you, where would Schoura be? . . .

I am delighted you are telling Pavlik he must move from that
flat. He is, I know, miserable there; and so is Allen. And how
can they work under those conditions? In the last letter I had
from Pavlik, he was mourning that he could not leave that flat,
and saying that he had to consider others, by which he meant

his father and mother and poor Schoura. I think his father is an
old vampire. How he has the heart to write and bully Pavlik in
the way he does, beats me. What other son in Pavlik's position,
and having been brought up in the way he was brought up,
would do so much for his father? I wrote and told him he *must*
consider himself; and when I come to Paris I shall join up with
you, and we will scold him well. For one thing, I am convinced
Pavlik must take more care of his health.

Oh how can you say I am less muddled than you? You always
go straight ahead, and keep your head; and I get terrified, and
do not know where I am.

That old beast of a father of mine has just paid £600 for a
fake Italian picture. I can't tell you what I feel about him. When
I think of an artist like Pavlik, and then see that old horror of
mine throwing money away like that! Of course he hates anything real, or new. He is odious to me, and at one time gave me
such a handsome allowance that I lived on bread and butter and
boiled beans and tea. Which doesn't matter, only he is an enormously rich man, so it doesn't do him credit. I never speak to
him if I can help it, neither does Osbert, who is a darling. I am
longing for you to meet each other.

How lovely, when I am in Paris I shall see your Julie, and see
for myself if she is going to be like her mother in her *heart* – and
I can't wish her anything more lovely. I do want to see her.
What fun we will have. And then there will be all the
rehearsals of *Façade*, which are always great fun.

Yes, if *only* poor Schoura has a chance of a happy life. Poor
little darling, she has got such a sweet nature, like a little very
trusting child, I think. How sad this must make you. How sad it
makes me. I wish I knew how she is. I shall telegraph and ask,
tomorrow. I left doing so for two days, because I know she is not
at the pension.

Poor Pavlik, I can't bear to think what burdens are on his
shoulders. I can't think, Stella, what that family would do
without you. It must be so wonderful for them to have somebody on whom they can rely absolutely, and who never loses
her head.

Bless you, dear.
Till the 24th – and how lovely that will be —

> Your loving
> Edith

Will you be at 84 Rue Notre Dame des Champs for some time?

---

105. *To Stephen Tennant*[7]

> 22 Pembridge Mansions
> Moscow Road
> W.2

[*c.* June 1929]

My dear Stephen,

You are a dear to have sent me such a *lovely* scarf. Thank you ever and ever so much again. I spend my days and evenings inextricably intertwined in it, for it is so lovely both by day and by evening. You will see, when you come home.

I am so happy to hear from Siegfried that you are so much better. Poor Stephen, it has been such a dreadfully sad winter and spring and summer for you, I know it has.[8] But soon you will be able to come home to the things you love. And it is worth so much, to get you strong again.

I wish there was any book of any interest to send you, but there is nothing. It is a flat year, and so there is not anything, really, that you have missed by being abroad. All the same, it will be so lovely when you come home.

I am plodding along at this book – if you can call it a book – on Pope. I can't help it if people say it is a bad book; they shouldn't want somebody who is simply born to play the flute, to play the harmonium. They *will* think it is the same thing. However, I shall return to my flute when this is finished.

Pavlik was so touched at your buying a picture of his . . . I think, believe, and hope, that things are changing for him. Oh I do hope so. It must change for everybody soon, I think.

I've had to reprove my old friend Mr. J. C. Squire for finding a little man called Mr. Twitchett and letting him be rude about my Gold Coaster. Really! – I've congratulated Mr. Squire, saying that though I knew water-diviners existed, I'd never heard of a milk-and-water diviner before I'd met *his* gift, which seems to be unerring. I've had no reply.[9]

There seems to be no news of any kind. You aren't missing much, I tell you. . . .

---

106. *To Georgia Sitwell*

22 Pembridge Mansions
Moscow Road
W.2

Sunday [1929?]

. . . The journey back [from Weston] was hell. Three children (travelling by themselves) got into my carriage and shrieked like parrots the whole way. They shrieked so loudly that it 'set off' the children in the next carriage, rather like something catching fire. The children in the next carriage started others in neighbouring carriages, and soon the whole train was a shrieking yelling hooting whistling mass of infant imbeciles. As you know, I haven't the unnatural love of children that afflicts some women (always excepting Reresby, for whom I have a real passion) and by the time I arrived I was longing for another Herod. . . .

107. *To Stella Bowen*

22 Pembridge Mansions
Moscow Road
London, W.2

Tuesday [*c*. December 1929]

Darling Stella,

I miss you terribly, there is no other word for it. I think of you
so much, and of your problems, and of your courage, and way of
facing the bleakest weather without showing you feel the cold.
For it isn't really the thunder storms, it is the bleak weather
which counts. Well, you face it, and so you will not come out of
it weather-beaten. You have preserved your natural sweetness,
and have added to it the experience of wisdom. I don't know,
really, if it helps anyone in your case to know that. But that is
the truth.

I should have written to you yesterday, but life has been
rather like that led by Robinson Crusoe when he *first* reached
the Island, before he had mastered the fauna and flora. We
arrived (after considerable upheavals) – to find that Helen's
letter saying what food we wanted on our arrival had only
reached our particular Good Man Friday by the last post on
Saturday. So we could not have the average food eaten by
civilised beings. Instead, we had a chicken which reminded
me irresistibly of your Mademoiselle,[10] all wry and gnarled
and gnawed and waiting for its centenary, bought from the
East End Flea Market – and consumed in unmitigated
gloom.

All the blankets bore stains of the Scourge which you and we
have suffered from, so we could only sleep in rugs, and that sleep
was disturbed by perpetual imaginary crawlings and nibblings.
Revels, apparently, have been held in *my* bedroom, and Helen's
is patterned with dirty finger marks. I don't mind telling you
that I am *fearfully* cross.

Also, my uncle died the night I arrived – Veronica's father
(my uncle by marriage and my first cousin once removed by

birth).[11] So now I shall have to slip *into* mourning when I see
the family, and out of it when out of sight. . . .

1930

*Letters 108–10 show ES attempting to raise money for Tchelitchew and
Stella Bowen by arranging the sale of books and manuscripts. Her efforts,
however, nearly exposed her, in one instance, to an accusation of receiving
stolen goods. Allen Tanner had asked her to find a buyer for a book given by
Thomas Jefferson to the Marquis de Lafayette. Tanner had no receipt for its
acquisition from a man named Vladimir Semenoff, who had obtained it
from Count Louis de Lastéyrie. When the book was sold at Sotheby's, the
Count claimed the proceeds.[1]*

108. *To Stella Bowen*

22 Pembridge Mansions
Moscow Road
London, W.2

[c. 19 March 1930?]

Darling Stella,

Thank you ever so much for your letter, which I was so
delighted to get.

I should have written before, but I've really been feeling too
ill. My *first* feeling, and it lasted for hours, on receiving this revelation, was pain for Pavlik – pain for the destruction of his
perfectly legitimate hopes (since he knew *nothing* of the origin
of the book, and *nothing* of the sale, till I forced Allen's hand),
pain for his worry. It was only afterwards, on a lawyer having
been consulted by a man friend, that I realised what Allen had
done to *me*. I am, to say the least of it, well known in London.
My poor mother has been in prison; but our characters as writers
have made this almost forgotten. Allen, by his lying and lying,

has not only risked my being prosecuted and perhaps impris-
oned, but it is absolutely *certain* that *had* there been a case or
prosecution, even with me only as Seller of Stolen Property
(and I could probably have proved my innocence), the *newspapers* would have raked up the story of my mother, even if the
lawyers did not. And in any case, it would have been the discussion of every Club and dinner party in London: 'Oh well, look
at her blood! Her mother,' etc.

Allen knew mother's history, because Gertrude told him.
And if *he* were any other man, or *I* were any other woman, I can
imagine how Pavlik's chivalry would have been aroused, and
what he would have had to say about Allen. But I'm not Diana
Fitzherbert,[2] or any of the other cheap little sluts who arouse his
chivalry. So it doesn't matter. He *says*, I am bound to say, 'J'étais
furieux que Allen vous a mis dans tout ceci' – but he goes on to
say, 'Cela m'attriste beaucoup que vous êtes si fâchée avec
Allen, mais je le comprends. . . . Je l'ai grondé bien pour cette
naïveté d'esprit qui va presque [à] la litteral.'

The facts are these. Allen began by writing me mysterious
letters asking me to go to Gabriel Wells[3] and tell him he (A.)
had a book of enormous interest to Americans. First of all, he
wouldn't send the book over; then, eventually, he did, and I
took it to Sotheby's. I must say he made no objection to my
taking it to Sotheby's, but he said he wanted the sale kept as
secret as possible, and *nobody* must know – certainly not Pavlik.
He had his reasons, which were quite simple, but difficult to say.
Would *I* say, that he had picked up the book in *Germany, on the
Quais*, or wherever I liked. (Thank God, at this point, I did *not*
go to Gabriel Wells privately, I *ask* you what would have happened. That would have dished *me*, anyhow, and I'm not
concerned about Allen, save as regards Pavlik.)

I forget what happened then: but a correspondence between
A. and Sotheby's began, and Allen then told me long and elabo-
rate lies, saying the reason he *did* not want the sale of the book to
get out, was because it had been *given* him by this old gentleman.
The old gentleman had given it him in a very nonchalant way,
four years ago, and probably would be *furious* at it fetching so

much money, as he was avaricious. That the old gentleman's reputation was very bad, and that his (A.'s) nom de jeune fille would be ruined if it were known in Paris that this old gentleman had given him the book. 'Oh lord,' he said, 'I hope to the Lord it will be taken far away and nobody will ever know.' And there was perpetual nagging that Pavlik must not be told, on *any* account.

I went to the Sale, so as to be further involved. *Then* all the abusive letters began, because I would not tell Pavlik that filthy lie about his having earned that money. Abuse after abuse, as I told you. He made me *quite* ill, by his threats about my ruining their lives by my conduct. Well I told you all about that. Now I get this letter from him saying: 'That damned book, I bought on the Quai for 600 francs.'

And it seems owing to his wish to preserve his nom de jeune fille, because this old man's reputation is bad, he had thought it better to say he had been *given* the book, instead of having *bought* it! – The logic! Really he is at once the biggest liar I've ever come across, and the most stupid one. I don't know what the real truth is. All I know is that he might have ruined Pavlik in Paris, and that he very nearly succeeded in ruining me here. *Think* of the talk at Sotheby's. I have apologised to them, and they have written me a charming letter, but this cannot have helped my reputation. Also it is quite obvious what they think the truth is!

Please, Stella, darling, write me a letter by return of post, even if you can only spare time for quite a short one, and tell me if Pavlik mentioned Allen's behaviour to me, and if so, what he said about it, and what his attitude to me is. It is most important to me to know. Of course, Pavlik would not believe Allen is a thief. He couldn't very well. If I did that (I don't say Allen has, I don't know) – but *if* I had, Helen would have to say she didn't believe I'd done it.

Poor Pavlik, I am so dreadfully sad that all those hopes of money have gone. Allen wrote me a glorious letter, all about his health and his nervous fatigue, and hitting me below the belt about their poverty, as though I didn't mind Pavlik's poverty enough, without that! I shall *never* forgive Allen for writing to tell me that if their hopes were ruined, it would be *my* fault, and that I could think about that when I was old.

I've been made completely ill, so ill that I couldn't work. My heart is absolutely galloping, I am so giddy when I go out I have to come home.

Never mind. It is over now. . . .

---

109. *To Stella Bowen*

22 Pembridge Mansions
Moscow Road
London, W.2

[*c.* April 1930?]

Darling Stella,

Thank you ever so much for your letter. First of all, to business: Mr. Wise[4] has written me a charming letter, regretting very much that he cannot buy the manuscript[5] (he wrote to *me*, because *I* wrote to him) – because he only buys *poetry*. He expressed great admiration of the work of Mr. Ford, but explained that novels were out of the line of his collection.

Don't be depressed, dearest. On Tuesday morning I will take the work to Sotheby's; and if *they* are not sensible about it, I could always try Elkin Mathews, but Sotheby's would be best, as I am sure a larger price would be given. *I will tell them to write straight to you at your new address*; that will delay it a few days, but we can't help that; we must on no account have letters lost. There was a delay with Mr. Wise, A because I had to get at his address, B because the old boy is ill. Will you decide about auctioning the book? If you put a reserve on the book, and there is not a bid quite as high as the reserve, then *you* have to pay (15% I think) but it would, perhaps, be as well to do it. I can't make up my mind. We must think it out. I am not going to Sotheby's till Tuesday, because the directors are never there on Saturdays or Mondays – they are too grand.

About Allen: I have received a long letter from Pavlik, saying, 'Je sais tout: Allen m'a tout dit.' He explains that the cause of the trouble is that *Allen* 'est trop droit' and that *I* have

'un petit défaut – de quereller facilement', or words to that
effect; and imploring me not to tell anyone, as if it gets back to
the old man they would have awful trouble.

And I have had a noble and very hysterical letter from Allen
forgiving me for insulting him. (The insult being that I called
the lie about his piano manual 'a *lie*' – instead of 'a beautiful
legend'.) He is also furious because, as he was in a state of raging
hysteria, I, terrified of what he would do, asked Peter Gorer to
write and tell him (without mentioning the cause of the trouble) not to quarrel with me.

Pavlik says Allen gave up his money, which had been given
him for piano lessons, to help Pavlik for the first two years he
was in Paris, and that he would never do anything to hurt P.
Perhaps A. *was* meaning to share with P. in the long run. But I
could *not* allow him to pretend he had done that work; and it
certainly didn't look at the moment as if he was going to share.
He has, of course, only told Pavlik about the sale because he was
afraid *I* should. And I don't believe for a moment he has told
Pavlik that the reason he is quarrelling with me is because he
wanted me to tell a particularly mean and caddish lie, bolstering
him up in his moral superiority. He is pretending that I accuse
him of keeping the money. So I have written and told Pavlik
that as Allen has told him everything, he knows, naturally, that
the quarrel is because I would not tell him (Pavlik) that I had
sold a manual that Allen had written, for £300. I have said that
I wish to hear no more of the affair, and that I refuse to quarrel
with Allen. But that I am ill (the doctor says my blood is not
feeding my brain, as the result of nothing but over-work; and
that means that I wake up every morning shaking from head to
foot as though I had Saint Vitus dance, and am fearfully sick . . .
I naturally didn't tell P. that, but am telling you); that Allen's
hysteria is affecting me painfully, and that during the fortnight
when the doctor says it is absolutely necessary that I should
have complete quiet and rest, all I get is perpetual hysterical letters from Allen, either abusing me or forgiving me, and a letter
from Pavlik himself saying the trouble is that Allen is 'trop
droit', that I quarrel too easily, and reproaching me for refusing

to tell him a lie. I then ended up by telling Pavlik that I have a very loyal and constant affection for him, but that he must not abuse that affection.

That is the gist of my letter. I assure you I am sick every time the post arrives. And it is a little tiresome, as there is no reason for it. Allen has got too beautiful a soul to work; I haven't. I work *very* hard (if I didn't, I shouldn't be ill now). And I want to feel well again, and be able to work. . . .

---

110. *To Stella Bowen*

22 Pembridge Mansions
Moscow Road
London, W.2

[25 April 1930?]

Dearest Stella,

I *would* have written to you yesterday; but when I returned from my first outing (in which I took the M.S. to Sotheby's, and also visited Osbert's housekeeper in hospital: she is ill as usual, appendicitis this time) I found messages from the *Evening News*, plaguing me for an article that very day.

My dear dear Stella, I am afraid that you will receive Sotheby's tiresome letter before you receive mine. How I *hate* to be the bearer of disappointing news to you. They swear that there is not the *faintest* chance of getting £350 for the M.S. They say it will not fetch more than £40 or £50; but of course if you liked, they could *try* if it would fetch more. They were very gloomy, and depressed me so much, I could have cried. I left the M.S. with them, pending your instructions. They say *no modern* M.S. excepting Shaw and Barrie fetch anything *like* £350. I am sure they are wrong, but yet I suppose they know – it is their job. On the other hand of course, they told me that curséd book of Allen's would not fetch more than £150 (if that). They said that on the very day of the sale.

I *wonder* what one had better do. Of course, I am not at all sure that it wouldn't be wiser to send it to America, where Mr. Ford's principal public is. What *had* we better do?

I can't tell you, Stella darling, what I feel about this disappointment. But of course we must remember that Allen was told exactly the same thing; only it was put at £80 to *him*, and at £150 to the young Harmsworths whom I imported to watch and see the sale was fair. Are you willing to risk it? . . .

I feel very worried about the last of the free Australian capital being called in. But at the same time, I do think what you have done is a good investment – I am hoping, urgently, that Inez will find new sitters for you. With any sort of luck, when she returns to London, I shall have a good go for her again. And I *intend* to arrange that visit for you and Julie.

I can't help feeling, in my bones, that you are going to turn a fresh corner in your fate. This is the low point. Always, in my life, just when one couldn't bear the low point any more, something happened to bring one back to life. But that is poor comfort at the moment of the lowest ebb.

If this letter is idiotic, please forgive me. My head still aches pretty badly. I can't think how I managed (considering the shape of my face and head) to hurt myself in so many places. But I bruised the whole of the upper part of my face, down to my lips, and part of my head. I suppose I must have bumped *that* in falling. The cuts won't last. There may be a tiny scar under my hair, but that is all. The bruising was far worse.[6]

I am glad that you have seen P. and A. I do not consider that I have been well treated by P. It is a little irritating, considering what A.'s behaviour has been like, that P. should write and say the whole misunderstanding came from A. being 'trop droit'. And that *I* quarrel too easily. Of the only two times that I have quarrelled with P., one time was on occasion of his sacrificing me to please Diana Fitzherbert's vanity, and the second time was because I would not aid A. to lie to him in a particularly mean way. I have *told* P. that I was asked to tell that lie and refused. I am not quarrelling with P.; but whilst I was lying in bed after this accident, I have seen the last year pretty clearly.

How I should *love* to come in June, Stella darling, if I *possibly*

can. What an angel you are to think of it. How much I appreciate you, dear dear friend. *Don't* despair about the M.S., but
please write me instructions.

With best love
your loving
Edith

---

111. *To Stella Bowen*

as from
Weston Manor
near Towcester
Northants

Wednesday [n.d.]

Dear Stella,

What *can* you think of me for not answering your letter
before? But I know you'll forgive me when I tell you why I
haven't – Domestic troubles. Some maids who never come
because they have dying mothers, and who when they *do* come,
are deaf mutes and unable to speak coherently, or give messages,
or to telephone. Others again, who are charming but whose
telephoning is a disaster. As a matter of fact, there are only two,
but I feel there are dozens.

I do hope your journey to Switzerland was not too bad, and
that now you are there you are rested and are thoroughly enjoying yourself. And I do hope, most of all, that you are better, my
dear. I suspect you of not taking proper care of yourself, in fact, I
don't believe you *ever* think of yourself at all. You are always
immersed in other people's cares, and in doing things for other
people, and in comforting them.

I suppose it is the penalty you have to pay for having a beautiful disposition and for being so much loved. Yes, dear, I don't
wonder you feel like a large cake that has had too many slices
cut out of it. Everyone does it to you.

My social week (or last fortnight) has not been entirely a happy one, though it makes me laugh when I look back on it. First of all, a certain well-known woman pianist[7] came to tea and explained (so extraordinary) to a large company of people she had never seen before, that two men who have just got engaged to be married are only doing so because *she* had refused them a few days before. She gave their names, etc. *And*, dear, one of the men present is a cousin of one of the fiancés.! I couldn't stop her; there was no stopping her. It was like a runaway horse. Then Geoffrey Gorer[8] and Mrs. Vallance[9] had a perfectly *terrific* row about Shelley. Poor Mrs. Vallance had said, without meaning anything in particular, that Shelley was a *classical* writer. Geoffrey pinned her down: what did she mean by classical . . . Well, she didn't mean anything, but at last, driven against the wall, said she meant *national* when she said classical. This did not satisfy Geoffrey, and it went on and on. Finally, as she left, she said to Geoffrey: 'We will continue about this: I think I know rather more about poetry than *you* do!'

Oh dear, did my troubles end there? They did not. Diana Fitzherbert came to tea. We were all looking at Pavlik's picture of Mrs. Church, and Diana began telling everybody in the room that she (Diana) had sat for Pavlik the whole winter . . . ('Oh, how often I've sat in that armchair, etc., whilst he was painting me.') Geoffrey Gorer, instead of holding his tongue, said: 'You haven't sat for him as long as Mrs. Church. *She* sat for him for four months on end, and he has done lots of portraits of her.' Diana was *furious*. I, trying to make things better, said, 'I'm longing to see your portrait, Diana. I know it is lovely. Pavlik thinks you are so lovely. I hope to see the portrait when I'm in Paris.' You would have thought that would have soothed her, wouldn't you? Did it, just! Somebody, to change the conversation, started talking about how awkward the pianist's revelations had been. Diana, in a voice which was really cracked with rage, said: 'Women do that sort of thing when they are *ugly*, to explain why they are not married.' I said: 'Well, not in this woman's case, because she is, as a matter of fact, very beautiful.' Diana said: 'Well, that is generally the reason; and women lie like that when they've passed a certain age, and think they *ought* to be married, and aren't married. They try to explain. We shall have *you* doing that sort of thing,' she said, turning to me. She then said something so frightfully insolent to me, that I *can't repeat* it. I can't imagine how she dared, it was so insolent. In front of Geoffrey Gorer and young Draper.[10] Geoffrey, being a Jew, fled. *That* routed him, anyway. Young Draper said, in a cold stern voice: 'I wish people would learn dignity in schools. It might prevent them from making an exhibition of themselves.'

Really, really! And again, goodness me!

She then invited me to tea, and I accepted, but didn't go. Because, though I'm an intrepid woman, she honestly makes me feel a little shy. She was fearfully insulting to me in Paris, but Pavlik forced her on me again. He is, I think, taken in by her whining about how ill-treated she is (as though any first-rate woman would. Really, do *you* whine? I should just think you do *not*. No one who did not know you most intimately would have *any* idea that you had had any sadness in your life). I've delivered an ultimatum to Allen. I've said she has been fearfully insulting to me *twice* (both times, it was too horribly vulgar to repeat) and that I won't have her forced on me again. Pavlik can scream as much as he likes; but out she goes.

The sequel was terrifying. On the afternoon I was supposed to go to tea, I led Ethel (the new 17-year-old maid, whom I am teaching to telephone) *to* the telephone and told her to repeat my message. Ethel, having got on (she is terrified of the telephone, it might be a lion) – said in a stern reproachful voice: 'Is that you, Bitch'erbal? Bitch'erbal, is that *you*? This is Miss Sitwell speaking, and she *won't see* yer!' Sensation, curtain! 'Ethel,' I said, when I had recovered from the shock, 'you mustn't speak like that. You mustn't call Lady Fitzherbert Bitch'erbal.' 'Why not?' enquired Ethel, sullenly. Why not, indeed. 'Because, Ethel,' I said, 'we have to try and respect Mr Manners.' It is the *2nd* time something like it has happened. Altogether, I'm feeling worn out.

Added to which, Pavlik is imploring me to get my father to

help about his visa for Italy. And my Papa, who is a curious old gentleman who spends his whole life dodging paying taxes, says that if *any* attention is called to him, he will have to pay taxes in Italy. Meanwhile, Pavlik has galloped light-heartedly off to the Italian Consul's, and *has* called attention to the poor old gentleman. I simply daren't think what will happen.

Pavlik's visit to London was not an undiluted success, was it? In the end, he practically trod on my face. But I've now realised that what can't be cured, must be endured. He's got a very good new trick of behaving first of all as though I were the Tower of London, complete with the death-mask of Queen Elizabeth and loving sets of thumbscrews, and *then* of behaving as though I were dead and he were laying me out. But he is such a marvellous painter; and there is something very sweet and childlike about him, so that we shall always be fond of him.

On Friday, I go to stay with Sachie and Georgia. I am *hoping* for a little peace there, but one never knows.

What a long letter, all full of nonsense. Do write to me, Stella dearest. You don't know how much I treasure your friendship. It is such a great happiness to me. A great, great happiness.

Bless you, dear friend.

With much love from your
Edith

---

112. *To Christabel MacLaren*[11]

22 Pembridge Mansions
Moscow Road
London, W.2

7 May 1930

Dearest Christabel,

Thank you many and many times for your letter, which was so personal and so like you. I shall always keep it.

I am thinking of you so much this evening, being kind and so absolutely right to everyone who is your guest. And I want to come, yet I am too shy, because I don't dance and shall not know anyone, and because I shan't be able to speak, for more than a second, to my hostess, who is the one person there whom I most want to speak to. But you will understand all that, just as you do understand everything. I've had such an unhappy letter from Osbert.

Best love,
your affectionate
Edith

113. *To Stella Bowen*

[10 June 1930?]

Darling Stella,

. . . Just before I became seedy, what I can only express as a phenomenon appeared in my sitting room! I was having a tea party, when the door was flung open, and in walked two complete strangers. A stout middle-aged woman with very tearful blue eyes – the kind of woman who leaves a card saying Mrs. – has cast-off clothing of every description and invites immediate inspection; she was dressed as what I can only describe as a Pageant of Empire: ostrich feathers from South Africa, fruits and flowers (on her hat) from Australia, specimens of the skins of all the fauna of the Empire. With her was a grubby boy of about twenty-one, who spoke no known language (he was tried with French, Spanish, Italian and German) and all he could say was Pliz? The phenomenon advanced and shook hands with me, and the lady said, 'You see we have come!' (Yes indeed). I racked my brain as to *where* I could have seen them, eventually coming to the conclusion that I must have met them at some lecture, and fallen asleep, and asked them in my sleep.

Presently the lady said, very coquettishly, to me: 'You *paint*! I see it on your face!' I said I beg your pardon, rather surprised. I don't. I only powder. 'But you are arrrtistic?' I nearly said I'm damned if I am! Well eventually it transpired that they had just happened to hear that there was a woman called Miss Edith Sitwell who knew all the young composers, and as *they* wanted to know them too, they had just come!! Simply that! I think it was so kindly and friendly of them to come and see me without knowing *anything* about me! I might have turned out to be not the sort of person one knows – or anything.

Can you *beat* it?

Do write to me, Stella darling.

Very best love
Your loving
Edith

114. *To Edmund Blunden*[12]

22 Pembridge Mansions
Moscow Road
London, W.2

13 June 1930

Dear Mr. Blunden,

My publishers have sent me your postcard.

The truth is that my brothers and I have been treated with such impertinence lately by your women-reviewers that we have had to make it a rule that no further books of ours shall be sent for review to the *Nation*. Of course, if you would care to have a copy[13] for yourself, I shall only be too delighted to send you one.

Yours sincerely,
Edith Sitwell

115. *To Edmund Blunden*

Renishaw Hall

5 August 1930

Dear Mr. Blunden,

I cannot tell you what delight and pride your review of my *Collected Poems* in the *Fortnightly Review*[14] has given me. I have not felt so much pleasure for a very long time. And not only did it delight me, it gave me a fresh impetus to work. It was most kind of you, and I am very grateful.

Yours sincerely
Edith Sitwell

This letter attempts to mend fences with Sydney Schiff, whose friendship ES had neglected for some months. Both felt betrayed at this time by the artist and writer (Percy) Wyndham Lewis (1882–1957), who had been a friend of the Sitwells from about 1918. ES had been the model for one of his most famous portraits, but she had also rejected his sexual advances (see Glendinning, p. 85), and this became his 'mean personal reason for hating me'. His novel The Apes of God, *published in June 1930, satirised the Sitwells and many other friends, including the Schiffs, who had helped him financially during the 1920s.*

116. *To Sydney Schiff*

Chez Madame Wiel
129 Rue Saint-Dominique
Paris 7e

26 September 1930

Dearest Sydney,

I started a long letter to you three days ago, and then tore it up, for I found it very unworthy. Now I have received your second letter, registered and forwarded from London. Dear

Sydney and Violet, whom I count among my dearest and best friends, *never* believe of me that I *could* desert you, or doubt you, or betray you, or let you down. If there is a long silence, then it must be for a very different reason. This reason is, that I have been very ill. I have not stopped in bed – if I had, I should have been better, but I've been so ill that I have had to have oxygen and gas injected in my shoulder twice a week. Early this spring, just before Easter, I had two very bad shocks, one straight on top of the other, at a time when I was very overworked. This resulted in all my glands becoming badly poisoned. I did not go to a doctor, for I thought it was just nerves, but tried to go on with my work; but I had terrifying attacks of giddiness, so bad that I did not dare go out. At that moment Osbert's house-keeper and his soldier servant were taking it in turns to have operations, and the one that was not having an operation at the moment used to ring me up on the telephone (which is in the flat next door) in the middle of the night telling me that the other was dying. One night I was alone in the flat, and waking up, thought I heard this happening. I went to the door, but overcome with giddiness, fell, crashing with my face and head against some panelling, and was picked up an hour and a half later, unconscious. My face was black down to my chin, and I had a large dent on my forehead. But the fool of a doctor who was called in, instead of realising I had had concussion, didn't, and I had to get up four days later, cover my face with a veil, and attend the death-bed of Osbert's housekeeper (though I wasn't there when she died, poor soul).

On the top of all this, I've had to finish a book, and correct the proofs; and writing used to give me such a black and fright-ful headache, that I have written no letters.

And that, dear Sydney, is why I have not written before, and why I am only now starting your very lovely new work, about which I shall write you a long letter when I know it properly. I have been unable to read anything this summer, and should have written nothing if I had not been forced to finish my work on Augustan poetry.

I value your and Violet's friendship most dearly; as I have said

before, you are among my very few *real* friends; with the exception of Arthur Waley and three other people, you are now the
only people whom I come to see, or *will* see, in London. And I
am incapable of destroying or spoiling such a friendship. If
people slandered you or Violet to me, I should not listen – I
should tell them to go to Hell. I should never believe for an
instant that you or she would be capable of unkindness or
treachery towards me, – such an idea would make me laugh! I
have seen too well what the friendship of both of you can be,
when that friendship is given. You have been badly betrayed by
two friends to whom you gave that unquestioning loyalty, but
you never will be by *me*.

I admire you most deeply as an artist; you have everything I
personally want in a novelist – beauty, deep insight, compassion, and absolute integrity – and these will be remembered and
honoured when all the foolish creatures who try to injure you
are forgotten.

I am longing to see the translation, which I know must be
not only a great translation, but a great monument to a great
friendship.[15] But I shall be glad, too, when it is finished, because
it is taking you away from your original work.

Lewis' book *is* about us. Everybody who is envious or who dis-
likes us all has been eager to tell me so. I shall not read it. I shall
certainly not read the part about you and Violet, for my rage
would be too great. Somebody has shown me a page about
myself, in which he says I am nothing but an old charwoman,
and which contains an insulting description of my personal
appearance, coarse to an unparalleled degree, and which blames
me for being over forty years old! But the person who showed it
to me was bitterly disappointed, I am afraid. Poor Lewis! Does
he *really* think that such a thing could hurt me? The things that
hurt me are ethical things – lies about my life, etc. (though he
has lied about that too, I believe). What he has tried to do to
you and Violet, I do not know, because I refused to look at any
page dealing with you. He has behaved monstrously to you
both. To me, he owes nothing. He has a mean personal grudge
against me, a mean personal reason for hating me, but I shall

never tell anyone what that reason is. You and Violet, he cannot forgive, because you have helped him.

I find this letter is less a letter than a conversation; but I *want* to talk to you both.

I am returning to London in the middle of November, and I hope, more than I can say, that you will both be there then. As I say, I am beginning to work without trouble, and to read again, and your book, which arrived when I was ill, is the first book I shall read – and with how much delight.

I think, Sydney, that we can afford to forget what Lewis has tried to do to us all. The difficult thing to forget is his awful treachery towards you and Violet. But he is evidently mad.

My *Collected Poems* will reach you soon – but without the inscription, which will be written in the book when we meet.

My love to you and dear Violet
Yours affectionately
Edith

---

117. *To Siegfried Sassoon*

As from 22 Pembridge Mansions
Moscow Road
W.2

5 December 1930

My dear Siegfried,

I am told that you are feeling terribly hurt with me, and that you believe that I didn't appreciate or understand your friendship. Do you *honestly* believe that? I can't believe it. You were one of my most intimate friends, and I have missed you more than I can say.

I have believed that it was *you* who did not appreciate or understand *my* friendship. And I, on my side, have been deeply hurt. I know I wrote you two violent letters, but only after I believed that you had deserted our friendship, because you had

made no effort to see me for several months. The events since
then haven't been my fault. And I've still kept my manuscript
book with the [illeg] workings of my best poem in it, for you –
(though you'll have to choose how it shall be bound, so that I can
have it bound for you, before I give it to you). And I *did* appreciate the box you made, and was deeply touched by your making it;
and it now contains various things that I value particularly.

I do suggest now that we should both dismount from our high
horses, the riding of neither of which seems to give either of us the
slightest pleasure, and continue our friendship where we left it off.

I go back to London tomorrow, and shall be there till the
17th or 18th, when I go to Paris for three weeks or so. Will you
choose a day to come to tea with me, and receive my *Collected
Poems*, suitably bound (for once) – and look at the M.S. you
shall [have] when you have chosen *that* binding, and, in short,
make it up?

Yours ever
Edith

118. *To Pavel Tchelitchew*

22 Pembridge Mansions
Moscow Road
London, W.2

Vendredi [n.d.]

Mon cher cher Pavlik

Voilà un tout petit mot pour vous apporter tout mon amitié
fidèle, et pour vos souhaiter un heureux week-end avec notre
cher Geoffrey, et de bons conseils, cher ami.

Avant hier, j'ai telephoné Geoffrey, et maintenant je viens de
lui écrire une nouvelle [*sic*] mot, car ce sera tellement compliqué
en français, que je ne pourrais jamais expliquer les conseils
d'Osbert en français. Enfin, darling, si vous voulez – si vous
jugez bien, d'avoir cette petite exposition seulement

temporaire – et pour le moment seulement – de dessins, tout le monde qui est à moi travaillerait pour vous comme des nègres. Discutez cela avec Geoffrey, qui est très très pratique, et qui vous donnera bon conseil.

Chéri, je fais mon mieux pour votre bien, et avec tout mon coeur, croyez-moi.

Je vous embrasse

à vous toujours
Edith

Geoffrey vous expliquera pourquoi l'exposition de dessins aura lieu chez Duckworth au bien que [*sic*] chez Georgia. Je prendrai le déjeuner avec Diana et Brian Guinness[16] aujourd'hui, et je parlerai des portraits.

1931

119. *To Allen Tanner*

22 Pembridge Mansions
Moscow Road
London, W.2

[23 January 1931?]

My dear Skipper,

The Skipper has done *nothing*, either unintentionally or intentionally, to cause this silence. What has caused it is good old-fashioned influenza, of the gastric type, but also with a bad cough, and a very high temperature. I started it on the train on the way to Calais, and think I got a chill coming off the boat, on top of it. Helen has had it too. I sat up for an hour yesterday, for the first time, and today am going to try and dress and sit up, but am so weak.

And in the middle of all this, I was informed that there has

been the hell of a row in the *Times Literary Supplement*. I mis-
quoted some Baudelaire in my *Pleasures of Poetry*,[1] as a matter of
fact, as a poet, I'm convinced Baudelaire *would* have written
that particular thing *if* he'd got it in his head, because, the effect
is very subtle and beautiful. I put

> 'Mon ange, ma soeur
> Songe à la douceur'

instead of

> 'Mon enfant, ma soeur,
> Songe à la douceur.'

The misquotation is, I still hold, infinitely more beautiful and
strange. Anyhow, some suburban spinster caught hold of this
and wrote a *furious* letter to the *Times L.S.* A young man I
know, Mr. Heywood, whom you also know, happens to be the
person in charge of all the letters to the paper. He, very generously, flew off to T. S. Eliot, and T. S. Eliot dashed down to see
the editor of the *T.L.S.*, whose name is Bruce Richmond,[2] and
said he would not allow anyone to be rude to me, that it was
obviously a mistake. Mr. Richmond, whom I don't know, but
who admires my work a lot, was extremely kind, and handed
the whole affair to Tom Eliot, who proceeded to manage it by
writing Mr. Richmond letters about the lady, letters which were
invariably forwarded to her. She got ruder and ruder, but none
of her letters was allowed to be published, and in the end, Tom
told Mr. Richmond, as far as I could make out down the telephone, laid, *simple, et sans complication*, that the lady was just a
suburban bore. The letter, of course, was sent to her, and she
has now shut up finally, because Tom's name is the most
impressive name in modern literature, of the younger generation.

I'm going to be made an honorary Doctor of Literature in
June of next year, I'm told, and everyone is trying to get the
rules altered about Oxford Professorships, so that I can become
Professor of Poetry there in three years' time. Of course,
whether *that* will happen or not, I don't know. Because I shall be

the only woman who has ever held that post, if I *do* get made it, and, also, a very young professor, though aged as a person. It won't bring in any money, though. . . .

---

120. *To Sacheverell Sitwell*

22 Pembridge Mansions
Moscow Road
London, W.2

5 May 1931

My darling old boy,

It seems there has been a complete muddle, as far as we are concerned, about the selling of those shares (about which I spoke to Georgia). I saw the Public Trustee and the Financial Expert yesterday, and what they wrote to me about was the selling of the shares which make up my £2,000 odd. Apparently it doesn't affect your or Sister Edith's[3] money at all. Mine is in shipping and electricity; and when the shares were bought, the former were a splendid investment, but now both the Financial Expert and the Public Trustee say they are really dangerous; and they are most anxious, indeed insistent, that my £2,000 odd should be put into safe investments, otherwise the whole lot may be lost. This won't affect you, because, should I pop off suddenly, and the market be safer, you can always buy something more spectacular. I daren't risk losing this money, because what I got from Aunt B.[4] has practically all gone, owing to having speculated in those damned nickels.

I can't tell you how much I am longing for *Far from my Home*.[5] Such a wonderful book; and the last story is, as I've said a hundred times, the greatest short story since Tchekhoff.

I'm feeling rather irritable today; because Master Riddle, who is Henry Ainley's[6] nineteen-year-old son, has landed me – with great skill – into going down to Sadler's Wells Theatre, with Tom Balston,[7] to see him dash on to the stage, in *King Lear*, and say either: 'Hail, my Lord', or else 'Hark the Bugles', or else 'Lo, the Moon!' – after which the crowd shouts 'Slay him', and he is, as I think very rightly, just dragged off the stage and killed, behind scenes.

Also, this book on Bath[8] is *such* a bore! My only pleasure is the thought of coming down to Weston on the 15th, and seeing you and Georgia and Reresby, and (oh *joy*), *Mr. Roxburgh!*[9] How awfully jolly! Awfully ripping of you, Mrs. Sitwell, to drive your sister-in-law over. Now, Sachie, you are *not* going to cramp my style. I am going to talk to Mr. R. about manly men and womanly women, about Good Influences, Healthiness, and the next war being won on the Playing Fields of Stowe. He is trying to forcible-feed us. But I have said *NO*. Tea, I expect, we shall *have* to have. But nothing else shall be crammed down our throats whilst I live to defend us. Shall I wear Mr. Andrew Clark?[10] Will you give Georgia my best love and thank her ever so much for her letter, and tell her I'll write to her tomorrow morning.

Very best love
ever your loving
Edith

And a kiss to Rory [?].

---

121. *To John Collier*[11]

22 Pembridge Mansions
Moscow Road
London, W.2

4:30 Monday morning.
June 14 1931

Dear Mr. Collier,

I was so really stunned with pleasure, though not entirely with surprise, at meeting you again, that I could not tell you just how pleased I was. I have missed your coming to see me, very much. Several people stopped coming to see me, but you were the only one I missed, and I did not know where *you* were, so could not write to you.

His Monkey Wife isn't a work of talent: it is a work of genius – or the word genius doesn't mean anything. Anyhow, it is what *I* know to be genius. And I feel badly that I have only read it in its third impression, but that is because I've been out of the world to which we both belong for six months. Then Osbert told me about it. And I asked: 'Is it my Mr. John Collier?' But Osbert, who had not then got into communication with you, said he thought it was not.

I don't think I know a work that contains more wisdom and more terrifying destructive and constructive wit. The word 'wit' has been debased from meaning Swift to meaning that wretched buffoon Noël Coward. But *you* have wit as Swift understood it. You are the only man under thirty (and one of the only men *over* thirty) who, to my belief, is anything. And *I know* that you have genius. And I never use that word lightly.

I don't think anything is left to be said now either about men's attitude towards women, or about women's inmost thoughts. I have always liked you very much, but I think you are a most terrifying young man. How on earth do you know so much! I'm overwhelmed by the scope of the book, and its almost appalling insight. . . .

Honestly, as exposing the point of view of a man towards an accustomed woman, and of the secret view a woman takes of herself, I don't know anything to touch the fancy dress ball scene. And of course, the description of Emily's sex appeal in the British Museum scene joins up with the Carmen episode. How *have* you managed to convey the sense of modesty and virtue, by the very construction of the sentences relating to or spoken by, Emily! It is quite extraordinary. . . .

122. *To John Collier*

Hotel de la Bourdonnais
Avenue de la Bourdonnais
Paris VIIe

26 September 1931

Dear Mr. Collier,

What you have said of my poem makes me feel it was worth while writing it. Anything I might say of 'Three Men in One Room' and of 'Address to the Worms' would be so inadequate as to be foolish. I know these poems, now, and every aspect of them, and I understand, in the fullest sense, how completely and absolutely the spiritual part of them has found the natural body of them. They are at once so new, and so world-old (like all beauty . . . a word which we are being taught to hate – still the real thing exists, in spite of all the palaver), so experienced and so creative, that one is at once astonished and assured by their certainty. . . .

I spent yesterday in walking from gallery to gallery, and saw the varying but splendid Degas[12] exhibition, two Cézanne[13] landscapes, in which the air was as living and pulsing and conscious a creature as you or I, a divine and innocent Douanier Rousseau[14] (a portrait of a tiger galloping through a jungle and a thunderstorm, with the lightning and the [illeg.] taking on exactly the same movement as the tiger, and with the lines of rain having the same texture and fierceness and tenderness as the hairs on the tiger's pelt) – and an exhibition of Rouault;[15] the very great young painter with whom I looked at these believes Rouault to be the greatest living painter. I came back to the hotel wondering how on earth people can be taken in by Matisse,[16] for instance, with his false naïveté! And where *will our* great ones go when they die? With whom will Mr. Hugh Walpole and Messrs. Maugham, Coward, Galsworthy and the Misses Dane and Sackville-West[17] hob-nob! Gosh! What a prospect! We shan't have to know then, anyhow. They will still be able to look down on us from their altitudes. . . .

1932

123. *To Sacheverell Sitwell*

129 Rue Saint-Dominique
Paris VIIe

Monday [*c.* January 1932]

My darling Sachie,

I can't tell you how delighted I was to get your letter, which reached me yesterday morning, the Sabbath not being a Day of Rest for Postmen in Paris, as it is for us. I was most frightfully disappointed not to see you and Georgia in Paris, and it was so maddening, as I had left a note for Georgia at the hotel, also full directions in a message for the Concierge here, who, of course, never gave it.

Is there any chance, whatever, of your both coming out here again soon? I do *hope* there is. If not, and also, if so, I do hope you are both expecting me some time in February?

Thank you *so* much, my darling, for the most lovely and kind things you say about my suggestions for the poems. I do wish I really thought I could be of any use to the greatest poet of our time. I think the loveliest of all the new poems, perhaps, is the 'Giant Orion', which is amongst the most wonderful mysterious-sounding and strange poetry that either you, or anybody else, has ever written. (Perhaps I should say 'they are', instead of 'it is', but I don't, because it is a marvellous whole.) This miraculously beautiful poem has that strange atmosphere – like that of music – which you alone of the poets of the last hundred years (if we except Swinburne, and a few lines of Tennyson) produce. I mean, it has not only the sound, but also the *meaning*, of music. *Please can you let me have a copy of the 'Giant Orion' as soon as possible, for various purposes*, both for my own delight, and because I hope to read it aloud.

I think it will be madness if you do not publish the *Canons of*

Giant Art. Please do so, immediately.[1] Can you, when you send
me 'Orion', send me that wonderful passage on Death which
comes in one of the Cantos of *Donne and Gargantua*. It was not
in the Cantos you gave me.

Will you give the last Canto of *Donne* (the last one I made
suggestions for) another overhauling? Being a female, I could
not *weight* the *blanks* properly (as you know, I never attempt
blanks myself, because I am sure they don't lie in a woman's
physique). I think the poem needs tautening up, in various
places. *Donne and Gargantua* is such a tremendously Great
poem, that nothing ought to be allowed to pass.

I shall be really *wild* if you don't publish the *Canons of Giant
Art*. You MUST. My darling, I am more proud and grateful than
I can say, of the dedication. You know what I believe of your
poetry. And, if I may say so without conceit, I am not speaking
ignorantly.

This flat looks charming, and it is very comfortable. Evelyn[2]
is kindness itself. The poor thing is *not* going to leave her office,
because she can't afford to. She is going to stop on there, and
now they are increasing her work, but not her pay. It really is
slave-driving. . . .

---

124. *To John Collier*

22 Pembridge Mansions
Moscow Road

26 March 1932

Dear John,

This very strange silence on my part, when I had wanted to
express my delight in John Aubrey, and your part in John
Aubrey,[3] was due A. to the death of poor Mr. Monro,[4] B, to fury
at having to correct proofs of, quite definitely, the worst book
that has ever been written, and, C, to exciting adventures with
a lunatic lady. A. and C. meant that I had to dash round and
round and round London, like a squirrel in a world-sized cage,

and, when B. was added to the rest of the fatigue, you can imagine my state.

Your preface to Aubrey is as delightful as it is learned, and Aubrey himself astonishes me more and more. Has there ever been a writer with more economy of phrase, or with a better gift for describing characters and appearances in two or three sentences? He seems to me to give every essential, and to cut off every wrapping which would take away from that essential. He is so companionable, too.

I do think your valuation, your criticism, of him is one of the most discerning and enlightening pieces of criticism of our time, and I cannot tell you how grateful I am to you for giving me this book, so full of life, of warmth and of light. . . .

David Horner (1900–83), socialite, occasional author, and RAF officer during the Second World War, was the lover and companion of OS from 1929 to 1964. ES maintained outwardly amicable relations with him until the 1950s, when his treatment of OS, by then afflicted with Parkinson's disease, led her to believe that he had merely used the Sitwells for social and financial advantage. Her correspondence with him was generally amusing rather than intimate.

125. To David Horner

22 Pembridge Mansions
Moscow Road
London, W.2

[28 March 1932]

Dearest David,

. . . We had a very exciting time yesterday. A certain lady[5] (Osbert will tell you who I mean) came to tea without her husband. As she entered, a strange smell, as though four bottles of methylated spirits had been upset, entered also, followed, five minutes afterwards, by Georgia and her mother.[6] Nellie (the maid) who was once what is known as an Attendant, enquired if she might speak to me on the telephone, and, as soon as she got me outside, said (looking very frightened): 'If she starts anything, Miss, get her by the wrists, sit on her face, and don't let her bite you. Don't let her get near a looking glass, or near the window.' I said 'What *do* you mean?' and she replied that what I thought was an accident with the [methylated spirits] was really the strongest drug given by Attendants when the patient is so violent that nothing ordinary has any effect!! She concluded, gloomily: 'Often, it has taken six of us to hold one down.' – You can imagine my feelings. And when I got back into the room, I found that Mrs. Doble had offered the lady a cigarette, and had been told that the lady *never* accepted anything from strangers. It was too dangerous. Poor Mrs D. was terrified, as she thought that the Patient was going to spring at her throat. Georgia was terrified too, and tea was undiluted hell.

But a wave of insanity seems to be sweeping over the country. I have just received a letter from a lady I don't know, inviting me, in an airy manner, to dash down to her house in Hertfordshire 'by the 8.10' train, walk for five minutes, unaccompanied, down a lonely country road (in these days when elderly ladies are hit on the head and their handbags taken, at every turning!) listen to her private performance of *Façade*, and then return to London by the 11.49. It only takes three-quarters of an hour to get there by train, dear! And I am not to be allowed anything to eat in the house, although I am one of the authors.

Thursday. I began this letter yesterday, but did not feel like finishing it, as I saw a poor little boy of eight or nine, knocked down and killed. I saw him running, and then I heard screams from people on a bus, and after a while two policemen came running, and he was lifted up and put on to somebody's coat. I see in the paper that it was a lorry that killed him, but I thought it was the bus. It was just by the Tube in Queen's Road – Bayswater Road. I was quite close. . . .

John Hayward (1905–65) was the highly influential and notoriously waspish critic and editor who would later share accommodations with T. S. Eliot in Chelsea. ES broke off her friendship with him in 1935 over his comments on her Aspects of Modern Poetry *(see Letter 150), but they were reconciled in 1944 (see Letter 228).*

126. *To John Hayward*

22 Pembridge Mansions
Moscow Road
London, W.2

[31 March 1932]

Dear Mr. Hayward,

It was so charming of you to send me your anthology,[7] and this long delay in writing to thank you for so delightful a present, is due, first of all, to a series of lectures, and a reading, and then to the horrors of proof-correcting. For I did not want to write until I could do so with a full realisation of the delights of the book. It is particularly interesting to me, because, although your anthology and my second, and third (forthcoming) anthology cover the same period, we rarely cover the same ground. I am jealous, as well as happy, that you have included the four heavenly Keats Odes, and Shelley's 'To Night', one of the loveliest of all poems, and the beauties from 'Prometheus Unbound'. I am especially delighted, too, with your Tennyson, because, with the exception of 'Tears, idle tears' we touch different ground again, and that means that, when I am travelling, if I take *your* anthology and *my* anthologies, I shall be rich with nearly all the beauties I could need.

We touch the same ground, again, in the inclusion of Rossetti's 'The Woodspurge', but our choice of Christina Rossetti is different, for I have gone completely mad, and have included the whole of 'Goblin Market'.

Your anthology includes more poets than mine; your taste, I think, is more catholic. But under the influence of your anthology I am beginning to feel positively *calm* about Matthew

Arnold – a state which I did not think would ever be mine, on that subject.

Indeed, I am most grateful to you, both for having sent me the anthology, and for the pleasure it has given me. As for mine, it won't appear till the autumn; when it does, I shall send it to you, if I may.

These last two weeks have been very distressing, with poor Mr. Monro's death. Did you know him? His wife has been quite wonderful, but her agony of mind has been very great, yet she has behaved with greatness and dignity.

With kindest regards, and most grateful thanks,
Yours sincerely
Edith Sitwell

---

127. *To George Russell ('A.E.')*[8]

22 Pembridge Mansions
Moscow Road
London, W.2

2 April 1932

Dear Mr. Russell,

It was exceedingly kind of you to write to me about my very unworthy review of the most beautiful book – the most revealing book on the poet's mind, and on how poetry springs into being – of our time.[9] I cannot, if you will allow me to say so, think of any essay since Shelley's which tells so much, and with such beauty.

Your letter gave me great delight, and I should have written to thank you before, but when it arrived, I was away lecturing, then I had a most tiresome attack of influenza, and after that, the husband of an old friend died.

My review of *Song and its Fountains* was wretchedly inadequate, I felt at the time, and feel now. For I had only three days in which to read, and then write about, that most beautiful book, before my review must go to press, and in those three days it was not possible to write about it as I should have wished.

When I spoke about the difference between the Celtic and the Saxon spirit, what I meant was, that the images which spring to our minds are, to some degree, different, necessarily, since our mythologies, our legends, our landscapes, are different. But once you have produced for us, from your dream and your creative impetus, those images, they become ours as though they had sprung from our dream also.

Poetry moves on such differing wings, and grows as naturally as a plant grows from the earth. Your noble tribute to all poetry, your revelation of the poet's mind, this lights all poetry, and should, even, teach those people who would like to love poetry but cannot because of some blindness in their nature, why *we* love it. . . .

---

128. *To Allen Tanner*

22 Pembridge Mansions
Moscow Road
London, W.2

Friday [29 April 1932]

Dearest Allen,

What a monster you must think me for not writing before; but I have been feeling like the yokels who sit on a gate throughout the short summer day, watching, with their mouths wide open, the snails racing! I mean time has consisted of nothing but lumps of indigestible boredom punctuated by weeping widows and other bores. And I am going to set out on a career of crime, and be completely heartless with these persons, for it has now come to a point where, either I rush for miles to hear them grumble, and do no work, or I don't rush for miles to hear them grumble, and they are huffy – but I *do* work.

I am still surprised at one statement that you made in your last letter: i.e. that Men in Australia listen to Melba[10] singing

'God Save the King' on the gramophone! No such thing. It would be a travesty of their manhood. No, they gallop forty miles through the Bush to hear Melba, in person, sing 'Land of Hope and Glory'. In the evenings they drowse over a pipe, or write a letter to the Old Folks, for they have to be up at four, cutting down such of the bush as has grown in the night.

Stella has already found that America does not produce manly sports of this kind. She seems to be enjoying herself very much there.

Allen, dear, I do wish I knew how life is treating you at present. I am afraid, I feel in my heart, that everything must be very bad, because it is with everyone, more or less. I do wish to heaven this nightmare would pass, and that the world would become sane again. It will never do for us to lose even a drop of faith, of belief, and of hope. But I *am* beginning to dislike the rich, heartless, and completely selfish people. They are as ugly in their minds as they are in their faces (which is, generally, saying a good deal).

And that reminds me. Pavlik tells me he has been seeing Lady Fitzherbert. I hope she has bought a picture. She has well over £3000 a year, and nobody to consider but herself (as you know, she had, according to the law case, £5000, which is enormous)[11] and I think she could afford to cultivate her mind, as well as to get clothes. However, that is not my business, as she is Pavlik's friend, and not mine. However, I thought I'd suggest to you that she should go to *The Galerie Vignon.*

Geoffrey has gone abroad. I always get my geographical facts rather mixed, so I daresay I'm wrong in thinking he has gone to the Red Sea. If he has, I hope to heavens there won't be an accident. I mean, it would be awkward for the other people, if the Sea suddenly parted, and the boat got stuck.

My best wishes, my dear, for a very happy Russian Easter. *And write to me, you wicked creature. You never write.*

Much love from your old friend
Edith

129. *To Allen Tanner*

Long Itchington .
near Rugby
Warwickshire

[6 August 1932]

My dear Allen,

I started this letter a week ago, and then the horrors of turning out everything in the flat,[12] storing most things, and packing others, sorting manuscripts – and the sadness of leaving my home, became too much for me.

The reason why I have not sent this poem to you before, is that I have been writing and re-writing it, softening it, rounding it, etc. Oddly enough, my absence from poetry for so long seems to have *broadened* my technique. This, if I may say so to another artist, never lacked a kind of violent strength and vigour, but extreme breadth and peace was difficult to me.

When I go up north, which I shall do shortly, I am going to set about getting that photograph I promised you from Cecil Beaton. This would have been done before, but first of all, Cecil was in America, and *then*, when he returned, he kept on asking me when I would go and stay with him and his sister Nancy in the country, saying I had only to choose my own time. Well, I cannot, fond as I am of him (he is extraordinarily nice), do that, because he lives near all sorts of people whom I do not like, so I have to wait until I am out of the way, to ask for that photograph.

How are you, dear Allen. I heard rumours of you giving a series of concerts in the autumn. Is that true? I do hope so. I think it would be so lovely if next summer, or next winter, you gave a concert in London. I have been thinking so much of that. For I do think the financial situation here will be better soon, and that then it will be possible for artists – *fine* artists, in all the arts, to make more money. I am very much determined that you *shall* and *must* give a concert here, Allen dear. We shall have to wait a bit, because everything is so frightful at the moment, but you must and shall have a concert, as soon as things are better.

This is a most exquisite, very tiny Elizabethan house, with a long low front, very pale timbers, and whitewash, and latticed windows, and the front of the house covered with jasmine, great hedges of sweetbriar, and everything exquisite. Georgia sleeps in the bedroom that Queen Elizabeth stayed in, in 1572, on her way to Kenilworth. There are two ghosts here. One is what the servants call 'a man in a top hat, with a strange thing round his neck, and who complains.' This is a man who was implicated in the Gunpowder Plot, and who was caught in the cellars here, and the 'top hat' is a top hat of that age. The other ghost is Queen Elizabeth, who, whenever a woman of our family (we should have been her cousins on both my mother's and my father's side) comes to this house, whizzes over here and opens the wardrobes to see what sort of dresses her cousin wears. She hasn't done that to me yet, but if she does, she will find only dresses of the year before last. . . .

Oh, how I wish that the general world finances would clear up, so that we could all have a little peace and prosperity. Speaking of world finance, my beloved Father is over here, and is 'after' us like a fox after chickens.

Much love to you, Allen dear, and to the whole family

Your friend
Edith

I may live in this house, soonish, and you will be dragged here to pay me long visits. What a lovely time we would have.[13]

1933

130. *To Sacheverell Sitwell*

129 Rue Saint-Dominique
Paris VIIe

[24 May 1933]

My darling Sachie,

I am still absolutely spell-bound by the *Canons of Giant Art*. There is certainly no poetry of our time which can even *attempt* to stand beside it, and certainly no poetry since Swinburne at his very best. All I can say is, if it is not great poetry, then we have never had great poetry in England. It is, of course, on a much bigger scale than Swinburne, whom I have just mentioned, being on the same sort of scale as Milton. It is also so miraculously varied, and so strange. The difference in texture between the lovely, soft wilderness of roses in poetry on page 35, and the terrible hopeless wilderness of death in 'Agamemnon's Tomb'; the incredible sweetness of the description of the bees at the beginning of the 'Fugal Siege', contrasted with the strange whirring sound of the page devoted to 'The iron men drink; it is a feast of wasps', melting into the lovely harvest moonlight – all these things are real miracles. And why do I think of snow, or of hail falling, when I read about

> *'Priam and Paris, all the heroes of the siege,*
> *with Cassandra and Hecuba, Hector and Achilles'?*

'Aeneas hunting Stags upon the Coast of Libya' is incredibly beautiful. And the lines in 'Cephalus and Procris':

> *'But it was an ilex-tragedy, those boughs of mourning*
> *Are ever dark for Procris, her very name*
> *In broken syllables is spoken by the leaves'* —

is nothing short of absolute magic. Nobody but a very great poet could have written anything to touch all this, and I, personally, cannot think of anything to exceed it. I haven't the faintest doubt that you are one of the greatest poets we have ever had (and, although she doesn't deserve it, England certainly has had some great poets).

All this I had been meaning to say to you if I'd seen you on your way back from Mimizan. I did hope you were coming, but I suppose it was some confounded rushing from station to station that prevented you.

My darling, once again, I am more proud than I can possibly say to have this great poetry dedicated to me. You know what poetry means to me, and you know what I have always known your poetry to be.

Will you please send Yeats a copy? I don't know his address. But *please* do that, and let me know when you have. The Old Old Man will probably lay hands upon you as a result, but that you will have to put up with.

What Hell Renishaw will be this year. I've seen the Gingers, to whom I've given a thorough fright. As for the Russian busy-body, she is in disgrace. Ginger suddenly rounded on her, saying: 'If you can have received Such a letter from My Daughter, Madame Snooks' (or whatever her name is), 'you must have done something unforgivable.' Her Ladyship, having put her up to the whole thing, ratted as usual, and left her to it, and now throws doubts on the legality of the Russian's marriage, and Madame Whatever her name is telephones day in, day out, to Allanah weeping down the telephone, and saying: 'Oh, where is my letter – *Where?* Restore it to me! Oh Give! Tell my Good Friends I am not what they believe!' – You see, she had gnawed her way into the house, and was intending to stay there eating for the rest of her life.

Oh dear, the Gingers *are* a pair!

I am having a fearful time in the papers about my *Eccentrics*[1] with an arch man with clanking rows of teeth like barbed wire entanglements (as I told Osbert) who thinks I stole his silver tooth pick when he was brought to tea with me, and so now he is avenging himself.

Very best love, my darling, to you and Georgia and Reresby,
and please *do* write.

ever your loving
Edith

---

*In 1933, ES assumed a much more sympathetic view of Tanner, who had
been replaced in Tchelitchew's affections by Charles Henri Ford (b. 1913),
a surrealist poet and the co-author, with Tchelitchew's future biographer
Parker Tyler (1907–74), of a sexually explicit novel entitled* The Young
and the Evil *(Paris, 1933).*

131. *To Allen Tanner*

Renishaw Hall

[15 August 1933]

Dearest Allen,

I do hope so much to have news of you soon – and good
news. For both your last letter, and the impression left on me by
my last visit, made me feel that you are most bitterly unhappy.
But I do know, and am sure, of one thing: you *are* loved by the
people whom you love, although, at this moment, you believe
you are not. But I also know, and understand, what you feel at
this constant procession of gimcrack figures, or not even figures,
empty clothes of a taking gaudiness. I know what it is, because I
have felt it too, but at the present time, I mind no longer, for I
have had too much, and am too tired in every way.

I do wish you were here, excepting that the rows are continual. I am writing what *should* be a satisfactory poem, but am
interrupted every other moment, and on every trivial pretext, so
that it is impossible to see the poem whole. My mother who has
an absolute mania for the Greek satellites of Greek royalties,
imported, recently, the aide-de-camp of the ex-King of Greece,
a bald, watchful man of almost unexampled boringness. Osbert

and Sachie refuse to talk to him, so I have to look after him
from morning till night, as he will not countenance being left
alone. He is a very early riser, and is of an untiringly enquiring
disposition. Luckily, I have been able to tell him so much of the
conditions in the mines, and among the miners, that he wishes
he had never mentioned either. Life is also enlivened by my
father walking up and down the lawn, just outside the windows,
dictating letters to his secretary: 'Messrs. Humdinger,
Humdinger and Humdinger. As I remarked in my last letter:
Worm. Worm. Worm. Read what you've got.'

I do not know where I shall go, when I leave here at the end
of the month. Probably to stay with Inez Chandos-Pole near
Derby. And after that, I simply don't know. I have no news,
excepting that Osbert's new unpublished novel[2] is absolutely
brilliant, but will, I should think, land him in three different
libel actions. He is perfect on the subject of the D. H. Lawrence
ménage – but they really deserve everything they have got, for
Lawrence's scandalous attack on Osbert.[3]. . .

Later

The most frightful series of rows between Osbert and
Sachie – *v.* my father (or rather the other way round) have now
ended in such a scene that I can't conceive what will happen
next. Very possibly, I should think, a law-case. Father is trying
to force Osbert and Sachie to tie down their money to such an
extent that should they, and Reresby, die before Georgia, all the
money will go to a 6th cousin, and she will be left with £300 a
year, plus what her father gives her. The whole thing is too disgraceful for words, and if it *does* come to a law-case, there will
be an appalling scandal. *But don't tell a soul*, as we want to avoid
a scandal, and extra trouble, if possible.

This is a frightfully dull, as well as a gloomy letter, but I feel as
if all my blood had been sucked, and my brains eaten by clothes
moths. What I would give to be able to work uninterrupted!

How is *your* work, my dear Allen? Pavlik told me in his letter
that you are working very hard indeed, and I do hope that you
are pleased with the work? Let me have some news of you, for
goodness sake, in spite of the inexpressiveness of this letter. If I

am left in peace after lunch (which I doubt) I will copy out some lines from my poem for you, if not, I will send those under separate cover. The poem is in fragments at the moment, not having been formed into a whole.

Best love to you and Pavlik and Schoura,

Your friend
Edith

---

132. *To Charles Henri Ford*

Renishaw Hall

23 August 1933

Dear Mr. Ford,

Thank you for sending me your novel. I think that there is much good writing, and that you have a strong visual sense, but I *do* get tired of the perpetual pillow fights. Frankly, don't either of you young men know *anybody* who is capable of getting into his own bed and stopping there? If you do, for goodness sake cultivate his acquaintance, and write about him next time for a change. Also, calling a spade a spade never made the spade interesting yet. Take my advice, leave spades alone, or if you must mention them, then mention the garden too.

All the miners round here – they are not an expressive race – use words which recur over and over again on your pages. But I don't find they add anything to my consciousness.

No, no, you [should] develop your talent along different lines, and let us have some more writing like that page about the girl and the sailor – with the last phrase left out.

Yours sincerely
Edith Sitwell

P.S. I mean that our forefathers, though an ignorant lot in some ways, were no more ignorant of the processes of excretion than are their descendants today. But apart from medical treatises, these things do not in themselves make interesting reading.

The prose rhythms of your book really deserve a more worthy subject, next time.

---

133. *To Allen Tanner*

Radbourne Hall
Derby

[August 1933]

Dearest Allen,

I can't imagine what you must think of me for not answering your very sad letter before, but just a day after it arrived there was such an *appalling* battle that I was, and have remained, completely shattered. The lack of consideration is frightful. The fact that certain people knew that I was nearly dead with fatigue and worry and apprehension did not prevent them from worrying me nearly out of my wits with the least little thing.

My poor dear friend, I *know* what you have been through. You are the most loyal and devoted of friends. But I *beg* of you not to do anything rash. You *cannot* part company – you can't do it. He is absolutely devoted to you, and you are absolutely devoted to him. You have *great* wisdom, and your wisdom will carry you through. I too have known great sadness and bitterness, but I think I know it no longer. Neither of you, Allen dearest, would be able, as I see it, to endure life apart. Your lives have been too closely knit together, in a great and noble friendship. I wonder if you ever realise how deeply I appreciate you, and with what affection.

Something so strange is coming my way, unless I am very mistaken, though it won't be immediately – probably not for some time. I am sorry to be so mysterious, but it wouldn't do to be explicit to even you until, and if, it materialises, because speech drives events away sometimes.

There does not seem to be any news, as far as I am concerned, excepting that I have written the enclosed poem, and seem to be on the verge of writing another. Then, I suppose, I shall have to return to my treadmill.

It makes me more wretched than I can say, knowing you have been so unhappy. As I say, you are the most loyal and devoted of friends. He told me once – more than once – that your friend-ship had been, and was, with his painting, the greatest thing in his life. So you must *never* believe, at any moment, that he does not love you, for he does, deeply. His trouble is that he gets taken in by cheap flimsy little horrors of people.

By the way, that book which was sent me to read is both boring and inexpressibly foul. Forgive this sinister dark stain on the paper. It *isn't* spilt blood: it is gum. For this is the last piece of paper on the block, and I can't get hold of any more at the moment. *Do* write to me. I go on the 21ˢᵗ to Badminton for a few days, then on the 28ᵗʰ back to Renishaw.

Bless you dear friend.

With love
Your friend
Edith

You *must* forgive the delay in answering. When I got here, I collapsed completely.

---

134. *To Allen Tanner*

Renishaw Hall
[4 October 1933]

Dearest Allen,

I do hope my wire arrived safe, though it was a day late. I know you'll forgive me when you know why. For a month I had had a swelling on my gum, and felt curiously ill. So when I went to London, I rushed to the dentist, the day before your birthday. He said it was an abscess which had eaten from one tooth under another, and fastened on the bone, and that I had to have it out that moment. They gave me a new anaesthetic and *cut out*, not

pulled out, the tooth. I was under the anaesthetic for one hour
and twenty minutes, instead of half an hour, and they thought I
was not coming round. Well, I was helped back home to bed (in
the hotel where my beloved parents were staying) and lay, too
weak to move, for two days. Then I came back here (because I
couldn't stand Mother's whining any longer) and went to bed
here. I have got *three* abscesses, as well as the one on the bone.
So that was why I seemed so heartless over your birthday, my
dear friend. But I wasn't really. And this letter brings you my
fond love and all best wishes for the coming year. I hope nothing will be *quite* so unhappy as this last year has been. I would
not live through it again, for a good deal.

I should have enjoyed being at Badminton a great deal, if it
had not been for feeling so ill. I saw the loveliest houses. I do
not know any part of England which is so beautiful, it is really
incredible. Louise Beaufort[4] is a perfect dowager, I don't know
such a perfect one, and perfection is always amusing, and Mary
Beaufort,[5] my younger cousin-by-marriage, is delightful
(although she is the Queen's niece, and dangerously like her).
The park has a strange Tchaikovsky-like quality, with a mock-
gothic gamekeeper's house called Ragged Castle, and a pleasure
house surrounded by avenues, called Swan Park, and a walled
orchard called Cherry Gardens. The Beauforts are fearfully poor,
so most of the house is shut up.

We went over to tea at a very beautiful house (of the time of
James II) called Dyrham, and inhabited by an old gentleman of
eighty-two with a black plush nose. The house had the most
beautiful mahogany doors I had ever seen, with strange gilt key-
holes shaped like suns, curtains of red velvet that were as soft
and deep as rose-petals, and cabinets made of nutmeg-wood.
Outside there were huge terraces with magnolia trees. The old
gentleman is descended from the War Minister of James II,
William and Mary, and Queen Anne; and when Queen Anne
kicked him out, he went off with all William of Orange's private
maps for his march to London, so there they are now at
Dyrham. The old gentleman was affable to *us*, but three days
before, Gerald Wellesley[6] and three other diplomats (I explain

that they were diplomats because of what happened) were sent over to tea with him, and stopped rather late, as the house is full of interest. So the old gentleman, in a clarion voice, because he is deaf, inquired of the cousin who keeps house for him: '*Faut-il les inviter à diner?*' At the sound of this cryptogram, so inexplicable to diplomats, they fled madly, as you may imagine.

From Badminton we went on to stay with Violet Gordon Woodhouse,[7] the harpsichordist. She is very beautiful and delightful. And an old and reverenced friend came over to see us, William Davies[8] the poet. He is one of the four finest living English poets, and I was so happy to see him again. We sat talking till 2 in the morning, and I am afraid our hostess was worn out.

I have just received a letter from Pavlik which has hurt me terribly. I did not need this extra blow to convince me, to prove to me, that he has lost any affection he ever had for me – if indeed he ever had any. When he has been betrayed by the last of the cheap worthless people by whom he is so dazzled, perhaps he will realise the kind of friendship that mine is, and with what loving care I have watched over him and tried to help him in his worries, and comfort him. But who knows that it will not then be too late.

Amongst other things, he is angry with me because I sent him those birthday prognostications. But I had the strongest reasons for doing so. In the first place, *I know* that his present friendships can only lead to fresh disasters for him (I am *not* referring to little James[9]), and secondly I dread either him or you going to America, because it will only mean fresh rats in the woodwork, and, at this time, it will not mean money. Again, he is furious with Osbert for suggesting that ballet. I cannot see why it is any worse for Osbert to suggest that than it was for the other ballet to be suggested. Osbert thinks it part of the duty of any artist to suggest what he thinks will be advantageous to other artists. He does, for me, all the time, *and* for Sachie, *and* for Willie. And so he did for Pavlik too.

I have no other news, excepting that Mrs. D. H. Lawrence's daughter has just telegraphed to Osbert asking for permission to photograph this house for a film which is to be made of *Lady Chatterley's Lover*!!!!!! Words fail me. You realise, don't you, that Osbert was portrayed as the cripple in that filthy novel – in unprintable words? We have telegraphed back saying that her request is as gross and coarse as it is libellous.

My love to you, dear Allen. And *please* write to me. I am feeling more ill than I can say, and very despondent about everything, for I have had a terrible letter from Helen. My best birthday wishes and my love to you all

Your friend
Edith

ES's letters to the Jewish novelist Charlotte Franken Haldane (1894–1969), then married to J. B. S. Haldane, reveal her firm views on the rise of the Nazis in Germany. Her letters do contain occasional anti-Semitic flippancies (see, for example, Letter 111), but, unlike some of her modernist contemporaries, including for a time SS and OS, she had no sympathy whatever with Fascism.

135. *To Charlotte Franken Haldane*

129 Rue Saint-Dominique
Paris VIIe

[19 November? 1933]

My dear Charlotte,

I should have answered your most kind and charming letter before, but have been so plunged in worry and gloom that I could do nothing. One of the two life-long friends with whom I share a flat here (they are sisters) has had two operations for the most terrible of all illnesses, and her aspect now, and her weakness, frighten me.

What you said about my poems made me feel very happy about my poetry. I myself think it traditional poetry, descended

from Spenser, Milton, Marvell and Dryden, and completely
unrelated to the later poets. It is descended, too (as far as
English poetry *could* be descended from French poetry) from
Baudelaire.

I am going to read *Brother to Bert* and *I bring not Peace* at
once. For about three years now, I've had to read nothing but
books about Pope, and books about Bath, and books about
Eccentrics (the last two subjects greatly against my will) and
now I am going to do a little reading which gives me *pleasure*. I
look forward to reading both those books tremendously. And I
look forward, too, to the new one when it is ready.

Yes, the years between twelve and seventeen do make a
tremendous impression on one, but so do the years between four
and seven, when one's senses have the most extraordinary
acuity. I can still smell the mimosa trees and the fields of nar-
cissi at Cannes which I smelt when I was four.

To go back to Marvell, I do think 'The Nymph and her Fawn'
is a perfect poem, and 'The Bermudas' almost so. But as for
poetry altogether, I think there are very few perfect poems,
though 'The Eve of Saint Agnes' is, for one.

Thank you so much again, and I am so glad we are going to
call each Charlotte and Edith

Yours
Edith (Sitwell)

---

136. *To Charlotte Franken Haldane*

129 Rue Saint-Dominique
Paris VIIe

5 December 1933

My dear Charlotte,

I cannot tell you how much pleasure your letter gave me. I
should, too, have answered days ago, but for about three weeks
now I've been having the most fearful headaches, which are

getting worse and worse. Why don't I see a doctor? Because he would tell me to take exercise, ride on horseback, eat cabbage, drink (like an unfortunate friend of mine) luke warm Vichy water instead of early morning tea, lead a healthy life, sleep with my window open, and, most of all, *not think* about anything. Ah! I know them!

I have sent for the novels, and am longing, too, to see your essay, your theory of aesthetics. (Meanwhile, why don't you take it to Richard de la Mare[10] of Faber and Faber?) I shall be most interested to see it, and it delights me that you have written about my beloved Carroll and Lear.

What a dear you are to say you will write an article on my poetry at the time of the medal-giving.[11] I can't think of anything which would give me more delight. It really *would* please me more than I can possibly say.

I've been feeling terribly unhappy lately, and our correspondence is one thing which I look forward to. I've seen people behaving in such a dreadfully ugly way just lately. And I never can get used to it. I mean, in my personal life it has been very bad, oh very bad. And outside, these horrible lynchings in America, and the departure last week of the French convict ship for Devils' Island, have upset me terribly. Nineteen hundred and thirty three years after Christ, and the 'righteous' are still behaving like this!

To go to other subjects: I believe Willie Walton's symphony is going on very well, though he still swears about the slow movement. (When I see you, I shall tell you an exquisite joke about that, but I can't write it.) He has gone down to spend the winter with Sacheverell and Georgia (Sacheverell's wife). Georgia in a letter to me the other day said: 'I hope to heaven he'll behave!' I was so amused at your description of the pianists at the concert you went to. How I hate this tickling and milking of the piano! It makes one fly to vulgar but robust pianists like Artur Rubinstein.[12] Anyhow he is a real *homme du métier*. He can *play* the piano.

I love Bach, too. But though I admire Mozart, I love him less, which is my fault, preferring infinitely, Gluck, because he is less sweet. Bach is my god. He seems to have created a perfect world, in which there is no sin, and in which sorrow is holy and not ugly.

I do hope that poor girl about whom you wrote, is better. I know how terrible rheumatic fever is. My poor friend has had a second operation for cancer. She is one of the bravest women I have ever known.

Please answer my letter as soon as you have time, as soon as you can. I know how busy you are, but please find time soon. This letter would have been written sooner, but I couldn't think.

With love

Edith

---

137. *To Charlotte Franken Haldane*

129 Rue Saint-Dominique
Paris VIIe

[December 1933]

My dear Charlotte,

I was more moved than I can possibly say when I received your first letter, and was made most happy and proud by the second, which I got this morning. Indeed, I scarcely know what to say first – there is so much to say. I do not know whether to thank you first for your exquisite delicacy of feeling in writing to me as you did, or your noble defence of my poetry.

I love to think of your reading my 'Romance' to a friend whom you love so much, and I am so happy that it was real and true to you both. Someone, an owl called Philip Henderson,[13] who has always been rude to me in the papers, wrote, the other day, saying that nothing roused any real feeling in me, as far as my poetry was concerned, but Love, Age and Death! Can you beat it? And he went on to say that nobody knew *who* were the two people in love, in my 'Romance!' – Had I not received your letter and your essay on my poetry this morning, I should most certainly have written and said that the lady's name is Miss Perkins, but that I am pledged not, for the moment, to reveal that of the gentleman, because he is employed in a department of one of the West-London Stores! But I decided, after reading what you had written, to keep silence and my temper.

I cannot tell you what it means to me that you have written as you have about my poetry. It is the only real happiness I have had, apart from writing 'Romance', for very long.

My former letter to you was so inexpressive. Indeed you are right in speaking of the primal horror of Germany at present. It makes my blood boil. I did not know that you are a Jewess, but with the exception of one person, all my dearest friends (I have very few) are either Jewish or in part Jewish. So apart from the rage and horror I feel in the cruelty of the Nazis, I understand the crétinism of it. To ill-treat and turn out a gentle and faithful people – certainly the most faithful of any I have ever known! But do not fear, dear Charlotte, that such outrages against decency and sense will ever occur in England. We know too well what our Jewish citizens have done for us. But I know the anguish you must feel in contemplating Germany.

I will return your essay on my poetry tomorrow, and also the devastating 'Note on American Literature', which really made me laugh till I cried. There is nothing left to be said, either about Gertrude, or about Americans. I am so glad Geoffrey Gorer asked you to send it to me. I have read it over and over again. As for the essay on my poetry, it seems to me more than perfect, and has made me happy and proud, and has made me feel more inclined to write poetry than I have felt for a year. There is only one thing: the fashion plates of the 'Elegy on Dead Fashion' were really mine, and not Tom Balston's.

Osbert was here for two days, on Sunday and Monday, on his way to Pekin. That was so lovely for me, but I was very sad, too, because I shall never see my home again, for reasons which I will tell you when I see you.

My love to you, and so much gratitude, dear Charlotte. I do hope you are better –

Edith

138. *To Sacheverell Sitwell*

129 Rue Saint-Dominique
Paris VIIe

[December 1933]

My darling Sachie,

A very, very happy Christmas to you, my darling, and I do *wish* we were all together, you, Georgia, Osbert, Reresby, and me. Bless you, my darling, I hope in about three weeks' time to *be* with you, if you'll have me. For I come over about the 12th, to receive my Medal on the 24th. How heavenly it will be to be with you again. And oh what fun about the Royal Society of Literature, who are black with rage at having to have me. But a strange wave of popularity has flowed over me, I imagine as a result of it. Mrs. Epstein,[14] having forgotten me for four years, has asked me to a thé dansant – (and I must say I'd have given worlds to have seen it). Mr. W. B. Maxwell[15] who met me at lunch four years ago, has never seen me since, and didn't see me then (if you know what I mean), has asked me to his daughter's party. Why? *Why?* That is what I ask myself. And one will never find out – that is what is so sad.

I had a letter from Blunden two days ago, in which he says that you and I live 'far from the noise of the Poetry Contractors, with their electric drills and demolition gangs'. Nothing could be better expressed. I am being allowed, by the *Morning Post*, to half murder Leavis[16] and his gang (though *not*, alas, wriggling little Grigson,[17] because he writes for them).[18] And I'm doing it in grand style. So keep a look out. I've also 'paid' little Spender[19] for his impertinence to you. I've said he has a slight, pretty gift for poetry, but has not produced any work of any importance, and that he is grossly overrated.

Life here is hell. Poor Helen is so terribly weak and ill. She is perfectly dreadful. On Saturday last we had a fearful time with her, and I honestly thought it was the end. I saw Osbert on his way to Pekin, and he gave me the lovely black red and green amber he has foreclosed on. *You* know where from. The author and only begetter of the amber,[20] by the way, is trying to make out he is breaking up, conveying that impression by stooping, wobbling his head from side to side with a perpetuum-mobile movement, and emitting, from time to time, a hollow, owl-like cough. Her 'Ell,[21] by the way, seems to be playing a very funny game in all this.

Did you ever get Lascelles Abercrombie's[22] letter about your poetry? Do tell me. I think the thing to do is now for us to join up with all the people like that, and simply 'go for' all the little worms like Spender etc. (only *not* Auden, because he *can* write, and *is* respectful) in company with them. After all, we mayn't go mad with enthusiasm about Blunden, Abercrombie, etc., but at least they *do know what poetry ought to be like*. And they *are* scholars.

Have I any other news? No, none. Excepting that I can't write. Are you working hard?

Very best love, my darling, and how heavenly it is to think that I shall be seeing you so soon.

Ever your loving

Edith

---

139. *To Rée Gorer*[23]

129 Rue Saint-Dominique
Paris VIIe

[December 1933]

My dear Rée,

. . . I've just had, between ourselves (and, naturally Geoffrey and Peter) the most perfect experience with Allen. I've only been to their flat twice or three times since my return, because Pavlik is much occupied, and I think Russians only *really* like idiots, prostitutes and dressmakers – preferably people who are all three in one. However, he is now relenting a little towards me, because it is obvious that if my life goes on in this way much longer, I *shall* be an idiot (or at least mad), even if I can't attain to the other ideals. So I asked the whole family to dine with me on Christmas night. They accepted. But ten days after, I got a letter from Allen saying could I have them to lunch instead, or, alternately, he would arrange to take me to the house of a dear American friend of his for dinner, as this gentleman had now invited them to dine on Christmas night, and he thought they would go there!! He did this, I may say, without Pavlik's knowledge. I have been extremely firm, not to say cross, and have said that I am not in the habit of going to strangers' houses for my dinner at Christmas.

I saw Osbert on his way to Pekin. His dear old father has now cut him and Sachie out of his will, and has left a codicil saying how badly and vilely we have all behaved. We shan't know *what* we've done until the old gentleman dies and the will is read. But may that day be soon, for I confess to curiosity on the point. . . .

---

140. *To Georgia Sitwell*

129 Rue Saint-Dominique
Paris VIIe

Thursday [December 1933]

My darling Georgia,

A very, very happy Christmas to you, and how I do *wish* we were all together, my darling. I do miss you so much, and although I have been very bad about writing these last few weeks, it isn't my fault. Life has been undiluted hell, and I simply haven't had the spirit. I won't tell you the tragedies, because it would be too depressing for you.

I do so hope your acidity is better. Poor darling, I do sympathise with you; it is awful [to] have blains of any sort. I've come out in a plague of boils, like Job, all over, which annoys me. Do ask the doctor if it wouldn't be a good thing if you drank orange juice neat six times a day. Because when I was 17, in Germany, I had much the same thing, and was tormented with it, and the doctor cured me by that – alternate orange juice and lemon juice, neat.

The Royal Society of Literature is behaving about the giving of the medal, as if they were Catherine of Braganza being 'forced to receive' Lady Castlemaine.[24] This tragedy in their history will take place on the 24th of January, so I shall come to England about the 12th, and please, darling, may I come to you about the 14th or 15th? That howling Missionary Woman Edith Olivier[25] is trying to make me arrive in England in the middle of the night, so as to stay with her – at least at 8 in the morning. I wonder. Do I want to wander about the Quais of France at 2 in the morning, in this wintry weather?

I had a letter from Siegfried in which he told me that his fiancée's 'maid had confirmed him in his belief that he was rescuing her from the horde of bores who had been the cause of her having a very bad nervous breakdown about four years ago.' I was so shocked I haven't answered it yet. Did you *ever* hear such a conglomeration of pretentious bosh? It is so complicated, too, in its implications.

Have you heard any more about the injured old Baronet? – I am delighted and happy to say that Osbert has taken some of the dear old man's black, red, and green amber and given it to me, to make into a bracelet.

Do keep a watch on the *Morning Post*. I am just about to roll on Mr. Leavis and some other critics in it. Osbert's savagery simply won't be in it. I am not being very delicate, either. Amongst other things, I am saying, 'Most modern critics, when writing on poetry, combine the attitude of a dear old country clergyman preaching a sermon on the Woman taken in Adultery, with the powers of expression of those interesting but amorphous persons who are placed in charge of the female household of a Sultan.' And I say, as well: 'Alas that what is believed by admiring Aunts and a friend from the University to be the Roar of the Lion is so often but the Squeak of the Pip!'

Cecil sent me such a sweet snapshot of Reresby the other day, looking *such* a man.

Very best love, my darling
ever your loving
Edith

1934

141. *To Charlotte Franken Haldane*

129 Rue Saint-Dominique
Paris VIIe

[January 1934]

My dear Charlotte,

I can't imagine what you must think of me for not writing before to thank you for – and express my delight in – your exquisite country bouquet, which is now framed and hangs opposite to me as I write to you. It was sweet of you to send me the bouquet. And I should have written so long ago, had it not been for one disaster after another. My poor friend who is so ill had a terrible attack of illness just before Christmas, and then, the very day after, a shocking tragedy in her family. In addition to these major things, 'they' have chosen this moment to set a giant machine in the ground of the house next door but one to 'creuser la terre' and make an underground garage. The noise is like that of a gigantic dentist's drill, and goes on from 7 in the morning till 5.

How nice it is to think I shall see you so soon. I arrive in England on the 16th, and I am asking Rée Gorer if I may come to her for the presentation of my medal.

A lecture was given at the American Women's Club here the other day, on the subject of Gertrude Stein, and I am *told*, though I cannot vouch for the truth of the rumour, that Gertrude wore a white Grecian robe, with her various chests surrounded by a gold – cestus, I think is the word – anyhow you will know what I mean. It must have been an impressive spectacle, and I can't think how she managed about her lingerie, for she usually wears dark grey knitted plus fours underneath everything.

Speaking of writers, do you know Wyndham Lewis, of the *Apes of God*? If so, the enclosed post card may amuse you. It is actually a photograph of two actors who were at Scarborough when we were children, but both (and especially the one on the right) are *exactly* like Lewis. The same slouch hat, dark spectacles, look of mystery and would-be romance, the same shaped hands – everything. And, if I may say so, the look of dirt. So, as Lewis insulted us in the *Apes of God*, Osbert had post cards of this photograph taken, and we bombarded Lewis with them from various parts of the globe, each post card bearing the same mad inscription: 'So there *are* two of you, Lewis?' etc. We also sent him telegrams. One ran thus: 'Achtung. Nicht hinauslehnen. Armoured Committee man about due. Better wireless help. Last night too late. Love. Ein Freund.' Another ran (he was having a nervous breakdown at the moment), 'We got your ticket. You report here next Saturday or we go for you. Nerve blather no excuse. Cold isn't it.' And Osbert's secretary lost a gold tooth, which was promptly done up in a jeweller's case and sent to Lewis, with Sir Gerald du Maurier's[1] card enclosed – (Osbert happened to have one).

I expect I shall be hearing Willie Walton's slow movement next week. The rest of the symphony is quite beautiful, and I do hope the slow movement is successful. He is spending the winter at Sachie's. He has lived with us, you know – with the exception of the last two years, ever since he was seventeen.

This is an inordinately long letter, and, I am afraid, a very boring one, for my mind is flat and dead. – And oh, if I don't write a poem soon!

My love, dear Charlotte, and thank you so much,

Yours
Edith

142. *To Osbert Sitwell*

Do not let the Gingers know I am here. (La Spezia)

Excelsior Hotel
Levanto
(La Spezia)
Italy

8 May 1934

My darling old boy,

I was so absolutely delighted to get your letter. And thank you ever so much for the really marvellous photograph of the actor as an ape. It is quite terrific – one of the most impressive things I have ever seen in my life. The depth of wisdom and the tragedy in the eyes is so extraordinary, and that heavy crown with the kind of furry dusty baubles attached to it. He must be a very great actor.

I came here a few days ago, because poor Helen has to have some sun. The sea is lovely, but the town is a triumph of ugliness, rather like the outskirts of Nottingham. However, the hotel is nice, the English people haven't found out who I am – or if they have, they don't care, and I can work quietly. I am at work at (besides that bloody Victoria[2]) a small book on modern poetry, in which I am simply going to 'let the devils have it'.

I wish you'd come back from China. Christabel complained to me that when one writes to you in China, one feels one is writing into space, and it is true.

I am sorry the English inhabitants of Pekin have been 'mad mud'[3] by my behaviour, but I can't regret the behaviour. There are some people it is impossible to snub. There is a ghastly American in Paris, quite young (a friend of Pavlik's) who pesters me with his poems, and I have half murdered him, but he still continues to dog my footsteps.[4] He showed me a sonnet the other day which began thus:

> 'Fatigue sits in your breast like a spring hare
> Gnawing the gross red cabbage of your heart,

> *Until, entreated by the spurious dart*
> *To leap into the room and be trapped there.'*

The other night, I went to Cocteau's[5] play on the subject of
Oedipus Rex. I don't want to be unkind, but I should have
thought *that* play *had* been written. But no, Cocteau comes
along with his little bourgeois mind, and dwarfs it from a vast
tragedy into nothing at all. The queen isn't like a queen, she is
like 'la patronne'. There is a ridiculous phosphorescent ghost
that moans and groans, the Sphinx is a dear little chorus girl
with curly hair. And in the end, when the afflicted pair finally
amble off the stage, I was more pleased to get rid of them than I
was to see the last of any pair, barring the Gingers. The play is
what one might describe as 'mignonne'.

Did I tell you that when I was in London I met someone who
knows the Leavises? He had been down to see them at
Cambridge and had dined with them. Mr. Leavis is small and
harassed-looking, and does 'coaching'. Mrs. L.[6] wears an emer-
ald green jumper and has a dyspeptic looking nose, and
eyeglasses. She is, of course, bobbed, and has black hair. Before
dinner, Mr. Leavis asked this man if he would like a drink, and
upon him replying he would, he was given a glass of Cydrax. I
don't know if you know what that is, but it is *non*-alcoholic
cider.

Before I left Paris, I went to a tea party to which Allanah
brought Mrs. 'arper. She was in grand form. She was looking
more like Hannen Swaffer[7] than ever, and was dressed with her
usual splendour – covered with tulle bows, ropes of pearls, diamond beetles, lucky gold pigs, lucky gold shoes, bangles, etc.
But, as a homely touch amidst all this splendour, she wore large
check bedroom slippers. These caused a certain amount of interest, but it transpired that Mrs. 'arper 'ad 'ad her foot bitten, by
whom or what she did not say, and was therefore obliged to
encase the wounded member in a bedroom slipper. A sense of
symmetry had caused her to wear the pair. On being told that
Pavlik is painting a new portrait of me, she said, in a burst of
uncontrollable enthusiasm: 'Ah, *Ow* I would love to be

deported to Yncient Greece, where burning Sappho loved and sang', then, looking round the room and feeling something had gone wrong somewhere, she added, 'And where the *Boys* were the Ryning Beauties and *all* the Ryge.' Sensation. Curtain. Shortly afterwards, she was withdrawn from circulation (much to my grief) by Allanah, who was very red in the face and had a steely glint in the eye.

Give Harold[8] my love. Poor Harold. I am sorry he is so poor. What an old beast his father is.

Very best love, my darling

ever your loving
Edith

My love to David, and thank him for his letter. Tell him I'm writing to him.

---

143. *To Osbert Sitwell*

129 Rue Saint-Dominique
Paris VIIe

[June 1934]

My darling old boy,

I was so delighted and happy to find your letter waiting for me when I got back from (hush) Italy. It is lovely that you are in England again, and perfect to think that, D.V., I shall see you in about a fortnight, for I shall come to England half way through July. Darling, I need not say that I shall *love* to come to Brides-les-Bains with you. It will be so lovely being with you again, and I can't tell you how much I am longing for it. What fun we will have, and what a sell for Ginger! If you don't mind, don't let's go to a hotel that is too expensive, as (as usual) I have to watch my step, or the 'dock'[9] would be after me.

Are you pleased or sorry to be back in London? I loved David's description of your conversations with the Chinese University lights, and your revealing to them the secrets of the private life of our new Savonarola.[10] Please give him (David) my love, and tell him I am writing to him, and should have done so before, but I wasn't sure where I should catch you.

Please don't tell Her 'ell you've heard from me, as she is pestering me out of my wits, and I am pretending I'm away. That pair is a real problem. They are getting more and more like Blake's *Book of Tiriel*:

'And aged Tiriel stood before the gates of his beautiful palace
with Myratana, once the queen of all the western plains
. . . the aged man raised up his [right] hand to the heavens,
His left supported Myratana, shrinking in pangs of death.
The orbs of his large eyes he open'd, and thus his voice went forth:
"Serpents, not sons, wreathing around the bones of Tiriel!
Ye worms of death, feasting upon your aged parents' flesh!
Listen, and hear your mother's groans! No more accursed sons
She bears . . ."'

etc. ad limitum.

If you will re-examine the *Book of Tiriel*, you will see it is exactly like the little problem we have to face. . . .

Does her 'ell telephone to you day *and* night? – I hear she has been fairly active with Mrs. Greville.[11] I didn't tell you. Everyone at Levanto was very scathing, and wouldn't speak to me, until an old lady turned up who knew I am the daughter of a baronet – then, you should just have seen the rush, which I am afraid rather missed fire.

How lovely it is, I shall be seeing you in about seventeen days from now, and how lovely it will be, our going away together in August.

Very best love, my darling

ever your loving
Edith

The pageant at Badminton is put off till *next* year. You must get going about it.

ES's *Aspects of Modern Poetry was published on 15 November 1934. It contained, in addition to attacks on Lewis, Leavis, and Grigson, essays on Hopkins, Yeats, Davies, Eliot, SS, and Pound. Although regarded as an important poet by some critics, SS was closer in his aestheticism to Swinburne than to Auden and Spender, and so was never likely to be celebrated in the 1930s. He was bitterly disappointed by the mixed reception, which included a savaging by Grigson, of Canons of Giant Art in 1933. His sister's essay, though it lavished praise on him, dwelt more on Dr. Donne and Gargantua than on the Canons, and so, in his view, compounded the neglect of his best poetry. He soon withdrew his complaints and apologised. ES wrote at length about the Canons in an essay on SS's poetry prefixed to his Collected Poems (London, 1936). See Bradford, pp. 250–1.*

144. *To Sacheverell Sitwell*

as from Hotel Excelsior
Levanto
(Spezia)
Italy

[November 1934?]

My darling Sachie,

Your letter hurt me most terribly; indeed, it upset me so much that I have been unable to answer it before. I cannot conceive how you can so have misunderstood my essay on you. The book was largely written so as to include that essay. I gave infinitely more thought, more care, and more time to it than to any other in the book, and everyone who has written to me about the book says it is one of the best.

I weighed everything *most* carefully. I could not *call* you a poet of genius because you are my brother, and it would have let loose a million little hounds at your throat. But I think I have *proved* you to be a poet of genius. I don't know how you can say I prefer Pound's *Cantos* to yours, because I hardly mention yours. There are sixteen pages about *Donne and Gargantua*, which to me is one of your greatest poems. It was, actually, more useful to me in proving my points than *Canons of Giant Art* would be, because it is easier to 'lift' quotations from it, than it is to lift quotations from the *Canons*. The texture of the *Canons*, line by line, is so intensely interwoven that a quotation would be like something torn. I deliberately chose the lyrics which I have discussed, because of their flawless shape, as a contrast to the nonsense which I *have* contrasted with them. I picked two points of contention with you, because I was determined that nobody should say 'here is a sister carried away by the fact of the poet being her brother.' I have, I think, combated and *absolutely* disproved *all* the charges which fools may bring against you.

When writing of Pound's *Cantos*, I made it clear that the first, which I single out for admiration, is a translation of a 15th translation of Homer!

I am terribly sorry you are having this awful worry with your overdraft. I also am in the soup as usual, and the 'dock is clamouring for an interview.

Tonight I am going to Levanto, to write *Victoria*.

Very best love,

Ever your loving
Edith

I think in my essay, I proved where your place is. With Milton, on one side, and with Marvell on the other.

1935

Aspects of Modern Poetry *plunged ES into, arguably, the most damaging controversy of her career. G. W. Stonier, in his review in the* New Statesman *(24 November 1934), noted that ES, even as she dismissed Leavis, made arguments extraordinarily like his. H. Sidney Pickering (1 December 1934) provided further instances of apparent plagiarism. In the issue of 8 December, Geoffrey Grigson levelled similar accusations, while ES and OS wrote separately to deny the claims. In the issue of 15 December, Grigson pressed his points again, now joined by Wyndham Lewis, while the literary critic and barrister John Sparrow (1906–92) disputed the contents of Grigson's first letter. On 22 December 1934, a letter from ES appeared disputing that of Pickering. Sparrow reviewed the book favourably in the TLS on 13 December 1934. Letters from Grigson and Lewis to press the case for plagiarism appeared in the TLS on 20 December 1934. Writers in various publications also identified misquotations and misattributions in the book.*

145. *To Georgia Sitwell*

Hotel Excelsior
Levanto
(La Spezia)
Italy

[c. January 1935]

My darling Georgia,

I wish you with all my heart a very happy New Year, my darling, and Sachie too. . . .

Thank you ever so much, darling, for your letter and the *Times Lit. Supp.* I was too late to answer in this issue, but have sent the enclosed letter to the editor, and hope it will come out in the next. I think it is a little beauty, I must say.

I can't *tell* you how kind John Sparrow has been about all this. He is the man who wrote a very brilliant book called *Sense and Poetry* about two years ago. I met him this summer when I was in London; and now he has absolutely come to my rescue. Perhaps you saw his letter to the *New Statesman*. It was he, also, who wrote the review in the *Times Lit. Supp.* and who, with the greatest possible skill and cleverness, answered Grigson's impertinence. The attacks on me have made him absolutely furious, and he has taken endless trouble and pains. He went to the editor of the *Times Lit. Supp.* and talked to him about it (he says the Editor is being most sensible and helpful); goes about 'spreading indignation', as he puts it, and, finding I had said something he thought unwise in a letter to the *New Statesman*, went to them and said that 'out of common decency' they would have to leave it (the paragraph in question) out. I really don't know anyone else who would have taken so much trouble. *Don't*, however, say to anyone that he reviewed it for the *Times Lit. Supp.*, as it must not be known, for all sorts of reasons. . . .

---

146. *To the Editor of the* Times Literary Supplement

[published 3 January 1935]

Sir,

Mr. Grigson accuses your reviewer (for no reason whatever) of being 'superficial, ill-informed and prejudiced'. The attack seems to have been made solely because he refuses to be a bore, and this naturally surprises Mr. Grigson. Your reviewer did not think it worth while to dwell upon what must be obvious to every reader – the fact that, owing to hasty proof-correcting (since my book was late for the press), there are a great many lamentable printer's errors. As for the 'plagiarisms' from Professor Read, I have said elsewhere, and I repeat again, wearily, that I see no reason why, because Professor Read says that Sprung Rhythm is *not* an innovation, I should say that it *is*. I repeat again, that because Mr. Grigson, apparently, was unaware until he read Professor Read's admirable *Form in Poetry* that Sprung Rhythm is the rhythm of Piers Ploughman and of Skelton, he should not therefore deduce that I was in the same state of ignorance. Thirdly, when I referred to Hopkins's 'acute and strange visual sense' I explained how, to my mind, he produced those acute visual impressions that help to make his poetry so remarkable. In this, I have taken nothing from Professor Read. Fourthly, Coleridge is not, as Mr. Grigson seems to think, an unknown writer!; and I have been in the habit of quoting the particular extract from Coleridge to which he refers over and over again in my lectures for the last ten years – and in much the same connexion. Fifthly, 'the principle of modern poetry' and 'the need for inherent form' mean two completely different things. I only wish to heaven that inherent form *was* a principle of the latest poetry.

As for Mr. Grigson's accusations about my 'queer debt' to Dr. Leavis, your reviewer has proved, and I have explained, over and over again, what must be obvious to any fair-minded reader. That is, that I am unable – and any critic would be unable – when writing of either Mr. Yeats or Mr. Eliot, to avoid referring to certain facts which are common knowledge. I am unable to see why the fact that Dr. Leavis has read Mr. Yeats's *Autobiographies* and *Essays* should have made it incumbent upon me not to. And to take two passages from *The Waste Land*, I did not need Dr. Leavis's book to tell me that the title of this poem was taken from Miss Weston's *From Ritual to Romance*, or to tell me that a passage in *The Burial of the Dead* refers to the Tarot Pack. Mr. Eliot's notes to the poem establish both these facts. Were I to begin mentioning the names of every critic who has referred to these matters of common knowledge, I should never have finished. . . .

---

147. *To Ronald Bottrall*[1]

129 Rue Saint-Dominique
Paris VIIe

16 March 1935

Dear Mr. Bottrall,

Your very kind and charming letter has only just reached me, for the reason that I was in Italy, staying a few days here, a few days there, and so for some time my letters were not forwarded to me, for fear they should be lost.

I was particularly glad to get your letter, for I was intending to write to you when I returned to Paris. I think I cannot have made my meaning plain enough with regard to what I feel about your poetry, in my *Aspects of Modern Poetry*. I had hoped my meaning was clear, but perhaps it was open to misconstruction, and I am very sorry.

I think your poetry has deeply moving qualities, and most *certainly* is a living thing; of that there cannot be any possible doubt. The line, for instance,

> *'Is it worth while to make lips smile again?'*

is a really beautiful and most moving first line. The lines

> '. . . *recant*
> *Our late betrayal and plant*
> *Within the shadow of the rock*
> *Our bloodless bodies . . .'*

are equally beautiful and moving.

When I spoke about a 'lesser gift for bareness of statement', I expect it sounded much harsher than I meant it to be. When one has a great deal that is really valuable to say, as you have, it is extremely difficult to eliminate. And elimination in poetry is both the devil and all (as I know only too well), and absolutely necessary. I do feel at moments that there are phrases, lines in your poetry, which are not in their place in poetry. And I'm not trying to put forth a plea for poetry that is a hysterical outburst, nor am I asking poets to write unreal bosh like

> *'I did not know the Dead could have such hair!'*[2]

(I've always wondered why on earth they shouldn't. What *can* Mr. Philips have thought he meant?) But there are certain facts of our daily life which are deeply significant in novels, but which I firmly believe are not *quite* right in plays, and are certainly not right in poetry. But a great deal of your poetry has moved me deeply, and I find the rhythms invariably beautiful, significant, moving, and born from the subject. In some, I find a changing of the scale, though, from something great, pregnant, significant, to something temporary and smaller. (I'm always flying at my brother Sacheverell for doing that too.)

Now I'm reading *Festivals of Fire*,[3] which I had sent for before I got your letter; it was most charming of you to offer to send it to me, and I think it remarkable, and it is obvious that you are a real poet. As I said before, the rhythmical quality of 'The

Loosening', its fluidity and perfect control, was most remarkable, and I never doubted that you have a most remarkable mind; all I wanted was more sifting of the material. When I know *Festivals of Fire* properly, I shall write to you again. And I shall ask the Editor of the *London Mercury* if he'll allow me to review your next book, so as to correct any false impression about my true outlook on your poetry which my *Aspects* may have given.[4]

I am scarcely the author of the book: the *printers* are. I could not have believed, I would not have credited, such a state of affairs. If they didn't like a word – or a whole line – they simply deleted it. They actually re-wrote quite a lot of Hopkins; they left out a line in Milton, the stressing in the same passage is *their* stressing, *not* what I wrote (and corrected, over and over again). They took matters into their own hands from the very beginning, and broke my nerve, very effectually, by changing Mr. Yeats' lines (page 86) to

> '*She that has been wild*
> *and barren as a* broken nose!'

And a phrase at the end of the essay on Mr. Pound, to 'a living evocation of the modern *hall*.' But Heaven protected me and I was able to remove these errors.

I think, speaking of Mr. Pound, that your essay on him in *Scrutiny* is by far the finest I've seen.[5] I was overwhelmed with admiration. Thank you very much for pointing out the mistake I made about Stephen. And, to revert to your letter once more, what you say about the 'ordinary' throws an entirely new light. It was incredibly stupid of me, though, not to have realised it.

I'm so very glad you agree with me about Messrs. Grigson and Read.[6] The latter seems to me not to have the remotest gift for poetry, and his ideas about it seem all wrong. The former is simply a noisy nuisance. He was *furious* about the first chapter in my book, and so was Wyndham Lewis, and the pair of them howled themselves hoarse. I'm shortly going for them again in a pamphlet, which is to be called *The May Queen*.[7] And my theme songs are two. The first is that Mr. Lewis resembles that other starry-eyed adolescent, the heroine of Lord Tennyson's poem 'The May Queen', inasmuch as both of them are always just *going* to be crowned Queen of the May, or *were* crowned Queen of the May a year or two ago, but neither of them are ever Queen of the May at the moment. And both want the whole wide world to be there, so as to witness their little triumph. The second theme-song is that for years Mr. Lewis has been howling that if only we all pay him sufficient attention, he'll produce rabbits from under his hat – that until now, nothing has been produced but an absolute cloud of bats from the belfry – but that now suddenly he *does* produce a genuine, if very small rabbit, in the shape of Mr. Grigson! There, I think, we have the matter in a nutshell.

I am venturing to send you my anthology *The Pleasures of Poetry*, simply because it's a useful book to travel with.

I hope we shall meet one day – it would give me enormous pleasure.

And please believe I mean to clear up publicly the muddled statement I made about your poetry.

> Believe me
> Yours sincerely
> Edith Sitwell

---

148. *To Cecil Beaton*

129 Rue Saint-Dominique
Paris VIIe

18 March 1935

My dearest Cecil,

I was so delighted to get your letter, and hear what a wonderful success Pavlik has had and is having. He thoroughly deserves it, but still, one doesn't always get one's deserts. Poor Pavlik, he was so unhappy, and everything was so beastly, it is lovely to know that all that is over. But I hope he'll keep them in their place, and remember how they've behaved. It must have been a wonderful experience, that enthusiasm after the ballet. And I hope now it will go on and on, and that money – apart from everything else – will come rolling in.

It is lovely for him your being there, and it makes all the difference to him, having a great friend with him. I do wish I could see the newspaper cuttings.

I am so glad you are having such fun, but kindly remember, Mr. Beaton, that you have had an operation, and don't go and overdo it. When do you come?

I'm literally dead of overwork. By May, I shall have written 130,000 words in one year, and I'm really worn out. Never mind.

I've just had a letter from Osbert, who has got involved in a fishing-row between two octogenarians over a worm. He says the correspondence is endless.

I really do feel so happy for Pavlik's sake. And I am also so happy you are with him. This is a very short note because I'm feeling very seedy and have had to go to bed.

Best love, dear
from
Edith

---

149. To Walter Greenwood[8]

129 Rue Saint-Dominique
Paris VIIe

25 March 1935

Dear Mr. Greenwood,

I have just read *Love on the Dole* and *His Worship the Mayor*, books which were sent me by a friend a short time ago, for the second time, and I feel impelled to tell you that I know you to be, not only a born writer, but a great writer (and I never use the word great lightly). I do not know when I have been so deeply, so terribly moved and so strongly impressed as I have been by these two superb novels.

How on earth you succeeded in combining the beauty and the unutterable tenderness of these books, their beautiful and inevitable form, with such an appalling indictment of our present damnable civilisation, I don't know. You are such a writer that the terrible tragedies of starvation, the people whose poignant and shining love, love between boy and girl, between husband and wife, love between friends, seem to me to have been known to me all my life.

There are really unbearable things in both these books, and those things are written with such restraint that they become more terrible still: 'As for that lad o' thine, Sal, lass, don't you wish him back.' . . . The words of Mrs Shuttleworth after the husband she loved had been murdered by this cannibalistic system – for that is all it is: 'Ay, y' don't know what me widder's pension'll mean to me, Jack.'

Shuttleworth and Hardcastle, by the way, are names from my part of the world too, though I come from a little south of your part of the world. My home is between Chesterfield and Sheffield.

I wrote to my brother Osbert yesterday, and before that a week ago. I said: there is a really great new novelist and his name is Walter Greenwood; and now I am going to write to Siegfried Sassoon, from whom I see you have quoted, and who is a very great friend of mine, because I have not seen him for some time and I want to know if he has read these books. It is not only that they are terrible indictments – they are also superb works of art.

Yesterday I wrote about them in the *Sunday Referee*; but next time a book of yours appears, I want to review it. Would you please have the kindness to tell me beforehand when you are about to produce a new novel, so that I may have this pleasure and pride.

Believe me
yours sincerely
Edith Sitwell

150. *To John Hayward*

129 Rue Saint-Dominique
Paris VIIe

25 March 1935

Dear Mr. Hayward,

I am sorry to see your article about my *Aspects of Modern Poetry*, which appeared in the *New York Sun* and which has just been sent to me by my eldest brother. I am sorry for your sake that you have done such a cheap and unworthy thing. It is obvious from your article that you have either not read my book, or not read that of Dr. Leavis, and in writing as you have, you descended to gossip-column levels.

You should not have attacked my brother. I think you do not know him, and he has certainly never done you any harm. Consequently your affront to him is as wantonly malicious as your statement about him is untrue.

I must ask you not to answer this letter: there is no apology that you can make to me, consequently there is no excuse for you to write to me.

I am

yours faithfully
Edith Sitwell

---

151. *To Walter Greenwood*

129 Rue Saint-Dominique
Paris VIIe

3 April 1935

Dear Mr. Greenwood,

. . . This shows what a writer you are: I have just been reading and digesting Engels' *Conditions of the Working Classes in England*, in intention, heaven knows, a noble work; but he can't write, so it raised anger in me, instead of grief. Then I read about Sam Hardie and the temporary lean-over. Well, I can't tell you how I felt about that.

I'm telling my publishers to send you my *Collected Poems* because of the last poem in the book, *Gold Coast Customs*. I wrote it at a time when three men in London had actually dropped dead of starvation in the streets, and when certain rich decadents were giving 'original' parties, costing goodness knows how much. Some actually gave a joint party on a barge anchored to the Embankment where destitute people were sleeping out. They had the infernal impertinence to invite me, of all people in the world. My answer was such that I must say they run for their lives now when they see me coming. *Gold Coast Customs* had a very amusing reception. It was at once perceived that there is only *one* form of cannibalism, and that there is only one Gold Coast . . . (the actual negro part is only the outward and visible sign of an inward and spiritual grace).

Believe me
yours sincerely
Edith Sitwell

---

152. *To Ronald Bottrall*

129 Rue Saint-Dominique
Paris VIIe

15 June 1935

Dear Mr. Bottrall,

Thank you so much for your charming letter, which I should have answered a long time ago, only I have been rather ill, first with influenza and then bronchitis straight on top of it. Such a bore! And I can't write either letters or anything else when my head feels stuffed with cotton-wool, so please forgive this delay in answering.

I hope you enjoyed your holidays very much. Pekin must give

one the strangest experiences, and I have always longed to go there. So far, I've never been out of Europe.

I've written to the editor of the *London Mercury* asking to be allowed to write about *Festivals of Fire*. I do think it is too bad of Tom Eliot not to have seen to the book properly, as he promised. I am very fond of Tom, but he is now absolutely *infested* with clergymen, and it is doing him no manner of good. I am not surprised to hear the book had practically no advertising, however, for I do find that Messrs. Faber (who publish much of my work), though charming people, keep one's books a little *too* much of a secret – no doubt out of a sense of delicacy. They *are* delicate. Whenever I publish a book, I'm always reminded of the Lewis Carroll verse:

> '*Don't let them know we liked her best*
> *For this must always be*
> *A secret kept from all the rest*
> *Between herself and me.*'[9]

I am much relieved, not to say delighted, to hear that you are not a Scrutinyite . . . The first work of yours that I read was the essay on Pound in *Scrutiny*, and I was more than puzzled to find what I consider by far the most brilliant and illuminating essay on his work that I have seen, in that magazine. Most of the people writing for it seem to me positively to dislike poetry, and also to approach it from quite the wrong point of view. They got into an awful row the other day, by the way, which may amuse you, if you haven't already heard of it. Somebody calling himself 'Ephraim Pundit' wrote what John Sparrow tells me is a very coarse, vulgar, and quite unlettered parody of Pound; and in a review of this work in *Scrutiny*, the reviewer lightly proclaimed with no grounds on which to base the assertion that the book was by John Sparrow, and that 'it demonstrates a lot about him, but *not the sort of thing that can be mentioned in a review!*' Can you beat it? Mr. Sparrow is a lawyer, and he handled the affair in a grand way, and the reviewer and Dr. Leavis had to apologise, though they did so very grudgingly.[10]

All Dr. Leavis's kind synthetic Aunties are very angry with

me for teasing their darling, but really it was irresistible, and it is very good for him. I shall do it again presently.

I couldn't agree with you more strongly about Spender. He is simply W. J. Turner[11] come again, and when he is not sentimental he is hysterical. As for the pylons and the young miners, I don't know what the young miners *would* say in answer to the unrequited passion – or rather, I can hazard a guess, though my native modesty makes me shrink from dwelling upon it. I came, you see, from the place where the young miners grow (between Sheffield and Chesterfield) and I can't see them putting up with Mr. Spender for a moment. I also wish he wouldn't wear those sort of collars, and look like a Greek god. In the last generation or two, Rupert Brooke is the only poet who has done that, and look at the poetry he wrote! Wilfred Owen didn't go in for that sort of thing, nor does Tom, though there was once a rumour that the latter had powdered his face green in the middle of a domestic crisis. I don't know if the rumour was true. (And of course, Mr. Pound, alas, does go in for a Little Lord Fauntleroy costume . . . but still.)

Mr. Grigson is a born nuisance – speaking of Mr. Spender, I have noticed he has been extremely rude to you several times, and I hope you'll go for him. He is encouraging the worst nonsense that is being written, and trying to suppress everything that is good.

Do send some poems to the *Mercury*. I look forward immensely to seeing them. And I look forward tremendously to meeting you when you come home at Christmas of next year. I do hope it will be for good, and that we shall have many talks, which I shall enjoy so much.

Yours sincerely
Edith Sitwell

I am rather disappointed at the origin of the name of Raffles College.[12] My illusion brought a touch of colour into my, at present, rather dull life.

153. *To Christabel Aberconway*

Renishaw Hall

[11 September 1935]

Darling Christabel,

It was so sweet of you and Harry to send us those delicious grouse, and thank you ever so much. They were so excellent; we had them for dinner last night. It was so kind of you both to think of sending them.

Just *how* depressed are you feeling? I am on the verge of suicide, and the news seems to be getting worse and worse. One can settle down to nothing, I find, with this horrible dread hanging over one. Don't you find that?

Your friend Mr. Sacheverell Sitwell has willed on us a gentleman named Captain Bobby Jenkinson. Osbert says you know him very well – (Captain J., I mean), so I have decided to complain. Really, I can stand almost anything in the way of boredom, but Captain J. is too devitalising, and Osbert and I have been so tired since he left that we have hardly been able to totter upstairs to our rooms when bed time comes. Also Captain J. kept on picking ticks off his retriever's coat at meal-times, and throwing them under the dining-table, wrapped up in pieces of fur to keep them warm, with the result that I imagine my feet are being bitten the whole time. . . .

---

154. *To Marie Adelaide Belloc Lowndes*

Renishaw Hall

[c. 11 September 1935]

Dearest Marie,

Thank you ever so much for your very sweet letter, which pleased me more than you can know. I, too, *very* rarely make friends now; I have only made two new ones in the last ten years or so, and when you came to stay here, I felt, indeed knew, that I had found a third one. It is the rarest and the happiest thing.

It is so sweet of you to say you are sending me a gift; I shall value it so very much; it is so very kind of you.

We did love having you here, and missed you so much when you were gone. Osbert and I were saying to each other yesterday that we hope now you have been here, you will feel like coming as often as you can – that it will become a regular habit. . . .

155. To Mrs. Almer[13]

[n.d.]

Dear Mrs. Almer,

After five years, you have again been kind enough to ask me to luncheon. The reason for this is that I have just published a successful book: the reason I have had a successful book is that I do not go out and waste my time and energy, but work hard, morning and afternoon. If I accept your kind invitation, I shall have to leave off earlier in the morning, and shall be too tired to work in the afternoon. Then my next book will not be such a success, and you will not ask me to luncheon; or, at best, less often. So that, under these circumstances, I am sure you will agree it is wiser for me not to accept your present kind invitation.

> Yours sincerely,
> Edith Sitwell

1936

Having initially disliked the work of the Welsh poet Dylan Thomas (1914–53), ES became his leading promoter. On various occasions, she found money for him, and endured a good deal of outlandish behaviour from him and his wife Caitlin, who were both spectacular alcoholics (see, for example, Letters 236–9).

156. *To Dylan Thomas*

[January 1936]

Dear Mr. Thomas,

Though we have never met, I am unable to resist writing to you to tell you, however inadequately, with what deep admiration and delight I have read your very beautiful poem which begins with the line

'A Grief ago'

and the beautiful and strange poem in this quarter's *Life and Letters*.[1] It is no exaggeration to say that I do not remember when I have been so moved, profoundly so excited, by the work of any poet of the younger generation, or when I have felt such a deep certainty that here is a poet with all the capabilities and potentialities of greatness. I am completely overcome with this certainty and this admiration. Only a young man who is going to be a great poet could have written the lovely, true, and poignant poem in the programme – (the first one also, has a fine quality) – I cannot recover from it. I think I am learning it by heart. – And as for the poem in *Life and Letters*, only a poet with real greatness could have written those extraordinary second and third lines of the passage which begins:

> 'What is the metre of the dictionary?
> The size of genesis? The short spark's gender?
> Shade without shape? The shape of Pharaoh's echo.'

Or the wonderful two lines which begin the poem, or the line

> 'Death is all metaphors, shape in one history'.

I have just finished writing about 'A Grief ago' for the *London Mercury*.[2] My friend Mr. Herring[3] writes me that a new book of yours will be appearing soon. I have already told my agent that I wish to review it, but I would be most deeply grateful if you could tell me who is publishing it, and when it will appear so that I may make certain to have the delight and honour of writing about it. I have a great admiration, too, for many of your 18 poems, but your two latest have excited and delighted me beyond measure. I must confess that the first poem I read of yours I did not like, technically – and felt it my duty to say so though without mentioning your name, taking the former only as an example. I know now, without any possibility of doubting it, that in you we have a poet from whom real greatness may be expected.

This is a very inadequate letter. I hope we may meet one day. There are innumerable questions I want to ask you. Your work has, I can assure you, no more true admirer than

> Yours sincerely,
> Edith Sitwell.

---

157. *To Sacheverell Sitwell*

129 Rue Saint-Dominique
Paris VIIe

Saturday [1936]

My darling Sachie,

I miss you and Georgia dreadfully, and I do hope poor Reresby is better, and that no fresh mumpers are appearing. It was so lovely staying with you, and I did love it.

I am making a list of all the poems I suggest, and will send it as soon as I've gone thoroughly over it again, with suggestions as to where they should go in the book. Nobody knows how enormously I am looking forward to it.[4]

This is *really* to tell you about Mrs. Gertie Waddyer and her latest adventure. (Mrs. W. must not be confounded with 'dot girl' who left 'der grave ontonded'. No, she is the wife of the Parsee millionaire.) 'Madam,' said Mrs. Reek,[5] 'dot mad girl Gertie, dot Mrs. Waddyer! What *do* you think? Yesterday, she ring up, and she start crying and screaming, and she say "Ma (she call me Ma) I'm in ter terrible trouble, and Mr. Waddyer he innocent as der new-born babe." I say "Gertie, *never!*" But dot Gertie, she scream and she cry, and she make no response. Then comes Underwood, der chauffeur, wid der Rolls Royce and a note. Moddom, *dot Rolls Royce!* You should see it. Puffoction! *Der taste!* Poffect! Large as a house, der paint cream, and dot Gertie's initials in gold all over der door. All der fittings in ivory and gold – der cocktail bar, der wireless set – *all.*

'Oh Moddom, dot Underwood's *face* as he tell me der events of der day before: Dot mad girl Gertie, she put dot boy she says her brother (but he her *son*, moddom, born before ever Mr. Waddyer come along! And oh, if *ever* Mr. Waddyer find dot Gertie out . . . you know these Heathen Blacks) – she put him in an establishment for Hair-Dressing, Beauty Culture and Manicure in der Upper Road, Islington. Dot *establishment* . . . Purfoction! Der salons for der beauty in green and silver for der psychological effect – (der soft colours, der soft voices, der soft lines smoo-oo-oothing away der wrinkles) – But dot Mrs. Waddyer, it being Opening Day she stand on der steps, with der Rolls Royce and der chauffeur in attendance, she stand in der Upper Road Islington, with der mink coat and der diamond bracelets *above* der elbow, and she shout to advertise de establishment: "This way, Ladies, for der free Manicure!" But Modom der ladies rush, and in der green and silver salons they *fight* for der free manicure, dey scream, dey break der glass basons, one break a glass door wid her umbrella . . . Der peace, der psychological effect, all spoilt because of der Free Manicure and who

have it first. And dot boy he so furious, he rush out and he
shout at Gertie: "I wish you six foot under der sod!" (Moddom,
der *ungrotitude*!) And dot Mrs. Waddyer, she scream and she
slop der boy's face, and he cry and he scream and he shout
"Murder. Police!" And der Police come running. And dey say to
Gertie: "Moddom, we *summons* you on account o de disturbance
and dot boy having his face slopped." Dot Mrs. Waddyer, she
reply – "I'll see you *B—'d*," she say to der Police, "before you'll
summons me." And she step into her Rolls Royce, she throw
back her mink coat, and she cry "Underwood – home!"'

I must say, I think it is a pleasing story, and it tells one such a
lot *about* such a lot.

Very best love, my darling, to you and Georgia

ever your loving
Edith

---

158. *To Osbert Sitwell*

Weston
But as from
The Sesame Club
49 Grosvenor Street
W.1

5 March 1936

My darling,

You must think me *A* a lunatic, and *B* a beast, for not having
written for so long; but since I arrived in London I've been
nearly rushed to death; and also, a great deal has been happening.

First of all, *Victoria* is having a violent success; I couldn't have
believed it possible, but there we are! When I left London a
week today, it was selling at the rate of 150 copies a day, and ten
days after publication, although the 1st edition had been a very
big one (4,500 copies), they started printing a second edition.

America is printing *separately*, too, so with any sort of luck, I may perhaps make some money. Anyhow, de la Mare is half off his head with excitement.

Do you remember my telling you in the summer, about a wretched deformed semi-dwarf, starving and with no prospects of ever doing anything else, whom the Beevers[6] introduced to me in order that I might try to get him a job as a reader? His name is Burton; and the very night I arrived in England I opened the paper and saw he had been *arrested for murder*. He had hit a boy of twenty-one on the head with a hammer, and over, of all people in the world, Mrs. Sylvia Gough. At first I felt terribly sorry for him, thinking his privations had turned his brain; but now I feel less pity, owing to the circumstances and also the wretched murdered boy must have gone through tortures. I've been having a *very* worrying time about it; for Mrs. Beevers lost her head, and gave the murderer's brother my address *without asking my permission*, and he rang me up and said he *must* see me, and wouldn't I *help*, and couldn't I find, beg or borrow, £1000 for the defence. I told John Sparrow, who advised me to keep out of it (he is a barrister, as you know) though he had not read the case, and he in his turn told Mr. Searle, who is a great friend of his. He promptly rang me up and told me most strongly to have absolutely nothing to do with it, because it was going to be a horrible, sordid case. So I was extremely firm. The poor creature is obviously mad; but I do think it is a bore to have such a fright-ful worry thrust upon one simply because one had tried to do a kindness, and when I've only seen him once. I can't go into all the ramifications of it in a letter, but poor Mrs. B. was pining for me to dash into the witness box and say he was mad when I saw him. As if that would help! I only saw him once. And I'm not dead keen on having my name mixed up with Mrs. Gough's. If it were a question of saving the man's life, it would be different. But I am assured it would have not the faintest effect.

As for our Griglet! Have you had the cuttings yet? I thought you would have seen the *Observer*, otherwise I would have sent you the cuttings. Now, alas, I have not got them. What hap-pened was, that I weighed in with the accusation that Grigson was scarcely the person to give his opinions about poetry, since he writes extremely incompetent verse under the name of Martin Boldero. Grigson replied under his own and also under Boldero's, denying this, and saying they were no more each other, than I am one of Mr. Cochrane's Young Ladies or the World's Sweet Heart. (It is so typical of Grigson that he would think one would *want* to be.) I then wrote two letters, one repeating the joke about G. being the rabbit from under Lewis' hat, and the other repeating my accusation that he *is* Boldero; and adding, 'Perhaps, though, neither of this gentleman is either himself or each other, but is simply an automaton worked by a pair of Spirit Controls, one being a Babu, and the other a house-maid who has "passed over" in a fit of hysterics after being dismissed for impertinence.'

The correspondence caused a lot of joy, and I have been egged on by such diverse spectators as Eddie Marsh and 'the Bystander'. Now dear Mr. Minney[7] is allowing me to go for Lewis, Grigson and Coward in Sunday's *Referee*. He says I can say whatever I like about them; not only that: on the opposite page he is going to publish the exquisite postcard you had printed, under the heading of 'Sex Appeal'. I'll send it to you, and when I get back to London I'll go to the *Observer* office and get the correspondence for you. It doesn't sound funny in my letter to you, because I've had to boil it down, but believe me it *was*!

John Sparrow has had a most frightfully insulting letter from Grigson because he dared to praise Victoria in the *Spectator*, and because he dared to ask for Mr. Boldero's address!

I am returning to London on Saturday, and shall be there for a fortnight.

Do write to me, my darling. Your letter about Eleanor Smith[8] did make me laugh so much.

Very best love, my darling
ever your loving
Edith

159. *To Georgia Sitwell*

129 Rue Saint-Dominique
Paris VIIe

[1936]

My darling Georgia,

. . . I am feeling dreadfully sad. Poor Helen, poor poor thing. She has started something under her other arm, *and* Hartmann has found something under the skin of her neck on the side on which she was operated. He says the thing under the arm is a little better, and so he is not going to operate yet, because both the places may go down, but of course the sooner we go to Spain the better, because she will have country air and sea-bathing. It makes one feel so hopeless and dispirited. . . .

160. *To Georgia Sitwell*

Monasterio I
San Feliu de Guixols
(Gerona)
Catalonia
Spain

[June 1936]

My darling Georgia,

I do hope you had a lovely time in Madeira, and that it took your mind as much as possible off poor darling Reresby going to school, for I know how fearfully you must miss him. I do hope, poor little boy, he has made friends and that everything is going on alright. And I do hope you found Trajan[9] well.

Do let me know as soon as you can what your address is in London. How I am longing to see you, my darling. And unless anything awful happens, such as poor Helen being much worse, I hope I shall in just over a month's time. I gave Sachie the wrong date when I wrote yesterday; the date I *do* hope to arrive (to 49 Grosvenor Street) is *Monday the 6th of July*. Oh, how heavenly it will be. If only something awful doesn't happen.

Like an idiot I didn't tell you when I wrote last that I had not been able to get the address of that wool-shop in Paris from Schoura. But the moment Pavlik gets back, I'll ask him to find out. He is sure to be able to.

The garden here is really heavenly – huge palms, five [?] magnolia trees, pomegranates, roses, two lemon trees, a medlar tree, and crowds of nightingales. But for three days it has been raining, with a lot of noise on a zinc roof, and I feel rather like Willie's girl friend Mrs. Opp . . . 'It is raining – raining – raining – so I have told him everything.' Also Guy Little is on my track. He says he knows I think he is a bore, but when he was young he was brilliant. And he wants to tell me some more about his brother-in-law's floating kidney. For some reason he thinks I take an interest in this migratory organ, and he tells me at great length all about its Odyssey, and just how many knots it makes an hour, as if it were the Queen Mary.

Also there is a plague of fleas, imported, according to one school of thought, by cats who come into the garden after the birds. That, I must say, is simply hell. . . .

---

161. *To Sacheverell Sitwell*

129 Rue Saint-Dominique
Paris VIIe

[*c.* 1 October 1936]

My darling Sachie,

If everybody who reads *The Dance of the Quick and the Dead* does not realise that here is a very great work, then we will know that greatness cannot be recognised in this stunted age.[10] I do not know when I have been so deeply impressed and moved: the book seems to me to have every single quality that goes to make greatness, a deep and flashing beauty of imagery, or rather transformation of everything seen and heard into beauty,

splendour, or at other moments, a moving softness of phrase (so
that when soft, the prose falls like velvet) strength and bold-
ness, or a sweet gentleness of rhythm, as well as every mood. I
think it is undoubtedly the most beautiful work in prose that
you have produced. There is so much to single out, I scarcely
know where to begin. The first part of the 'Paradiso' has the
same kind of magical sensuous beauty as the sensuous phrases
and rhythms of the *Canons of Giant Art*: the whole of Part III, of
the Masqued Ball, too gigantic to write about after only a week's
reading, is on these vast lines, and is sometimes luminous, sometimes fiery, with beauty. As you say: 'The world burns in
astonishing brightness.' And this changes into the melting
beauty of the chapter about Swinburne and Mrs. Rossetti, with
its moving gentleness of rhythms, in the most lovely way. The
wonderful chapter about Kean, which is just as much 'lit by
lightning' as Coleridge says the plays of Shakespeare were when
acted by him, the appalling indictment of the penal system, how
can anyone who reads these chapters fail to realise the temper
and splendour of the book they are reading. The part about the
little chimney sweeps in the Kean chapter, the whole of the part
about Australia, make one sick with horror, and yet it is utterly
unexaggerated in both cases.

All this praise is so miserably inadequate. I shall write to you
about the book, if it does not bore you, in much greater detail. It
is far too huge in conception to be written about in a letter like
this.

All the details are wonderful: the passages, say, about the
auriculas. I honestly do not know a prose book so crammed with
beauty, and it does not seem crowded. Everything is floating in
an air of its own. I do wonder how all the transcendental owls
will take it.

And how I *long* for the poems to appear. I can hardly wait for
them.

Is Dick de la Mare being delicate-minded, or is he, for once,
being properly *coarse*? I honestly don't know what anybody is
going to do about it. I should think all the Pipsqueakery are
wringing their flippers. As for me, I am really *floored* by it. It just

is a great work, and there one is. I get breathless with it, as one does when one is out in the wind.

Very best love, my darling, and my most proud feelings, and my very best love to Georgia.

Ever your loving
Edith

I am more touched by and more proud of your most *beautiful* reference to me in the chapter on Miss Siddall, than you will ever know. I can scarcely write of it.

---

162. *To Nancy Pearn*[11]

129 Rue Saint-Dominique
Paris VIIe

[November 1936]

Dearest Ann,

Thank you so much for your very kind letter.

I feel an absolute beast for saying I can't do what you suggest, after all your great kindness to me. But a poem on anything to do with Victoria or her reign is something I feel I simply cannot do. First of all, I've never written a poem on a subject *given* me in my life, and shouldn't do it well, and secondly, to be frank, I've had enough of the old girl to last me. If, when I start writing poetry again Nash's would take a poem, I'd be very pleased, of course. But I don't feel I can do Victoria. I am *so* sorry, as I say, to shirk doing anything you ask me to, and thank you very much for suggesting it all the same.

I'm starting a roaring cold, so forgive a very stupidly vague letter.

Best love from
Edith

Throughout her life, ES was a devoted admirer of William Butler Yeats. Her preference for his Oxford Book of Modern Verse *(Oxford, 1936) over Michael Roberts's* The Faber Book of Modern Verse *(London, 1936) is unusual, and may be partly owing to personal loyalty or to Yeats's considerably larger representation of her work. She did, in any event, hold firmly to the view that Roberts's anthology was grievously defective (see Letter 292).*

163. *To William Butler Yeats* (fragmentary draft)

[December 1936?]

Dear Mr. Yeats,

Thank you so much for your kind and charming letter. I am [illeg] pride and delight to me than I could possibly say that you should have chosen poems of mine to appear in the *Oxford Book of Modern Verse*, a most inspiring book, full of beautiful works which I did not know before. I have learnt a very great deal from it – both from your Preface, and from the verse itself. I did not, for instance, know Senator Gogarty's[12] splendid and heroic and beautifully shaped poems before, nor did I know Mr.[?] Higgins.[13] Nor had I ever, until I saw them in this collection, been able to appreciate Bridges.[14]

I am absolutely shocked and horrified at what you tell me about the enormous sum which has had to be paid to authors, and the fact that a large part of the payment will devolve upon you. What *can* they be thinking of? They can have no sense either of reverence or of gratitude. I think it is quite disgraceful. But I was much amused by the behaviour of Robert Graves and Laura Riding, who were content to figure largely in the *Faber Book of Modern Verse*,[15] surely the worst, most tone-deaf and fumbling collection of modern verse ever printed.

164. *To Marie Adelaide Belloc Lowndes*

129 Rue Saint-Dominique
Paris VIIe

Tuesday [December? 1936]

Dearest Marie,

Helen Rootham, one of the friends with whom I share a flat here, has just gone to London, and she has asked me most urgently if I will give her a letter of introduction to you. I said that I would write straight to you instead. If you have a moment to spare, it would really be angelic of you if you would allow her to go and see you. She is an enormous admirer of yours. And also, having, for the last twenty years, shared a flat with me, *she knows what a writer's time means*, otherwise I would never, no matter how fond I am of someone, introduce them to you.

She is very anxious to consult you, as both a famous writer and a Catholic, about a publisher for a translation she has just finished of a religious work. She is a very fervent Catholic, and also a very good translator. She did all Rimbaud's *Illuminations* into English. This translation of the religious work is the authorised one. She is staying at

> Durant's Hotel
> Manchester
> Square.

Incidentally, you did meet her years and years ago, when you came to a party we both gave in our flat in Bayswater.

I was *so* disappointed I did not see you this summer. I saw none of my friends, and everything grew more and more gloomy. Everyone I really cared to see – and there were very few – was either ill, like yourself, or away. And I was racked with anxiety, so that I couldn't settle down to do anything. My two friends with whom I share a flat here (H.R. and her married sister Evelyn Wiel) and I had taken a house in Catalonia, with one of the most heavenly gardens I have ever seen in my life, crowded with swarms of huge roses and nightingales (two of the latter

nested just outside my bedroom window), lemon trees and
mimosa trees, a fantastic grotto with a creeper falling down it
covered with large bell-flowers of a dark orange-pink, a big
clear-watered reservoir with a pomegranate tree hanging over it,
the coral-coloured flowers and brilliant leaves reflected in the
water, tubs full of gardenias, two magnolias, one a winter one
covered with scarlet flowers, etc. etc. . . . and . . . Then . . .

I left Spain three days before the revolution broke out!! But
the wretched Helen and Evelyn were caught by it, and as they
had omitted to register their names with the Consul, they could
not escape for ages (one chance they missed). At last, the local
Doctor managed to get them out, at half-an-hour's-notice, and
they escaped on a cargo boat, after *weeks* of terror. When they
did escape, it was discovered that poor Helen was most terribly
ill. For she should have had an operation in May. Luckily she
seems better now.

Osbert stayed a few days in Paris, on his way to Vevey. It was
lovely seeing him.

Are you as bored about Mrs. Simpson as I am? Thank heavens, we now have a Queen who does *not* contract friends who,
at the age of seventy or more, dye their hair blue, and then
stand on their heads. I hope we shall now have a little more
decorum, a little more – as I heard some woman say – of the
dog-collar. At the present moment, a great many engagements
seem to be taking place between people who are already married
to quite different partners.

Now, I see no chance of arriving in London before July,
because I am crawling along on hands and knees after my
novel.[16] But when I *do* come, I do *hope* I shall see you, in
London, and at Renishaw. I do hope you are very well, dear
Marie, and are working happily, but not so as to half kill yourself, and I do hope you will have a very, very happy New Year.

With best love
Yours affectionately
Edith

165. *To Georgia Sitwell*

129 Rue Saint-Dominique
Paris VIIe

[December 1936]

My darling Georgia,

. . . Really, I don't know *what* we are to do with the protozoa;
they are getting worse and worse, if we except the behaviour
about the *Dance of the Quick and the Dead*, which (with the
exception of Herbert Read[17]) was reviewed solely by intelligent
people. But with the poems my preface seems to have unloosed
on the wretched Sachie an absolute flood of abuse. And as for
what both Yeats and I are getting over the *Oxford Book of
Modern Verse*. The bitterness! The hatred! The squeals of rage.
Robert Nichols has dug up poor old Goethe and turned him
into a ventriloquist's dummy, and a damned stupid one at that.[18]
I was *so* angry about Herbert Read, that as soon as I can find a
stuffed owl of a moderate price (they seem to be regarded as
luxury here) I shall send one with my compliments to the Editor
of the *Spectator*. That paper has now been turned into a soft
downy nest for baby owls. The last time I saw Arthur Waley he
said to me: 'I did not know owls could have so many habits. But
every week for fifteen years the *Spectator* has discovered a fresh
habit for owls.' And now, wishing to study them at closer range,
the *Spectator* has converted itself into a nest, whence Messrs.
John Hayward and Parsons and the parent owl, Herbert Read,
hoot defiance.

G. M. Young has, in his long review of the *Oxford Book of
Modern Verse*, said the most wonderful thing about the *Canons
of Giant Art*.[19] I am ordering the *London Mercury*, in which the
review comes, to be sent to Sachie.

There is such a noise going on, I can't think or write.

Very best love, my darling, to you all
ever your loving
Edith

1937

166. *To Sacheverell Sitwell*

129 Rue Saint-Dominique
Paris VIIe

[15 February 1937]

My darling Sachie,

I have just got the press-cutting of young Spender's review of your poems, and I am going to write to him and tell him not to talk nonsense. I shall point out to him that when he says that Agamemnon's Tomb 'lives in the world of Endymion', he is only using other words for saying that you are a very great poet.[1] And that if propaganda is the only reason for a poem, then it knocks out Milton, Keats, Marvell, etc. as poets. We are left with nobody excepting Shakespeare (it is true), Shelley, Blake and Wordsworth. And at least he must admit that the reason they wrote great poems is, *not* their interest in politics, but because they were great poets, and produced great beauty. I can't find one word of propaganda or what he calls 'pressure of thought' in either Milton or Keats. When Keats does a bit of thinking he produces embarrassing truisms like 'A thing of beauty is a joy for ever' or

> *'Beauty is truth, truth beauty; this is all*
> *Ye know on earth, and all ye need to know.'*

Of course I shall put all this far better in my letter to him, because I shall think it out for hours and hours first.

I adored the *Times Lit. Supp.* I loved the reluctant way in which the darling old Country Clergyman who wrote the review was forced to admit that the poems are full of heavenly beauty, and that perhaps there is something in beauty after all.[2]

I read the poems almost every night of my life. And if it was possible to think them more heavenly even than I did when they were completely new to me, I should say that I did. But it *isn't* possible.

Poets are being treated now and regarded by the public as the Jews are treated and regarded by the Nazis. Look at the blasted impertinence Yeats is having at the moment. Woosh! He *is* getting it and so am I, because he dared to praise my poems. And every pipsqueak who has ever drawn breath is simply allowed to come along and insult us all.

Mr. Young tells me he is urging you to translate Pindar. He seems fairly determined that you shall. How will you get out of it?

I have absolutely no news at all, excepting that I hope to go to Levanto in a fortnight's time. I am being very nearly driven mad by bores here, pawing the doorstep and howling to get at me and prevent me from working. I am being firm, but it is very difficult.

My very best love to you both, my darling. I long to be with you. I hope we shall be for absolute ages in the summer. Last year was so lovely.

Do write to me

ever your loving
Edith

---

167. *To Georgia Sitwell*

Hotel Excelsior
Levanto
(Spezia)
Italy

[February 1937]

My darling Georgia,

Well here we are, that is to say, Helen and me. We arrived on Sunday, and I should have written before we set off, but was feeling so frightfully tired and none too well.

How are you, my darling, and how is Sachie? *Do* write to me when you have time. I *long* for letters.

I don't think I have any news, excepting that I had a bit of a dust-up in the train with an Italian General of the Air Force (who tried to be impertinent) and drove him out of the compartment by giggling at his medals, with which he was covered from head to ankle. Only his boots were left undecorated. Helen then fell with a crash onto his hat, which he had unwisely left on his seat (and which was a dainty little affair of gold lace). He was at the moment trying to quell me by the power of the eye (through the window and an eyeglass), I allowed it to be seen that I was delighted by the fate of his hat, and the victory was complete. . . .

---

168. *To Richard Jennings*

Hotel Excelsior
Levanto
(Spezia)
Italy

3 March 1937

My dear Richard,

I have been wanting to write to you for ages, but have had influenza twice since Christmas, which makes cerebration difficult. In fact, at one time, I thought my mind was going to swing about in empty space for the rest of my life.

How are you? I do hope *you* haven't had it? (Influenza I mean.) They've got a nice new form in America, which causes one to lose the use of one's hands and arms for a while. A friend of mine who is in New York had it, and it lasted for ten days.

The last time we corresponded, it was on the subject of Master Thomas, who is rapidly heading for having his ears boxed. I can feel the tips of my fingers tingling to come into contact with the lobes of his ears. And it would do him a lot of good, for he was evidently insufficiently corrected as a child.

What a tiresome boy that is, though a very gifted one. Having given us all that trouble, caused me to pester you and to write dozens of letters to busy people who must now curse the name of Sitwell, he has disappeared again, disappeared without leaving a trace. I have received reproachful letters from this person and from that, reproving *me* because *he*, after getting *me* to ask *them* to give *him* an appointment, hasn't kept it. But not a word can we get from him. This disappearance trick seems to be a habit with the younger generation. They ought to join Maskelyne and Davenants,[3] for they'd make the fortune of the place, and we should see a recrudescence of interest in magic.

I'm practically Master Thomas' secretary now, as everybody who can't find him (and nobody can) addresses his letters care of me, and I have to readdress them.

My only other piece of news is that I had a short sharp dust-up with Bob Nichols in *Time and Tide*. It was only fun on my part, but Bob took it seriously. He always does. It began by Bob printing a conversation between himself and Herr Goethe on the subject of the *Oxford Book of Modern Verse*, and ended by Mr. Alfred Austin descending (apparently) from Heaven to defend Bob. Can you imagine a man called Alfred Austin being such an owl as to interfere? I can imagine Bob's feelings when he saw that well-known name signing a defence of him.

Helen and I arrived here a few days ago. She is better, but they have not been able to destroy the root of the trouble, poor unhappy woman. I am so dreadfully sorry for her. She is so wonderfully brave, and never complains.

It is piercingly cold here, but very beautiful, with fields full of glittering peach-flowers. I expect to be here for about three months, unless poor Helen is taken ill again, in which case, of course, we shall have to return to Paris immediately, so that she can renew her treatment. Then in July I hope to come to London.

Osbert is having to pretend to go on a cruise round the world, because Ginger is on his track. This involves a lot of ingenuity, because of posting letters, but Osbert enjoys these problems, and working them out, though he pretends not to. I remember the time when he and Sachie were at Amalfi, having told Ginger

they were in Greece, when suddenly they saw a well-known face
and form ascending the long flight of steps to the hotel. With
great presence of mind, they told him they had just come off
Gerald Berners' yacht, pointing out a yacht in the bay. The
problem then was how to prevent Ginger from trying to board
the yacht and bearding a complete stranger, so they said someone was ill on board, and so the affair was smoothed out.

Have you seen Mr. Noel Coward's Autobiography?[4] I can
believe almost anything of him, but this exceeds my wildest
hopes. Of course, he is undoubtedly the biggest pup (as well as the
biggest puppy) that has ever been sold to this innocent nation,
but I can't believe even the English will swallow *this* book.
Amongst other triumphs, he has a very good chapter about how
romantic and what a wonderful experience it was to go to Venice
for the first time with Miss Elsa Maxwell!![5] Shades of the Doges!

I look forward so much to seeing you in July, though it is a
wretchedly long way off. Goodbye, dear Richard,

> Yours ever
> Edith

---

169. *To Rée Gorer*

> Hotel Excelsior
> Levanto
> (Spezia)
> Italy

12 April 1937

Dearest Rée,

You must think me a monster – I have not written for so
long. But I've been half dead with fatigue over my novel, which
is progressing better than I could have hoped, and with which I
am very pleased, but that doesn't mean it isn't very tiring. The
actual manual labour is terrific, and by the time evening comes
and I want to write letters, I'm too dead to the world to do it.

However, today, thank goodness, I've taken a holiday.

How are you, my dear? I do *hope* you've had no more of these wretched colds, and that you have been taking proper care of yourself, which I suspect you (not without reason) of never doing.

Did you enjoy your cruise? I do hope so. I must say, I never knew a more adventurous family in my life. I am sure that if you and Geoffrey had lived in the 15th century, it would have been you, and not Christopher Columbus, who would have discovered America! (*Was* it the 15th century, by the way? I never can remember.)

What news have you of Geoffrey? And when does he return? It isn't only countries he discovers, but writers. It was he who told me to read George Orwell, and I am really overcome by his *Keep the Aspidistra Flying*; it seems to me one of the most moving novels I have read for years and years. Have you read it?

I'm in constant danger. My beloved parents are installed in Florence, quite close to here; and there was a horde of interfering women staying here who dashed off to Florence and told an old girl called Lady Dick-Lauder (*what* a name), who is a crony of my Mama's, that I am here. Why *can't* they mind their own business? Ginger thinks he is ill, and six specialists were called in, but according to Henry,[6] our lifelong butler, who wrote on the subject to Osbert, 'they could find nothing wrong, so the undertakers have had to take the box back again!' . . .

---

170. *To Nancy Pearn*

Hotel Excelsior
Levanto
(Spezia)
Italy

28 May 1937

Dearest Ann,

I was so glad to get your letter, and should have answered it days ago, but my daily output of actual handwriting (invention and copying,) is rather over 4000 words. Which means that I am more dead than alive when it comes to anything but work. I never begin later than 6 o'clock – having made myself tea before – and sometimes as early as 5.30.

In answer to your sentence about the years ahead of us – (unless the Great Reaper intervenes), I am much older than you, but I look forward to a long prospect of stumping into your office with an ebony stick – but not, I hope, an ear-trumpet – up till the age of ninety, for the purpose of discussing new contracts. Do you suppose we shall still have as much fun, then?

Oh, I've just had a letter from Messrs. Harrap – a very charming one – asking me *will* I write a Life of Queen Mary, 100,000 words or so, written in the style of my *Victoria*. Mr. Harrap[7] says he would 'be prepared to make a contract with you which I feel would make you satisfied. If necessary, I could come to Paris to further discuss this proposition.' This made me see stars. I have returned the answer that contracts forbid, but that perhaps one day I shall have the pleasure of working for him. Because really his letter couldn't have been nicer.

Have I any news other than this? None. Excepting that my bedroom seems to have been turned into a sort of public resort. I have retired to it for good and all, because the English visitors *will* pester me when I'm tired. But do you suppose that keeps them away? Not a bit. They walk in at all hours of the day, saying they've come to cheer me up. And five Italians of both sexes, with a grim 5-year-old American child chewing gum, have just got in, 'by mistake'. I've fastened up a notice saying: 'This room can only be viewed by the general public between the hours of 5 and 7.' In Italian, English, German, and French.

I should be so very grateful (to return for a minute to business), if you would ask Mr. Webb[8] to send me the cheque from *America* when it comes (I mean for *Victoria*), irrespective of what has been happening with Messrs. Curtis Brown; which I'll bother you about when I come to England. I am looking forward to that, after many months of hard work and seeing none of my friends.

Best love,

Yours ever
Edith

---

171. *To Richard Jennings*

129 Rue Saint-Dominique
Paris VIIe

[29 June 1937]

My dear Richard,

. . . The last three or four months were hell. Helen and I were at Levanto, which used to be heavenly, but is now given over to the most awful people with legs like flies, who come in to lunch in bathing costume, flies, centipedes, an idiot boy who has been given charge of the church bell, which he rings *literally* all day on Sundays, barking dogs, people who bang doors, and an incessant wireless. They also tore up the road just outside our bedroom windows whilst we were there. And we couldn't move, because the wretched Helen had acute spinal neuralgia. We've got away at last, but she is *still* in bed, and has been for three and a half months!! There were times when I felt my brain rocking in its orbit. But I have nearly finished my novel.

By the way, have you read a man called George Orwell? He is gloomy and often displeasing, but really rather good.

I'm half dead – 4000 words a day is my average handiwork, though it isn't all invention – sometimes copying.

The Secondary Schoolmasters of England are about to cage me, for three days in August, with Humbert Wolfe[9] and Middleton Murry[10] at their Summer School at Cambridge. It'll be a happy three days, as regards my fellow lecturers, for Umberto won't speak to me because he thinks I've egged on Siegfried to tease him, and Middleton Murry won't speak to me because Osbert called him Muddling Moral. I don't know why it should be supposed that I'm a lion-tamer, and I'd have to be, to be able to keep either Osbert or Siegfried off their prey. I remember when Siegfried wouldn't speak to me for two years – indeed he cut me dead at a party – because Osbert had mistaken an enlarged photograph of W. J. Turner for a map of Vesuvius.

I don't think I have any news. Nothing ever happens here excepting hard work. . . . Oh yes, I *have* some. I'm going to deliver two of the Northcliffe Memorial Lectures at London University, and am to speak on modern poetry. I'm going to deliver *such* an attack on the political propaganda poets. . . .

1938

172. *To Sacheverell Sitwell*

129 Rue Saint-Dominique
Paris VIIe

[16 February 1938]

My darling Sachie,

. . . No news excepting that Helen seems a little stronger. But she is absolutely helpless. She can't move one leg at all. And she has to have morphia twice a day. She cried this morning when I took her in her early morning tea, because she said she wondered if she would ever walk again. And I said of course she would. But the doctor told Evelyn he thought she would *never* walk again. We have to keep that from her at all costs. He says the poor thing is not dying.

Life here is absolute hell, and that is all there is about it. . . .

173. *To Sir George Sitwell*

129 Rue Saint-Dominique
Paris VIIe

[March? 1938]

My Darling Father,

Thank you ever so much for your two letters, which I was so delighted to get. I hardly know where to begin in answering.

But first of all, I must say how happy and relieved I am to hear that you are, at least, a little better, I was awfully worried – we all were – about you in the summer. You *must rest* as much as possible, and I'll promise not to worry you at Montegufoni.

I can't tell you how touched I was by your second letter, about the champagne for Helen. So was she, poor thing. You are so kind. At the moment, I am afraid she mustn't have it, she isn't allowed any alcohol excepting a teaspoonful of brandy in her tisane, but perhaps she may be a little later. But the dreadful thing is, darling, that I am forced to *beg* you to lend me, as an advance from mother's money which you are so generously handing over to us, another £150. I know only too well what a large sum it is to borrow, and how much it is asking of you. But that wretched woman now *has* to have three injections of heroin a day. The morphia no longer works, and she has to have the stronger drug. And there are other reasons into which I can't go in a letter, for which nurses *have* to come in. If she does not have the drug, her agonies are perfectly unendurable. The illness is gradually taking possession of her whole body. Since writing to you last, it has now attacked her kidneys, and the nurses say it will be the intestines next.

So you see, darling, I am forced to beg you for this. I do *hate* doing it. I *hate* worrying you, and I have always tried my best not to be a worry to you about money. But what else can I do, now? One *can't* let her go through these frightful agonies. If you could see *her* whilst she is waiting for the drug, when the effect of the last injection had worn off, you would know. Well, I feel sure you will, anyhow.

It is so lovely to think of seeing you so soon. It is only just over three weeks now. I would be very grateful if I could be met at Pisa. Not knowing a word of Italian, changing trains would be a bit difficult. And I shall come straight to the Castle. Nothing would induce me to waste time by spending a night in Florence!

Forgive this badly written letter, but I've got such a headache I can hardly string two words together.

Very best love, my darling

ever your loving
Edith

---

174. *To Helen Rootham*

Agencia Egidi
28 Via Vigna Nuova

[15 April 1938]

My darling Helen,

This is just to tell you how much I shall be thinking of you at Easter, and that I hope you will have as happy a one as is possible, poor darling, when you are so ill. I have asked Evelyn to get you some lovely flowers from me.

I do *hope* you are better, dear. It is so lovely to think I shall be seeing you in ten days from now. I shall (D.V.) leave here on Sunday the 24th, and reach Paris in the early morning of Monday the 25th. How heavenly it will be. Will you please tell Evelyn from me with my best love? I am longing to be home again, though I admit that it is very lovely here.

I suppose that pest Inez turns up next week. How like her to come just now!

Oh, how I do hope you will like the Crucifix I am bringing you. It really does seem to me to be lovely. One of the arms of the Cross is, unhappily, damaged, but it is so ancient one can't wonder. The carving and the dim colour are really beautiful.

This is only a short note. There is no news, and, in addition,

I am being pestered A. by an old gentleman of 87 who was once a servant of the Worsleys, and wants to know if I'm a relation, and B. by Tom Balston. I rather resent the former, which seems to be an imposition.

But before I finish the letter, I do want to say one thing. I had a long talk with Father yesterday, who fully understands how *very* ill you have been, and *will* need building up for ages. He says I am never to *hesitate* to ask him for more money the moment it is needed for you. And that you are on *no* account to spare expenses. You are to have everything that could possibly be needed to build up your strength and make you well again as soon as possible. So please, dear, bear that in mind. There is no conceivable money worry for you, and anything you could possibly want, you are to have at once. When this £150 is done, more will be forthcoming. And it won't only be forthcoming for the actual illness, but to build you up after.

Very best love, darling, to you both, and kiss Cat. Tell him I pine for Children's Hour, and am longing to be with all three again.

Ever your loving
Edith

---

175. *To Sacheverell Sitwell*

129 Rue Saint-Dominique
Paris VIIe

5 May [1938]

My darling Sachie,

I've just got the invitations for the 19th of May. My darling, how lovely it will be to see you and Georgia. I am *longing* to. This is just a tiny note to tell you that, and to tell you, too, that poor Helen is dying. I got back from Montegufoni ten days ago, to find her delirious, and – well, the rest I won't harrow you with. She is constantly delirious, and when she isn't, we have death-bed scenes. Three times have I been sent for, because the nurses and Evelyn have thought she was dying.[1]

I am obliged to tell you this, but don't be too miserable. And *don't* come, darling. There is nothing on earth you can do, and it is unnecessary for anyone who doesn't *have* to see and hear all this, to see and hear it.

No more now, because I'm absolutely worn out. I do *long* for the 19th.

Very best love to both, darlings,

ever your loving
Edith

---

176. *To Marie Adelaide Belloc Lowndes*

Renishaw Hall

Tuesday [n.d.]

Dearest Marie,

Thank you *ever* so much for the perfectly exquisite bed jacket, which has been a heaven sent blessing last night and this morning, when it was very cold, and which is exactly the colour of a new nightgown which is just made. How very, very kind of you to think of sending it to me; I do appreciate it so much.

We are all feeling very despondent and gloomy here, about the Italian situation, which seems to get worse and worse. And it is very difficult to do any work. I am trying to occupy myself with teasing Mr. Wyndham Lewis in *Time and Tide*, by way of light relief.

With much love from us both, and ever so many thanks

Yours always
Edith

My *Collected Poems*, I hope, will reach you tomorrow; they are being sent with my best love and warmest admiration.

1939

177. *To Raymond Marriott*[1]

129 Rue Saint-Dominique
Paris VIIe

26 February 1939

Dear Mr Marriott,

Thank you so much for your very kind letter. I was so glad to get it, and to recover your address, which is now safely written down.

How very dreadful, how anguishing for you, about Mr. Roberts. At twenty-eight! The sense of waste, as well as the terrible sense of your personal loss! What a dreadful, dreadful thing. *Of course* you couldn't possibly have begun to recover from it yet – the grief, and the shock, and the feeling of emptiness. It is terrible that this should have come to you when you are young. It is all wrong that one should be unhappy in youth.

My poor friend I couldn't wish back. She suffered six months of unspeakable torture, and as she was nursed in this tiny six-room flat, both her sister and I were worn out. What *I* am suffering from, is delayed shock. One gets over that. Only I ought not to have done any work for a time, and was told not to, by Lord Dawson.[2] But I *had* to, and so did. And I expect the same happened with you. In time, I hope and believe the anguish with you will be – covered over. That is the only way to express it. It is like new skin covering a wound. That doesn't mean that one forgets the people one loves who have gone away.

I do hope you will like my *I Live Under a Black Sun*. It is an allegory, in a sense, as you will see. The reason I put Swift into modern clothes is because the spirit of the modern world is power gone mad. And Swift is power gone mad. I have tried to show the futility and barrenness of hatred. It is a terrible book, I think. I felt as if I had been through an earthquake, after I had written it.

I shall be very much interested to hear what you feel about it,

when you've read it. I am so happy that you like my work.
I look forward very much to seeing you in July.

Yours very sincerely
Edith Sitwell

---

178. *To Rée Gorer*

129 Rue Saint-Dominique
Paris VIIe

[March 1939]

Darling Rée,

We've all (by all I mean Moby Dick,[3] the maid, and myself)
have been down with influenza, or I should have written ages
ago to say how enormously I am looking forward to our trip to
America next January. *What* fun we will have, and how very
happy I am that I shall be going with you. I simply couldn't face
it if I were not.

At the moment I am having a protracted argument with the
agent, Mr. Colston Leigh,[4] on the subject of whether I am, or
alternatively am not, a trick cyclist. As far as I can make out, he
would like me to bicycle round and round the platform on the
tip of my nose, with my feet in the air, intoning at the same
time on the effect that texture has on the caesura. In other
words, he is making everything as difficult for me as possible, by
insisting that I must not *read* my lectures. I have no memory,
and as the lectures on poetry are highly technical, and any slip
would be fatal, I have said that I am *going* to read them.

How are you, dear Rée? I do hope you have escaped
influenza, which has been very bad here, but I hear has been
worse in London. It was lovely seeing Geoffrey and Peter when
they were over here. I do wish you had been with them.

I'm getting on grandly with my anthology, which will be
finished fairly soon, and with which I am really satisfied. (But it
isn't improving my handwriting, as you can see. I have such an

enormous amount of copying to do.) Of course that infernal influenza put everything back. Poor Moby Dick had it worse than me, and succeeded in producing the phenomenon of, at the same time, trumpeting like an elephant and spouting like a whale. Poor old soul, her appearance, her *cosmetic* system, getting more and more peculiar, so that she no longer looks as if I had gone in for a lucky dip in the most louche quarter of Port Said, and had brought out something very special, but as if she were Lamia before she changed into a lady:

> *'She was a gordian shape of dazzling hue,*
> *Vermilion-spotted, golden, green, and blue;*
> *Striped like a zebra, freckled like a pard,*
> *Eyed like a peacock, and all crimson-barr'd;*
>
> . . .
>
> *She seem'd at once, some penanced lady elf,*
> *Some demon's mistress, or the demon's self.'*

She has taken a great fancy, too, to the works of Dr. Cronin,[5] which makes everything still more difficult.

Pavlik has appeared. He is looking very thin and ill. He is furious with me for not having written to him for six months, and hints that I have broken his faith in human nature by deserting him when he was ill.* He will never be the same again, he says, never. Either to me, or in general. I think he must have forgotten last summer. However . . . He is now ill with influenza.

Best love, dear Rée
Your affectionate
Edith

My love to the boys, and please tell Geoffrey I am writing to him.

* Pavlik says the doctors tested him to see if he was getting cancer, which upset me horribly.

179. *To Osbert Sitwell*

1 2 9 Rue Saint-Dominique
Paris VIIe

16 August 1939

My darling Osbert,

I should have written to you ages ago, but have been in such a whirl with indexing my anthology, and the absolutely unending letters asking for permission to include poems. My word, I've got into correspondence with some pretty big boys lately. Dear old Sir Arthur Quiller-Couch,[6] of course, is a mere child of seventy-eight, but Mr. Wilfred Meynell (who really must be one of the sweetest and kindest old men in the world) *must* be rising 100. His wife was born in 1850. He really *has* been too kind for words, letting me use poems of Thompson's for which he usually refuses permission.[7] I am now so ashamed of having torn his wife limb from limb.

I have also written letters and cabled madly to two old gentlemen who both died twenty years ago. Which gives a pleasantly necromancical air to the proceedings. . . .

Oh by the way, I do think we ought to read Lady Eleanor Smith's autobiography. I saw quoted a very good ghost story from it. Apparently when Frances Doble was rehearsing dancing for Ballerina, 'a little white figure' crossed the stage, stopped, looked at Frances, then '*crossing herself*', walked into the wings. This was the ghost of Pavlova!! Can you beat it?[8]

I have no news excepting that apparently dear Dr. Goebbels has written to the King and to the principal inhabitants of Ramsgate, saying that old Mr. Gladstone and I both agree with him about the British Empire.[9] In support, he quoted what I said in Victoria about the mid-Victorian English wanting to interfere with everyone who had a different pigmentation of the skin. But why Ramsgate? That is what I ask myself. . . .

ES returned directly to Britain from Levanto after the Nazi invasion of Poland on 1 September 1939. She left almost all her manuscripts, paintings, and possessions in Paris, where Evelyn Wiel was stranded throughout the war-years.

180. *To E. M. Forster*

Renishaw Hall

1 October 1939

Dear Mr. Forster,

I cannot tell you with what delight I found your lovely his-tory of Alexandria,[10] and your most kind letter, awaiting me when I returned here on Thursday. (I was delayed in London) the book has a beauty that makes one feel calmed – (at the moment I am reading the section on literature) as one feels calmed when looking at certain statues and listening to certain music. I am deeply grateful to you for sending it to me, and am most proud to have it inscribed in your handwriting.

I wish you could know what pleasure I feel in reading the book. Whilst I was in London, I found people tearing about, and declaring they could read nothing but newspapers. What a strange way of trying to retain one's sanity! For myself, I have been reading Nashe's *Lenten Stuffe*, and now I am reading *Alexandria*.

By the way, did you get to see the Russian ballet *Symphonie Fantastique*, with Christian Bérard's[11] décor? There is a miracu-lously beautiful act – (the second, I think) – which was, I am told, inspired by the neighbourhood of Alexandria. I expect you know this, and have seen the ballet. But on the very remote chance you have not seen it, I mention it, for it is most strangely lovely.

I was most delighted to meet you at the London Library the other day, and have even a short talk. I do hope we shall meet again soon. When in London, I am always at the Sesame Club, 49 Grosvenor Street; and next time I come up, I shall write in the hope that you may also be in London. (I've lived in

Paris now for years, nursing, on and off, my poor friend who died.)

With great trepidation, I am venturing to send you a book of mine, *I Live Under a Black Sun*. But I beg you to believe that I *don't* consider it a novel. It is an allegory. I hasten to tell you this before the book arrives, which it will do in a few days.

With my homage and gratitude,

Yours very sincerely
Edith Sitwell

This letter, which was vetted by R. A. ('Rab') Butler, then Under-Minister for Foreign Affairs, was part of a propaganda skirmish in the months leading up to the beginning of the Second World War. Through the summer of 1939, Commander Stephen King-Hall produced five newsletters, which were mailed, then smuggled, into Germany in an attempt to counter the 'encirclement' theory being used by the Nazis to persuade the German public of the need to occupy neighbouring territories. Goebbels responded to these newsletters, citing ES, Victoria of England, p. 156, in 'Antwort an England', Völkischer Beobachter, 14 July 1939. See Stephen King-Hall, Total Victory (London, 1941).

181. *To the Editor of* The Times

[published 11 October 1939]

Sir,

Some weeks before the present war broke out Dr. Goebbels, in a diatribe against Britain addressed to Commander King-Hall, was good enough to drag in my name as a witness to the truth of his accusations.

Dr. Goebbels quotes me as having written: 'Unhappily, side by side with this increasing enlightenment on the part of the governing classes, grew a wish to interfere with all nations

possessing a different pigmentation of the skin – purely, of
course, for their own good, and because Britain had been
appointed to this work by Heaven.' This quotation is correct;
but he omits to say that I was writing of the years between
1833 and 1843.

It is understandable that Dr. Goebbels finds it difficult to
believe that a nation can improve, and can become more
humane, in 100 years. But it is a fact. All nations have, I am
afraid, been guilty of great cruelties and injustices in the past
(some of the deeds in the years of which I wrote are indefensi-
ble): but I am unable to agree with Dr. Goebbels that this makes
it right and advisable that any nation should commit cruelties
and injustices in this age.

Dr. Goebbels is shocked, I presume (one can do no more than
guess at his meaning owing to his rather turgid and over-emo-
tional style of expression), at the idea that, in the benighted
years of which I wrote, the British should have wished to 'interfere' with other nations. Let me point out to him that side by
side with this 'interference' has come a great amelioration of
conditions among the people interfered with. Can the German
Minister of Propaganda claim that the German 'interference'
with people of another race, the wretched, stricken Jews, has
resulted in any amelioration of their conditions?

It must astonish Dr. Goebbels that when this war was forced
upon us, the Indian native rulers, without one exception, made
offers of help and of treasure to the King Emperor. It must
astonish Dr. Goebbels that the whole of the Empire, and the
Dominions, have declared themselves as standing by our side.
But this may no doubt be the result of the horrible cruelties and
persecutions to which they are subjected by Britain. Just as the
rising of the valiant Czecho-Slovak nation against their
German 'protectors' may be a tribute to one year's experience of
the gentle loving kindness of these.

I am, Sir, yours faithfully,
Edith Sitwell

P.S. This letter will, of course, be represented as part of a new

Jewish plot, although I am 100 per cent Aryan; or else as an attempt to encircle Dr. Goebbels and the Beloved Leader.

1940

Hamilton Fyfe, in his review of Edith Sitwell's Anthology *in* Reynolds News *(14 February 1940), had said of the Sitwells: 'Now oblivion has claimed them, and they are remembered with a kindly, if slightly cynical smile.' The Sitwells sued for libel, winning their case against the newspaper in February 1941.*

182. *To Sacheverell Sitwell*

Renishaw Hall

[3 March 1940]

My darling Sachie,

Osbert telephoned to you yesterday, explaining about *Reynolds* and the Libel. Will you please write immediately to Mr. Frere[1] confirming that you will join with O and me in the action we are taking. He has consulted counsel, who says the paragraph is libellous. And, being sick of this sort of thing, O and I think, and know you will agree, that it is about time that people *paid money* for indulging in malicious lies with the intention of injuring us. They want a lesson, and money is the only thing that teaches them. This only a very short note, darling, because I have to write to Mr. Frere too, but I just want to send it off to you. . . .

The historical novelist Bryher (1894–1983), who was born Winifred Ellerman, arrived in England on 28 September 1940, having escaped from Switzerland via Portugal. She and her lover, the Imagist poet Hilda Doolittle ('H.D.') (1886–1961), became close friends of the Sitwells. Bryher, who was heiress to the shipping magnate Sir John Ellerman, became patroness to ES, giving her, among other things, a house in Bath, which ES never actually occupied. She remained ES's most devoted supporter for the rest of her life.

183. *To Bryher (Winifred Ellerman)*

Renishaw Hall

15 October 1940

Dear Bryher,

(Yes, I am delighted we are going to call each other Bryher and Edith) – thank you so very much for your letter. I *did* enjoy your visit so much; the only fault was that it could scarcely be called a visit, it was so short. And I hope the next one will be a proper one. It was the first time I have ever had a real opportunity of a talk with you, because as you say, there was a crowd on both occasions when we met before.

Hate parties! Osbert says I have a kind of drawing-room phobia. I hope we shall meet again very soon.

Before I go any further, I must tell you that I can really *never* even *begin* to say what I feel about your extraordinary kindness in helping me like this about poor Evelyn Wiel. If you knew what a relief it is to my mind, having this hope of getting in touch with her. It has been horrible, thinking what the poor woman's plight must be. I can't even begin to say what I think of your great kindness, and I can't even begin to thank you. . . .

Your journey must have been frightful, with a spiritual horror added to the physical discomfort. That circling round and round and not finding one's way, those depths below where people, at four in the afternoon, are crouching, waiting for the night. Do you think a new being will be evolved, dead white and blind like the races of insects that live in cellars?

That poor Czech,[2] unable to speak any language but his own:
how hopeless he must feel!

Wednesday morning, 8.30
    Robins has just come in to say there has been a new and most
appalling raid on London last night. I hope with all my heart
you are safe. *Please* leave London as soon as you can. You really
must not stay there. It will be a great relief to know you have
left. . . .

---

*This letter responds to Doolittle's account of the break-up of her marriage to
the poet and author Richard Aldington. Doolittle, whose relationship with
Bryher began in 1918, gave birth in 1919 to a daughter, Perdita Aldington,
whose father was generally believed to be the composer Cecil Gray.
Aldington himself had affairs first with Dorothy Yorke from about 1917 to
1928, then with Brigit Patmore from 1928 to 1936, and then with her
daughter-in-law Netta Patmore. Once Netta became pregnant, Aldington
sought a divorce from Doolittle, which was granted on 22 June 1938.*

184. *To Hilda Doolittle ('H.D.')*

Renishaw Hall

Tuesday [1940?]

My dear Hilda,

    I appreciate your letter more than I can say, and the friendship
that prompted it. My dear, how can I ever tell you *how deeply* I
understand and feel all this wretched suffering that you have
endured? The whole story of those dreadful months is agonising.
All I can say is, I am thankful you had Bryher, and I am thankful
Bryher had you. What would either have done without the
other? It is truly most frightful to contemplate. It frightens one.
    I am *very* thankful you have your daughter. Nothing makes
up for the agony you have passed through, but you *have* got
something precious.

I knew something of how monstrously Mr. A. had behaved, but not all these new lights. That 'Who is Hilda' is terrifying! What can he have meant. I don't believe for a moment he had shell-shock!

Some years ago, when I was in Paris, I was introduced to Miss Yorke, but did not know who she was until afterwards – I mean the part she had played, because I did not hear her name. She was – perhaps you know – practically chucked out by Mr. A., in the end. He brought what Osbert calls his 'synthetic grannie', Mrs. Patmore, to live in the house, and when Miss Y. wouldn't bring them up early tea, he told her to get out. He just gave her her ticket, and threw her out. She was in a deplorable condition when I saw her. Despair had made her into a hopeless (so they said) dipsomaniac. In the end, of course, Mrs. Patmore was left, too.

Oh dear! Well, I can't say how thankful I am that you left him. To think of someone like you in all that, is too much.

Oh Hilda, your divorce must have been so dreadful for you, such a frightful experience, as though all the rest had not been enough. It is a wild and horrible thing that someone who has endured what you endured, should have had to go through that too.

But above all, I feel it is wonderful that you and Bryher, in your different despairs, should have saved each other in that way. What strength and reliance it must give to both. But *that* story is terrible.

I am very glad to know all this – glad in spite of the fact that the misery goes to my heart. Because it does put an extra bond between us. I feel we were friends during all that awful time twenty-two years ago, if you see what I mean. Very deep-rooted friendship. All that was a horror of misery. But you have come through it as the woman and poet you are. . . .

185. *To Sacheverell Sitwell*

Renishaw Hall

Christmas Eve [1940]

My darling Sachie,

What a confounded nuisance it is for all three of us, each of whom is *just* starting a new book, to have this law-case coming on. But I don't see how we could have allowed this man to say we have sunk into oblivion, and 'if we are remembered, it is with a kindly, if cynical smile.' If we had allowed it, the sentence would have been repeated in paper after paper, in the provinces, and all over 'the Empire'. It is a pest, but I don't see what else we could do.

Dear Mr. Slade,[3] our Counsel, is a bore of a real Sir Arthur[4] magnitude, is an extremely clever, wary old boy, and is, apparently, one of the two greatest counsel for libel.

I have felt too wretched to write any letters for Christmas, so you and Georgia must forgive. The two raids here were truly *appalling*, Sunday, though shorter, being the worst. And one thought every second or so would be our last. We got it again in the middle of the night on Saturday and this Sunday, but nothing to compare to the two big raids, which, 'they' say, were worse than Coventry.

I've just heard from Veronica, telling me, amongst other things, her boy, Reresby's friend, has gone into the Army, in the ranks. He is the only child and she does adore him. I can't bear to think of it.

Have you any news from Mr. Fermor,[5] in Greece?

Gerry Wellesely [*sic*] (I can't spell this morning) came over here for a night, about a fortnight ago. He is really *very* nice when one gets to know him. But he takes knowing.

I comforted myself last night when I couldn't sleep, by reading those truly wonderful passages about the shells and sea-nymphs in *Sacred and Profane Love*. What *miraculous* beauty.

Sir Edward Marsh came to lunch on Saturday. His toothiepegs give him and everybody else a lot of trouble; sometimes they sound like galloping horses, at other moments they hiss like a boa-constrictor. Osbert waited till he was just going, and then flew at him about Mr. Churchill, which nearly reduced him to tears.[6] He – Sir E. – is now exactly like a bad actor taking the part of a gaffer in a play by Eden Philpotts.[7] I think, poor old boy, he must have had some kind of a fit.

Very best love, my darling, to you and Georgia, to whom I am writing, also Reresby. How *dreadfully* you must both be missing little Francis.[8]

ever your loving
Edith

1941

186. *To Sacheverell Sitwell*

Renishaw Hall

6 January 1941

My darling Sachie,

Here is a little *extremely* cheering news from Philip Frere. In a letter received from him this morning, he says: 'I take a very confident view, and so does Mr. Slade. The libel seems to me to be obvious and I think we *must* succeed on that. Moreover, malice is strongly indicated in which case we ought to obtain more damages than the amount paid into court which carries with it the costs of that issue as well.'

Which will be a treat, won't it? So I strongly advise you to go into the matter in the way in which the Elizabethans went for the King of Spain. 'Now then,' as Mrs. Addey[1] wrote to me when inviting me to a tea party at which the great-nephew of a former editor of the *World-Wide Review*, a young man who had written a book about Boy Scouts, and the Deputy Town Clerk of Islington were to be present: 'Now then, will you be *tempted?*' . . .

There seems to be no news. I am still having real hell with neuralgia. Sir Edward Marsh came and twittered over here the other day. But perhaps I've told you that, already. Osbert accused Leslie Hartley,[2] who was sitting in front of the fire in a great-coat, of 'trying to look like Carlyle's Grannie'. There my information stops.

Very best love to you and Georgia and Reresby, my darling. Bless you.

ever your loving
Edith

A young man who is here, Captain Dru, says that lovely stone head on the mantelpiece is exactly like you. *Of course* it is. I'd always wondered who it reminded me of.

---

187. *To Marie Adelaide Belloc Lowndes*

Renishaw Hall

14 February 1941

Darling Marie,

So many *most* grateful thanks to you and to Elizabeth for your kind and cheering telegram, and so many thanks to you for your lovely letter. It did hearten me to get it.

Nobody knows how the Defence behaved, in that filthy case. Their whole attitude was a disgrace. And the papers have garbled the reports in such a way that, for the most part, reading them, nobody would guess just *how* we won. They have given no clear idea, for instance, of the Judge's summing up, of his sternness towards the Defendants designedly keeping out of the witness box, and, indeed, towards the way in which I was insulted, personally, during my cross-examination.

Incidentally, during Mr. Roberts's[3] speech for the Defence,
we were told that Blackmail would be alleged against us, if it
were not that we have a little money! So that, you see, only the
rich can afford to defend themselves and their reputations. We
felt it an absolute duty to fight the case, not only for ourselves,
but for all artists. Perhaps, now, when these sort of people are
feeling idly malicious, they will be a little careful of what they
say, for their own sakes.

I wish you could have seen them. The editor is a horrible
furtive-looking grey rat of a man – grey in everything but his
hair, which is a dusty black. He has a mouth that droops at one
corner, owing, I imagine, to chain-smoking, and twitching
yellow-stained fingers. The solicitor (I suppose it was the solicitor) is a woolly Australian bushman type of young man. Both
were very dirty. On the other hand, Mr. Hamilton Fyfe was far
too clean. The latter sat swallowing and rolling his eyes like a
chicken with the pip, all the time that our counsel was saying
what he thought of him for not going into the box. The Judge
was absolutely *charming* to us. Nobody would have thought that,
from the reports of the Case!

Mr. Fyfe had a singular objection against it being known that
he is *Hamilton* Fyfe. Now, *why*? Do you suppose he has been up
to something, before this?

Mr. Wilson,[4] of Bumpus, who, kindness and chivalry itself,
came to witness for us, told Bryher (Sir John Ellerman's
daughter) that he thought he was used to 'tough' people, but
he had never encountered anything to touch the people on
the paper.

I'm so glad it is all over, for it was a horrible strain, and the
fact that I was in acute pain nearly all the time, with this
wretched sciatica and neuralgia of the spine, didn't make it any
better.

Will you please give Elizabeth my love, and tell her from me
that Osbert keeps on saying she – Elizabeth – keeps a verse of
mine in her bag. He doesn't tell me *which*. I wish she would let
me know (when she feels inclined) so that I can write it out for
her. I would love to.

Darling Marie, you are always so sweet to us. And we think of you as such a *great* standby and support –

Best love

Your devoted
Edith

---

188. *To Sir Hugh Walpole*

Renishaw Hall

8 March 1941

Dear Hugh,

Thank you so much for your extremely kind letter. Osbert and I are more overwhelmed than ever by your kindness in giving so much of your time and care to this affair, when we realise that your flat has been bombed. We are horrified to hear it. We are only so *thankful* that you were not there at the moment. It is terrifying to think of. I do hope that your collections of pictures and of books are in the country, and have not been damaged?

You and Mr. Shaw have so succeeded in quelling the rioters.[5] They are very subdued, sad, but resigned, now that they realise there is nothing to be done. I shall send your letter on to Sacheverell, and should have written to thank you before, but I have been suffering torments with acute sciatica. He will be delighted and most gratified by your suggestion. He certainly should and must bring out a book of selected poems, and now he will feel encouraged to do so.

With most grateful thanks again.

Yours ever
Edith Sitwell

189. *To Leonard Woolf*[6]

Renishaw Hall

4 April 1941

Dear Mr. Woolf,

No words can express our feelings at this dreadful heartrending thing.[7] We are absolutely overcome. All our thoughts are with you. What *can* you, and Mrs. Bell,[8] be enduring, with the pain and the grief and the shock.

It cannot help you in the least to know how many people must be feeling a desperate sense of loss. I know that *we* do, here, but that does not help you in the least. Nothing can.

Perhaps the day will come when we shall think, 'At least she was spared seeing people sink lower and lower, and all the new desecrations and shames'; but at the moment that doesn't help at all.

When I think of that noble and high spirit and mind!

There isn't anything one can say, and one must not intrude on your sorrow. But all my life I shall remember the feeling of *light*, and of happiness, that she gave one. As a person, as well as in her art. Everything seemed worth while, important, and beautiful.

With my deepest feelings for this cruel grief that has fallen upon you,

Yours sincerely
Edith Sitwell

You must not think of answering this.

190. *To Bryher (Winifred Ellerman)*

Renishaw Hall

5 April 1941

My dear Bryher,

That wonderful edition of Pope has appeared: and I can never thank you enough. You cannot know what a delight it is to me. It is truly *wonderful* for me to have all his works in this singularly beautiful edition. And apart from the joy of having it, it has come at a moment when I am about to collect, enlarge, and put together, all my notes about his poetry, for this book on poetry I am working at.

I am very glad, too, to have it from *you*. I hope you will inscribe it for me, when we meet. I have not nearly finished looking through it, even, yet. Osbert and I are so very disappointed that you are not coming here as soon as we had hoped. We had believed and hoped that you were coming for Easter. I do hope you will be down here again very soon, *and* staying with us.

Osbert tells me that you have given the *Times* a good ticking-off, a copy of which you have sent to Robert,[9] who will show it to us. I am delighted to hear it. Their behaviour has been quite monstrous. I cannot help feeling that it may have had something to do with poor Virginia's frightful death. After all, she was so delicately balanced, she was utterly unused to the kind of baiting most of us have had, and this sudden charge that the war is due to the particular group of intellectuals of which she is a member may only too well have been too much for her.[10]

The creative artists and the higher intelligences are now having to pay for the behaviour of the *New Statesman* and *Spectator* stickleback, who are, I admit, enough to aggravate a saint with their spurious superiority. But why blame *us*? They are just as full of contempt for us as they are full of contempt for the 'Common Man' (whoever he may be), and are infinitely more harmful to us.

I am hoping soon to get the proofs of that anthology which is ostensibly for children,[11] but am much troubled by a longing to put in various lovely poems which might have a deleterious effect on the brats – might, in short, 'put ideas into their heads'. My principal temptation is a very lovely Lullaby of Skelton's. But I can imagine the life of parents and teachers if I gave way: 'Mummy, *what* is "deadly sin"? Mummy, what did the lady mean when she said the gentleman had forgotten it?'

I don't much care for children, and, as a rule, don't much care for their parents either, and feel that this would be a good come-back on them. Still . . .

With love and most grateful thanks. I cannot tell you what a delight that lovely edition is to me,

yours ever
Edith

Also the temptation of Marlowe's 'Hero and Leander'!

---

191. *To Nancy Pearn*

Renishaw Hall

22 July 1941

Dearest Ann,

What a lunatic you must think me. Here is the spare page of that letter, which has just been found by the housemaid, carefully put away! I enclose, also, a letter from Miss Horsman, which I should have sent you some days ago, but I wanted to think over it, first.[12]

I am now very seriously vexed indeed with Messrs. Gollancz. I have *not* referred to it, to them, as I do not want any trouble. But I am firmly determined that, contract or no contract, they shall *never* publish another book of mine. It is nonsense, the excuse they give: every week, I see books of theirs advertised – novels and political works. I cannot work for them, I consider they have made it quite impossible. (They have had that anthology for a *year*: *since last July*.)

I am told that all we have to do, is to ask them a price that

they will not pay, for the next book, and that I shall then be
free. In any case, I am *absolutely determined* they shall *not* have
another book of mine.

Rache Lovat Dickson[13] has been staying here – (he leaves
today) – and is enthusiastic at the idea of my going to
Macmillan's. So am I. I have talked to him of a small book of
poems to be published this autumn (October):[14] and, in a day or
two, he is going to ring you up, or write to you, about this. I
have told him I can let him have the manuscript at the end of
August, (I want to put in one or two more). So will you, please,
like an angel, make arrangements with him.

What about telling Messrs. Gollancz that I imagine they will
not want to have the option of publishing the *poems*; but that they
will have the option, instead, of a book I am going to start, immediately, about Queen Elizabeth (Tudor). Then, when the option is
put forward, will you please ask a sum that they will not pay.

I no longer take the slightest interest in that children's
anthology, it has been treated in such a way. And I am *determined* to have a book of my own poems out, this autumn.

Gosh! I *am* cross with Messrs. G. . . .

Incidentally, I am having to put all thought of that novel
aside: for I now find it would get me into *frightful* trouble. I have
not broken it to Madame Martin[15] yet – so this is in confidence
(unless you have to tell Messrs. G.) but the book *might* land me
in a libel case, and certainly would land me in trouble of a very
bad kind.

But I hope you will be pleased about Elizabeth! You *always*
wanted me to write a book about her! I am wild with excitement
about the book of poems. It is going to be called *Street Songs*.

Dear Ann, you are always so full of understanding. I know
you will realise that I simply *cannot* write again for Messrs.
Gollancz, after their behaviour.

Best love, most grateful thanks for everything

Yours affectionately
Edith

192. *To Amalia Sackville-West* (draft)

6 November 1941

Dear Amalia,

Thank you for your letter. I am grieved that I have to grieve you: but I must abide by our lawyers' advice. I cannot throw it aside.

The terms of the legal contract I should have to make with the publishers and which is invariably made between authors and publishers contains this clause: 'The author guarantees to the Publishers that the said work is in no way whatever a violation of any existing copyright, and that it contains nothing of a libellous or scandalous character, and that he will indemnify the Publishers from all suits, claims, proceedings, damages and costs which may be made, taken, or incurred, by or against them on the ground that the work is an infringement of copyright, or contains anything libellous or scandalous.' It is impossible for me to sign that legal agreement with my publishers under the circumstances.

From the very beginning I have known and it has been obvious that my manuscript and the general synopsis would *have* to be seen by my lawyers.

Now, as I say, I must abide by their decision. No useful purpose would be served by sending all this to other lawyers, and throwing the advice of my own lawyers aside. It is out of the question, even if it were possible, which it is not. No agreement between you and me exists that I would take this dreadful risk. Nor has there been any contractual arrangement.

I hate writing this to you. I know only too well how deep is your grief and disappointment. I am terribly distressed to think of it.

> Yours
> Edith

193. *To Sacheverell Sitwell*

Renishaw Hall

Wednesday [late 1941]

My darling,

. . . How sickening it is the *Festivals* being put off by Faber's till the New Year.[16] But I suppose, in a way, anything is better than a great book like that, getting into the Christmas rush. My poems[17] are having to be put off till the New Year, too. But at the moment I am sick of them, and don't care.

But though your great book has to be put off, and although my poems have to be put off, that does not stem the rush of Poetry. Dear Mr. Faber[18] has sent me his own poems, and I have written to him praising their Integrity. That is my stock phrase now, and I think you might also find it useful. It saves a lot of trouble; and Integrity is a retriever-like, faithful quality that I find very trying. However, nobody knows that. Dear Wilfred Wilson Gibson has also sent me *his* book. Again I have commended its Integrity, adding that it has *Force* – in the scientific meaning of that word. That means that it is binding. Well, they shouldn't do it. . . .

---

194. *To Sir George Sitwell* (incomplete)

c/o Post Box 506
Lissabon
Portugal

22 November 1941

My darling Father,

Osbert, Sachie and I are terribly distressed because we gather, from a letter recently received by us from a Lady Crump, that none of our letters has reached you for some time. How this can have happened, we do not know. We can only hope that this letter will reach you.

Darling Father, you are in all our thoughts, always. We are dreadfully unhappy that we are separated from you, and most unhappy knowing how ill you are. We long for the time when we shall all be together again. If only we could hear that your health is better, how happy we should be. We think of you every day.

Osbert sends you his very best love. He asks me to tell you that there are difficulties now about his writing to you. And we all beg you to believe that a lack of letters from us means no lack of affection or of thought for you.

We are fairly well, including the [ends here]

---

195. *To Veronica Gilliat*

Renishaw

30 December 1941

My dearest Veronica,

Just a line to wish you and Frank and David a very happy new year, as happy as anything could be in such a nightmare time.

My dear thing, how *are* you? I have a kind of feeling that either you haven't got a letter of mine, or that I haven't got a letter of yours, but I don't know which is which. The only letters which ever seem to get here are bills, and letters containing devastating news. Did you ever get my letter, thanking you for your poems? Oh ages ago, now? I particularly enjoyed the one about the sisters – so did Osbert. . . .

I have been having a grand time with Amalia Martin, née Sackville West, re that novel. She has been threatening me with breach of contract, and her letters were menacing to a degree. Luckily, in the course of them, she was very rude about our solicitor, Philip Frere (who is also a personal friend of ours) – so he has taken a thorough dislike to her.

I have just started my book on Elizabeth. But am I allowed to write? Of course not. The Clergyman's mother says will I choose

my own day to go and have tea with her; and complete
strangers stationed in the neighbourhood say they will come
over here and bring their verses with them. Robert Herring badgered me to go to tea until I couldn't avoid it; the motor, having
delivered me there, went away, leaving me helpless, and I had
two hours closeted with a friend of Robert's, a female mental
defective, who said to me these words: 'Oh Miss Sitwell, what a
beautiful name you have. I think S is such a beautiful letter. It
makes me feel I am getting underneath something. Don't you
often feel you would like to get underneath something? I often
long to get underneath everything!' At this moment Osbert
arrived, and asked the lady if, in two days' time, she would
come to tea with us.

I must say I really blasphemed!

Best love, my dear thing, and all my very best wishes for the
New Year.

Ever your loving
Edith

Love to Frank and David, and best wishes.

1942

196. *To Edmund Blunden*

Renishaw Hall
25 January 1942

Dear Mr. Blunden,

Thank you so much for your most kind letter. Your praise of
my 'An Old Woman' made me very happy and proud. For some
reason it was a very difficult poem to write. I am most happy
that you like it.

I *hate* to realise that you are again in uniform. What an outrage it is, that you, who ought to be doing your own lovely

work, should be involved in this misery and wretchedness.

Poor Osbert is now almost a semi-invalid (he was invalided out of the army in the last war). By that I mean that he gets recurring attacks, which anything is liable to bring on. He sends you many messages.

It seems a very long time since we met. The last time (at some club) we were both struggling to get away from a very long-winded American from the west who had lassoed us, and who evidently made a collection of poets. I do hope we shall meet again soon, and without such disadvantages.

With all good wishes

Yours very sincerely
Edith Sitwell

---

197. *To Henry Treece*[1]

Renishaw Hall

9 September 1942

Dear Mr. Treece,

Thank you so much for both your charming letters, and for *Kingdom Come* which I am delighted to have. I have read your Statement on Poetry with great interest. There is a great deal to think over. The paragraph which *begins* with the sentence: 'It might now be asked: If Neo-Imagism, Leftism, Surrealism and Georgianism are to be reconsidered, what then is left to British poetry' – is, I think, very important. I shall be writing about this, and about the essay in general, a little later, when I have read it several times. (I have, actually, already, but I want to read it still again.) . . .

So far, from reading your statement, I agree with a great deal you say. Though not, I think, with 'the poet should show in his images psychological symbols, his own disease, and by uncovering them effect his cure.' There are far too many silly though nice young people who think they have some psychological malady, and *must* therefore be poets. Oh, why *won't* people realise that poetry is a specialist's job! . . .

I didn't realise, stupidly, when I wrote to you first that Robert Herring is a friend of yours. My brother Osbert and I are very fond of him as a person. When he was bombed out, he came and spent three or four months with us in this house, and was one of the most delightful, charming, kind and thoughtful guests one could imagine. I dedicated a poem to him because of my appreciation of those months (in which, incidentally, we went through the two bad Sheffield raids together) and because it came out in *Life and Letters*. . . .

---

198. *To Denton Welch*[2]

Renishaw Hall

25 October 1942

Dear Mr. Welch,

I am so truly sorry not to have written before, but I have been rather ill, so you must please forgive me.

I cannot tell you how *delighted* I am to hear your news. It is splendid that the book has been taken, and I do hope it will have an enormous success. I am looking forward tremendously to reading it. If it is anywhere near as good as your adventure with Mr. Sickert, it will be very, very good indeed.

Yes, Mr. Read is a most delightful, kind, and charming being. He was a shy and charming youth, and was part of the happy life of my youth, when I lived in London. We used to have large tea-parties on Saturdays, and Herbert Read and two others, sometimes four others, of our very intimate friends used to stop on afterwards, and help cook the supper. Herbert Read was a constant and delightful companion, and we always felt happy with him.

When will the book appear? I hope very soon. I have to pull myself together, and get my notes on poetry ready for the publishers. It is a terrific job, because some are rather abstruse – or would be to persons who do not habitually read poetry. They seem to me clear as daylight, but the publishers always want one to explain the unexplainable.

You must, I think and hope, be feeling extremely happy that your book is coming out. It is a wonderful event in one's life, when one's first book comes out. My first book was one of ten pages; it had dark brown paper covers, and I paid £5.10s. – a vast sum to me at that time, to have it published. It came out at 6d. – its name was *The Mother*, and it is now worth anything up to £10 a copy!! Isn't that strange?

This is a very dull letter, but I still feel very odd. I will write when I feel better and more alive. But I did just want to write you a note to tell you how delighted – truly delighted – I am to hear your news, and to send you all my very best wishes,

Believe me
Yours very sincerely
Edith Sitwell

During the war, one of ES's chief anxieties was the distress of Evelyn Wiel in occupied Paris. She had almost no means of support, and ES could not find a way to send her money through the Red Cross or other channels. In Letter 201, ES threatens to use publicity against bureaucrats and diplomats who were obstructing her attempts to relieve Wiel.

199. *To Evelyn Wiel*

25 October 1942

My darling Evelyn,

No words can say what I felt when I received your dear letter, which has just come. Nobody will ever know my feelings. I had tried over and over again to get in touch with you, but all in vain. And now to get a letter from you! It seems too good to be true, and I can *never* be grateful enough. I miss you every hour of the day. I could cry with relief and yet sorrow at your news that you are making money by knitting. When I think that £10 a month has been sent you every month, and that you have not received it!

You wrote a letter that Osbert rightly says is 'a most noble and wonderful letter'. And it *is*. You must have thought I had deserted you, and neither Osbert nor I can get over the nobility of your letter. Darling, I *never* would desert you. *Never*. I cannot conceive why the monthly allowance has not reached you. It is sent by the usual official way permitted by the governments, and my bank pays it every month. Dearest Evelyn, have you been to the place where the money is paid? I do not know which neutral government pays the allowances now. But have you tried the place where the English are given their allowances, and the place where the Norwegians are given their allowances – if it is at a different place? Try both. If it is not there when you call, do not despair. But continue to go there again and again. I say this, because stringent enquiries are being made as to why the money has not reached you, and during the time while the enquiries are being made, no doubt the money may be held up temporarily. But at least £190 should have been paid to you in all these months, and the allowances will go on being made, as soon as the enquiries have been settled. So keep on trying, darling, knowing that we are leaving no stone unturned.

I am afraid it is not possible to send the money through the Red Cross, as it is against the regulations.

Oh my poor darling Evelyn, it makes me feel terrible, to think how poor you have been, and then to read your noble-minded letter. You are a wonderful woman. I think of you unceasingly, and long to see you. I think of you going about your daily life with such noble-mindedness. How well I see the rooms in the flat. I dream, continually, sometimes every night, for weeks on end, that I am back in the flat. And then I wake up in an agony of mind, wondering how you are, and how my darling little angel,[3] whom you did not mention, is.

I am so happy your legs are well. To think of being in pain, as

well as poor! I have been frantic about you, and so has Osbert,
who has done everything he could to insist the money must be
got to reach you. . . .

---

200. *To Rée Gorer*

24 December 1942

Darling Rée,

  . . . My beloved parent has succeeded in getting out of Italy,
and making his way to Switzerland, accompanied by a nurse.
There, he is teaching an unfortunate pair who scarcely knew
him, before the war, what life can be. The wife is the daughter
of that world-scourge, Inez Chandos-Pole, the husband is a
charming, practical, quiet Swiss.[4] The old gentleman simply
descended on them like a blight. He inhabits their house; he
has changed all their modes of existence. He won't let them go
to bed at night, because he wishes them to sit up with him; he
insists on having a hot meal of roast chicken at 4 o'clock in the
morning, so that the cook has to sit up too; and when he wants
anything expensive and they say that they have no money, he
makes a clucking sound, puts his head on one side, tossing it
irritably, and says, 'I'm afraid I can't help that!' The nurse quar-
rels with, and gets rid of, all their servants. And altogether, life
is a real wow! Of course he *is* nearly 83, and his mind is going!
Poor Osbert gets letters calculated to drive him really barmy. I
don't know how he stands them.

  His host, incidentally, called forth that great phrase from his
mother-in-law (when he was still engaged), which nobody who
once heard it could ever forget. She said: 'Dear Berny is a social
hermaphrodite!' She said it at tea, at Pembridge Mansions.

  Did I tell you – oh ages ago, that my old home in London is
no more. It was blown up when a gas-work of some sort caught
fire, and every single person in the building was killed. Most of
them were never found, including the old lady who used to

watch out of the windows on the ground floor. She was blown
to dust. There is something really terrifying in something of
such a kind happening to a house in which one's daily life was
lived for so many years. . . .

1943

201. To S. J. Warner[1]

[c. 22 February 1943]

Dear Miss Warner,

I write you personally, because Lord Titchfield,[2] who took up
the matter of Madame Wiel with Sir Richard Howard-Vyse,[3] sent
me your very kind letter on the subject, dated the 13th January.

In this letter, you told Lord Titchfield that you had
telegraphed to the International Red Cross Committee at
Geneva, asking them to ascertain if this British-born lady, married to a Norwegian subject who, many years ago, deserted her,
leaving her destitute, is in very great need. You said that were
this the case, you would apply to the authorities to have her
case reconsidered. (Although the Trading with the Enemy
Department of the Board of Trade had, about six months after
the Fall of France, in December 1940 or January 1941, given me
leave, owing to the sad circumstances of Madame Wiel being ill
as the result of two major operations, old, deserted by her husband, and destitute, to send £10 to her each month, she has
never received a penny. And early this year, Sir Harold Satow[4]
of the Foreign Office, under what is quite evidently a misappre-
hension, ordered the permission to be *cancelled!*) . . .

Madame Wiel is evidently, as I said, destitute. I have supported
her entirely for years. She has no other means of support. I am
willing to go before a Commissioner of Oaths and swear to that
effect. And if called upon to do so, I will ask the Bank Manager

who, each quarter before the war, received, on Madame Wiel's behalf, an allowance paid by my Bank, to do likewise.

May I now, under all these circumstances, beg you to do as you told Lord Titchfield you would do, if necessary: apply to the Authorities, *most urgently*, that Madame Wiel's case should be reconsidered immediately.

The information received by Sir Harold Satow was, to put it politely 'incorrect'. Though I am a professional writer, I confess the situation now leaves me without words in which to express my horror. The situation is now made infinitely worse by the fact that this poor unhappy woman has been given the impression that the money is coming to her – when it has been cut off by the orders of Sir Harold Satow.

I do not know *what* she eats – *when she does eat.*

If nothing can be done otherwise, I must, of course, consult with Lord Titchfield as to what could be done by raising the matter publicly. I cannot let it rest. . . .

At a poetry reading at the Aeolian Hall on 14 April 1943, organised by the Sitwells, chaired by Vita Sackville-West and attended by the Queen and both princesses, Dorothy Wellesley failed to appear on stage and was found drunk by Sackville-West and her husband Harold Nicolson. Later, Wellesley telephoned Sackville-West repeatedly, denying she had been drunk and threatening to commit suicide. See Glendinning, p. 323.

202. *To Vita Sackville-West*

as from
Renishaw Hall

20 April 1943

Dear Mrs. Nicolson,

I only received your most kind letter today, forwarded to me from Renishaw (where I am returning tomorrow). I can't tell you how much your letter touched me. Osbert and I will never

cease being grateful to you both for averting a frightful scene.
(It was pretty bad, as it was . . . but my goodness, what it *might*
have been – if the platform had been reached! . . .) It was you
and your husband who saved any situation that *could* be saved;
you both were really wonderful in dealing with it. We were so
terribly sorry for you both.

Poor woman. Oh I do think it is too dreadful that this should
have happened. I feel exactly as if I had been in a motor that
ran over a dog. 'You mustn't mind . . . it was the dog's fault. The
dog got in the way.' Yes, the dog did – but still! And if *I* feel
that, what can you and your husband feel! It was far worse for
you two, than for anyone at all.

I can't bear to think of her waking up in the night and realising that something dreadful had happened, and that she was
lying under disaster, and not knowing quite what it was.
Though of course it will be less dreadful if she does not realise.
Will she *ever* be allowed to forget this episode? What can one
do to help her wipe it out? . . .

You read *magnificently*, there isn't any other word for it. And
the audience was most deeply impressed. I know *I* was, and I
hear that everywhere. We were more grateful to you than I can
say, for coming. If only this dreadfully sad thing hadn't happened, the afternoon would have been a real splendour.

With great gratitude

Yours very sincerely
Edith Sitwell

---

203. *To Lady Gerald Wellesley* (draft)

21 April 1943

My dear Dorothy,

Thank you so much for your letter. Before we go any further,
I will tell you straight out that you yourself can hardly have felt

this disappointment more than Osbert and I did. My dear, if you will forgive me for saying so, it really *was* your own fault, not that it makes it any easier to bear. We told you very clearly that it would be perfectly all right for you to sit in the audience in the *first* half of the programme, but that you *must* come up with us on to the platform in the second half. Osbert even went so far as to make out a chart about where we were all to sit, with full instructions to you, and to put it in the artists' room.

In the interval, you told him you felt you did not wish to read after all. You had been (and still are) very ill with neuritis: I, for one, thought, when you did not appear, and when I heard what you had said, that you were in a wave of terrible pain, which would make it impossible for you [to] read, or, alternately, that your strain about your daughter was so intense that you felt you simply *could* not read without crying (as you said in your letter to me). I didn't know.

It was impossible to stop the proceedings and find you *and* bring you up on to the stage. Exactly the same thing would have happened to any of the rest of us if we had not come up, leaving aside the fact that you had said you did not wish to read.

My dear, people sometimes do feel they can't go through a performance. In the last war, a friend of mine was giving a concert on behalf of the Serbs, and she suddenly announced that she could not sing. There *was* a pianist, otherwise the whole thing would have had to be put off.

What *nonsense* and *utter rot* you talk about my not wanting to see you again. I have every intention of doing so, and when I *do* see you, my girl, you are in for the most frightful ticking off from me about not taking proper care of your nerves. Do you suppose I don't know what nerve-strain is like? And acute neuritis and sleeplessness doesn't help anyone.

I literally *cried* with disappointment when this happened. But now, Dorothy, go straight ahead, write more poetry, take care of your health, and don't give a hoot for anything else.

204. *To Stephen Spender*

Renishaw Hall

26 May 1943

Dear Stephen,

I am more delighted than I can say by your letter, and by the three magnificent Sketches for Sonnets. I am most proud to have these. I think they are superb, and deeply moving.

> '. . . *we are, we have*
> *Six feet and seventy years, to see*
> *The light, and then release it to the grave'*

has a simplicity and concentration and strength like Chaucer's.

> '*Mortals are not aeons, they are not space,*
> *Empires or maps; they have only*
> *Their bodies and their graves'*

has the profundity of the deepest root in truth. As for the lines that end the third sonnet, they are absolutely magnificent. The identity of the sonnets is grave and splendid, and the poems have the magnificence that a sonnet should have, – and they have a deep life that is one with the sonority. Thank God the small way, 'the close and observant small kind of poetry,' will never be *your* way.

When you say you 'can't do what you can do' I do follow your meaning. But I think you *can* do it, and superbly. That does not mean that you have not all kinds of unexpected developments to look forward to. That is what is so grand. For you, there is no blind alley. . . .

In your letter you speak of the sufferings one undergoes when one is divided. I know that suffering only too well. One is pulled all ways at once. There is the mental suffering, some-times so bad that one feels one is being eaten alive – at seeing the hopeless poverty, the social injustices. There are things I have seen that I shall never forget.

It amuses – but at the same time infuriates me – the idea that certain reviewers have, about my lovely Ivory Tower, in which I have lived unspotted from the world! . . . I left home (my home was a very terrible one, excepting outwardly, and excepting for Osbert and Sachie) and I have been very poor. I lived like a poor workman; and I have, amongst other activities, nursed somebody who died of cancer of the spine (the worst and most agonising form of cancer) in a tiny flat of five rooms with no bathroom. I never bother to tell anybody this, but it comes natural to tell you. That ivory tower of mine was simply practising technique, – that, and nothing but that. Obviously women never had any technique till now, and a man's technique is quite unsuitable to our muscular system. So if one is a woman one has to work like hell to develop one. I have always felt social injustice with a vulgar violence thoroughly unsuited to a lady! . . .

To go back to what you say about 'universal subjects.' What fools people are, to think greatness suspect. Of course it is dangerous – naturally. But then danger enhances the life of the soul . . .. As I was writing this letter to you a letter arrived from Pavel Tchelitchew. It begins with these words:

'I think stupidity is terribly curse of heaven.'

I don't know why this profound truth is so much funnier, and, at the same time more telling, when couched in that very Russian English! . . .

Just before your letter came, I found what I think is a great example of the difference that poetic genius makes. I was reading Donne's sermons, and found this from Sermon CXVIII: 'Hast thou found honey says the Holy Ghost in Solomon; and he says it promiscuously, and universally, to everybody; eat, as much as is sufficient.'

Then I turned up these lines in *Proverbs* (XXV.16) from which he took it, and found, amongst a lot of commonplace advice, this: 'Hast thou found honey? Eat so much as is sufficient for thee,' etc., etc. *No* mention of the Holy Ghost. The Holy Ghost was left out, in every sense!! And the Holy Ghost does make a difference. I like the idea of the Holy Ghost telling us all to eat honey. What an extraordinary beauty the thought of it has.

Then I found this, from St. Hilary, quoted by Aquinas: 'The Lord having taken upon him all the infirmities of our body, is

then covered with the scarlet coloured blood of all the martyrs.'
Putting down my honey-comb for a moment, I see the spring
like that, – like Christ covered with the scarlet coloured blood
of all the martyrs. What splendour. Nothing is lost . . ..[5]

---

205. *To Denton Welch*

Renishaw Hall

27 May 1943

Dear Mr. Welch,

I do hope you are as pleased with the reviews as I am. I say
'pleased' – delighted would be the better word. In my own opinion,
they really *could not* be bettered. Do you belong to a press cutting
agency? And if not, do your publishers send you the notices?

If not, James Agate had an admirable review in the *Daily
Express*. I *saw* it, but could not get a copy. If you have not got it,
ask your publishers to send it to you. It was really splendid, and
should be a perfect 'selling' review. And the *Sunday Times* had
this, also, a perfectly admirable review.

I can't tell you how delighted I am. I think you have every
reason to be *really* delighted, and to feel that your career as a
writer has begun splendidly.

I long to know how the book is going. I hope the publishers
are pleased with the book. They most certainly should be. I
can't think of a first book that had a better reception.

This is only a tiny note: I shall be writing again in a day or
two. I'm having my usual 'correction of manuscripts nightmare'
at the moment. But I can't and won't let another day pass without telling you of my very real happiness that the book has been
so splendidly received.

With many congratulations

Yours ever
Edith Sitwell

206. *To L. P. Hartley*

Renishaw Hall

8 June 1943

My dear Leslie,

I can't tell you what *delight* your most kind review of my *Notebook* has given me. I have never had a review that under-stood with such acuity *everything* I am trying to do, and that must so convey it to the reader. I really am more *grateful* to you than I can possibly say.

Among other things, what delighted me so much was what you said about 'she looks for a universal not a personal emo-tion.' And what you say about Blake coming nearest to being my ideal poet. Nobody excepting you has ever understood what I feel about Blake.

It is a really wonderful review to have had – so deeply encouraging, because it is extraordinary, comforting and heart-ening beyond words to be understood so completely. I wish you knew how much happiness it has given me. . . .

There doesn't seem to be any news. D.W.[6] has been pestering me again, and has sent me masses of poems, including one *extremely outspoken* one named 'Maelstrom'. It might more aptly have been named, simply, 'Whirlers'. The refrain reminds me very much of a passage in one of Ronald Firbank's novels (I can't remember which). In it, a great prima donna is practising an aria from a new opera. The words run thus:

> '*Say will you love me when my hair has flown,*
> *When my teeth have fallen*
> *And my cheeks are wan.*
> *Say: will you love me then?*
> *I will love you, said he, for ever and ever,*
> *For ever and ever and ever and ever,*
> *For ever and ever and ever and ever.*
> *For ever – and ever.*'[7]

Poor D.W. I am awfully sorry for her, but she really is a great nuisance.

Like D.W., I am sending you some poems. You will remember, perhaps, 'Harvest' in an incomplete, *very* bad form in the *Times Literary Supplement* about a year ago.[8] It had been ruined by Alan Searle[9] and his dog ('Who is a Woogy Boogy? Who is a Tiddler?'). But since then I have worked at it, and am now reconciled to it.

I hope to hear from Osbert, as soon as he gets back, that you are coming here *immediately*!

With love, and such appreciative gratitude

Yours ever
Edith

---

207. *To Alec Guinness*[10]

Renishaw Hall
Monday [1943]

. . . How *maddening* it was that I missed you, on Saturday. I left the Club at 9 in the morning, and had one ceaseless rush all day. Then, I had to leave to go to stay with Mrs. Gordon Woodhouse, the harpsichordist, at Stroud, to see her, and also because I am hoping to be given – yes *given* – a house in Bath . . .[11]

It is very like a Tchekhov play, the idea of the house in Bath. Either one will go on talking about it forever, and not buy it, or will buy it, and not have the money to live in it! However, the thought of it is fun. I *may* buy (all this is between ourselves) Mrs. Thrale's[12] house in Gay Street. It has a very bleak, ornate, Beardsley 19th-century façade looking on the street – two huge rooms with enormous bay windows looking out on a long paved garden at the back, which, again, looks on a park, and it is at present inhabited by an old lady of 96, who is going to be moved from the house next month, because a nurse cannot be found for her. Doctor Johnson frequently comes and tries to browbeat her by glaring at her, but I shan't mind that, for I have a theory that we shall get on well together. I am a born listener, and have a sense of respect. So I don't expect to be 'tossed'. Nor will *you* be.

It was delightful staying with Violet Woodhouse, who is a very old friend, and not only a *very* fine artist, but a most remarkable and enchanting woman – very beautiful, too. One has no idea what Mendelssohn's music for the *Midsummer Night's Dream* is really like – its wonder – until one has heard Violet play it on the virginals. It is then shown as having been woven by one of Shakespeare's own fairies out of cobwebs. She played me Henry VIII's own setting of 'O Western Wind, when wilt thou blow'. Have you heard it? That man simply had genius as a composer – (whilst being a very bad and boring poet) – what a strange character. I can believe anything of him. That particular song is exactly like the sound of a dark soft south wind blowing among flowering trees. . . .

———————————

The poet, critic, and publisher John Lehmann (1907–87) was one of ES's staunchest admirers and defenders. ES wrote to him several times a month for more than twenty years, and relied heavily on his criticism of her new work. The warmth of their friendship can be traced to her outpouring of sympathy at the death from leukaemia on 9 March 1944 of his friend, the Greek poet and philosopher Demetrios Capetanakis (1912–44). Lehmann was, from time to time, a happy participant in ES's literary intrigues, and could often be relied on to answer her critics. He was the author of A Nest of Tigers: The Sitwells in Their Times *(London, 1968), which remains a valuable work of critical biography, and editor of ES's* Selected Poems *(London, 1965) and (with Derek Parker) of her* Selected Letters *(London, 1970).*

208. *To John Lehmann*

Renishaw Hall

8 June 1943

Dear Mr. Lehmann,

I was delighted to get your letter, and should have written to thank you for it two days ago; but I've been suffering from the most violent neuralgia – of the kind that tears one's head to pieces as if it were a tangerine, and then puts it together again in order to repeat the performance.

I look forward to writing those articles immensely. I shall now think out *immediately what* exactly I am going to write about, in the first. As soon as I have done that, I shall be able to know how long it will take me, and I will write and tell you – this will be in a few days. I hope to be able to let you know at the beginning of next week.

I think it might be interesting to write about the necessity for sharpness and a kind of crudeness, in women's poetry. (Not that there *are* any women poets, that I can see; though I *hope* I am a poet.) I could then speak about the necessity of studying *very early poetry*, and the necessity of studying *Verlaine* because his rhythms, his movements, are suitable to women's muscles. Is that the sort of thing you want, to begin with? This is merely a tentative idea. I'll write to you about it either at the end of this week or the beginning of next. *How many words should there be?*

I am most excited at the thought of writing these [articles].

> With best wishes
> Yours very sincerely
> Edith Sitwell

P.S. I should think I ought to be able to send you the first article in about three weeks. But I'll write more definitely about this in my next letter.

---

209. *To Demetrios Capetanakis*

Renishaw Hall

9 June 1943

Dear Mr. Capetanakis,

Here is the new poem I said I would send you. At least, part of it is new. It appeared (a little of it) in a very incomplete and unsatisfactory form in the *Times Literary Supplement*, about a year ago. It had been ravaged by a bore, who had drained my vitality and who had done something to my hearing. However, by dint of hard work, I've got it, at last, to be something. I hope you will like it.

I feel sure the 'note' from Pindar is outrageously badly translated.[13] I *cannot* forgive the fact that I wasn't taught Greek. I know one should begin as a small child. It is terrible what I have missed. Will you, one day, read some Pindar to me, that I may hear the *sound*?

My very best wishes to you, and to your poetry. This is only a note. I am tortured by a headache, and have been for days.

> Yours very sincerely
> Edith Sitwell

Mr. Lehmann has asked me to write for *New Writing*. I cannot tell you how much I look forward to this.

---

210. *To Evelyn Waugh*[14]

Renishaw Hall

27 June 1943

My dear Evelyn,

This is just a line (on no account to be answered) to say how much I am thinking of you, in your grief and loss, and how very deeply I feel for you.

I remember so well your father's great sweetness amid the acerbities of Sir Edmund Gosse's tea and dinner parties. And it shows what quality was in that sweetness, for Sir Edmund never turned upon it or tried to instil acidity.

With very deep sympathy to you and to your family, and with love,

> Yours ever
> Edith

Sir George Sitwell died on 8 July 1943 in Switzerland, leaving conflicting wills in England and in Switzerland. According to the English will, ES was to receive a miserly £60 per year, and according to the Swiss will the still ungenerous sum of £200. His children believed that Sir George had favoured his grandson Reresby at their expense, and the episode sharpened long-standing tensions between OS and SS.

211. To Lady Colefax

Renishaw

9 August 1943

Dearest Sibyl,

I was so deeply touched by your letter: it was so like you, in its comprehension, its deep kindness, and its strong sense. It was a great help to me getting it, for this has been an ugly, *repulsive* time in many ways; your letter said what was the truth, and said it at the same time with pity; and it made me feel much better.

It really has been a horrifying spectacle of waste, and of petty ideals. I will tell you about it when I see you, which I hope will be very soon. It is very difficult to write, because it is too immediate, and too raw on my past life.

I am glad he died peacefully in his sleep, without pain, and without (I think) knowing he was dying. He was frightened to die. I shall remember about him that he was truly kind to my poor friend Helen and indeed behaved like a human being to her; and that he did *not* prosecute two employees who each embezzled £200 from him. I shall remember these things, and I shall try and think that he could not help certain things which grew in his nature. But – he remained to the last what he has been for the last thirty years. He had, of course, a miserable married life. But then, so did my mother. Poor old man! But they *were* a pair, and the trail of what they have done is still all over everything. The last three weeks have been very ugly, excepting for the beautiful behaviour of everyone intimately concerned. They, at least, *couldn't* have behaved better. . . .

212. *To David Horner*

Please burn

Renishaw Hall

[23 December 1943]

Dearest David,

. . . You may, or may not, have noticed that I had a slightly strained look in the eye on your last day here. This was due to the fact that I was in a passion, and was trying to keep the fact dark. Knowing that S's new book was coming out,[15] I had *ordered* it. It arrived – (the copies he is sending O and me have not come yet). Most of it is magnificent, as usual, to a degree. But the last chapter, 'Songs my mother taught me' is devoted largely to Mother's admirable qualities as a mother – her mother-love, etc.!!! She is represented as a gentle, sweet woman brimming over with mother love. So careful was she that her child should not be hurt mentally or morally, that she turned S's head away when there was a street-accident etc.

I really haven't any words to say what he has done to *me* by that chapter. I do not need to tell you that by this, he has succeeded in leaving me alone with the hell of my childhood (he was never in it) – has succeeded in conveying that it was all *my* fault (I suppose *I* ill-treated *her*, when I was a child of eight and nine, a child of thirteen!).

Why do you suppose he has stuck a knife into my back in this way? Out of mawkish sentimentality – and because, like his father before him, he cannot see anyone else's life, or his own life, honestly. . . .

1944

213. *To Sacheverell Sitwell*

Renishaw Hall

4 January 1944

My darling Sachie,

I hope you will have got my wire by now, to say that
Splendours and Miseries has arrived safely. I have been seedy ever
since just before Christmas, and could not throw it off, otherwise I should have written sooner.

I do not need to tell you that I think most of the book is on a
very great scale indeed, and is full of splendours. The chapter
about the beggars, the chapter about the three actresses, are
magnificent, and most profoundly impressive. I am just as deeply
impressed by these as when I first read them. I felt exactly the
same impact, and felt their splendour as if I had not read them
before.

The chapter on Madeleine Smith has an astonishing
romantic beauty, of a most exquisite kind. The birth of the
Anti-Christ has great grandeur. And all the time, flashes and
sounds like thunder and lightning break over one . . . as with
those terrific sentences about the multitudes of the yellow men.
One of the most grandiose and terrifying passages, surely, that is
imaginable.

It is a great book. – I cannot, of course, see the last chapter as
an outside person would see it, and do not know, therefore, how
it will strike them. It is not how I see the situation. My nerves
were completely broken, and my nervous system ruined for life
before I was ten years old. This was perfectly well known to the
doctors who attended me then, and to the doctors who have
attended me since. One doctor (Vernon Jones), after an interview with the then family lawyer, told Father, in terms that
even *he* could not misunderstand, exactly what he thought of

him for allowing it; and told him what would be the result for them both if anything happened to me. My health has never recovered.

When Osbert was twenty-two, our mother nearly succeeded in ruining his life also. Father then, with the squalid sentimentality and hypocrisy that were his distinguishing features (nothing mattered unless it touched *him personally*) – assured her that she had saved Osbert's life in so doing! I have forgiven Mother a long time ago, and it needed some forgiving.

Let us please *never* refer to this again. I have had just as much, in one way and another, as I can endure. I realise, my darling, only too well from this chapter, that you have been suffering from great unhappiness. Many things have gone to make this up: loneliness at school; the first war coming while you were yet so young; your young friends being killed; the dreadful 1915 incident; *this* war; and, I think, too, the extraordinary wave of idiocy that has swept over the country on the subject of poetry – all these miserable incompetent little bungalow boys being treated as if they were Shelley.

But don't you realise this last has *always* happened? I honestly think I shall make a Calendar, specially for you – with a thought for each day in the year about what has happened to other great artists.

You are surrounded by people *devoted* to you. You are at the height of your powers. Don't take refuge in some dream of childhood. Don't allow yourself to pulled down by imbecile publishers, either. Go straight ahead, and leave these dreams behind. Now is the time to write more poetry. You owe it to us that you should.

And the tide is turning.

Very best love to you and Georgia.

ever your loving
Edith

214. *To Maurice Bowra*[1]

Renishaw Hall

24 January 1944

Dear Dr. Bowra,

. . . It would be quite impossible for me even to begin to say what great pleasure your essay on my war poems[2] has given, and is giving, me, or how profoundly grateful I am to you. I wish I could express what it means to me to have my poetry so understood – understood so richly and completely. It is a great happiness to me.

There is so much to say, and so much to be grateful for, that I scarcely know where to begin.

What you say about my technique fills me with gratitude. It must surely now enter the heads of your readers that perhaps someone who could work so hard – work with such endurance and patience – may have something to say. I am very glad that you chose my poem 'Poor Young Simpleton' to speak about in that connection. It was extremely difficult to manage – or would have been if I hadn't got my technical muscular system under control.

I am deeply grateful to you for pointing out that my vocabulary is deliberately unpretentious and my poetry simple. Oh, what I feel when I hear the words Russian ballet used in connection with my poems! I could really commit an act of violence. I am hoping that your essay will correct this nonsense once and for all. Women's poetry, with the exception of Sappho (I have no Greek and speak with great humility on that subject) and with the exceptions of 'Goblin Market' and a few deep, and concentrated, but frightfully incompetent poems of Emily Dickinson, are *simply awful* – incompetent, floppy, whining, arch, trivial, self-pitying – and any woman learning to write, if she is going to be any good at all, would, until she had made a technique for herself (and one has to forge it for oneself, there is no help to be got) – write in as hard and glittering a manner as possible, and with as strange images as possible – (strange, but believed in). Anything to avoid that ghastly wallowing.

What you say of 'Still Falls the Rain' is so moving that I feel again as I felt when I first wrote the poem. I see that *at last* 'Street Song' is going to be made clear to readers. It is a poem that for some reason gives me a pang – again, as though I had just written it. I think it is one of the saddest of all the poems, in spite of the ending.

It is a dangerous thing to say, but I can say it to you. Sometimes, when I begin a poem, it is almost like automatic writing. Then I use my mind on it afterwards. It was so here. For that reason, partly, it means several things to me, whilst being deeply experienced. Sometimes I think a barrel organ was playing in a street, and a young woman passing it, hears through it the voice of her dead lover, killed in battle, and buried – a little hopeless sound. Or else she hears it just in the sounds of the street, of the children playing, and the people selling and buying. In any case, it is meant to be a love song from a dead man to a living woman, or from a man who is about to die – but I think dead – and seeing the world as it is now, and seeing the woman who had been his peace and his night of rest. Then he sinks back into his deeper night, and she realises that the counsel of despair, sounding through the words of love, was perhaps only that of the ruined world speaking. As you so finely say: 'It is possible that the cry is really from the depths of the human heart as some brutal tyranny pursues its relentless way; but it is no less possible that the present agony is some little understood process of change in the world.'

What you say of my 'assertion of positive values' is very true, and it has been very rarely understood. Your sentence 'The earth is more than a garment of God: it is a manifestation of God Himself' is wonderful, and it is the truth that lies beneath all my poetry.

I said before, but must repeat again: 'I do *not* know how to express my gratitude to you, or the happiness the essay gives me, and the feeling of strength it gives. I am overjoyed to read in your letter that you will not only 'hasten with publication', but set to work on a much longer article 'for your book'.[3]

This is a very wonderful thing for me, and the thought of it, the encouragement it gives, makes me inflexibly determined to work as hard as I have ever worked. It wouldn't be possible to work harder, or I should do it.

With my deepest gratitude

Yours very sincerely
Edith Sitwell

Following the death of Sir George, it became evident that his Swiss host, Bernard Woog, had probably swindled him. By April it was confirmed that £60,000 was missing from Sir George's trust fund. Woog had been made sole beneficiary of the trust under dubious circumstances in 1941, and continued as beneficiary until his death in 1948. Although the Banque Populaire of Zurich accepted chief responsibility, Woog, who had been their employee, was never held accountable for the lost money. ES suspected, very implausibly, that the banker, wishing to avoid detection, had actually murdered the old man. The best evidence she could muster was the opinion of a medium who viewed the tragedy of Sir George as 'gruesome and appalling'. See Bradford, pp. 312–21; Elborn, pp. 162–7; Glendinning, pp. 231–3; and Pearson, pp. 366–72.

215. *To Sacheverell Sitwell*

Renishaw Hall
[24 February 1944]

My darling,

I've just got your letter. I heard from Osbert the day before yesterday the *full* extent of that frightful old man's wickedness. And I had to wait until to-day to pull myself together sufficiently to write to you. For I have been made physically *sick* by his behaviour.

My darling, no words can *possibly* tell you what I feel about it, or what I feel for the behaviour, and how I feel for you and Georgia. *Vile* old man! However, my darling, I do from the bottom of my heart believe that Woog can be forced to dis-gorge, at any rate, something. I should think a whole lot can be proved against him: and if you ask me, I should think it quite probable that there were strange incidents surrounding the end. Do you take me? My own feeling is that we can easily prove that old Iniquity was mad. I spend my nights thinking (as well as my days) how to circumvent that little area sneak.

My darling, remember this – as far as the old man's *conduct* is concerned, this is a continuation of his base persecution of us all that has been going on for about thirty years.

Nothing – nothing can put his conduct right. But *do not let this* – however hard it may be (and I know only too well that is) – *interfere at this time of your great and extraordinary triumph* with your spirits in such a way that it *hurts your great and wonderful work. Go straight ahead.*

You have had this great and deserved triumph: go straight on, and let *nothing* stand in your path.

I am sending you and Georgia 1 doz. claret from Hay's. It is the only thing I can think of to send you at the moment. I do hope it will be good. I am telegraphing to *you* to telegraph to Hay telling them where to send it, because of I know of the difficulties.

I love you so much, and am more *proud* of you than you can ever know. It would – and I am not saying this lightly, I mean it – break my heart if this monstrous wickedness had the slightest effect on your work. It cannot be allowed to have. As Osbert said in his letter to me: 'Our work is the true answer to such conduct.' I *wish* we were all together.

This letter is most dreadfully inexpressive. What *is* one to say? I only set all my forces and will together for the winning of the action. I am writing by this same post to Georgia.

My darling, no one knows how much my thoughts and love are with you both.

Very best love

ever your loving
Edith

216. *To Demetrios Capetanakis*

Renishaw Hall

1 March 1944

My dear Demetrios,

It made me so happy to receive a letter in your own hand-writing. Though I was terribly sad to read between the lines and know how great is your suffering. It is so feeble when one tries to show the sympathy that one is feeling. For one who is suffering so greatly must think: 'How can they know?'

But the sympathy *is* there, the feeling is there. And we try by some invisible means to give you strength. I hope with all my heart that the blood-transfusion has strengthened you. But Beryl[4] tells me it was terribly painful.

I am most *thankful* that you will soon be in a private room; although it made my heart ache to read 'alone between four walls with my suffering'. If there is anything we can do, you must let us know. Please. Tell Beryl to.

Yesterday I wrote and told Fortnum and Mason to send you some turtle soup. It is extremely strengthening. I told them to be quick about it, as you were ill and needed it for your health. Please tell Beryl to let me know as soon as you feel like having books sent to you.

Isn't *Our Mutual Friend* wonderful? Leaving everything else aside, the characters are so amazingly funny . . . Lady Tippins is a dream. I know someone just like her. Have you read *Hard Times*? It is one of his slighter books, and not as tiring [to] read as the greatest ones. If you haven't read it, I will try and get it for you. But a good many of his books are out of print. It, also, is quite wonderfully funny.

We think of you *continually*. Believe that the thoughts of all your friends are with you. It will be so wonderful when we know that you are *really* better. Beryl says already you have more strength. And that will grow and grow.

Yours ever

Edith

217. *To John Lehmann*

Renishaw Hall

15 March 1944

Dear John,

Your letter came by the *second* post yesterday, then it was too late for me to get an answer off to you. You have never been out of my thoughts, with the nightmare of pain and bewilderment, the feeling of blind waste, that you are enduring. One is help-less against such pain. I *still* cannot believe it, for I never thought it would happen – one *could* not believe it, somehow.

How well I know that feeling that one must deaden the pain somehow, temporarily. I think you are an extremely courageous person – otherwise I would warn you: 'don't try to deaden it: for if you do, you will never be the same person again: for if one deadens anguish, some part of one remains numb.' But I do not think that will be so with you: I do not dread it for *you*, in the very least.

How thankful I am that you were spared that last afternoon: it would only have been an anguishing memory for you. Osbert, who has seen a great many men die, says he believes *all* people want, at that moment, is, not to be surrounded. No human con-tact can appear to them real, and it is only an added cruelty.

Poor Beryl was stricken by it. The beauty and nobility of that good and high-minded face must have been so great when you saw it – all pain gone. I am very happy to hear from Beryl that he has been photographed, and Beryl has said she will try and send me a photograph, which I should treasure.

In all your pain, in all your sense of waste, try to remember that your friendship was to him one of the most wonderful things in all his life. It must have made his life in England a beautiful thing. So that he was not a foreigner or stranger; but was surrounded with warmth, and had exactly the intellectual companionship he needed.

I am so glad you were with him on that afternoon when he could still talk, and could still receive warmth and a feeling –

for all he said about optimism – that all might still be well.

It is agonising to think of that unfinished work, and the pain for you, of collecting it, will be great – I know. But after the sharp pain of handling the manuscripts, you will know that this is the highest tribute that could be given him.[5]

I shall miss him more than I can say. What must *your* loss be? Tell me when there is anything I can do to be of the least help.

This is a stupid – stupid letter. But it is none the less actuated by a deep knowledge of the dreadful pain you are enduring. It is terrible not to be able to help in the very least; and that all words are quite powerless.

Yours ever
Edith

P.S. I had written this, when I heard that there has been another raid on London. Oh, that on top of everything else for you. I hope all is well. What a horror this is.

---

218. *To John Lehmann*

Renishaw Hall

21 March 1944

Dear John,

I was so glad to get your letter this morning. I have worried very much about you, knowing the desperate sadness you must be feeling. I say 'have worried!' I *do* worry.

There isn't anything one can say which is of the slightest use. At last, though, a skin does grow over the wound. One never thinks that it would or could, but it does. First of all, one feels it is almost an unfaithfulness to one's friendship, to believe that that could ever happen. But it isn't so. It is just healthy growth. One never ceases to be fond of one's friend, and one always feels them beside one for, I am sure, the rest of one's life. I do believe that when one returns to that growth of life which is cut off for a time by sorrow, one is, in a way, giving the person who has gone a part of one's life, just by the very fact of living fully. Meanwhile, until then, it is dreadful for one.

Oh it is dreadful, there being only those notes about the Plato and Kierkegaard, and only those dozen or so poems. But I am happy to hear there is this lecture on Greek poetry, with beautiful translations. I am very proud and happy that you should ask me to write one of the memorial articles. I need not say that *of course* I will do so. When would you like it? I mean, what is the *latest* I can send it? And please is there some chance that I could see the lecture on Greek poetry, and those translations, before I write the memorial article? For I would like to write about the translations, as I feel that they must be of the greatest beauty, and so valuable from so many points of view.

I cannot tell you what I feel about all this. Such a sense of waste. It would be merely foolish to begin to say how much I feel for you, who were his greatest friend.

Yours ever
Edith

---

219. *To John Lehmann*

Renishaw Hall

[13 April 1944?]

Dear John,

Forgive a tiny note. I'm now ill as a result of shock. It is something most dreadful about my father, who died last July. It is too bad and too serious for me to write about in a letter.

Thank you ever so much for sending me those poems of Demetrios. I didn't know them. It would be most kind of you to send me his poem about 'Cain and Abel', which I particularly want to quote, and also the 'Detective Story' poem. I would be most deeply grateful for the photograph of him. I had them but somebody must have walked off with the book. It is so annoying of people to take books without permission.

I am sending you, under separate cover, my new small Anthology,[6] compiled to amuse myself.

Yours ever
Edith.

The Penguin 19 is grand. *When will it be out?* What a beautiful photograph of Demetrios.

---

220. *To John Lehmann*

Renishaw Hall

13 June 1944

Dear John,

Your letter, with its great kindness, touched me so much. You know I am indeed *very* deeply grateful to you for all you are doing for my poetry. I can't tell you with what joy I read that there is a chance of your writing about this new book. It would mean an enormous amount to me if you can – from more than one point of view. For one thing, in order to be able to work, I do need sympathy and comprehension. And you are one of the very few people on whose help in that way as in others (technical problems, clarity, being among the other ways in which I should most deeply value your advice . . . many others, those particularly) I should greatly rely. I do hope you *will* have time. But I do not want you to feel hunted, either. . . .

Poor John, how *sickening* for you having your work unhinged and your poems driven away like this. Nobody understands one's feelings in that matter, better than I do. It is like a new Gestapo torture – like being deprived of sleep. Because poetry does refresh and remake one, and, in that way is like sleep. I am hoping your poems, the ones that have been driven away temporarily, will come back. But that doesn't mitigate what one goes through at the time.

It must have been dreadful for you writing about Demetrios. It gives one a stone in one's breast, which gets larger and larger as fresh memories accumulate. It is horribly unfortunate that you had to do it now. Although the pain would always be as bad, it wouldn't be so dreadfully unaccustomed and raw, later on. And of course *that* must have numbed your power of writing poetry at the moment. 'Recollected in *tranquillity*' isn't quite right. But recollected long afterwards *is* right.

Oh the war and the misery and horror. All those young men; and the young women at home whose lives will be broken. My young maid (a village girl from here), who came when she was 16, and left at 21 to go into the WRNS, got married here, three days after Demetrios died, to a boy of her own age in the Air Force. They had three weeks' leave for their wedding and honeymoon, and a week after they went back to duty, he was posted missing.

It is simply frightful to see that poor child, to whom I am devoted, and who is devoted to me. She was given com-passionate leave, most of which she spent in my room, not speaking excepting to say from time to time, 'Oh Miss Edith, Miss Edith.' She is back at work now, which I think is the best thing for her.

I think there is still *some* hope; but not much. . . .

---

221. *To Sacheverell Sitwell*

Renishaw Hall

[3 July 1944]

My darling,

Ever so many thanks for your letter. There is so much to say I scarcely know where to begin.

A If you *ever* say to me again that you will never write any more Poetry – *I seriously do not know what I shall do to you*.[7] It is an absolute *crime* to say such a thing. Your genius for poetry is a transcendental one, and I am measuring my words. I am not exaggerating, and I mean exactly what I say.

You say that you have re-read your poetry and are dissatisfied with it. I can only reply that this is just one more proof that you

are a great poet. Naturally any great poet, re-reading his work
after a lapse of some time, is dissatisfied with it. That follows. All
it means is that one's critical sense is growing and developing, and
that one is going to do new and great work. Don't you know that
Keats was dissatisfied. Poor boy, he had no chance to do any more,
because he died at twenty-six, but his dissatisfaction does not
prove that 'Endymion' was not a work of sheer wonder. It was.

You have to write poetry. And never let me hear you say again
that you will not. . . .

---

222. *To Georgia Sitwell*

Renishaw Hall

Friday [1944?]

My darling,

. . . I want to say one thing to you most *firmly*. I know you
have been very unhappy lately, owing to so many causes that
one cannot even begin, in a letter, to write of them all. I also
know that cruelly inconsiderate people have been worrying you
and making you miserable by telling you things which they
must *know* would drive you half frantic, and which I am
absolutely certain are quite unfounded.

I want to beg you, if and when anything of that kind, or any
other kind, which makes you miserable, happens, *to write
straight to me*. Do not allow your mind to be driven into a frenzy.
When one is as dead tired as you must be, from your war work,
and all the frightful worries you have had, one is so apt to
believe things more easily, because one's mind is too tired for
resistance. And there is all the miserable side of people *repeating*
things – all wrong, having misunderstood everything from the
beginning. And then all the fools coming back from Canada,
and telling you God knows what – and I am convinced all
wrong. If, when this happens, you find a moment and write to
me, I am certain I can get the real hang of things, and be able to
make you less miserable.

Now for instance, this about Sachie's worries, not of the money kind. We only had a most *interrupted* conversation, but I found from him that he most truly had not realised what Osbert said to him, at Weston, about writing. Osbert *frequently* urges me to write a long poem upon a given theme. He suggested for instance, that I should write a long poem about Sophocles (I think it was Sophocles) being killed by an eagle dropping a tortoise on his head, thinking it was a stone. And another suggestion was that I should write a long poem about the discovery of America. He frequently urges me to try completely a *new style. This is not because he does not admire my present style, for he admires it greatly, but because he thinks it is good for one's work to vary it, because it keeps it more than ever living.*

That is all that Osbert was saying to S. Osbert told Beryl, in my presence, that Sachie had as great gifts as Shelley, or Keats, or Milton. And he did not say this once. He elaborated it. So you see how little reason there was for misery on that score.

If there is *ever* any misunderstanding, *come straight to me.*

About financial worries, I think you will see that these are soon bettered. I feel, and have felt, absolutely miserable about all you have both gone through, my darling. You must know there is nothing I would not do for you. Always remember that.

Reresby is without doubt the most beautiful young creature I have ever seen. Like a Michelangelo. Sculptors, I should think, would go quite mad about him, painters also. Oh that moving book of youth, which almost brings the tears into my eyes. And he has such a lovely nature. And he does love you so deeply.

Perhaps in less than two months from now, you and I may be sitting side by side at the Sesame. I have a feeling this really *will* be so.

How I do wish I could ever express what I really feel, in anything excepting poetry. For I *do* feel, you know.

Very best love

ever your loving
Edith

223. *To Hilda Doolittle ('H.D.')*

Renishaw Hall

Thursday [1944]

My dear Hilda,

I should have written to you such days and days ago, but have been feeling wretchedly seedy (A) and then (B) had to copy out some pages of my lecture which were really indecipherable for *Life and Letters*.

I was so cross at being balked in my attempts to telephone to you on Wednesday morning before I left. First I was given the wrong number, *then*, just as I was about (I thought) to be given the right one, B the Peril[8] got on to me and talked for twenty-four hours or so on the subject of her wrongs, which were of a mysterious and singularly boring order – and then I had to telegraph to someone just arriving in Lisbon from America, and then, of course, it was time for the train. I really did curse B.-P. I am fond of her in many ways, but she is awfully like a sleepy fly, settling on one's nose.

I miss you *very* much. I especially enjoy morning visits, I think. They seem very intimate and young, in a way no visits to anyone else ever seem. I am sure you know what I mean. I *wish* you were here.

Bryher and Robert[9] came to lunch the day before yesterday, and are coming to tea today. It *does* cheer me to see Bryher. And makes me feel more real, because she belongs to the real world of the mind and spirit. And I'm being bored and distracted by our invasion (between ourselves). Dear good Gerald Berners. He is very nice, but I do get so dreadfully bored by *never* being able to speak about anything serious, and by little mouse-trap jokes.

I thought the last party was hell – mainly because of Sir John Squire. He came uninvited, and really was so querulous and dictatorial, imprisoning people in corners, and forcing them to write out lines in the manner of a schoolmaster, and 'insisting' that he *must* go – as if we were trying to kidnap him.

I don't think I have any news at all, but feel vaguely

harassed. The weather is bad and cold. Anyhow Bryher is coming to tea today, so I have got some reality to look forward to. I wish you were here.

Best love, dear Hilda,

Edith

---

224. *To Natasha Spender*[10]

Renishaw Hall

3 August 1944

My dear Natasha,

I am afraid you must be back in London, so am writing there. I do *hate* to think of you both being in that dreadful place at this time;[11] I worry about you frightfully, and think of you all the time. Indeed, it is the foremost of all my anxieties, your being there. Oh if *only* there wasn't that wretched work for poor Stephen. Is he hating it, apart from all the other wretchedness?

Enclosed is the poem[12] I want to dedicate to you, if you will allow me. It is fearfully gloomy – what my dentist calls 'a very serious *Grouse*' – and in that sense is a singularly unsuitable poem to dedicate to someone young and good. But for some reason I like the poem, and think it may possibly be my best for some time. But you mustn't hesitate to say if you would rather have a less sad poem. . . .

---

225. *To Norman Ault*[13]

Renishaw Hall

8 August 1944

Dear Mr. Ault,

Thank you so much for your most kind letter, which delighted me. I am really ashamed to have kept the discoveries so long, but I found myself returning and returning and returning again to them. Never, I think, has so much been brought to light about subjects that have long been mysterious. So I ask you to forgive me for having been so long in returning them.

The discoveries are really *enthralling*. I do beg of you, in spite of what you say in your letter, to put them all together in one book. Oh yes, I realise the paper difficulty! Have you thought of trying Messrs. Macmillan?

Before speaking of discoveries about the poems and the other matters, I cannot resist saying again what I said in my previous letter – (I feel it so strongly) – that I think you have done more for Pope as a *person* than has anyone at all. I know him well, but, as I said before, he is now an even more living being to me than he was before – even to me who have a profound devotion for him. And, as I said before, you write as if he had been your friend, and you had loved him. You write about him as Swift might have written, if he had not been black from bitterness – if only the good side of him had written.

Surely when this work on which you have been engaged for ten years is published, in book form, with these pamphlets and notes, no one will ever fail to recognise the kind of man Pope was.

Of the discoveries themselves: to me, your essay on Pope and Gulliver is one of the most enthralling of all. Not only is the poem itself one of the best among those discovered, but you have most surely proved it is his. For one thing, it has Pope's particular *weighting*. The parallels seem to me to make the authorship certain. The whole essay is so full of interest, of information, that both seem endless.

Speaking of weighting, is it not curious that anything by Pope should ever have been ascribed to Gay?[14] The whole muscular system is different. Gay, however delightful, walks, runs, leaps, like an amateur. But there is nothing that could be known about technical devices that Pope does not know. . . .

It is very curious, that 'reluctance' of Pope's, to which you refer, 'both to destroy his early poems and to acknowledge them'. The reluctance to acknowledge them would, of course, be due to his incredibly high standards of perfection. The reluctance to destroy I understand too, in a way. It is the result, I think, of physical illness, of debility. If a poet's health is not good, he will produce, sometimes, a line of value, or a phrase of value, in the midst of what seems to be worthless. And that phrase, or line, can be and will be used when he is better. But if he destroys the surrounding verse, before he is ready to use the line, the life of it may go. The 'deliberate re-working of old material' comes, I am sure, from physical debility (*not* mental debility). But that still doesn't explain why he should have published that whole poem anonymously.

Pope was the greatest of all tight-rope walkers. How he could remain balanced, throughout his life, in mid-air, on a lie or 'genteel prevarication', without falling to earth, remains a miracle to the ordinary fairly truthful person. And he didn't confine himself to one tight-rope. Even to watch that continual crossing from one rope to another makes one giddy. But the tight-rope walking is as nothing to his building of labyrinths round himself, his subject, and his motives. How somebody of such physical debility could have had the *energy*, is bewildering to a degree.

Your history and unravelling of the Miscellanies labyrinth is enthralling. I can see the object was the 'propagation of Pope's fame', but there is the mystery of the anonymity of his poems in the Miscellanies. Here again, do you think his physical debility had something to do with it? He wished, one presumes, to see them in print for *working* reasons, since this is the best way to judge what one has done right or wrong in poetry, and no doubt his debility had made him nervous, had made him, great artist, supreme craftsman that he was, temporarily uncertain of his rightness. . . .

I thought I had understood exactly the persecution from which Pope had suffered . . . Now, reading your 'Pope and Addison', I know that even with all my sympathy for him, I had not realised the perpetual movements of malice round him. It would have been enough to drive any man, not suffering from constant pain, not little and weak and in fear, half mad. . . .

226. *To Natasha Spender*

Renishaw Hall

18 September 1944

My dear Natasha,

I cannot tell you how sad and disappointed we are that you and Stephen can't come to us next week. We had *so much* looked forward to it – made such plans. We are only comforted by knowing that unless something unforeseen happens, we shall be seeing you in a month from then, – or less.

I am most *deeply* moved by your news, – moved, happy, worried about you, all at the same time and in the same instant. It is most *wonderful* to know that you are going to have a baby, – so right, so absolutely right for you both.[15] . . .

I am more touched and moved than I can say at your asking me to be godmother. It will be such a pride and happiness. I shall *love* the little creature, with warmth and tenderness. It will be most wonderful to see it grow in mind and spirit and body. I shall feel it a great responsibility of love, on my side, never to fail the child, and to help bring it to its own vision of the greatness of life, to help open its eyes and let it see for itself.

I hope the child will manage to be exactly like you both. I cannot imagine more ideal parents, from every single point of view. The child will start its life with all the makings of the most noble human being imaginable. It will have all that in its nature. And beyond that, what a lovely childhood it will have, with such parents. What a horizon, what treasures of mind and spirit!

I *hope* I shall be a good godmother. I have managed to keep my seventeen-year old nephew Reresby's love and confidence. He trusts me, – and he has a very difficult life in some ways, poor child, through nobody's fault. Anyhow, he talks to me with a feeling of safety and assurance. . . .

One practical detail. As time goes on, would you like me to *knit* for the baby? I may tell you that I am the Knitting Queen . . . ('a beautiful little knitter,' I am told by experts. Why 'little'? I think it is an expression of approbation.) And no doubt you two will be wanting wraps and things. Blast the coupon-system! . . .

---

227. *To T. S. Eliot* (draft)

[*c.* 31 October 1944]

Dear Tom,

I cannot tell you how proud and happy I am, to have this great poetry given me by you, and inscribed by your hand. I am deeply grateful to you.

I thought I knew each of the *Four Quartets* as well as it would be possible for anyone excepting yourself to know them. I have often read them together. But seeing them together in a book is a very great experience.[16] At this time when horror has taken the place of awe, I feel awe return to me, with this work.

Osbert sends his love. We are both so delighted you can come on the 24th, and look forward tremendously to seeing you.

Yours ever
[Edith]

---

228. *To John Hayward*

Renishaw Hall

29 November 1944

Dear Mr. Hayward,

I am writing to you for my brother Osbert and myself. I have long wanted to tell you that I feel towards you exactly as if there had never been any interruption of the friendship, and Osbert, who hasn't met you yet, excepting just to say how do you do, but who would very much like to, joins with me in asking if you don't feel, with us, that the whole episode should be forgotten and treated as if it had never existed.[17] I think it would be one of the nicest things that could happen.

Yours very sincerely
Edith Sitwell

I am sending you a book of poems, under separate cover, because the book will be much slower in reaching you.

---

229. *To Evelyn Wiel*

Renishaw Hall

15 December 1944

My darling Evelyn,

I have just this afternoon received your letter of the 12th November, and it just made me feel like crying. If you *ever* talk again, as you talked in this letter, about money, *I do not know what I shall do.* I simply can't bear it.

You will receive your allowance, darling, as soon as the bank can get it arranged. Already £50 has been sent through Coutts' agents, by permission of the authorities, and I am *hoping* that we shall be allowed to send through £16 a month (sixteen pounds per month). I cannot *bear* to think what you have been through. Nobody knows what horror and grief Osbert and I endured thinking of what *you* must be enduring. All I can tell you is, that when, *after over a year* during which we were assured most solemnly, in answer to our repeated enquiries, that you were most certainly getting the £10 a month which is allowed to be sent, and which Coutts paid over every month – when we got that *terrible* telegram signed Herlain saying your situation was 'désespérée', Osbert *cried*. He had to break it to me, because he was at Coutts when the telegram came. I can assure you that everything which *could* be done, *was* done. You can't think the scenes there were, or the people who took a hand. Osbert and I didn't let up on anyone for a single day. We tried *everything*.

When we meet, I will tell you all, and will show you some of the documents. It was an absolute *nightmare*. We imagined every horror. Indeed, when I say it was an absolute nightmare – well, I didn't dare sleep, because of the appalling dreams I got.

And now you say all this about money.

If you *ever* say it again, I do not know what I shall do. Your allowance will come through, as soon as it is humanly possible, and you will *now rest*, darling. And I won't hear a word about anything else.

I wrote to you the day before yesterday, and now I am going to write to you every few days. I know from this last letter that you have got *one* postcard, but do not know if you have got the others, or if you have got my two letters, or Osbert's letter.

Shabby? Poor darling. It is too pathetic and tragic to think of it. But let me tell you, everyone is shabby here, because of coupons!! I, being immense, can have no new clothes, and look like nothing on earth.

Oh won't it be *wonderful* if you can come for Easter! I think it must be you who comes over here, first, if the authorities allow people to move. Because it will change the scene for you after all you have endured. And *what* a welcome you will get. Everyone is longing to see you. I have new and *much* nicer friends, whom I know you will like, and whom [*sic*] I know will love you. My great new friends are Stephen Spender, the poet, and his wife; and John Lehmann (Rosamond Lehmann's[18] brother), the editor of *New Writing*. Besides Bryher Macpherson, whom I have told you about, and Hilda Aldington (H.D. the poet, previously married to Richard A. whom she has had to divorce).

Writing? Poetry all the time. My new book of poems, published in August,[19] has sold 5000 copies already; 2000 more are being printed, which means they are certain to go. This is tremendous for poetry. My previous book of poems,[20] printed in 1942, went into 4 editions! 'They' now say I have taken Yeats' place. But of course the pipsqueakery are still squeaking. They will, all my life. It would mean my poetry was dead, if they didn't. My poetry is now incredibly bigger than it used to be.

Oh, my *feelings* seeing your handwriting on an envelope, and the well-known paper. It really does seem too wonderful to be true.

I telegraphed to you, two days ago.

I was up in London in November. I can't remember if I told you this. Osbert, Sachie and I were giving a reading at a club for American officers. I'd just stood up to read a poem of mine about the 1940 air raids, when the warning went, and then the chug-chug-chug of the V.1 bomb; and the whistle blew. Which is the signal of imminent danger, i.e. that the bomb is coming down!!! I must say I *did* feel rather old fashioned, as the thing was just over the roof, where it remained chugging about *throughout* the poem, until the three last lines!!! However I continued to read as if nothing was happening. The thing by a miracle went away. But of course some other poor wretches got it.

I tell you this simply because it seems part of daily life, and you told me to tell you of daily life.

Christmas will be here in ten days. Oh how I *wish* you were here, darling. At any rate our hearts can be relieved, in comparison with last Christmas. And I am fixing my mind on Easter.

Very best love, from Osbert and

ever your loving
Edith

1945

230. *To Hilda Doolittle ('H.D.')*

Renishaw Hall

11 April 1945

My dear Hilda,

I hope you have got my telegram. I can only say, you yourself can't have been more excited than I was this morning when the book arrived, and the excitement *more* than remains.[1]

You are a lucky woman to have written XIX, XXIII, XXXVI – lucky to have written every poem in the book. XXIII and XXXVI in especial are to me miracles.

I say you are a lucky woman, because you did have your hand guided. It really is the flowering of the rood. Besides these, I, II, and IV are amongst those which I find most exciting (it is strange that something with an outer stillness can be exciting, but so it is. And it is very rare to find those two qualities together, am I not right?). I know this book so well, *and yet* print has given it even a finer body. One poem grows from another, and all in nature.

What a happiness the dedication will be to Osbert. He is at Scarborough, so he has not got the book yet.

Yours is the supreme apple tree, the flowering apple. I shall never forget the day when I saw those poems first, but the feeling remains exactly the same. I shall never see any flowering tree again without thinking of that revelation.

Best love to you and Bryher. And all my thanks for *Tribute to the Angels* – lovely name. I am longing for Monday.

Edith

This doesn't in the least adequately say what I feel. I am walking *entirely* in a spell. And that perhaps is the ultimate thing to be said for any poem.

---

231. *To Sacheverell Sitwell*

Renishaw Hall

[28 August 1945]

My darling,

I should have written before, but have been feeling *extremely* upset, as we all have, naturally; we have had enough to upset anyone – and also, really, pretty ill.

Naturally, I shouldn't dream of worrying you to do anything

you don't feel like doing, at this moment. But of course you are quite wrong about the poems. And about what would happen. (And incidentally, what on earth do you mean about those great and wonderful poems being 'old-fashioned', my darling? What *do* you mean? Poetry isn't a matter of fashion, excepting for a few fools, who do not count, and to whom *nobody*, now, pays any attention.) The fact that you haven't written any poems for 6 or 7 years, or, as you say, looked at them, doesn't point to anything. I didn't write poems for 10 years, but came back to poetry more fresh than ever.

Now is our time – the tide has turned, we have many and powerful adherents. And we *can't* let that filthy old man and his jackal[2] get us down. You speak of not being able to bear them being torn to pieces. I can assure you that amongst all the other many and powerful adherents I spoke of you have got one most *powerful* ally in Dr. Bowra, who, as I told you in my letter, would insist on that book being properly treated. And, to take one example from the past: just look at your poor sister: has anyone ever been more torn to pieces? But I am going strong. Very well. On regrette. *I know* what the fools who have insulted us in the past will look like in a hundred years' time. *I know what we are. And I'm damned if I am going to watch you throwing yourself away.* . . .

---

232. *To John Lehmann*

Do forgive the scratchings out on the next page. Robins keeps coming in and out, badgering me about a strap for my trunk. These things excite him unduly, and he will give me no peace.

Renishaw Hall

29 August 1945

My dear John,

Thank you a thousand times for your most kind, most understanding and sympathetic letter. It did me a great deal of good.

You always understand everything, with such intuition and heart.

I am delighted with the beautiful poem,[3] which is deeply moving. The fourth section is particularly lovely. And I find the idea of the reaper *very* moving and lovely: but there are, in this section (2) fair lines which I feel are not *quite* the equal of the rest of the poem; I am doubtful about these:

> '*And strained to watch them, while his lips repeat*
> *"Brave lads – the best of all . . ."*'

It is especially the second half line that I am doubtful about. Also,

> '*Poor blinking heroes, like those towns below,*
> *Their souls be roasting – though their lives were cheap.*'

I may be wrong. *Will you think it over?*

Dear me, how well you manage the A-B-A-B 10-syllable line. That scheme, like the open-shut open-shut scheme or its reverse, are extraordinarily difficult to handle. You do it with such ease that it is like a swan floating. You gain *great* effects of beauty from this complete ease, for the A-B-A-B 10-syllable line quatrain is very lovely when properly handled, and quite awful when badly done. When Emily Dickinson uses the same rhyme scheme in an 8-syllable line, she wobbles like a jelly. You always float, or fly.

Apropos of my beloved father's goings-on. Now, Osbert realises he (my father) actually got through at least £200,000 of the family money, above and beyond his annual income. It isn't bad, is it? And all spent on his own whims. Sachie is badly hit by all this. The old man played ducks and drakes with Sachie's money (*without* telling him, and he had no right to touch it) – he then, out of vanity, made up Sachie's income out of his own (my father's money) and now of course Sachie finds a large part of his income gone.

Osbert will not get the £1,200 a year he should have had. He will have nothing to leave, and the old man seized and squandered everything that was not entailed. Osbert with great nobility is giving up the £20,000 to Sachie.

I have my small family allowance. Owing to having had to leave home owing to my mother's conduct and habits, I had great charges of honour and gratitude, and so have had, in the past, and still have, to pay out a part of my income. But I have the house in Bath (a present) and I have an allowance, and I can earn money. And I never, never mention the charges I have spoken of, because it is so terribly painful to the helpless, generous and noble-minded person concerned – and was to the one who is now dead. I should have been lost if it had not been for them.

When I am told by the left-wing boys that I can't write poetry because I have not proletarian experiences, I often wonder how many of them, at the age of 17, have been sent to pawn false teeth – parental false teeth!!!!! You get 10/5 on them. And whisky was then 12/6d. My handwriting at that point became wonky from an attack of fou rire. Mind you, I couldn't sympathise more with the owner of the teeth, as regards that. The life would have driven anyone to it. But I did not lead exactly a 'sheltered life' as a child and young girl!

When do you get to Paris? I don't want to bother you about poor Evelyn Wiel, and if you have not the time to see her, I shall more than understand. If you *do* go, No. 129 Rue Saint-Dominique is between the Avenue Bosquet and the Avenue de la Bourdonnais. The house is exactly above the Fountain (a landmark.) The flat is the top floor right-hand one. Evelyn Wiel is one of the most wonderful women I know. (I lived in the flat before the war, and she looked after me like a mother. She is the sister of my dear Helen Rootham, who brought me up, and who is now dead.) E.W. may startle you by her *maquillage* effects. These are worn to prove to herself that *nothing* can conquer her, neither having starved in the past (she used to live on *25 shillings a week*) – *nor* having had frightful operations (*not* cancer, but terrible, anyhow) – *nor* being in constant pain – *nor* being old (she is nearly seventy, if not quite) – *nor* having been beaten and then deserted by her Norwegian husband, who was at the Legation in Paris – deserted with no money.

She is terrifically brave, and is covered with decorations for bravery as a nurse in the last war. The Germans bombed a hospital full of liquid-fire cases. All the nurses and doctors ran for their lives, excepting Evelyn and two doctors, who remained with the delirious patients.

She has no brain in particular, but a heart of gold, and one of the most lovely natures I have ever known. . . .

1946

233. *To John Lehmann*

Renishaw Hall

[6 February? 1946]

My dear John,

I was very excited to get your letter this morning, with its most important, and I think splendid news.[1] Personally, I could not have heard anything better. I am perfectly sure you are right to strike out on your own and to leave all this deadening Hogarth influence behind you. One could almost tell which were the books you chose, and which were the books Mr. Woolf chose.

You have the same kind of Impresario gift – leaving your other gift aside – which Diaghilev had. You most definitely and surely *are* a man who, not only spots winners, but trains them. Your influence is for the best, and it is wrong, and hopeless, and maddening, for you to be hampered by Mr. Woolf's crotchetiness and small outlook and timidity. I have always felt that about him. He has got all the Puritan Fathers' make-up, but without their fire and resolution and courage. That is how I see it, and I am sure I am right.

I think this is the best possible piece of news. You are a young man, and an extremely important one, and you should not be hampered . . .

---

234. *To Charles Henri Ford*

11 February 1946

Dear Mr. Ford,

I am perfectly delighted with 'A Night with Jupiter'. A thousand thanks for it. It was most charming and kind of you to send it to me, and it delights my imagination with its strange sharp unknown flavour. I am very happy to have it.

I have been thinking a great deal lately about a suggestion I am about to make to you. I am sure that it is time you had a book of your own poems published in England. Now, would you trust me to see to it for you? You safely may. What I suggest is this, if it meets with your approval. Would you, I wonder, *send me a certain quantity of poems and trust me to make a selection? – This is the reason.* As you may know, there is a frightful paper famine here; it is a *most* rare thing, almost unknown event, for publishers to print a *large* book of verse. I would have to see how much paper was going, and then would choose accordingly. And you could trust me to choose your best.

I do particularly want, amongst your *earlier* poems, the strange, living 'A.B.C.' and that wonderful, still earlier poem about the negro lynched. These among many. I do not want to lend the publishers my copy of 'A.B.C.' (they would return it covered with filthy finger prints, and in tatters). And I know you will understand this. I feel *very enthusiastic* about the project, and a lovely book should be made. It takes *ages* to get publishers here to move, and a year (when the book *has* been taken) for it to come out. But still, we may get it out before the scientists finish the universe in order to show how clever they are! . . .

235. *To Stephen Spender*

Renishaw Hall

16 March 1946

Dear Stephen,

Thank you so much for your most kind, sweet letter, and for the essay,[2] which reached me yesterday afternoon.

Nothing could please me more. Of course, one expected you to seize every aspect of poetry that is in the poet's mind. But that isn't all. You do, in this essay, definitely give me, for one among the poets you have written about, something to think over and to work on. You show me where I go wrong, and where I go right. Nothing could possibly be more valuable to me. It is constructive criticism, the whole way. When I was young, I suffered terribly from having nobody who could give me the real poet's advice. This essay does. I am never tired of working, never tired of learning and of trying to expand and to clarify – and to prune. (Pruning, actually, I have always been pretty apt at.)

Not only what you say about my poetry, but also what you say about Robert Graves and Mr. Auden is excessively valuable to *me* – so what can it be to *them*?

I am now asking myself this question: you say about Graves, 'There has only been a purifying down of a wider less discriminating poetic creative impulse into something within very strict limits.' I am asking myself whether *I* ought to go in, now, for a strict 'purifying down'. But on the whole, I don't think so, because a woman's problem in writing poetry is different to a man's. That is why I have been such a hell of a time learning to get out my poetry. There was no one to point the way. I had to learn everything – learn, amongst other things, not to be timid. And that was one of the most difficult things of all. And I think that if I started getting the thing into very strict limits it might bear the marks of a return to timidity.

I cannot tell you how valuable that whole essay is to me. I am profoundly grateful to you, my dear Stephen, for so many reasons connected with this: not only for explaining my poetry to the *Horizon* public in a way which really no one could fail to understand, but also for helping me with my own problems.

I think you are deeply right in what you say about the horizontal line and the vertical image. Oh it gives me a great deal to think about.

How strange it is, what you say (and you have said it before, to me) about the Spanish character of some of my poetry. I had a far-back Spanish ancestress, and I have always felt a strong physical affinity with the Spanish nature. I like the hardness and fire, and detest the milkiness and softness.

Please can I keep the essay? There is a great deal I want to think over. . . .

On 14 May 1946, ES, along with Eliot, Thomas and others, had partici-
pated in a poetry reading at the Wigmore Hall, which was attended by the
Queen and both princesses. The dinner party afterwards took place at the
Sesame Club.

236. *To David Horner*

Renishaw Hall

18 May 1946

Dearest David,

. . . I do miss you and Osbert so much. And did I – or did I not – miss you both at my dinner party after the Reading! All I can say is that, to quote my dear Mrs. Reek, der Heart it *trrram-ble* in der Brost like a little bird when I even think of all that happened. I asked S. and G. and I am thankful I did – if it had not been for them and for Betty K. Roberts[3] and Hedli MacNeice,[4] all of whom were towers of strength, the Lord knows what would have happened. Dylan was as *good* as *gold*, and simply sweet to me. But . . . Well. It wasn't until we got up from the table that I realised . . . Mrs T. said, 'Mother of God, dear, *must* we be moving?' and then said, 'Let me hold on to you, dear.' I then found she couldn't negotiate the passage. Betty and I got her along *somehow*, and got her upstairs somehow to the room where we have the parties. I *had* noticed that John L. had fixed me with two accusing blue flames from across the table, but this had not really struck me as particularly menacing.

It then transpired that Mrs. T. had spilt some ice cream on her bare arm, and had ordered John Hayward to lick it off. John H. refused. She insisted. He said he would lick it off any part of her body anywhere else, but *not* in the dining room of the Sesame Club. 'Mother of God!' she replied. 'The insults of Men! You great pansy. What for are you sitting in that throne, and twisting your arms like that.'!!!! She afterwards seemed to take a fancy to him, although she perpetually, throughout the evening, addressed him as Old Ugly. She would not be parted from him. She also took a great fancy to Sachie, who was very good with her. D. is an angel, really. He has such a sweet nature. He worships her, and it makes me so sad to think that I am afraid she will get worse – if that is possible: (it hardly is) and that she will lose him friends. She won't lose him my friendship, however. But he didn't turn up to lunch with me the next day (which I expected him to do) I suppose because he would have had to apologise for her. It was far worse than this gives you any idea of. . . .

---

237. *To T. S. Eliot*

Renishaw Hall

22 May 1946

Dear Tom,

You are kindness and goodness itself. I did not want you to have the trouble of writing about that wretched evening; but I am very glad to have your letter.

What a day! What an evening! Perhaps it was all done to

brace us for the future, and we shall all be the better for it. But I doubt it. Perhaps, again, it was better that we should have three hours of sustained shock and nerve-strain coming straight on top of the sheer horror of the afternoon (or most of the afternoon) than that we should have had the trouble in two doses. I don't know. All I know is that I shall never forget it.

Oh, of course, the actors were paid for torturing us. We must remember that that is what the public wants: it brings poetry down to their level, and they understand that the poet makes poetry as the shoemaker makes shoes.

I was *furious* at the thought of your reading in the midst of such deadness. The Committee – an extraordinary one – made a proper programme impossible. This was *not* Mr. MacNeice's or Cecil Day Lewis's[5] fault, or Dylan Thomas's. But – to give you one example: dear good Vita Sackville West said *women* were not properly represented. . . .

I hope so much that you will enjoy being in New York, and will not be tired and plagued to death. And I hope you will have a very good journey.

Thank you again so much for your letter, for which I am profoundly grateful.

Affectionately
Edith

I shall be in London in September. I do hope you will be there then.

---

238. *To Denys Kilham Roberts*

Renishaw Hall

22 May 1946

My dear Denys,

How *ashamed* I am not to have answered your most kind letter before. I should have, but on the way back from Chesterfield station, I had the narrowest escape of a really frightful accident. A child dashed across the road – fell, practically under the motor. To avoid it, we skidded right across the road (it was a cross [?] road) into a stone wall. It was so bad that the old driver cried for ten minutes (he thought he'd got the child). I was much bumped by my luggage, and we had the narrowest escape of being killed. I couldn't do any real work for 2 days, and have had 8,500 words of a lecture to write since (!!); hence, all my letters are late, and you and Betty must forgive me.

I cannot be grateful enough to you both for your *great* kindness and help at that awful dinner party. Indeed, I do *not* know what I should have done without you both. How you both must have hated it – as I did. The date of that evening will be found inscribed on my heart, after my death, as the word Calais was found (or was supposed to be found) on the heart of B. Mary.

What is so sad is I really *did* think I had obviated any possible danger by the arrangement of the dinner table. What a bore to have an evening spoilt. I am sorry for the poor child herself – it is sad. But I am *worried* to think to think how his friends will be driven away if she goes on like that. He is such a *wonderful* poet – a really *great* one, and has very endearing qualities as a person.

The afternoon was a huge overwhelming success. It was also great fun – there was a feeling of liveliness and excitement. I never saw a hall so packed, and I hear on all sides how much everybody who was there enjoyed it all.

With love to you and Betty, and most GRATEFUL thanks for your help beyond thanks.

Yours ever,
Edith

239. *To David Horner*

Renishaw Hall

Tuesday, The whatth? The 28th I think. [May 1946]

Dearest David,

. . . I didn't get the full horror of Mrs. D.T.'s behaviour at the Wigmore Hall. But was told by Denys K.R. eventually, that she got behind the Queen, somehow, and, unpresented, said to her, 'I say' (no Ma'am, or your Majesty) 'I say, do *you* like this? I don't. I think I shall ask for my money back.' She then used the Queen's dress as an ash-tray.

My dinner party began happily by G. murmuring to me, just as we were going into the dining room, 'Oh darling, I've just made *the* most appalling floater I've *ever* made in my life. Oh it is *too awful.*' I said, 'In the name of heaven, *what?*' But she said, 'Hush', and I went through a happy dinner wondering just who (and how badly) she had offended. It transpired that she had said to the company at large: 'Oh there is a woman in the cloak-room more *roaringly* drunk than anyone I have ever seen in my life.' And D.T. said grimly: 'That will be my wife.'

As, indeed, it was.

I must say, we never looked back. D.T. was as good as gold with *me*, but suddenly felt an inexpressible urge to fly at Tom Eliot on the subject of Milton. (This was not due to any outside, or rather, *inside* cause, but was the poet in him.) He muttered across me, to Tom, 'I'm surprised we were allowed *Milton* this afternoon; I thought he was dead.' Then, in a tone of unspeakable scorn, '*Dislodging* Milton with very little fuss – *Dislodging* Milton with very little fuss.' Tom said mildly: 'I won't be held responsible for what Leavis says.' 'Well, you ought to *stop* him,' said D. 'And look here, why does a poet like you publish such *awful* poetry. *You know* it is bad.'

After dinner, by the mercy of heaven I had got a private room. But as Rosamond Lehmann said, 'It haunts me to think of Mrs. D.T. and John Hayward; it was so macabre.' Poor John, for a sad and tragic reason, unable to move.⁶ Mrs. D.T. who *should* not have moved, for quite another reason, insisted on doing so, and then having been assisted to her goal (which was John H.) remained frozen to his side, alternately stroking his wrist (she had never met him before) and calling him 'Old Ugly'. 'God, ye great Pansy!' she said, 'Sitting there in that th-rrone! What for, in the name of the Mother of Heaven!'

I was only made conscious of something being *really* wrong in the middle of dinner, when I was suddenly transfixed by two blue *lightnings* from John Lehmann's eyes. I looked back, but he didn't remove the lightnings, but continued them. I am sure lightnings on Judgment Day will be just like that.

This paper is hell – quite impossible to write on. The pen won't mark.

Best love to you both. I am *longing* for your return.

ever yours affectionately
Edith

---

240. *To Denton Welch*

Renishaw Hall

15 July 1946

Dear Denton,

I have only received your letter this morning.

I am filled with a mixture of really *extreme* delight and some trepidation at the thought of your describing that lunch party of two. (Trepidation remembering your description of Mr. Sickert. But at least I did not, as far as I remember, dance or sing. Oh, how Osbert and I laughed over that description.) Well anyhow, trepidation or no trepidation, I am *enchanted* that you are going to do it, and look forward to it very greatly. Of course, I trust you to do exactly as you feel about it. I would love to see it if you have a spare copy, however, just for the sheer pleasure of seeing it. . . .

241. *To Charles Henri Ford*

Renishaw Hall

27 August 1946

My dear Charlie,

Thank you so much for your most delightful letter. I should
have answered it ages ago, but have been having blue hell
here – copying (with a hand with a strained tendon, very
swollen) acres and acres, which *must* be done before I go away
for the servants to have a holiday (on the 2nd September) – and
clearing things in order that they shall not be lost by the care-
taker (*sic*), a really lethal idiot.

There is a great deal to say and I hardly know where to begin.

First, I hope my message (sent in the telegram to Pavlik)
reached you intact. I shall be *delighted*, and really proud, to be an
advisory Editor of *View*.[7] And as well as being very truly honoured, I *will* take an active part – send (if you will have them)
heaps of work, and keep you wise as to any new planet appearing. (That, I must say, seems very unlikely.)

Thank you so much for your telegram. I do hate to think of
deleting poems; but of course David Higham[8] really does know
his ropes – he is an extraordinarily clever agent. He is also an
extremely nice and kind man. And he says that owing to the
infernal paper shortage, it is most unwise to send a book of
poems of that length to a publisher. He suggested that 'Distances
of Pain' and 'Epigrams' had better be the ones to be deleted,
rather than anything else. And if anything *has* to go, I can see
that it had best, at this stage, be the most difficult poems.
(Difficult, only because people are imbeciles. But they have to
be 'put on to' their mental food, like babies who have been fed
on the bottle too long.)

You are very good, very patient, and very amenable, to agree.

Oh, I *do* hope we shall soon hear the book is 'en train'.

In re *View*! Osbert says I am to *implore* you to keep it a
monthly, or, if that isn't possible, a quarterly. *Not* a yearly, and of
course he is absolutely right. It will lose all its quality if it simply

comes out once a year – though I don't see why the best work from it should not be gathered into a yearly.

(This is my first Advice as Advisory Editor). . . .

I have gathered together, and will send you as soon as it is copied, the Notebook. It doesn't only deal with the Arts, but also with certain aspects of the universe. There are the *most wonderful* quotations from Lorenz Oken[9] on the Flower, on Light, on Colour, etc. He has had a very great influence on my poetry. I believe him to be a great genius – and the rediscovery of him (by me, if I may say so) to be of great importance. His work – much of it – has an incomparably strange beauty. I am enthusiastic at the thought of it being taken out of its dull context, and made to shine, and that it should be rediscovered.

Do you know anyone who is a really fine translator from the German? Because Oken has been abominably translated – in about 1802. So abominably that it is sometimes almost impossible to trace the meaning. It would be an admirable thing if he could be retranslated.

He was a Professor at Zurich University. And my belief is that he may, *possibly*, have had some influence on Schopenhauer.[10] Perhaps I am wrong. . . .

---

242. To Lady Cynthia Asquith[11]

Renishaw Hall

8 October 1946

Dear Lady Cynthia,

Thank you for your letter. It is charming of you to ask me to contribute to your book. I am sorry I am unable to do so, as I have nothing suitable. I do not write for children. My last poem, which is about the Atomic Bomb, would be out of place (even if I could send it to you, which I cannot, as it is already being printed elsewhere), and when I wrote a 'Lullaby', it was of a kind that would send children screaming to their beds. I do not think they would enjoy a poem written by me – until they are old enough to go to war.

I am *so* sorry not to be able to help in this matter, and I hope the book will have a very great success, which it is sure to have.

Yours sincerely
Edith Sitwell

---

243. *To Sacheverell Sitwell*

Renishaw Hall

14 November 1946

My darling,

. . . I travelled down here with a woman who lives at Tupton Grange, near Chesterfield, and who is mad. There were two women in the carriage – not together – and they both started talking to me. The Chatelaine of the Grange said to me, 'Do you know what language Yum, Yum, Yum, Yum, Yum is? Is it Chinese?' I said, 'No. Oddly enough, just before I went to London, I was reading in *The Golden Bough* about islands near New Guinea, where the cannibals, when they are wanting to drink human blood, rush through the towns shouting "Yum, Yum, Yum, Yum." Why do you want to know?' But she gave two piercing yells. 'Oh – Oh! That is what "they" say to me every night. They snatch off my bedclothes in the middle of the night, and they whisper over me "Yum – Yum – Yum – Yum!"' When she had calmed down a bit, she said, 'And I hear other voices too. A woman's voice says "Prove it! Pro-oo-oove it." And a man's voice answers "*Prove* it."'

I wish you could have seen the face of the other woman, the head-mistress of a girls' school, and obviously used to these goings on with 'difficult' girls at a 'difficult age'.

Very best love to you and Georgia, my darling, and very best wishes for your birthday.

ever your loving
Edith

---

244. *To David Higham*

Renishaw Hall

20 November 1946

Dear David,

I am so sorry to pester you about this, but think I had better consult you.

As you may remember, I signed a contract with John Lehmann about my *Shadow of Cain* saying I would not publish it here in England before a year had passed after he had published it.

As I think I told you, *before* I gave it to John, I had given it to José Garcia Villa[12] for his Edith Sitwell number of *Viva* (to appear in America). John knew that.

There was after that a lot of fuss and bother and delay with publication, because José couldn't get enough paper. But I have now been sent another American paper in which I see the forthcoming E.S. number of *Viva* advertised as about to appear. (I am not at all sure, now, that *Viva* will not be produced in *book* form, as I believe it is rather too large for a paper. But about this I am not certain.)

Before I knew any of this, I had, at José's request, asked Rache Lovat Dickson if Messrs. Macmillan would distribute the paper when it appeared. Rache answered that they would like to do it (to help me) *if* possible, but there might be technical difficulties – something to do with what the government will, or won't, allow, with regard to importations. He said he would have to *see* the publication, before deciding.

I don't think the book or paper *Viva can* be coming out for some time – but if it does, what do we do?

Incidentally, I didn't tell *José* the poem was coming out in book form here, simply because I thought Viva would be out *months* before, and it was only while I was at Bournemouth in September that I heard he had had difficulties about paper.

I *am* sorry to trouble you about this. But I should think, by the time *Viva* is out, a copy sent over here to Rache, Rache's decision taken, *and* then (if favourable) the copies sent over here, the year will be up. In any case I must do *nothing* to annoy John. He has been a wonderful friend to me.

Most gratefully
yours ever
Edith

---

245. *To Geoffrey Grigson*

Renishaw Hall

16 December 1946

Dear Mr. Grigson,

Your honest and honourable letter reached me by this afternoon's post.[13] I shall, of course, reply to it at length; but in order to catch the post that goes early tomorrow morning I am writing, meanwhile, this brief note to thank you for your letter, to say that I appreciate it greatly, and that I accept it in the same spirit as that in which it was written.

May I say at the same time that I have always admired your strong championship of the works you care for.

Believe me
Yours sincerely
Edith Sitwell

1947

246. *To John Lehmann*

Grand Hotel
Locarno
Switzerland

27 January 1947

My dear John,

Here we are at last, but my hands and brain are numb with the cold. We are deep under snow.

We seem to be the only people in the hotel, excepting for a pair of unpleasant rude females – the kind of people who probably keep a sweated tailoring shop in the East End. But when we arrived (the day before yesterday) there was a Gala in the hotel which lasted till 6 in the morning, so the whole of the staff slept throughout the day, just waking up for a few minutes to give us our meals. But it is a charming hotel, and the staff is equally nice.

I have had no news, so send you a poem. Of course, I have had to give it to José Villa. That dear well-meaning boy has had a strangle-hold on all my poems for nearly a year, so that I have been able to publish practically nothing in England. I saw his paper advertised in another American paper, but a deathly silence has fallen otherwise, and there is a report that José had gone to Mexico!

I am still feeling terribly cross about Grigson. Really! To have had to *allow* that little pipsqueak to write to me about my poems in order to please dear loyal John Piper!![1] However, that way madness lies. Perhaps it isn't J.P.'s fault, – but surely no wife would bring out a magazine without consulting her husband, as he is a painter.

Anyhow, Osbert says we must show no sign of anger, as J.P. is illustrating his book. He feels it, because he was very fond of them. I feel very sorry for him. I am *wildly* angry at the position I have been put in, and find it very hard to bear. If I had followed my instinct, I should have told Grigson to go to hell.

Love
Edith

I should think Rosamond must think I am dead. I'm writing to her.

---

247. *To George Barker*[2]

Renishaw Hall
Thursday morning, the 11th [1947?]

My dear George,

I am more distressed than I can possibly say, to hear you are having these tearing and disintegrating worries and miseries. I know pretty well what those worries can do to one, so not only do I sympathise, but also understand *what* you are going through. How furious it makes me that a poet like you – leaving aside a person like you – should have this to contend with.

I enclose a cheque to help tide things over before something else can be done. I am an ancient person old enough to be your mother, and I feel in a maternal position towards those young poets who are producing great poetry (there are only two).

I shall be seeing Osbert at lunch time and will speak about it all to him (the Authors' Society). I can't get at him before lunch, because he has had to go to a neighbouring village, start-ing very early. And this letter has to be written this morning, because the Post Office has started a new trick of having the post go before it is possible to write an adequate letter.

Oh dear! How *wretchedly* worried you must be. And there is all the material misery attached to it. I suppose no sleep, or very little, and such a deadness of mind that you can't work, as well as all the other horrors connected with it. I am not surprised you have boils: of course it is the result of worry.

I *know* Osbert will do everything possible to help.[3] He has the greatest admiration for you, and in addition, such a great liking that he is always talking about you. And I happen to know that Denys Kilham Roberts is a very great admirer, too, and, also has a great affection for you. He said to me, last time I saw him: 'Dear George, I get fonder and fonder of him.' So I know if anything is possible to be done, it *will* be done.

I will tell you at the end of this letter (when I have seen Osbert) what he says. Meanwhile, cheer up. Something will certainly be done. . . .

---

248. *To John Lehmann*

as from Hotel Lausanne Palace
Lausanne

5 March 1947

My dear John,

How utterly ashamed I am that I haven't written to thank you for your most kind letter before. I was having to write an interminable lecture – that is why.

I *am* so sorry you have been ill, and do hope you are better. What was it? The result of dear Mr. Shinwell.[4] I do not see what people can do if they are ill, under these dreadful conditions. And now I see everyone is to starve, as well as freeze. Are you one of those unhappy people who derive all heat from electricity? I return on Saturday the 15th, and am longing to see you. All Sunday I expect I shall spend – at any rate most of it – in bed, as I am a dreadfully bad traveller, and have to lecture on Monday to lots of school teachers.

Could you lunch with me on Monday? 12.45. I think I shall ask nobody else, so that we can talk. I do hope you will be able to come.

Oh dear! *What* has Mr. Allen Lane been doing? I think there is a strong wave of insanity – and of a most unpleasant kind – sweeping over the country. Surely nothing else would explain the really extraordinary way in which so many people are behaving. I do think it is infamous to treat you in this way. When I think of what *Penguin New Writing* has done![5]...

I am so longing to see the copy of the *Shadow of Cain* that has arrived.[6] I do wonder when the whole lot will come. As I shall be in London in 10 days, perhaps it would be as well to keep the copies I want to send out until I arrive. (Anyhow, perhaps they will not reach you before I come.) Please may I have 40 copies?

John! You won't forget, will you, *not* to send copies, on *any* account to the *Observer*, the *Listener*, or the *Spectator*? All three are in disgrace.

I can't write, at this time, and it is like something nagging at one's vitals. How unhappy one is, when one can't write. . . .

I say! I think – I fear – that Herbert Read and his stooge Mr. Bonamy Dobrée[7] have both gone off their nuts. Herbert has written a most extraordinary letter to David Higham about poems of mine and their anthology (which they say will eclipse the *Oxford Book of English Verse. What* a hope!!).

With love from Osbert, David and myself, and we are longing to see you.

Yours ever
Edith

249. *To Charles Henri Ford*

Renishaw Hall

11 April 1947

Dearest Charlie,

. . . Oh, I am so sick of all the dreadful nonsense that gets talked about poetry over here – all the pompous little sub-Auden boys. They would give a lot to do us all in. But I'll see they don't!!

I wish that good man Gregory[8] wouldn't say my poetry is Baroque, by the way. What the hell *is* he talking about? It is

Greek. I hate and loathe the Baroque (excepting Sachie's book on *Southern Baroque Art*,[9] which is wonderful). Gregory said in a review that I am greatly under the influence of Crashaw! I read Crashaw for the *first* time (apart from the *Oxford Book of English Verse*) at the beginning of the 1939 war!! Demetrios Capetanakis, who was a most extraordinary creature, a Greek, said he thought my poetry was Sappho's, come again. He said even the movement of my lines were Greek, and had her (Sappho's) very accent. . . .

---

250. *To David Higham*

Renishaw Hall

15 April 1947

Dear David,

How nice to have such a large cheque! Osbert, of course, says it will all have to go on Income Tax. Anyhow, I am so very grateful to you for all you have done to get it for me. . . .

With regard to Charlie Ford. He has been so good to me (he has just done a fresh act of great kindness, on top of all the others. He has reviewed my poems which have been thrown down a bottomless pit, it seems, by dear sweet well-meaning, *maddening* José Villa . . . it is a long story, I'll tell you about it when I see you) – so good and so kind, I really *daren't* tell him, or have him told, his poems can't be published here, until we've simply tried everything, from cajolement to blackmail of publishers!!

So I am now going to *write* the preface, and then try and palm the book off, *personally* (perhaps slightly shortened) on Messrs. Duckworth. And, if I succeed in bringing anything off with anyone – *because* I am a poet, and perhaps they won't have the face to refuse them, to a poet's face – I shall beg you to come down and make the arrangements, as you did with José Villa's book.

Oh dear! And what about the publishers Dennis Dobson's?

What are they like? – I am hoping that one or other of them may want work of *mine*, and so would be amenable.[10]

Yours ever
Edith

---

251. *To Cyril Connolly*[11]

Renishaw Hall

17 July 1947

Dear Mr. Connolly,

Thank you so much for your charming letter, which I found waiting for me here. But before I speak of that, I must tell you what great happiness your dedication of this month's *Horizon*, and everything that you so generously and so *chivalrously* said, and indeed, the whole number of *Horizon*, have given Osbert and me.[12] It goes beyond pleasure, and is happiness. We are, both of us, deeply touched. And we shall remember it always.

I would love to write an essay about genius for you. May I think about it, and then suggest to you what writer I would like to discuss?

I am very pleased with your idea of a statue of Osbert for a London square. I think it should be one haunted by a great many Indians in straw hats; they would make a good décor for him, I feel.

I hope you will have a lovely holiday in Italy. And I do hope that when I am in London in September, you and Mrs. Connolly will come and lunch with me. I will write ages ahead, to ask what day would suit you both.

Osbert sends his love.

Yours very sincerely
Edith Sitwell

252. *To Nancy Pearn*

Renishaw Hall

9 August 1947

Dearest Ann,

Osbert and I really cannot allow the B.B.C. to offer us these gratuitous impertinences – and, at that, through you, who have the kindness to represent us.

Will you please reprove them – *and sharply*! Neither of us can possibly allow poems to be broadcast with an introduction so egregious, as well as so impertinent.[13] The person says that Osbert 'shares the family tendency to the ironical'. He is *never* '*ironical*'; he writes satires – that is a different thing. And every-thing he writes is not a satire. The family has no tendency whatever to be ironical.

They take my terrible poem 'Still Falls the Rain', which is about the Crucifixion and about the Air-Raids, and say it is 'strongly marked by my caustic wit and satirical play on words'. What do they mean? I have no wit – (I loathe wit), am not caustic, make no play on words, and I do not happen to think the Crucifixion and the daily and nightly new Martyrdom of Christ a subject for wit – or in the least funny! This person applies the same terms to my 'Lullaby' which is about the ruined world sinking into the state of the Ape.

The writer of the commentary has obviously not the slightest idea of what one has done, or our position in the literary world. Will you advise him to read the July number of *Horizon*, and not, in future, to offer writers of our standing, impertinences.

And should you ever receive such an application, couched in such terms, again, please return it at once to the people concerned, with a reproof, and without sending it to us.

By the way, I listened to the programme last night, in which Miss Gladys Young[14] recited my 'Dirge for the New Sunrise'. It was *appallingly* done – and the poem dwarfed and ruined. I have determined, in future, not to allow any woman (with the possi-ble exception of Miss Catherine Lacey[15]) to recite my poems on the wireless. They *must* be done by a man – and preferably by Dylan Thomas, when he is in England.

Best love

yours affectionately
Edith

Please tell the B.B.C. what I have said about the suggestion for the programme from the *Literary Supplement*. About the question of women reading my poems, we will wait until a programme is suggested, so as not to cast an immediate aspersion on Miss Young.

---

253. *To John Lehmann*

Renishaw Hall

13 August 1947

My dear John,

Thank you so much for your letter. Well, I'll be damned! Mr. Laughlin,[16] some time ago, when he thought Dylan was going to America – this is private, please – wrote a very foul thing about me to Dylan, about me personally, I mean. (In the same letter, apparently, he had said he liked my work.) It happened to be the *one* thing that I would most resent, and that would cause me the greatest pain. I cannot tell him I know, because it would give Dylan away. Also it might bring down something on the heads of the friends at whom he was hitting through me. I did not *see* the letter, because Dylan, in a fury, had torn it up. But it is true that he did write it. I have to endure what he did, for the two reasons I have told you. But you can imagine my feelings.

About a fortnight or three weeks ago, this gentleman wrote to me, saying he had not yet seen a copy of *The Shadow of Cain*, but, given 'the *usual* excellence' of my work, 'and its difference', he was wondering if it would not be *worthwhile* for him to reproduce it in a yearly book of his!!!!

I replied that if he wished to succeed as an editor and publisher, he had better not write that sort of letter to very eminent people; and that I was returning his letter to him with passages marked which would shock him most when he re-read them. (I referred, of course, to his letter about the S of Cain.) I added the following: 'Do you play the Truth Game? Though I have never met a friend of yours, I have heard a good deal about you lately, and I should not give you 100 marks for savoir faire.'

Charles Ford is publishing those poems in *The Song of the Cold* which have not appeared before in America, together with my newest poems. Did I give you his edition – the *View* edition of *Green Song*?[17] It is most beautifully produced. Do tell me if I didn't give it to you, and I will send it. I am sending Mr. Glover's[18] copy of *The Shadow* under separate cover.

How are you, my dear John? And what are you working at. I do hope you will be in London when I arrive, on the 1st of September. Evelyn is coming over to stay with me for five weeks, and we shall be in London from the 1st to the 8th. Then at Bournemouth for a fortnight. Then in London again from the 22nd for a fortnight.

I am – between a million interruptions – doing a little work!! Reading Blake (preparatory to the edition) pondering and making notes, preparing – or helping to prepare – a selection of Sachie's poems for the press.[19] I am even hoping to write a little poetry before the 1st.

Mr. Norman Ault is plaguing me to read his discoveries about Pope. He is, I think, violently huffy because I have had to tell him I cannot read these tomes before I reach Bournemouth. Oh, what it is like to be dragged from one's work, and plunged into an entirely different atmosphere. And what is more, I haven't a waste-paper-basket mind, like Mr. Grigson. (Mr. A. discovers something fresh every six months.)

I've just been violently slapped on the face by two butterflies. They were exceedingly drunk, poor boys, and couldn't steer properly. Eventually they went back to the budleia [*sic*] (if that is how one spells it) which had been the cause of this moral downfall and had some more! They were peacocks – and too lovely for words. There were about fifty of them there, simply carousing as if the government didn't exist, or care, or anything excepting honey and the sun and their own lovely wings. So angelic.

Love
Edith

What should we do about dear Mr. Laughlin?

---

254. *To Charles Henri Ford*

Renishaw Hall
15 December 1947

My dearest Charlie,

I wish you, with all my heart and power, a very happy Christmas and a wonderful New Year, filled with everything you have ever hoped for, happiness, new inspirations and poems, enormous success, (and success of every kind).

I do wish and hope all great and wonderful things will come to you. I shall be telegraphing, both to you and Pavlik, of course. But I am writing this, perhaps rather early, because I have to go to London tomorrow, for three days, for Osbert's triumphal day. He is going to be given, as Pavlik will have told you, the *Sunday Times* prize of £1000. I *do* think it is fun. All the mingy *little* prizes have always passed the Sitwells by, to be given to dingy little versifiers who write about thrushes singing on battlefields and robins covering the dead soldiers with leaves, and to frilly lady novelists with sweet smiles. But *this* prize is the largest there is.

I wish you and Pavlik and I were spending Christmas together. Perhaps we shall, one day. I am a bad Christmasser, however. For when I was a child, I was always condemned to look after deaf old ladies asked by my father, and then left by him in complete solitude, forgotten and uncared for. 'I think it would be *kind* to ask old Miss So and So.' Oh the melancholy of it all. It was almost beyond belief. My father had a large assortment of them, all with a history that nobody knew.

Mr. Laughlin has vanished, mysteriously, into thin air. It is rather like one of the smaller poems by Wordsworth. On the other hand, Miss R.[20] has very kindly sent me a parcel containing chocolate, etc. Poor girl. Otherwise she, too, has lapsed into silence.

Osbert is going thoroughly into the question of who is who in Mrs. Guggenheim's book,[21] by which we are really enthralled. Osbert's eyes start out of his head in astonishment. What *can* her two wretched children be like? I really think it very bad and sad that anyone should be brought up like that. I do wish, however, that Mrs. G., being the kind of benefactor that she *is*, hadn't disguised all the names. But I know who the *last* boy-friend in the book is. And how do you think I guessed? By the fact that he had a boxer dog. There is a piece of detective work for you.

I dread and abhor the thought of London, for I wish to see nobody at present. I am sad, and cannot write poetry. That is one reason why this letter is so appallingly dull. There is not an idea in my head.

It was seven years on Sunday since the worst Sheffield blitz. The Germans were recalled early, because of fog. Otherwise, nothing would have been left.

Best love, dear Charlie, and blessings, and a very very happy Christmas and New Year to you.

Edith

1948

255. *To T. S. Eliot*

Renishaw Hall

1 January 1948

Dear Tom,

All Osbert's and my warmest and most delighted congratulations. It was so exciting to be woken up this morning with the news,[1] and it has begun the year so happily, that I, for one, realise the Government can't be one single giant fool, as I had thought. But anything but a fool.

I had never hoped to see the greatest poet of our time properly honoured and reverenced. Well, I have.

Robins – Osbert's old soldier servant – rushed into our rooms, panting. He is an extraordinary man. Though nurtured on football, and inured by his daughter to crooning on the wireless – (I mean to listening to the horror) – the names of T. S. Eliot, Stravinsky and Picasso are part of his vocabulary. He is always bringing them out, with an air of pride. Osbert and S. always jump violently when he does. We feel like the people in Saki's story 'Tobermory' when the cat began to speak – excepting that Robins is a fox terrier, not a cat.

Love from Osbert,

Yours affectionately,
Edith

256. *To Northrop Frye*[2]

29 April 1948

Dear Mr. Frye,

Nothing could have given me greater pleasure than your letter. It is very important to me that you should have liked my *Shadow of Cain*, and I thank you for what you say of it.

I have written by this same post to Professor Bowra, asking him what can be done with the Oxford University Press about *Fearful Symmetry*. If he can put any pressure on them, I know he will. He is an exceedingly energetic man – like a short express train, complete with steam (he is also one of the most delightful characters imaginable, full of wit, and humanity). His enthusiasms are of the utmost exuberance, and that for *Fearful Symmetry* is boundless. Indeed, it determined him to lecture at great length to his students at Oxford, on the subject of Blake; *and*, this autumn, to the students at Harvard, where he is to be Professor of Poetry for six months.

I am very grateful indeed to you for having sent me *Yeats and the Language of Symbolism*.[3] I think this, also, a book of the highest importance. Really, it is most exciting to me to know that at last we have the critic we have been waiting for. But it goes further than that. I think you will also prove to be the religious teacher we have been waiting for.

In the way of criticism, everything you have to say on the subject of *The Vision*[4] is not only of the profoundest acuity related to the actual work, but also helps to resolve many other aesthetic problems. Indeed, the whole book does this. And it has made me wonder where one ought to begin again, as regards work, what paths one should avoid. Your warning against treating symbolism as a dead language is of high importance. The whole book is crammed with a life-giving power.

Sometimes I wonder – indeed, I wonder often – how poets as great *qua* poets as Yeats and Swinburne should have been, at moments, so shallowly silly. This is perfectly obvious from what you say of Swinburne's belief, and of Countess Cathleen.

I don't believe Yeats was "right in believing that he had developed special faculties for communicating with some unknown but objective type of intelligence." I knew him quite well, and he would often speak to me of spiritual matters. I have never known anyone who was more easily deceived, and I think that was because he *wished* to be.

I was reading a curious book called *The History of Magic* by Eliphas Lévi, the other day. And amongst a good deal of rubbish (or what seemed to be rubbish) found some remarks of a real profundity (again, as it seemed to me).

'Excessive passion is real madness, and the latter, in its turn, is an intoxication or congestion of Astral Light. The false miracles caused by astral congestions have invariably an anarchic and immoral tendency, because disorder invokes disorder. Mediums are generally diseased creatures in whom the void opens and who thus attract the light, as abysses draw the water of whirlpools.'[5]

I think this is true of certain genius. But I don't think Yeats was a medium. Nor do I think all mediums are diseased creatures.

What you said about my book on Blake, and *The Pleasures of Poetry* made my cheek mantle!! I *was* beginning that selection; but I also am contracted to write a preface, and it is quite impossible that I should have the nerve to write *about* Blake, immediately after the appearance of *Fearful Symmetry*. The book will have to wait.[6] . . .

I look forward with eagerness to your works on *The Faerie Queene*, and Shakespeare's Comedies, and Rabelais. This is an inordinately long letter. But it is profoundly exciting to me to write to so great a critic.

Believe me
Yours sincerely
Edith Sitwell

I am sending you my two other Atomic Bomb poems. They came out in 'Orion'.[7]

I expect Pavel Tchelitchew will be writing to you. He says *Fearful Symmetry* has helped him resolve certain very difficult problems of his own.

---

257. *To John Lehmann*

Renishaw Hall

Tuesday [c. June 1948]

My dear John,

I really do think you are an Angel to try and get *I live under a Black Sun* out by the beginning of September.[8] And I am more grateful than I can say. I particularly want it out, as I want to send it to hundreds of people – none of whom will know it – and make a splash with it. As I say, it is my prose ewe lamb, and I really do long for it to appear. . . .

Richard Church[9] has sent me his book of *Collected Poems* – 'all he wishes to preserve'. Have you seen it? 283 pages – and several poems to the page – twitter – twitter – tweet. He said it was sending a coal to Newcastle. There he is wrong. It wouldn't catch fire in Hell – but would go out like a damp squib.

Love
Edith

---

258. *To John Hayward*

Renishaw Hall

24 June 1948

Dear John,

Thank you so much for your delightful letter; and thank you again, most gratefully, for the exquisite *Seventeenth Century Poetry*.[10] I should have written about both before this: but first there was a wedding in the house – that of the young daughter of Osbert's old soldier servant and the housekeeper – then there was the comforting of the bereaved parents (who behaved exactly as if she had gone to her tomb), and the absolutely infernal noise of the houseparty gathered for the wedding. I am only just beginning to settle down to real life again – or what I consider real life.

Seventeenth Century Poetry is full of the most exquisite delights. Many I did not know – William Hammond's 'The Rose' for instance. (How charming it is, and it *might* have been nothing at all, instead of a fresh and lovely little poem.) I read Richard Leigh for the first time in a previous anthology of yours. I am delighted you have so much Rochester. I think 'The Mistress' especially an admirable poem; though I wish he had ended it with

> *'You had gone mad like me.'*

Do you agree?

The Dryden looks at its most magnificent. You really *have* an *extraordinary* gift for making poems shine at their finest. It is a strange gift, and hardly any editor has it.

I have an affection for my collateral ancestor Lord Herbert of Cherbury, as well as for his more famous brother. I really believe the one poem absent from this book which I would have liked to see there is Lord H. of C's strange sonnet 'Innumerable Beauties, thou white haire'. But as it is, I shall be the first to put it in an anthology. I shall do so, soon.

I believe you have read more than anyone in the world. And this book proves it. It makes one feel good-tempered though the weather is bad, to read this book. It seems to me *the only* anthology of the poetry of that century . . .

259. *To Jack Lindsay*[11]

Renishaw Hall

31 July 1948

My dear Jack,

It would be quite impossible for me, as I said in my telegram, even to begin to express my gratitude and my delight. Your understanding is the most extraordinary I know. I am amazed always by its depth, its sweep, and its comprehensiveness. Because every overtone is seized – not only the foundations and what Jung (I think) called 'the suns from below the horizon'.

That you should have written this essay[12] about my poetry is a very important thing in my life as a poet – one of the most important that has ever happened to me. And not only that. It has come in a moment of my life when I have been feeling great personal and creative despondency – being dead tired mentally – and this great illumination and belief is as much needed by my creative self, as water is by a plant, and sun is by a plant.

It is so amazing to have one's poetry understood in its completeness, and in every vein and impulse. Sometimes when reading a criticism of my poetry by other critics, I think: 'I *might* have meant that – but actually, I didn't mean *quite* that.' But with you, never.

You are one of the only two people who know what my early poetry means – Arthur Waley is the other. And you are the only person who knows what *The Shadow of Cain* means. What you have written about that poem is a wonder of insight. You might have been the mind and heart that wrote it. Only, *I* cannot explain it as *you* have done. There could be no possible excuse for anyone who has read this essay, to pretend they do not understand every shred of meaning in the poem.

At the end of September, I have to broadcast about *The Shadow of Cain*, and my later poems in general. Please may I ask one more great kindness of you? Will you allow me to quote you as saying what you have said about Lazarus and Dives – from 'Life is split to the core' (page 9) down to 'an achievement of peace, plenty, brotherhood' on page 10 – using this, of course, as a quotation.

I should be profoundly grateful. It is very nobly written, and I cannot explain that part as you have done. What does not my work owe to you? And what will not the work I shall do in future owe to you?

Thank you many times for the strange and beautiful lines you sent me – the translation of the *Sibylline Leaves*.

I suppose being a great scholar helps to make you the great critic you are. Being a poet doesn't necessarily make a man a great critic. Look at one whom we all revere as a poet – but who can only see other men's poetry through his own eyes.

Your second letter has just come. I am so happy that you should be pleased with what I said about *The Starfish Road*. I repeat, that I think it is one of the most important books of our time.[13]

Yes, I see, entirely what you mean about the Dadaist manifestations. And I see, too, that it is necessary, in writing a history of them, to give those manifestations.

You are very good about Sachie. It was only his comparison with Turner that I thought not accurate. I don't think, and didn't think, he came in with revolutionary poets. Entre nous, Osbert and I have rather a time with him, because he suffers so *appallingly* from melancholy, owing to the way he has been under-rated – (and I imagine owing to his having been at school when my mother was sent to prison) that he has now given himself an internal ulcer. He wouldn't – *wouldn't* – write poetry for ages. And – but I'll tell you about it all when I see you. He can't see that other people are under-rated too, and he hasn't got his sister's vulgar violence and natural arrogance and swank. . . .

In October 1948, ES and OS, accompanied by David Horner, undertook their first American lecture tour. Their itinerary included New York, Yale University, Boston, and cities through the Midwest. They were lionised wherever they appeared, and the highlight was a celebrated recital of Façade *at the Museum of Modern Art in January. ES remarked during the tour, 'Walt Whitman is my patron saint'; it seems that her bold and rhapsodic poetry was at this time more admired in the United States than it was even in Britain, where some younger critics were providing a foretaste of the negative reviews she would receive during the 1950s when the 'Movement' took centre-stage.*

260. *To John Lehmann*

The St Regis Hotel
1 East 55th Street
New York City

[23 October 1948]

My dear John,

A thousand thanks for your telegram to the boat, which made us feel slightly less like convicts bound for a Penal Settlement.

Oh dear! Well, here we are, after two bad days at sea, twelve hours' delay, and four and a half days – no I mean hours – (that wasn't a bad joke, but a slip) – in the station because all our large luggage had been lost. Eventually we recovered it, and arrived here at 11 in the evening, having had nothing to eat since 1, Osbert and I sat up till nearly 2 arranging the most lovely flowers – but bending over them has given me lumbago!

We dined last night with dear Alice,[14] who is at her very nicest and sweetest, and the height of her good looks. I like her husband[15] *very* much. I didn't when he was a boy, but he is extremely nice now.

The attack on me in the *Listener* is obviously by one of those twin pipsqueak poetasters, Messrs. Fuller[16] and Julian Symons.[17] I know all about their behaviour. They are inseparable, and are additionally bound together by their phobia against me. I have done nothing to either of these persons. I have not attacked them, or answered them. . . .

I cannot forget that Mr. Fuller, in order to insult me denigrated Demetrios immediately after his death, because *I* had praised him, a pretty low thing to do.[18] I think him a disgusting person. Every other man who served as a soldier or sailor, wrote *general* poems of misery, about the *general* sadness. This man wrote little pipsqueak poems complaining because just for once, he had been *forced* to behave as if he were a decent man of his particular age, and help to defend his country.

The man Symons had the temerity to try to get into Renishaw the other day, to interview Osbert. He thought Osbert had not seen the constant stream of insults he had poured out.

I *think* the review may be by Mr. Fuller, *because his name is mentioned.* It is a trick of which the *Listener's* reviewers boast, in order to put the poets and prose writers attacked in their anonymous reviews, off the scent.

On the other hand, it *may* be by Mr. Symons, because Alex Comfort[19] is dragged in (they are great friends, and he often does drag him in). It is *not* by Grigson, because Grigson, with all his faults, is too honest in his hatreds to praise Dylan, suddenly, in order to make an insult to me more pointed.

The nasty little man who is the literary editor disgraces himself by his perpetual, mean, anonymous attacks on me. *This* attack (and the one a few weeks ago) is obviously inspired by personal malice. I shall *never* answer them. But equally I will *never* forgive them. If I like, I can do them great harm. And believe me, I shall. By them – I mean the man Ackerley, and those abject little versifiers Fuller and Symons.

I miss you very much, and do wish you were here. I feel very melancholy, and the boat is still swirling under my feet. Love from us both

Edith

Iris Mountbatten,[20] my displeasing cousin, is after us.

261. *To Francis Sitwell*

St Regis Hotel
1 East 55th Street
New York City

[December 1948]

My darling Francis,

This is just a tiny present, wishing you a very happy
Christmas and New Year.

I hear you are soon going to Eton, which makes me feel even
more pre-diluvian than I generally feel, because it seems hardly
possible to believe that *you* are so ancient!!

Very best love, darling,

ever your loving
Dedey [?]

---

262. *To Charles Henri Ford*

Hotel Ritz-Carlton
Boston
Mass.

[December 1948]

My dearest Charlie,

A very happy Christmas and New Year to you, and every
lovely thing in the New Year for which you could possibly wish.
May you get a play finished and as you would wish it to be, and
may it be taken and bring you the greatest happiness and success.

Oh dear! I feel like a worn-out old cabhorse, so this is a very
dull letter. The wind seems to have got into my head, and be
whistling in and out of it, but there isn't an idea in it.

Last night Osbert and I gave a reading. Afterwards I had a
nice chat with Professor Theodore Spencer[21] and his new wife
about Miss R.[22] She – Mrs. Spencer – was at college with her.

Of course I was interrupted, so did not get as far as I could wish, but I shall yet know more, as I shall be seeing her tonight.

I don't feel about Boston as I do about New York. But there was no means of my stopping in New York, as Osbert has to be here, and everyone I know in New York would be out of it, in the country. I can stand a good deal in the way of gloom, but that would have gone beyond it, as I am not working at present. If one *is* working, one doesn't notice gloom in the same way.

I am now possessor of an instrument given me by Evelyn Waugh, which is advertised as a protection against burglars, thugs, and 'social embarrassment'. It lets off a piercing howl like all the air-raid warnings of a city, and doesn't stop for ten minutes. Evelyn, who has tried it (in the country) says it would disturb everyone ten blocks away. I am going to use it on the bores at my Club, when I return.

How delighted I am about the lovely news about your sister. I am longing to see her in this role.[23] Please give her my love and wish her a happy Christmas and New Year. And Osbert and I both wish you a very, very happy Christmas and New Year. This year has been in many ways a sad one. But everything changes – even sadness.

Best love

Edith

1949

263. *To John Lehmann*

The St Regis Hotel
1 East 55th Street
New York City

15 February 1949

My dear John,

I was so happy to get your letter, and hasten to answer it. I am all for Morgan Forster being given this grant.[1] It makes my blood boil to think of his being treated badly. Although he has, as far as I know, never had a cross word from the press, *of course* he ought to have had some recognition from the government. But as usual (excepting in the case of Tom[2]) they have passed him over in this insulting way, and do let us do something to show we resent it.

I long to see you. We shall be home next month. 'They' still won't let us know what day we start, which is maddening, as one must make arrangements, and I have to get a room.

Anyhow, we should arrive between the 12th and the 15th, I think, and I hope you will lunch with me the day after my arrival.

Poor little Denton.[3] It makes me so unhappy, and all the more unhappy since I was sent a – I don't know whether to call it an essay or a story – called 'The Luncheon Appointment', about his meeting with me. I wrote a letter to *The Times* about his death but do not know if they published it, because they have not replied. I shall feel very badly about it if they haven't, because his friends will think I have done nothing about it, and simply don't care, and can't take any trouble, which isn't true.

How is your sciatica? You scarcely gave me any news in

your letter, I mean of a personal kind, and are you writing poetry?

I am just (in the middle of the usual pestering) – writing my first poetry for ages. I will send it to you when it is finished.

There are, I confess, moments when I wonder why I don't go raving mad. But, as against that, I must admit that the Americans seem to have taken to us almost with violence. *Façade* was a wild success, and at the dress rehearsal, to which all the poets, artists and pressmen were invited, the whole audience rose to their feet when I came into the hall after the performance. And the *New Yorker* came out with the enclosed which you must admit is the stuff to give the troops. Is there *any* way in which we can get news of this to the Sprat-Heaver?[4] I think it might kill him.

Apropos of all the little nuisances, it may amuse you to know that Mr. Peter Watson[5] – I call him Mr. Watson, and not Peter – was here the other day. He tried to get into *Façade* without paying, but was balked of this. He met David in the hall, and said to him, 'Is it true that Edith' (Edith, too) 'calls me Bubbles?' David replied, 'I have never heard Dr. Sitwell call you anything.'

To return to *Façade*, I have just made gramophone records of them, which are much better than the previous ones, for Columbia.

Do you know Mrs. Jean Starr Untermeyer? I forget if I have grumbled to you about her before. She is most persistent, and fearfully patronising. Several times I have thought that Osbert, who listened in to her conversations with me, was going to kill her. And she wrote to a neurotic woman in England who writes mediocre poetry – a Miss Valentine Achland[6] – and caused her to write to me asking me if I thought she had deceived me by saying she was lonely. 'Loneliness is not only a matter of company.' Oh God! This occurred at a moment when I was rushing madly from pillar to post, and waiting to hear if poor Pavlik had to have an operation. I am thankful to say he hasn't. But he is very ill. Miss Achland says her 'delicacy was disturbed, and she hoped *I*

didn't think that *she* thought that *I* thought that *she* wasn't'
something or other. I have replied that, like all poets, I am the
hell and all indelicate. Much love from Osbert and

Edith

How lovely it is to think that I shall be seeing you a month from
now.

---

*Having been separated since the beginning of the war, ES's reunion with
Tchelitchew in New York proved calamitous. On her arrival she failed to
communicate immediate admiration for his painting* Hide and Seek. *He
subsequently came to resent the publicity she received and claimed that she
lacked 'femininity', by which Ford judged he meant 'passivity'. As her departure approached, he told Ford, 'I'd like to slap her face and have her kneel at
my feet and crawl like a worm.' For an account, see Parker Tyler,* The
Divine Comedy of Pavel Tchelitchew *(New York, 1967), pp. 460–4.
ES's letters of 28 March and 2 April are the most complete surviving drafts
of two versions of the same, apparently unsent, letter. Successive drafts
show an effort to eliminate anything pathetic or uncontrolled. There is, however, some uncertainty about which pages belong with which draft of the
second version of the letter.*

264. *To Pavel Tchelitchew*

Renishaw Hall

28 March 1949

Dearest Pavlik,

Your heartless and callous letter reached me this afternoon.
I should not reply. But your accusations against me are entirely
untrue. And there are certain things you force me to say to
you.

I thought from the beginning that mischief – the result of
spite and great envy – had been made by your 'artist-friends', as
you call them. Almost at the beginning you said that a woman[7]

formerly married to Mr. Edmund Wilson complained that she could not talk to me because I 'looked her up and down'.

That this was a malignant lie is proved by the *Life* photograph of her talking to me with gusto. My *Façade* records were not due to my meeting Mr. Lieberson[8] at Miss Marlowe's[9] house. They were arranged by the Museum of Modern Art.

I do not understand what you mean by Miss Marlowe's party 'for me' being a flop. I was unaware it was 'for me'. Also, that morning, I had to undergo an operation to my throat which took half an hour. A growth was removed, in such a condition that it had to be sent to be analysed, to see if it was malignant. It was not, but neither the surgeon nor I were in the least certain, at the time, that it was not. I was ordered to be in bed, was in considerable pain, and could not turn my head without great pain.

I do not tell you this because I think it would be of the slightest interest to you. There is no reason for your treatment of me, excepting your wish to rid yourself of me. I was aware of that wish from the evening after my arrival in New York. (Long before I ever met your 'artist friends' you looked at me with hatred.) You have indeed succeeded.

The complaints you have allowed these women to make of me are merely an excuse of which you have availed yourself. And those complaints are as unfounded as they are impertinent. You have a perfect right to choose what friends you please. Zosia,[10] Minnie[11] and Alice[12] are first-rate women. But as a rule, you do not like women of my kind. And that I accept. I have never made any claim upon you. I have neither the right nor the wish to do so. But you should be ashamed forever of the letter you have written me, and of your behaviour towards me.

I hope your health will soon be better.

Edith

I 'think of myself first'!!!

265. *To Pavel Tchelitchew*

Renishaw Hall

2 April 1949

Dearest Pavel,

I call you that since it is how you now wish me to address you.

I wish neither to disturb your work, nor you. And I wish I could avoid answering your accusations against me. But they are as untrue as they are unkind, and I am obliged to do so.

First, I have never, since I met you, put myself before you.

I have not changed, in the sense of which you accuse me of changing. The war was a little tiring, in England. It is a little monotonous being woken, almost every night, to the possibility of being killed. Alice is the only woman you know, beside myself, who went through it.

I knew, from the evening after we arrived in New York, that you had changed towards me. And as the days went on, this was made abundantly clear to me. I quite understand. Only I can't let you say this was due to my alleged treatment of your 'artist friends'. I had not even met them then.

Miss Marlowe's party – I did not know it was given 'for us' – was on the 16th of December – two months all but two days after our arrival. I had, unfortunately, to have an operation

[Two pages are missing at this point.]

Dr. Wind,[13] for whom I have a profound admiration, indeed, reverence, and a great personal liking, and Mr. Parker Tyler, who has no cause of complaint against me.

I do not know what you mean, when you say I turned my back on your left-wing friends, and spent my time with people you despise. It was Charlie who brought M. Cocteau to lunch.[14] And I thought you were Mr. Stravinsky's friend – (incidentally, I saw Miss Marlowe waiting outside the artists' room, I imagine in the hope of speaking to him, as we were leaving the artist's room. I do not understand, therefore, why you should quarrel with me and not with her.) You know, having been told so both by Osbert and me, our first reason for going to Monroe Wheeler's[15] house.

Ever since I arrived, you have hinted, persistently, that nobody likes me. This is both unkind, rude, and entirely untrue. Do you *really* think I do not realise how much you and Charlie have done for my work? I do not know how else I am to express my gratitude than in the way I have expressed it, over and over again. Osbert and I owe it to you entirely that we went to America. Do you think we should ever forget that?

Would it *really* give you such pleasure if my next book in America had bad reviews?

You have been turned against me by various people who are meanly envious because audiences enjoyed my reciting. I think it a little petty of them. If I could not recite, I should be ill-advised to do so. Interpretative art is unlike creative art, inasmuch as interpretative art *cannot* be misunderstood. If one is a good *interpretative* artist that is appreciated immediately. Interpretative art that is not appreciated immediately is just plumb bad. So nobody need resent people having liked my recitations. I was born for poetry, and was, as well, given the requisite instrument with which to express it.

You are wrong in thinking you have to make our personal relations clear to me. It is quite unnecessary. And I have neither the right nor the wish to make any claims upon your time. I have made no claims, of any kind at all. I have no wish to disturb either you, or your great work.

As ever, and hoping your health is already much better.

Edith

266. *To Zosia Kochanski*

Renishaw Hall

Easter Sunday [1949]

Dearest Zosia,

Thank you a thousand times for your most sweet, kind letter, also for your Easter message, which has just reached me. I should have written to you a week ago, but I had proofs of two books to correct, and as the light is really terrible here (we have no electric light, but it is too dark with rain, etc., to be able to read without artificial light in the day time) I got very tiresome sinus trouble and wretched headaches. Osbert has just returned from London, after a bad attack of influenza.

Life is dull – dull – dull – after America. But I am occupying myself with my American anthology.[16] One young man has written what seems to me a really great poem, Robert Lowell.[17] The poem is called 'The Ghost', and appears in *Lord Weary's Castle*. Nothing else he has done comes up to it, but that poem has a force, a despair, a wretchedness that is really great.

I am glad Pavlik is better. I thought he would be, as soon as I left America. His illness, of course, was entirely real, but I think it was brought on partly as a protection against having to see me.

He was working too hard to spare me any time while I was in America; but as soon as I went, he was – as I hear from everybody – just his old gregarious self. He need never fear that I shall intrude upon him again. He could not even *pretend* to want to talk to me, the evening after we arrived in New York, but, at Alice's party, spent his time clamped to one of his dressmaker friends, a woman whom he could have seen, and no doubt did see, every day during the ten years in which we did not meet, in six of which I might have been killed any night.

Having started off like this, he then allowed several nasty little women with inferiority complex, furious because I had a great success as a diseuse, to exacerbate his feeling against me.

Miss Marlowe, and in a lesser degree, Miss Mary McCarthy, are responsible for a great deal.

I really cannot help it if Miss Marlowe is one of the world's biggest flops, and that no amount of climbing, pushing and being a nuisance will make her anything else. She should play better.

I received a letter from Pavlik saying I think of nobody but myself!! He forgets the 20 years of my battles on his behalf! And that I have been neither kind nor polite to any of his artist friends! In fact, to nobody excepting you and Lincoln![18] He is always hinting that I shall lose my poetry, and now, in this letter, he says my next book will get terrible reviews (as a result, I suppose, of my lack of reverence for Miss Marlowe).

His discarding of my friendship has been a little public, to say the least of it, and has therefore been painful to me. It was even being discussed in Florida. And Cecil Beaton has brought the glad news to England, discussing it with my sister-in-law, who, with, her distinguished sense of delicacy, *allowed* him to discuss it, and lapped up all the details, eagerly. (She usually lunches and dines out on any happening which has caused me pain, and which is my private affair.)

I am therefore leaving Pavlik to his artist friends – Miss Marlowe, Miss McCarthy, Cecil Beaton and Signorina Fini.[19] A most distinguished galaxy of genius.

This anyhow for the present.

But I shall always do everything I can to be of use to him, and I shall always be interested in his welfare, and shall worry if he is ill or in any straits. Only, I am under no illusions about his feeling for me. I shall write to him, perhaps, when I have recovered a little from the various episodes I have had to put up with, and from his letter.

It is very difficult to get back to work, after America. But I have masses to do – so much, indeed, that I wander from work to work, which is bad for it.

Dear Zosia, Osbert and I miss you so much. How I wish you lived in England. When I have a new poem worthy of you, it shall be dedicated to you.[20]

Our best love to you, my dear, and all best, though belated, Easter wishes

Yours affectionately
Edith

---

267. *To John Hayward*

Sesame Imperial and Pioneer Club
49, Grosvenor Street, W.1.

[May 15 1949]

Dear John,

Thank you so much for your most kind and sweet letter, which I got by the last post yesterday. I am distressed that I showed low spirits. I had hoped I didn't, because it is too bad of one to inflict one's own gloom on one's friends.

Actually, I have been having almost unbearable worry lately – *not* about my own affairs; but, as you know, one gets involved in one's friends' affairs. This one seems to be endemic; we think it is over, and it comes back again, in a worse form.

And on top of it all, in the morning, a poor soul who has done work for me for over twenty years came to see me. Her husband (who used to knock her about) has just died of a tumour on the brain, leaving her entirely penniless, and with large debts through his illness. She is a very brave woman and will be all right, I think and hope; but it is sad. And she had just left, in tears, about five minutes before the lunch party. (She isn't a person who cries, or whines.) So perhaps I was looking harassed. But I had hoped not, because it is bad manners. You are so kind and so percipient, nothing could be hidden from you.

I believe and hope I am going to come back towards the end

of next month. (When I know exactly when, I will write and tell you.) May I come and see you? As I have said before, you are one of the people to whom I enjoy talking most.

Yours affectionately
Edith

---

268. *To Dorothy Marshall*[21]

Renishaw Hall

11 June 1949

Dear Mrs. Marshall,

It is a great pleasure to me to hear from Miss Pearn that you are going to be so very kind as to help me with my book on Gardens and Flowers,[22] and I look forward greatly to meeting you.

Meanwhile, I wonder if you will be so very kind as to search in the British Museum, and send me, extracts which you think charming from such books as Ascham's *Herbal*, Turner's *Herbal*, either recipes for scents, syrups, or such like (I have an exquisite recipe from Ascham about Syrup of Violets) or descriptions of flowers.

Also recipes for the same kind of things – scents, syrups, powders, sweet waters, from the Countess of Kent's *Still Room Book*, and *The Queen's Closet* opened by W. M. Cook to Queen Henrietta Maria. Also *The Boke of Secrets of Albertus Magus* (translated into English very early: 1560). This contains many strange things. Also recipes from the *Still Room*, by Mrs. Charles Randell.

My book will contain flower-recipes, as you will see from this. And queer things like the following recipe from Albertus Magus, 'To Raise a Rainbow':

'This herb [sage] yf left to putrefy with the blood of a serpent or a bird like a oysell, yf it be touched on ye brest of a man he shall lose his sence or felynge the space of fifteen dayes or more.

And yf the foresaid serpent be burned and the ashes of it put in ye fyre, anone shall there be a rayne bowe with an horible thunder.' . . .

---

269. *To Rosamond Lehmann*

Renishaw Hall

18 June 1949

Darling Rosamond,

It made me *so* happy to get your lovely letter. I found it waiting for me when I got back to Renishaw last night.

Never – never – *never* think I have 'gone away', as people do, sometimes. Alas! Don't I know it! Who better! If I am devoted to anyone, I am devoted to them forever, and never change, unless *they* throw *me* out. Even then, I don't change.

You *must* forgive these last few months' odd silence. I have been very unhappy and fearfully worried, and the days drifted on in a kind of mist, hopelessly. If people dug me out, wrote to me, or telephoned, I would drift towards them. But my own feeling made it appear to me that if they didn't, it meant they didn't want to see me. All my confidence in the possibility of gaining affection and friendship had gone. And I didn't want to inflict my own deadness on other people; they have troubles of their own.

Please don't mention this to anyone. Not that you would.

Well, anyhow, I am now beginning to revive a little. Only I have only written one poem for many months, and that, too, is dispiriting. . . .

---

270. *To Geoffrey Gorer*

Private

Renishaw Hall

[1949]

Dearest Geoffrey,

. . . Part of the trouble I spoke to you about, is on the subject of S²³ and our having gone to America. G says he was broken-hearted at not being taken, and that it brought on an ulcer. I really felt like a murderer. There is now – I find out from O – only this mustn't come out on any account – *every* chance of our going again next autumn. I have spoken to O, who absolutely refuses to take them along. You see G has really been very difficult . . . and mischief has been made otherwise.

I don't know *what* to do. If I don't go, it is simply throwing everything away, as D is certain to go, and will simply muscle in, in ways I will explain to you. I can't *bear* to hurt S, whom I love dearly. And the poor darling is dreadfully down, anyhow. Oh dear, what an impasse!

Of course I can see we can't go about like a troupe of acro-bats. S doesn't know of this plan to go next autumn. I think the only thing is for the agent to make him another offer. But I feel ill with worry. And there have been other troubles about him, too, falling on poor O.

I should not worry you about all this. But you are the only person I can trust, who has any sense.

Much love, also to your dear mother

Edith

When I spoke to O, he said, 'How *like* them, to get at you when I was away!'

The South African poet Roy Campbell (1901–57), who had in April assaulted Stephen Spender at a poetry reading, had now menaced Geoffrey Grigson with his walking stick at the BBC, supposedly in defence of ES's literary reputation. Both events were greatly embroidered in Campbell's recounting of them.

271. *To Osbert Sitwell*

Renishaw Hall

28 September 1949

My darling,

. . . There is great joy and rejoicing in London over what dear Mrs. Reek would call 'de event'. The Spanish Ambassador is *enthralled*, and sent a message asking me to lunch, although he does not know me. (I couldn't go.) Lord Beaverbrook[24] has been made aware of the facts by Daniel George.[25] The enclosed appeared in the *Express*.

Grigson has (as far as I can make out from Roy, who shrieked so on the telephone that I couldn't hear very well) asked the B.B.C. for protection. They asked Roy to promise he wouldn't hit him again. Roy replied that he would rather throw the whole staff out of the window than give such a promise. The head of the B.B.C. went and 'looked me (Roy) over' and asked, 'What do you mean by throwing people about outside the B.B.C.?' He replied that he did it from a chivalrous motive.

William Plomer[26] came to lunch with me I can only imagine in order to insult me. He was quite *odious*. He said – I can't remember his words in this instance – that it was nothing for me to have had Grigson slapped, as Roy had slapped Stephen. Evelyn[27] said, 'She didn't *ask* Campbell to slap Grigson.' No, he replied, virtuously, '*but Stephen is her old friend*'!!! I said, 'I suppose I ought to have asked him *not* [to] slap Grigson. Is that what you mean?' Disloyalty has always been my strong suit, and loyalty Stephen's, of course. I said, 'I have never asked anyone to defend my poetry.' He replied, 'Well, *you couldn't very well, could you?*'

No indeed. You think of what I did when he was being hysterical about Lillian Bowes-Lyon![28] And *he could* have protested against the non-stop anonymous insults in the *Listener* (the editor being one of his greatest friends) but he did *not*. I said, 'I am sorry that you are not pleased that this man was slapped for insulting me.' He replied, '*one cannot take both sides*'!!!

I imagine Rosamond has been whining; because she was present when Geoffrey[29] said what a good thing Roy's article[30] had been. *Really!* It is the only harsh criticism any of these little pipsqueak poets have ever had – I mean softy [?] Cecil[31] and so forth. Well! I think Plomer is very right to take the side of a great poet like Day Lewis instead of that of a *woman* who is the *poet I* am! And yet – I think I know whose poetry will be remembered.

I do not care to be insulted at my own luncheon table, and I shall not see Plomer again. After all, if I have to refuse to be defended, in order to please *all* the men Rosamond has dossed down with, my life would be a little difficult.[32] So Plomer can now go and tell his Mickey Mouse stories to somebody else. It was an ugly, ugly performance, and I am horribly shocked.

Darling, I am not meaning to disturb your holiday by telling you these things, but I thought you would want to know what is going on.

Alice Who[33] is in London; we shall have to be very careful. I said I was longing to work, so she said she was thinking of taking a house if I would go and stay with her. I said I could not work staying with people. She said, 'I would *never speak!*' She then insisted on motoring me to Sheffield. I said I would not ask her to Renishaw as you would not forgive me if *I* showed her Renishaw before *you* could. She talked ceaselessly. I think I have headed her off. Florence and she may be going to stay in London and worry me instead.

I think the old girl is very sweet in some ways, but she isn't 'right' over here. She was, of course, wonderfully kind in New

York. *Please show David this letter, and thank him for his*, with my
best love.

Very best love
ever your loving
Edith

Naturally, I was only an excuse for the hitting, which Roy has
been longing to do for years. But what a useful excuse.

---

*ES had challenged David Higham over an apparent conflict of interest in his
dealings with her. She discovered from him that his firm also represented
Geoffrey Grigson, and was irate that her own agent had arranged publication of articles and books which were plainly damaging to her literary
reputation. Higham responded on 25 October that his firm did not handle
Grigson's articles, only his books, and that a particular book ES had mentioned at lunch had been placed before it was written. Moreover, he
maintained that it was in the nature of the literary agent's business to remain
'below the battle'. See David Higham,* Literary Gent *(London, 1978), p.
203.*

272. *To David Higham*

Weston Hall
Towcester
Northamptonshire

22 October 1949

Dear David,

I have not had time to write to you before. I was much surprised and displeased by your attitude when you lunched with
me on Wednesday. I may say that it shocked my cousin as much
as it shocked me.

There can – or should – be only one point of view on the
subject discussed. I have a right to expect loyalty from you.

Apparently, you act for this person as well as for my brothers

and myself. Of course, if you think he is likely to be more successful, professionally, than we can hope to be, there is nothing
more to be said.

But I must ask: am I to understand that your firm placed this
man's articles about me, and the books in which he has attacked
me?

Yours
Edith Sitwell

273. *To David Higham* (telegram)

27 October 1949

JUST RECEIVED LETTER AS AM STILL AT WESTON
RETURNING RENISHAW TOMORROW QUITE
UNDERSTOOD AND ALL CLEAR EDITH

274. *To Richard Church* (?)

Renishaw Hall
30 November 1949

My dear Richard,

I am so grateful to you for your letter and its most valuable
enclosure.

Thank you, with all my gratitude, for what you have said
about my poetry. My gratitude to you is as great as it is
unending.

I am very interested indeed to read what you say of Edwin
Muir.[34] Do you know that I have never read him? I feel that
there is a gap and that I must and shall read him at once. When
I say I have never read him, that is not quite true. I did read a
few early poems, and found them unvital. Evidently something
has happened to him, as it has to several poets.

I find Miss Raine[35] dreadfully trying. In fact, I feel rather as Mr. Paul Robeson might do if confronted by somebody imported from the untrodden wilds of Central Africa. (Excepting that there is nothing wild or savage about Miss Raine.) I wish, if she *must* write verse (I see no necessity for it) she would stop trying to write *mine*. I cannot move, without her dogging my footsteps, helping herself to my imagery, and ruining it. First, she took the end of 'Still Falls the Rain' and ruined *that*. She then took all my rose and fire images, and my primitive images, and ruined *those*. It really *does* ruin images to have this lady's maid poetry imitating them, and so badly. I believe she is a nice woman. But her poems, to my mind, are not only small, but very messy. . . .

1950

275. *To Katherine Anne Porter*[1]

Renishaw Hall

4 January 1950

Dear Miss Porter,

I do hope that my telegram reached you safely, a telegram that expressed only too inadequately the great happiness and pride with which your review[2] filled me. *Nothing* could have made me happier, than to be so praised by a writer for whom I have such a great admiration.

The review reached me at a moment when I was in the greatest need of encouragement. It brought my poetry back to life in me again. It came at exactly the moment when it was most powerful to revivify, to strengthen. And indeed, I do not know how to thank you.

What generous warmth! What *complete* comprehension of everything I have tried to do, and of the spirit from which the poems sprang. It is a wonderful thing for me to have been so

understood, and by you. I am most deeply moved by all you
have said of my poems.

It was a great disappointment to me that you were not in
New York at the time of our visit; and a great disappointment to
my brother Osbert also. I hope we shall have the happiness of
meeting you when we come again, very shortly.

I waited to write this letter until the New Year had come in,
because the post office in England makes a point of losing
important letters at Christmas and the New Year!

With my deep gratitude.

I am
Yours sincerely
Edith Sitwell

---

276. *To Katherine Anne Porter*

Renishaw Hall

2 February 1950

Dear Miss Porter,

Your most delightful and kind letter gave me the greatest possible pleasure. And I should have answered it immediately, but
first I was ill, and then the household, one by one, went down
with the usual winter complaints (the climate is grim in this
part of the world) and so everything was disorganised, and one
is late with letters and with work.

I do thank you for your letter. I do thank you for what you
have done for my poetry (to *me*, as well as to my readers, for the
essay came at a moment when I was 'damped and benummed'
like the person in one of Donne's sermons). As for the long
study of which you speak! How *am* I to express my gratitude?
You cannot know what happiness the thought of it gives me.

There is no living prose writer for whom I have a greater
admiration and living feeling – for those depths on depths
render that wonderful shimmering surface that is like life itself,

and that is never separate from the depths, but a part of them.

I shall never forget the first time I read 'Pale Horse, Pale Rider'[3] – to me one of the greatest of short stories, as it must be to everyone. It was an extraordinary experience, living through that strange hallucination, the growth of it, the gradual development – a hallucination that seems as real to the reader as to the hallucinated – living through it and feeling it change to terrible truth, to the unbearable reality, the waking world. I had just been nursing a dying friend, going through her deliriums with her, and I know the appalling exactitude of fever that you produced.

How much my brother Osbert and I hope you will be in New York when we are there. I think we arrive about the 21st of September.

I hope my telegram reached you. But nothing can begin to express my gratitude.

With great admiration

> Yours very sincerely
> Edith Sitwell

Oh, what a *stupid* letter this is! Stupid-seeming, but most deeply felt!

---

277. *To David Higham*

Renishaw Hall

16 February 1950

My dear David,

I have just received the enclosed letter from Ted Weeks.[4] As you see, the matter is *still* not settled. If it *is* not settled, I shall have lost my contracts with Ted, and done my career in America infinite harm – and all because *for a whole year* Armitage Watkins[5] has refused to do what I asked him.

If he does not wish to act as my representative, all he has to do is to say so. But I cannot have my career spoiled because he will not do what I ask him.

It is a little difficult to write with moderation about this. I have waited – and waited – and waited. Who on earth do you suppose would put up with such a thing? I do not understand even his point of view in not breaking off the contact with the American Macmillan.

What poet of my standing would continue to work for a firm that has insulted all his or her most important work, and has been grossly rude by omission personally? Do you suppose Tom Eliot would? Do you suppose Mr. Yeats would have?

I am highly indignant, as you can well imagine. I dare not trust myself to write to him at present, but I shall as soon as I can control my very justifiable anger.

Yours ever
Edith

---

278. *To Minnie Astor*

Renishaw Hall
Renishaw
near Sheffield

12 March 1950

Dearest Minnie,

Thank you so much for your letter, which I was so delighted to get. And Osbert and I are so thrilled to hear about Kate Cushing Paley.[6] I am sure she must be an angel, and we are longing to see her.

Your family does produce the most enchanting women in the world, and the greatest wish anyone could have for her, is that she will be exactly like her dear grandmother, her mother, and her two aunts.

I should have written this days ago, but *the very* day when I got your letter, I received two enormous bundles of proofs – the size of the week's washing in a large hotel, *and* the typescript of my coming book for America – (a selection from my *Shakespeare Notebook* and my *A Poet's Notebook*, with additions to the latter).[7] All these had to be corrected at once, and ever since I have been at it, without stopping, with eyes pouring with tears, because the printers *will* put queries in the faintest pencil.

You know what the man McCann[8] did, when I was trying to write to you while you were in Jamaica last year? He gave me, as your address: Suncet Lodge – Yes, spelt like that – Jamaica. When Osbert told me that was insufficient, I wrote, and wrote, *and* wrote, asking for your proper address. No reply.

I have *never heard* such an infernal impertinence as La Chasseuse's remark to you! Never. Very well. Shall I tell you *how she* got a poem[9] dedicated to her? She *asked* me for it!!!! And not once, but over and over again. It is a thing that has never happened to me before.

I would have thought she would have been quieter, because I have had to reprove her. Please don't tell anyone. But what *do* you think she did? Her daughter is a weak, sweetly feminine composer. Without asking my permission, the daughter set two poems of mine to music. (I loathe this being done, unless the composer is a professional of the highest kind: and even then, I am very choosey about it.) One of the songs was quite pretty (the words are light) so I said that could be published, but the other mustn't be. La Chasseuse then said that Chasseuse Junior was setting my 'Lullaby' – the one ending

> *'The Judas-coloured sun is gone,*
> *And with the Ape thou art alone.'*

for orchestra and voices. I said I could *not* have this done. I wrote it, and received a reply from La Chasseuse on the subject. That was in October.

In January – to – to put it mildly, my *surprise* – I received a *gramophone record* of the rough setting (not completed) with a letter from La Chasseuse saying she could not help feeling it would help my career (!!) if this work were performed.

Did you *ever?* What she got back must have scorched the postman's hands.

The work consisted of a weak mewling like that of a darling little kitty witty who has shinned up a tree too high for it (which of course is exactly what Chasseuse Junior did do), and doesn't know how to get out of it.

Did you see Tom Eliot's *The Cocktail Party*? He has just sent me the book of it. I *do* think the beginning in especial is marvellous – so wonderfully funny, too.

I don't seem to have any news. Partly because I've been pinned with my nose to my proofs all this time. Thank goodness they are now finished. I do *hope* you are coming over this year? Only for a much, much longer visit. It is so lovely to think of America. We can hardly wait till September. . . .

---

279. *To Minnie Astor*

Montegufoni

29 April 1950

Dearest Minnie,

It is now so lovely here (after a freezing fortnight). I do *wish* you were with us. What fun we would have. It was so heavenly warm and sunny yesterday that we were able to lunch out on the terrace amongst the orange and lemon trees.

I have been here for exactly a fortnight. But I only began to recover yesterday from my journey, which was – let us face it – sheer hell! I left a trail of despair and nervous breakdown among all the officials from Victoria to Pisa (inclusive) and my name is mud. Their descendants will probably frighten their children with my name, three generations hence, as the English used to frighten their children with the name of Napoleon.

At Victoria I lost all my permits, and it was some time before they were found. Boarding the Train Bleu, I lost my porter and my luggage – again found with difficulty. At the frontier the train was held up owing to my misdemeanours, and I was hauled out in the snow at 7.30 A.M. to have a furious row with the

Custom Officials, who asked if I was opening a shop. At Pisa, where I had to alight, there was no motor. It is 2½ hours' drive over the mountains to Montegufoni, I can speak no Italian, don't know the way, there was a heavy fog, and it was nearly night. Also my luggage was (again) lost. Eventually I arrived, to find Osbert with a heavy cold and much badgered by ghosts. (A purple light got into his room at 2.30 A.M. and gave him gyp for ten minutes one night; and the next, he heard a dead person being wheeled in a trolley along the passage outside his room.)

However now all is well. The ghosts have quieted down, I have recovered my nerve, the fireflies are out, and the village band has begun to practise on lovely brass instruments under my bedroom window.

Are you coming to England this year, dearest Minnie? How much I do hope so. I am going to be in London during most of July – at least from the 10th onward. It would be so lovely if we could have some parties there and then if you could come to Renishaw.

It is heavenly to think we shall be seeing you *anyhow* (D.V.) somewhere about the 20th of September, I can hardly believe it. Please may I ask you, once again, if you will be an angel and ask the manager of the St. Regis to reserve exactly the *same* suite as we had before – on the 11th floor? Because we should be broken hearted, and they would too, if we were not looked after by the same delightful servants, Mary Rohan, Rose Haughton, Charlie, and Max (I don't know what their surnames are). . . .

---

280. *To John Lehmann*

Montegufoni

3 May 1950

My dear John,

I do hope you won't curse me when you get this letter. It is an S.O.S. You may or may not know that I am having a fearful row in the *Spectator* with an American called Harry T. Moore and several other ninnies, about the reaction of the American public towards English poetry.[10]

Mr. Moore, in his latest letter to the paper, says that not only was I not mentioned by Mr. Edmund (Piccadilly) Wilson in *Axel's Castle*,[11] but that Professor Bowra in 'his admirable book *The Heritage of Symbolism*'[12] didn't mention me either, although I am 'connected with the Symbolist movement'. Apparently he only mentioned important poets.

This letter appeared in the issue of the 28th [*sic*], and I have just seen it. Now I *can't* let it pass. *Maurice wrote a short book about my poetry*, as I think you know. I can't write up about it myself, and do not like to ask Maurice, as he might think I was trying to muscle in. I would be so *deeply* grateful to you if you would, with your invariable great kindness and chivalry to me, write to the *Spectator* pointing out that Maurice wrote this book about my poetry (subsequent to the *Heritage*).[13] The book was published in Paris by the Editions de l'Oiseau Lyre, 122 Rue de Grenelle. I really would be endlessly grateful. And as it is *you*, they will pay attention.

I do wish you were here. It is heavenly now, although it began by being freezing. But we can now lunch out. I return on the 1st June (a Thursday) and shall be in London till Monday. What day can you lunch with me?

You met the La Belle *Chasseresse*, didn't you? She has just written to say she is coming over to England *again*. (Osbert has asked her millions of times if they can't just be *friends*!!) It really is like having a tame bluebottle. Osbert has written to say he is going to Lapland, as people won't let him work in England. And I am going to write and confirm what he says, adding, 'Of course, there is that old attachment.' The idea of Osbert's life-long love for a Lapp is very pleasing, I think.

Love from Osbert, David
and
Edith

Having suffered from dizziness and a tremor in his arm, OS was diagnosed with Parkinson's disease during the summer of 1950. The comfort ES drew from the opinion provided by the eminent physician Sir Henry Cohen, later Lord Cohen of Birkenhead (1900–77), was misplaced. Despite an array of treatments, OS was gradually crippled by the disease.

281. *To Sacheverell Sitwell*

Renishaw Hall

Burn this

Tuesday evening [postmark 2 August 1950]

My darling,

In the greatest haste, because I want to get this off first thing tomorrow morning, expressed.

Sir Henry Cohen's diagnosis was *not* bad. Indeed, as things stand, I felt very comforted. It is the *condition*, *not* the disease. There is no reason why it should get any worse. Sir Henry thinks it will go on the same for 10 or 15 years. He is to go on with his normal life, as far as possible.

He thinks it was started by an illness O had at Montegufoni, after the first war, when he appeared to be poisoned. He felt very sleepy and was very sick for three days, then he went to Paris, where he had double vision. People often, apparently, have a slight touch of encephalitis without knowing it. Anyhow, though it is dreadful he should have anything at all, at least there isn't the awful horror that beast of a specialist terrified one with.

I thought it very dangerous to telephone. I've got nowhere, really, where I can, excepting the dining-room, and outside the kitchen, with people trampling in and out all the time.

Very best love to both

Greatest haste
Ever your loving
Edith

282. *To Sacheverell Sitwell*

R.M.S. Queen Elizabeth

[*c*. 20 September 1950]

My darling,

I am full of grief at your letter. I cannot bear for you to be unhappy. I love you *most* dearly.

Most truly, my darling, you have got all this *wrong*. First of all, I can see you think it is harming you, our coming first, our coming two and two. I *assure* you, and that most solemnly, that it is *not*. Everyone in America is expecting you to come next, and Colston Leigh is all set and prepared to make a contract for you. *Nobody* thinks for the fraction of a second that you are being ignored or not regarded as you should be. It is utterly *out of the question*. Nobody thinks of such a thing.

I wish, my darling, you saw more writers – I mean writers of your own position. Because they would assure you of that. Nobody, however well they know the world, understands the literary position unless they are writers and mix with other writers. By that I mean, that your friends who aren't writers can no more be expected to understand literary ins and outs than I could be expected to understand Bishops' affairs.

It is natural to go two and two, because we *have* to earn our keep. I shall never be able to go again. I am 63, and this last year have been feeling very old and tired – and do you wonder? Haven't we all had enough to make us, even those who aren't 63? O, equally obviously, won't, I think, be able to go again.

You are 10 years younger than me, and in your full force. And my darling, you really *must* accept Colston Leigh's offer. If you don't, it will really be most foolish of you – indeed, one can't envisage such a thing. You *must* go. Everyone is going to be told you are coming.

Don't, my darling, I beg of you, let people who are no doubt well meaning, but who can't resist jabbing nerves, and giving pain, put silly and *most wrong* ideas into your dear and wonderful head. We have quite enough to bear with poor O's illness, and with all the dreadful worries there have been.

And what *do* you mean by 'I still think I shall be remembered.' Are you out of your mind?

I love you dearly, and know you to be one of the greatest living writers. Do you think I would ever do anything that could harm you? Give Georgia my best love and thank her so much for her letter and the lovely flowers, and tell her I am writing.

Very best love

ever your loving
Edith

---

283. *To Carson McCullers*[14]

The St Regis
Fifth Avenue and Fifty-fifth Street
New York

21 November 1950

Dear Carson McCullers,

I am deeply grateful to you for having sent me *The Heart is a Lonely Hunter*, and *The Member of the Wedding*. You are a transcendental writer – there can be not the slightest doubt of that. I am most truly overcome by these books.

The Heart is a Lonely Hunter stabbed my heart and my conscience, as nothing has done for many years. The part about those three children on a burning summer day, with the pavement scorching Bubba's bare feet – the poor little baby's cap that was too small, but was put on him to give him face – the part about the change in Bubba – so that nobody ever called him Bubba again, the part about Bubba's bicycle – all the parts about Dr. Copeland, and the terrible passages about Willie's feet – the beauty of character and loneliness of Singer! The book is a masterpiece of compassion, of understanding, of writing. What a born writer you are! Only a born writer would have made Singer and his friend see that mad dog at a corner, and not on a straight road, thus making the hazards of fate more appalling. (I read that part when I was very feverish from an inoculation against typhoid, and I saw that mad dog running and biting, all night.)

As for *The Member of the Wedding* the beauty of it is so great that I am living in the summer of that book. One lives in it from the first page, with those 'trees of a bright dizzy green.' I have just finished reading *The Member of the Wedding*, and was now looking for that wonderful passage about the moths, one of the loveliest in the book; but as I am going to read the book straight through again, I shall soon find it.

What a great poet's mind and eye and senses you have – together with a great prose writer's mind, sense of construction and character. What would not a poet give to have written 'The long gold sun slanted down on them and made their skin look golden also' . . . 'The *long* gold sun . . .'

I have not been so excited by any books as by these, for years. In fact I am so excited by them, that I find it impossible to write coherently. . . .

May I send you my love – which indeed I do, and my deepest admiration?

Yours
Edith Sitwell

1951

284. *To Carson McCullers*

Fairmont Hotel
San Francisco

[6 February 1951]

Dearest Carson,

. . . You say you are horrified about my childhood. What do you suppose *I* am to know what *you* have suffered in that terrible house where you found yourself locked up. How *could* anyone have done such an appalling thing, to you, of all people in the world. The torture and terror of it. And that horror of being told that nothing one does, says or thinks, is 'normal'. Naturally, a genius does not think in the way in which an ordinary person thinks. For two years, once, I suffered from being told by someone who was, poor soul – she is dead now – devoted to me, but was getting cancer of the spine which altered her mentally – that I was 'going mad'. I was told that daily. I happened to be writing a very terrible book at the time, and naturally after a hard morning's work I *would* look as if I had had a terrible experience – because I had.

How *could* anyone have landed you in that place. When we meet, dear, I want you to tell me all about it. Nothing I could say could possibly express what I feel about it. The words you utter about 'the muted and terrible docility' under the menace of that treatment, really pierced my heart. I do not know how even such a noble spirit as yours could have passed through that time in safety. . . .

How wonderful it was for me to be told that I have helped, even a little, to bring poetry and the joy of life near to you again. And that is what you have done for me. I have had a dead year, very near to despair, and feeling very far from my poetry. And becoming friends with you has meant so much to me.

Though we are going back to England, I think we shall be coming to America very often now. Which is wonderful to look forward to.

Osbert was made very happy by what you said of his work, and asks me to thank you. He admires you very greatly.

Dear Carson, I send you my best love, my admiration, my belief.

Edith

---

285. *To Carson McCullers*

The John Ringling Hotel
Sarasota, Florida

15 February [1951]

Dearest Carson,

I found your letter waiting for me, to my delight. Oh' what a journey we had, including a railway accident on the Sunset Express between Los Angeles and New Orleans. The train in front was smashed to atoms, and so was our engine, also our train was set on fire, and the railway lines were smashed to bits. . . .

Carson, it is splendid about the film,[1] but you careless girl you ought to have ground the company down and got millions out them. I am sure you are not a good business woman!

I shall never be able to be grateful enough to Mr. Tennessee Williams for having arranged that party.[2] You know the moment I sat next him at dinner at Alice's, he said we must meet. And how right he was. I, too, was feeling fearfully shy at that party. I *am* very shy, which causes me to clasp my hands nervously. I am so happy to hear Mr. Williams' new play is such a success. So it should be. What a *greatly* gifted writer. I have seen two of his plays over and over again. The only long one I haven't seen is *The Glass Menagerie.*

Tomorrow, if only I can get to the post office, I shall be sending you two small anthologies.

Forgive the maiden-aunt-like vagueness and idiocy of this letter. All I can do is to sit with my mouth open staring at the wall, I am so tired. And I wish you could see the amount of work I've got to do before I return to England. How I shall ever get it done, I don't know.

Best love and bless you.

Edith

Next morning

Dearest Carson,

I had just finished the enclosed flippant letter, when I received your second letter, telling me of your visit to the doctor.[3] I am filled with sadness. Indeed, [I] do not know *how* to express it. If only I could do something, say something, to help.

You say what have you done to deserve it. I think, sometimes, that a noble and great soul is called upon to bear anguish as some sort of redemption for the world – as the greatest who ever bore flesh suffered anguish. I don't know, but it seems so to me. . . .

All my thoughts are with you.

Best love
Edith

---

286. *To David Lutyens*[4]

Renishaw Hall

24 May 1951

Dear Mr. Lutyens,

At a luncheon party in New York, in the presence of several witnesses, you uttered a grave and damaging libel on me. You said that my poetry is Fascist, and that I showed my anti-Semitism by the fact that I called a character in my *Gold Coast Customs* Lady Bamburgher.

I take a very serious view of these statements, which are calculated to do me great harm. . . .

I am so little a Fascist and so little an anti-Semite that at the beginning of the last war, I risked what would have been certain death or the horrors of a concentration camp – had the German invasion then expected at any moment materialised, or had the Germans won the war – by writing an open letter to Dr. Goebbels in which I reproached the Nazis for their ill-treatment of the Jews and other non-Aryans. That letter was published in *The Times*, and it was vetted, before I sent it, by Mr. R. A. Butler,[5] then under-Minister for Foreign Affairs. . . .

I do not understand why you feel this malice. I have shown you and your wife nothing but kindness. . . .

---

287. *To Jack Lindsay*

Montegufoni

[n.d. 1951?]

My dear Jack,

I by now daren't imagine what you and Ann[6] must think of me. But I've been driven almost demented for months. First of all, dear Beryl de Zoete was taken terribly ill. Then Jane Clark[7] had to have a really fearful operation and for six days or so was so gravely ill that – well, you can imagine. The very day that I heard she would recover, we got the news that dear Susan Robins, who has been housekeeper at Renishaw for 35 years (her husband was Osbert's soldier servant in the first war, and before, and has been with him for 40 years) was mortally ill. It was frightful, for she was in great pain, and delirious all the time. Robins nursed her at home. She died two days ago. Another friend is dying, I fear. Apart from our grief for her and for him, there are fearful practical worries, as it is impossible for us to go back to Renishaw at present, and I have to find somewhere to live. (Osbert has a house.) All our belongings are at Renishaw, including manuscripts and books!!!

I must say, this last year has been hell, beginning with Ann's illness. The whole thing has got me down to such an extent, that for months I have really done no work – excepting for that long poem, which I am going to send you as soon I hear you have returned to England. (I don't want to risk it getting lost, going across countries.) When I say I have done no work, it is not quite true, because I always work. But I haven't finished anything, as I feel too numb. When I get back to England I shall go into hiding, excepting for you and Ann and a few others, and try to get something finished.

I hear our dearest Dylan has been painting New York (literally) red. The centre of his activities being the Literary Salon of Mrs. Murray Crane,[8] the watchwords of the Salon being Decorum, Bonne Tenue, and the milder and more restrained forms of Evening Dress. At one of the interminable evenings of Culture to which one is doomed there, Dylan suddenly sprang at Caitlin, and (according to my informant) 'kicked, punched, and bloodily beat' her. Mrs. Crane shrieked and fainted – being revived with difficulty. There is then a gap in the narrative. I *think* Dylan was sent home, but do not know what happened to Caitlin. However Dylan soon reappeared, and demanded the money for his taxi. My informant wrote, gloomily: 'I don't suppose he will be asked again.'!!

I haven't *yet* got over that fearful evening when we met last. After I die, certain dates will be found inscribed on my heart, like the word Calais on the heart of B. Mary. . . .

1952

288. *To Marianne Moore*[1]

Hotel Cappuccini Convent
Amalfi
(Salerno)
Italy

2[?] February 1952

My Dear Marianne,

Osbert and I were so very happy to get your letter. You are an angel to have sent us those poems which are amongst the only beautiful and life-giving (as well as living) poems of our time.[2]

My copy has not arrived yet. Or, of course, I should have written immediately. But the English version – I mean edition: such a noise is going on that the right words fly out of my head in fright – has been more of a delight to me than I could say. I am trying to write about the poems at this moment. I can't tell you how much I am enjoying writing about the lovely warm assonances, and the roundnesses, of 'Nine Nectarines', which, of course, I have known for a long time, but am now writing about, Also about the amazing brilliance of the technique of 'The Buffalo'.

All this is giving me a lovely chance to tease my old enemy Geoffrey Grigson – the Laureate of the Winkle (which is what I call him, for his name is never mentioned by me) about 'exact expression'. What is the use of that, if one irradiates nothing? When *you* write about a fish, it is as important and beautiful as a star. Mr. G. goes on and on about winkles, and they are just something dull and dark on a barrow.

It is so *extraordinary*, that life-giving character that all your poetry possesses. I thought it would be impossible to admire and live in your poetry more than I did when I read it first. But it is even more a happy living and exquisite delight now than it was at the beginning.

We think of you so much, dear Marianne. And miss you. Shall we *ever* have you in England, I wonder? How much I hope, and with all my heart, that circumstances will change, so that you can come.

Love and admiration

Yours affectionately
Edith

---

289. *To Zosia Kochanski*

Hotel Cappuccini Convent
Amalfi
(Salerno)
Italy

4 February 1952

My dearest Zosia,

. . . I am deeply touched that you should have spoken to Pavlik again. Perhaps he *will* write to me again some day – but it will be too late. He will be writing to something that no longer exists. Not only did I feel the loss of a friend – which I had thought him for over twenty years – but he insulted me publicly. I forgave him for that (although I exercised a certain caution with him, as it was difficult to feel quite the same) as he was ill. He then waited till I returned to America, and then dismissed me *publicly* as a friend. He has done this *solely* under the influence of that woman Fini, and, too, to please the vanity of several other people who are nearly, but not quite, as low. I never think of him now, as it is bad for the soul to think of such conduct. But unfortunately, two days ago, Signorina Fini arrived in this hotel with two of the men with whom, I understand, she lives, and with a young Pole whom Osbert and David knew. I was able to avoid the disgust of having her introduced to me, but unfortunately her presence in the hotel where only two other people were staying, did bring all Pavlik's conduct back to me. She is a *horrible* looking woman – looks as horrible as she is. I was going to say that she looks like an epitome of the Seven Sins. But that would be paying her a compliment – imputing to her a certain greatness. There is no greatness. She is just an open slum.

Osbert caught her looking back through a glass door to see if I was looking after her, which amused me. I wasn't. I see with great concentration when I choose. And I took her in, in two glances, otherwise, I never rested my eyes on her. . . .

---

290. *To John Hayward*

Hotel Cappuccini Convent
Amalfi
(Salerno)
Italy

7 February 1952

My dear John,

What *have* you been up to? What have been your errors, heresies, crimes against Good Taste, Sensitivity, and Adult Awareness? When did you fail to wince, or condone an ill-placed comma? Or do you think the Doctor's diatribe against you (which I haven't seen yet: I base my letter on Raymond's review in the *Sunday Times*) is due merely to your companion-ship with Publicans and Sinners such as myself?[3]

Really, what an impossible man he is! And I see he has had the impertinence to turn on Tom.[4] Actually I think it is only a question of time before he retreats into the shades of a Lunatic Asylum, driven there by mingled conceit and thwarted ambi-tion. Of course, some time ago, Queenie was complaining that Tom hadn't got him canonised. What he (Tom) ought to have done, apparently, was to order an immediate massacre of all poets, critics, scholars – in fact of all men of letters, leaving Dr. Leavis in sole possession of the world.

I look forward to reading the book – I have sent for it. I

understand I am in trouble again, but then hot water is my native element, as far as Dr. L is concerned. . . .

I read, somewhere, that Dr. Chalmers said of Carlyle when he was young: 'That laddie is a lover of earnestness more than a lover of truth.' And I think the description fits *this* laddie exactly. Better even than Carlyle. . . .

---

291. *To Katherine Anne Porter*

As from
Montegufoni

15 September 1952

My dear Katherine Anne,

I can't tell you how delighted I am that we are going to call each other by our Christian names. I have wanted to do this for a long time.

The housemaid – who is, to my letters, what clothes moths are to one's most prized materials – has got hold of your letter, although I had hidden it. So I am not sure when you return to New York. I am sending this, therefore, to New York.

You are so sweet about Sachie. What you said about him made me very happy. He is bringing you his poems in person. . . .

I wonder if you saw Carson McCullers in Paris? It was *said* she was marching on London, which caused a certain amount of fear and despondency, rather like that caused by Attila in the dim past. But the days passed, and calm still reigns.

With love and I do *hope* to see you soon

Yours affectionately
Edith

---

292. *To John Heath-Stubbs*[5]

Montegufoni

18 October 1952

Dear Mr. Heath-Stubbs,

Very many thanks for your letter. I am very sorry, but I cannot reconsider my decision about the inclusion of those poems.

In conjunction with the *Faber Book of Modern Verse* – one of the worst anthologies I have ever seen, although Mrs. Ridler,[6] coming in at the end did her very best to improve matters, and it is not her fault that she couldn't – no idea whatsoever would be given of my poetry. I am very sorry to have to refuse anything for which you ask, as I like you, and I like your work.

My poems are now in the Penguin series,[7] and I do not really need anthologies – nor have for a very long time, now. They are useful, of course, to the young and lesser known.

I hope you are keeping very well. I have injured a knee and am in tortures.

All best wishes and many regrets,

Yours sincerely
Edith Sitwell

293. *To Hal Lydiard Wilson and Boodie Wilson*[8]

The St Regis Hotel
1 East 55th Street
New York City, N.Y.

2 December 1952

My dear Hal and Boodie,

I do hope my telegram reached you safely. And this letter would have been written days ago, but I got caught up in an entanglement of business interviews and telephone wires as soon as I arrived.

Thank you so much for that exquisite luck-bringer, which I

carry about with me. I am sure it *will* bring me luck. It was so
sweet of you both. . . .

I was deeply disappointed at missing a talk with you both –
seeing you both, for my few minutes with Hal *were* only a few
minutes – before coming here. But immediately I returned from
Italy I got bad influenza, and then had to recite with the
London Symphony Orchestra!! Then a press conference, and
then America.

On the way over, Osbert frightened a sweet blackamoor
bell-boy of about seventeen nearly out of his wits by falling
asleep with his head pressed to a bell. Irving – for such is the
blackamoor's name – rushed in and woke Osbert up. Osbert
denied hotly that he had rung the bell. The blackamoor withdrew, whereupon Osbert promptly fell asleep again with his
head pressed to the bell. Irving rushed in again, and again
Osbert denied having rung the bell. After that, until we
soothed him, Irving's teeth would chatter and he would roll
his eyes when Osbert sent for him, as he thought Osbert was
teasing him.

We are coming home in April, I think, (if still alive).

My love to you both.

Yours affectionately
Edith

1953

Having contracted in 1951 to write a screenplay of Fanfare for Elizabeth,
*ES made extended visits to Hollywood in 1953 and 1954 to work with the
screen-writer Walter Reisch (1903–83), under the eye of George Cukor
(1899–1983), who is best known as the director of* A Star is Born *(1954)
and* My Fair Lady *(1964). The collaboration was unsuccessful, and the film
was never produced.*

294. *To Geoffrey Gorer*

Sunset Tower
Hollywood
California

21 February 1953

Dearest Geoffrey,

. . . There has been a heavenly heat-wave here. But as I am working like a slave, I never get out, excepting when dragged out by the inhabitants. There is also a very bad epidemic of rabies – the worst for very many years. One mad dog was disposed of in this street. About twenty people have been bitten. They killed five mad dogs in three days, and one got into a schoolyard where the children were playing; however, all those particular children escaped.

The publishers Little, Brown have asked me to do an English–American anthology of 2000 pages, which is exciting. I shall put in *some* modern poems – but hardly any, excepting Wystan and Dylan.

The film treatment is progressing, but, to my fury, George has gone to Paris for a fortnight. Osbert says Groucho Marx has founded himself entirely on George. For instance, in placing one foot on the ground, when sitting, in such a way that he can spring to his feet and escape at a second's notice. The other day, the man who is collaborating with me, speaking of one scene, said, 'That is the scene where you have those Cardinal-guys threaten the King with eternal damnation, and you have the King say, "That's O.K. by me, boys! I am the King of England, and you can go tell your boss the Pope to hell with his damnation."' (But he said it for fun.)

I get back to England on the 5th of April, and am longing to see you. How is your dear mother?

I don't seem to have any more news. Osbert is at Palm Beach.

It is so nice seeing dear Aldous and Maria Huxley[1] – two of my oldest and greatest friends. Aldous hasn't changed at all since he was 23 (when I knew him first). He drove me to tea with Dr. Hubble,[2] the astronomer, the other day, and on the way kept up a long grumble – the drive took 40 minutes, on the subject of Coleridge and Wordsworth. 'Really, Edith, that any man *reputed* to be sane should have written, *quite* deliberately,

"I need not say, Louisa dear,
How glad we are to have you here,
A lovely convalescent . . ."'[3]

Best love
Edith

My poems come out in either June or July.[4] The heat is terrific today, and my brain feels melted.

---

295. *To John Lehmann*

Renishaw Hall

Sunday [May 1953]

My dear John,

I was so delighted to get your letter, although I did wish you had told me more about yourself – more about your plans in general.

I am *still* furious with the B.B.C. and shall remain so.[5] I am delighted, however, to hear that you are going to go to the country and will be able to work at the autobiography and the poems. That will be lovely for the Prima Donna, too (to whom my fondest love).[6]

I should have written before, but have really been more dead than alive. I worked like a slave in Hollywood – had a journey from there to New York of three days and three nights, followed by fresh incessant work at the film and making records; then an absolutely frightful crossing, ending with having to leave my bed at 4:30 A.M. and, when [I] arrived in London, there were all the damned reporters and press photographers, at the station, and waiting for me at my Club.

I must say I thought that awful Tracy woman's attack on

Rosamond in the *New Statesman* the outside limit.[7] It was the kind of thing one would expect in 'Town Topics' – if that still exists.

I have just written and told Dr. B. Ifor Evans what I think of him for a vile attack on Osbert in *Truth*.[8] (I know Dr. B . . . What do you suppose B stands for?) I told him he was actuated by class prejudice (*That* will annoy him!), and by a mean and petty envy.

I've just accrued a very bad new lunatic (he is quite raving). He sends me enormous quantities of 'poems' – all in indecipherable pencilling, and letters from famous writers ticking him off, and telling him to be less conceited. (One is from Morgan Forster, and it is the only time I have ever known Morgan to lose his temper.) The lunatic is a Russian boy, aged, I should think, 24. He says he is of European importance, far greater than Rilke, and probably as great as Shakespeare. He says I cannot be expected to criticise him, as he is above criticism (his very words). And that if I do not return immediately a magazine called *Poetry Liverpool*,[9] with whose editor he is having a row, he is going to insist on the Queen instituting a personal search in my room. I have told him to put the whole thing before Dr. Leavis, who, I assured him, would be bound to admire his poetry. He hasn't a vestige of talent, there is nothing there at all.

I am waiting to get on with my film. But meanwhile [I] am working at an anthology of English and American poetry for Little Brown – of 2000 pages, which is exciting.

I long to see you. I am coming to London on the 16th of July, and shall be there for some little time, so I hope you will be in London then.

I don't think I have any more news.

I have not seen the Searles since my return, nor shall I be seeing them after their monstrous conduct.[10] But that is private.

Love from
Edith

and please stroke the Prima Donna's ears, for me.

296. *To Minnie (Astor) and James Fosburgh*

Sunset Tower
8358 Sunset Boulevard
Hollywood 46

26 December 1953

Dearest Minnie and Jim,

I am so ashamed that this letter is so late, but it is so for two reasons, into which I will go later. Thank you a *thousand* times for my most lovely presents, *so deeply* appreciated.

I do hope you had a wonderful Christmas – but I know you did, for I have never seen two people so happy, with a heavenly happiness, that spreads to everyone round you. My best love to you and best wishes for the new year that should be the happiest you have ever known.

The reasons for my being so late in writing: A. I had, like a fool, come away without your address, and had to wait till Osbert and David arrived to get it, as I was not sure where Betsey was, so could not send it to be forwarded. B. I have had to work *all* day (copying in the morning, being roared at by Walter in the afternoon) including Christmas Eve and Christmas Day. C. I have had a very bad shock – (coming straight on top of Dylan Thomas's death:[11] it was I who found him, so to speak, and it was I who made his very great fame).

The other day, at the St. Regis, as we were leaving the restaurant and Natasha[12] was coming in, she introduced a play-wright called Peter Ustinov[13] (Osbert knew him already). I *thought* his manner was most odd: he behaved exactly like a blackbeetle that thinks it is going to be killed – tried to crawl into the wall. (Excepting that he was like a fat white slug.) Well, a few days after I arrived here, I found out *why*. On the 2nd of December, or 3rd, he produced a play of his at the Savoy in London, *written for the purpose of grossly insulting Osbert and me.* There can be no question it was meant for us. We are given the name of *D'Urt*!!!

Miss D'Urt is a famous 'poetess in a turban' (I used to wear these many years ago). Sir Mohammed D'Urt is a famous writer who is a baronet, and they have an eccentric old father. Both of us, apparently, are sex maniacs of an advanced kind. The baronet was described by one paper as 'a lecherous pontiff', and I hunt unwilling gentlemen in and out of bedrooms. The *Daily Express* has said, *in so many words*, that it is meant for us. Can you imagine anything *so foul* as to do this to a poor man who is known, by the whole of London, to have a most terrible disease that is made *infinitely* worse by any kind of shock or worry?

However – the play was booed off. On the first night, every entrance of the actors and actresses was booed and yelled at by the gallery. One line of Miss D'Urt's ran, 'We forgive everything' to which a voice replied, 'We don't. We'll never forgive this.' The brave Mr. Ustinov who has insulted a helpless cripple had to hide in his box. The play was withdrawn after nine days. . . .

George said I was to give you his love when I write. He hadn't got your address, which I shall now give him.

It is heavenly weather here, but I have been too busy to go out more than three times – I having dined with George, who is working fearfully hard all day. I have given a strong impression, in George's household, that I am, to say the least of it, not quite in my right mind. (I *am*, of course, rather dotty, but there is nothing *actually* wrong with the grey matter.)

Immediately on my arrival, I received a telegram from the *Sunday Times* asking me to fly straight back to London at their expense in order to be third mourner (after his wife and mother) at Dylan Thomas's Memorial Service arranged by them. It was in that paper that I made his fame originally.

I told you I would keep a kind of diary for you, Mrs. Whitney and Natasha. So far, there has only been one *really* terrible scene. That was at dinner with George, two nights after I arrived. The enormous black poodle – the size of a large cart-horse (I adore him) – was chasing one of the dachshunds across the sofa, over my lap (trampling on my appendix) backwards and forwards. George mentioned Miss Jean Simmons, where-upon Walter, who hates her, began to shriek imprecations in a really piercing manner. I have never heard such yells. George

said, 'Damp down, Walter, damp down.' After about five minutes of this, the dachshund suddenly turned, just as it was being
chased over my lap, and put its head into the poodle's mouth,
where it became fixed – I thought irrevocably. The poodle's eyes
were distended with fear and suffocation. Walter stopped yelling
and pulled, violently, at the dachshund's back legs. The dachshund, thinking Walter was trying to tear it in two, as its head
was held as in a vice, shrieked down the poodle's throat –
making the poodle's fear and suffocation far worse. George tried
to prise open the poodle's mouth. Myrtle, George's housekeeper,
who worships the poodle (as do I) was standing outside the door
with her hands clasped in an agony of apprehension. For some
minutes the commotion was indescribable. I *still* cannot think
how the dachshund was dislodged, but it was, at last. George
said, rather huffily, when I expressed wonderment and condo-
lence, that it is always happening.

I am sending you Dylan Thomas's great and wonderful poems,
from the Gotham Book Mart.

Best love to both and all, *all* best wishes for the happiest New
Year you have ever known. A million thanks for my lovely
present.

Edith

1954

297. *To the Editor of the* Spectator

8358 Sunset Boulevard
Hollywood 46
California

[published 22 January 1954]

Sir – To my great amusement, a Mr. Anthony Hartley,
reviewing my *Gardeners and Astronomers*,[1] states: the last lines
of 'A Song of the Dust' show a greater measure of disintegration:

> *'If every grain of my dust should be a Satan,*
> *If every atom of my heart were Lucifer –*
> *If every drop of my blood were an Abaddon,*
> * – Yet should I love.'*

'Anyone reading this,' Mr. Hartley continues, 'is bound to feel that it verges dangerously on bathos. The assertion is too grotesque to convince, and what has happened seems fairly evident. The imagery has taken over and developed itself into extravagance, affecting the meanings communicated to the reader. One image leads to the next, but the ideas behind them do not follow. Quite the reverse. They are destroyed and made ridiculous.'

It is good of Mr. Hartley to teach, not only me, but the late John Donne, Dean of St. Paul's, how to write. By a most unfortunate accident, which nobody regrets more than I, and which will be rectified in my next edition, a note was omitted from the book, telling the reader that the passage of which this gentleman complains with such vehemence, is an adaptation from one of Donne's Sermons.

Would it not have been wiser for your reviewer, before being quite so impertinent, to have read more widely?

I shall, no doubt, be told that little Mr. Tomkins (or whatever his name may be), this week's new great poet, does not incorporate in his work, phrasing from the past, giving them a twist, and importing new meaning. That is so. But more than one great poet does. And it is useless to deny it.

Mr. Hartley says: 'If Dr. Sitwell had some idea in mind as the particular appropriateness of peridots and beryls to the sap of a tree, she has failed to communicate it.'

To Mr. Hartley. *Not* to others.

I was brought up in the country. I suggest that one day in spring Mr. Hartley should try breaking off a twig from its branch.

Yours faithfully,
Edith Sitwell

298. *To Kingsley Amis*[2]

Sunset Tower
8358 Sunset Blvd.
Hollywood 46, California

8 February 1954

Dear Mr. Amis,

I admire your *Lucky Jim* so greatly that I cannot resist writing to tell you how much pleasure it has given me. I have read it twice since its arrival ten days ago.

You are a born writer. Your natural gifts, your observation, your insight, are exceedingly remarkable, and your handling of language is nothing short of brilliant – Margaret is a masterpiece; so is poor Professor Welch.

I do not remember when I have read a more vital and vitalising first work in prose, and I shall watch your career with the greatest interest: it will be, I am convinced, of very high distinction. . . .

With best wishes for the great and deserved success of your book.

I am
Yours sincerely
Edith Sitwell

---

299. *To Osbert Sitwell*

Sunset Tower
8358 Sunset Boulevard
Hollywood 46

[8 February? 1954]

My darling,

Thank you so much for your letter, which has just arrived. Long before getting it – about ten days ago (or I should have done as you asked) I wrote a very calm and dignified letter to the *New Statesman*, just contradicting some of this impossible person's inaccuracies.[3] But the letter will not do anything to set people against me. It was most calm. I had not then seen Tom Driberg's and Mr. Pudney's letters to the N.S. giving them blue hell. It really does do them both the greatest credit. And John Lehmann, who had promised to do a portrait of Evelyn Waugh, has written to K. Martin[4] saying he cannot write for a series that has been 'fouled by such an offence'.

I have had an extraordinarily nice letter from Alan Pryce-Jones[5] – not *ostensibly* about that, but of course, really, about it. So I shall now forgive him and make friends with him again. I was really very touched by his letter.

There is an – I think *extraordinary* – new novelist. Very young. His name is Kingsley Amis, and his book, *Lucky Jim*, is the funniest first novel I've read since *Decline and Fall*. I'll lend it to you and David as soon as we meet in New York, and give you each a copy as soon as we get back to London. In the novel there is a female hysteric who is as good as any of that old beast Perks'.[6] The book is beautifully written. (He is not spiteful, like Perks, just observant.)

The temperature is 88 today, and was, yesterday. Tomorrow, George and the second in command at the Studio are coming round here to listen to Walter yelling. Walter has discovered that the name of Lot's wife was Edith; he has also found that Savonarola's last words, as he was about to be burnt, were, 'I am in love with fire.' Therefore, the other day, yelling because I had told him we couldn't use the word 'décolletage', but must say 'bosom' – hanging head downwards over the sofa, he shrieked 'Oh, Dr. Stillwell! Oh, Miss Atkin! Oh, Mrs. Lot! Oh, Signorina Savonarola! Oh, you bosom-fetichist ('bosom' twice in three pages)! Oh, shades of the Hay office! Oh, shades of Harry Cohn! Oh, what shall I do?' (straightening himself, suddenly) 'What are you laughing at?'

Very best love to you and David

ever your loving
Edith

300. *To Kingsley Amis*

as from
The St Regis Hotel
1 East 55th Street
New York City

8 March 1954

Dear Mr. Amis,

Thank you so much for your letter, which I should have answered before, but I was suddenly taken ill.

Do not feel the slightest discomfort. When you come to the luncheon party I shall give for you, you will find me completely oblivious that this has ever happened.[7]

I think your book *highly* remarkable, beautifully written, and with extraordinary characterisation, and I prophesy for you a most distinguished career.

To return, for the last time, to the *Spectator*: the whole affair is too extraordinary for words. *Not one* of the persons who has had the impertinence to attack me has even a germ of talent for poetry. They simply can't write. And it would never enter the head of a poet of any stature to discuss their verses. Not only I, but all my fellow-poets of any importance (as I know from their letters to me on the subject), are entirely amazed that they should have dared to behave as they have. They cannot harm me. All that has happened is that they have made an abjectly ridiculous spectacle of themselves, and are being laughed at, not only all over England, but also in New York.

I look forward with great pleasure to our luncheon party. . . .

301. *To Geoffrey Gorer*

The St Regis
Fifth Avenue and 55th Street
New York

3 April 1954

Dearest Geoffrey,

. . . Goodness me! I wouldn't go through these last few months again for anything in the world! My film has been wrecked for the *second* time, and all my time has been wasted. I was simply left to my own devices by George C., who was busy filming with an ass whose name is, I think, Judy Garland, and who screams and cries and hits people with her shoe all the time. George thinks this wonderful! She won't work for more than two hours a day, so I (who was made to work 8) have had to hang about wasting my time until her Ladyship made up her mind to finish the film. Consequently, Walter has wrecked it again, as he screams so loudly that I can't make myself heard.

Last year, George left me to my own devices (and Walter's) in order to fly to Paris and spend a month there working on the script of Miss Garland's film (a masterpiece called 'A Star is Born') with a Mr. and Mrs. Kazan or Tarzan.[8] *They are now trying to make me go back to Hollywood in July. And I am not going!* . . .

Pavlik is now trying to make it up with me – via Minnie Astor-that-was, Fosburgh-that-is. He wrote to her, 'Please tell Edith I often dream of her – not have forgotten her – hope she hasn't forgotten me. Give her please, my love and when I see her all will be all right again.'!!!

Wystan and Chester lunched with us yesterday. Wystan was looking very well. I am delighted to hear he will be in England in July. . . .

302. *To Cecil Beaton*

Renishaw Hall

23 June 1954

Dearest Cecil,

Thank you so *very* much for your most kind sweet letter of
congratulation. It is great fun being a Dame[9] (I'm one already,
officially, unlike poor men who have to wait for the accolade
before they become knights).

I was most disappointed not to be able to come to the Foyle
Luncheon in honour of your book. But I've got to recite at the
York festival next week (*Façade*) and have been dead tired
lately. This has now been added to by my poor secretary getting
flu!! Needless to say, I shall love to be photographed by you
when I am in London, which will be in August; and I hope, too,
that you will lunch with me.

All success to the book, and I hope the luncheon will be
great fun.

Love from
Edith

303. *To Maurice Carpenter*[10]

Renishaw Hall

26 June 1954

Dear Maurice,

So *very* many thanks for so kindly sending me your book on
Coleridge; I look forward to reading it with a real sense of
excitement. I am sure it is admirable. You have a great gift for
plunging right into the very heart of a subject.

My dear, *of course* you have not done anything to offend me!
How could you? I like and respect you very much, and value
your friendship. For several years now, I have been much
separated from those friends who actually do not live in

London, and who do not write me letters, by the fact that for a great deal of the time when I was not in America, I have been here, and have made only fleeting visits to London. I have been and am in great and permanent grief, owing to the grave and tragic illness of my darling Osbert (this is in confidence, please) and this grief brought on, with me, sciatica in its most acute and chronic form.

Again, I had to wait until you communicated with me, because I had mislaid your address. Now – would it be possible to be such an idiot – I have mislaid it again, so I write to you c/o your publishers. . . .

My love to you both, also my Godchild.

Yours ever,
Edith Sitwell

304. *To L. P. Hartley*

Renishaw Hall

18 July 1954

My dear Leslie,

How very kind and sweet of you to write and congratulate me on being made a Dame. I must say it *is* fun – after all I have been through with the Pipsqueakery, who have been quite intolerable throughout the autumn, winter, and spring.

It will amuse you to know that as I advanced towards the Queen to get my decorations, the band played 'Annie, Get your Gun'. . . .

305. *To J. R. Ackerley*

Montegufoni

18 September 1954

Dear Joe,

Thank you so much for your letter. Osbert and I are infinitely touched and grateful that you should have taken such an infinity of trouble about Alberto de Lacerda.[11] It really is more than good of you, good of you anyhow, and especially considering how busy you are.

I am afraid that, as you say, it does not sound hopeful; but I am still hoping. And in any case, the fact that you should have showed such kindness is most heartening.

I hope you will have as wonderful weather as we are having for your holiday. (I hardly dare mention the weather.) With the exception of one day of raging thunder storms we have been able to lunch and dine out every day, and we eat figs that are really almost the size of small melons, and with seas of honey in them. I bought the children of the young man who is butler and everything else, a trumpet, and loud and melancholy sounds reach us from the dungeons in which they play on it – their father having told them that dungeons are the proper place for a trumpet.

I am nearly driven bats trying to finish an Elegy for Dylan Thomas that I had promised an American magazine. But I am so horrified and really heart-torn by the ghastly wickedness and cruelty of the rabbit-plague that I can hardly write. What a *hellish* crime![12]

I do hope you will be back in England before Osbert and I go to America. (I think we sail on the 9th of November, but am not sure yet.) Because I do want to get you, Morgan Forster and William Plomer to lunch together.

Again, our very deep gratitude

Yours
Edith

306. *To Jean Cocteau* (draft)

[1954?]

Dear Jean,

I am profoundly grateful to you for sending me *Clair Obscur*.[13] The book only reached me the day before I telegraphed to you, because of the eccentricities of a housemaid – a confirmed enemy of books. She never forwards them to me, and, owing to the fact that she thinks I have second sight and therefore know of their arrival, she remains mute on the subject. I had to write to her about something, and asked if any parcels had come for me. 'Oh yes, several books – some arrived weeks ago.' I am horrified to think how long she can have hoarded this book. She did the same to a book by Tom Eliot. I only found that on my return, after it had been [there] for three months!

I believe these poems to be among the finest you have ever written, with their deep-seeing electrifying wisdom, their flawless elegance of form, their extraordinary revivifying of every object seen, so that one realises its identity for the first time. Never have you ridden that winged horse of beauty and of terror with more surety. Jacob certainly conquered the angel – or perhaps *became* the angel.

'Foudroyer', 'Pour les Vierges Calculs', 'Rouge', 'Champêtre', and the unbearably moving 'Quel est cet Etranger' seem to me miracles of poetry. If only the young Englishmen making dreary poems out of pieces of grey blotting paper could be reached by this power of germination that is yours. Never – since the minor poetry of the Augustan age – has English poetry been in such a deplorable state.

We do hope you have completely recovered from your serious illness, the news of which grieved us very much.

I send you (under separate copy) my *Collected Poems*, my gratitude, my affectionate and very deep homage,

Edith (Sitwell)

307. *To Stephen Spender*

Montegufoni

1 October 1954

Dearest Stephen,

Nothing has ever given me greater pride and happiness than your letter, which reached me last night. (It has been eight days on the road.)

How *deeply* proud I shall be to have a section of the *Collected Poems* dedicated to me.[14] I am overjoyed. It is a most wonderful thing to happen to me. Thank you, dear Stephen, for this lovely proof of your friendship.

Yes, Edith Sitwell is right.

I am so grateful to you for sending to me the exquisite 'Sirmione Peninsula.' What a lovely poem! You are one of the only living poets who can attain to gentleness and yet keep their strength. I think the phrase 'the wings of the water' is most wonderful in connection with the two lovely last lines:

'With her hair blown back by the winds of the whole lake view,
Lips parted as though to greet the flight of a bird . . .'

Don't tell me you will be en route for your tour[15] before I reach London on the 21st. I long to see you both.

Yes, we did hear from Mr. Richmond,[16] and have cabled to say we can go to Washington in March. But we have had to say that *parties* must be considered 'out' – because (I haven't yet told Mr. Richmond the tragic reason) Osbert simply is not fit for them. They tire him out, he cannot bear to have his tremble remarked, and any fatigue makes him worse. What an awful thing it is! . . .

---

308. *To Georgia Sitwell*

as from
The Sesame

[October 1954]

My darling Georgia,

. . . In re Pavlik. I beg of Sachie not to show anything, as the whole thing is going to be a fearful strain and *most* painful for me, and I don't want anything to happen which would be an extra strain. I have been asked to *open* his exhibition, on the 26th.[17]

What I am doing, I am doing simply because he is a very great artist – for no other reason. I am afraid I do not feel the same. I shall be very amiable to him, but, as I say, I do not feel the same. . . .

1955

ES, OS, and David Horner visited the United States through the winter of 1954–55. Horner, here referred to as 'little Lord Fauntleroy', spent much of his time with the painter Brian Connelly, and his conduct gave rise to talk that he and OS were breaking up. In December, OS had apparently explained to ES, who had a limited understanding of homosexuality, the nature of his love for Horner. She took a severe view of Horner's infidelities, but OS, who was emotionally dependent on him, would not tolerate her outbursts. See Pearson, pp. 437–8, and Glendinning, pp. 312–14.

309. *To Sacheverell Sitwell*

Private and Confidential
Destroy
Let Silence be the Watchword

> The St Regis
> Fifth Avenue and 55th Street
> New York

17 January 1955

My darling Sachie,

I should have written ages ago, but have been having A hideous worries and B bad insomnia. I do hope my Christmas present reached you? I believe you were in Portugal at the time, but I sent it at the same time as I sent Georgia's.

Now, my darling, *please do not mention this to anyone excepting Georgia, and tell her not to mention it to a soul.* If you do, it will get back, and will precipitate a hideous family row, as O *does not want it talked about.* And I have had so much to put up with, I can't take a family row, which will fall upon *me*, on top of the rest.

Dear little Lord Fauntleroy has *not* been in New York during the whole of our stay, but has been staying with a friend in the country. (He did lunch once with O.) *Nor* has he gone with O to Florida. O has gone with a very nice young man, a friend of Lincoln's, who was a naval nurse during the war.[1]

I am afraid I really let myself go to O on the subject of the little Lord's behaviour, and this has not made me popular. To have chosen this moment to let O be looked after by strangers!!!

I did not tell you until I could control myself, because it is dangerous for us if we fall into rages over it, because he will come back when there is something to be got out of it. After all, any social position he has, comes through us.

Do not mention this on any account to O. For *God's sake.* But of course, he has been entirely seen through. On *no* account tell Tony.[2]

You see, the creature is coming back to England with us, and will infest the house again. O says we have to behave the same, otherwise our domestic life will be hell, because we shall have him there, just the same, but hating us. O says one must show nothing.

Well there, my darling, is my news. And you would have had it before, but, as I say, I had to control myself before I could write and tell you.

I had a most extraordinary experience yesterday. I went to a lunch party, and after lunch, sat talking to Mr. George Copeland,[3] the great pianist (he was one of Debussy's closest friends). I know him fairly well, and like him very much. A man whom I had never met before came up and started talking to us. He said to me, 'Of course your father would never give any money for housekeeping, would he? So your mother forged his name on a cheque and was jailed for it.' I said, 'My mother did not forge my father's name on a cheque.' He said, 'Oh surely she did.' 'She did *not*.' 'Well, she *was* jailed, wasn't she? What was she jailed for?' I said, 'My mother was sent to prison. But don't you think perhaps it is a little painful for me to discuss it?' I then turned my back on him. But he continued to speak to me. During this episode, poor Mr. Copeland, who is half Cat's Whiskers Boston and half Spanish, and very much a gentleman, sat looking as if he had been struck by lightning. From time to time, he opened his mouth, but no words came. He said to me afterwards: 'I *tried* to think of something to say, but couldn't think of anything excepting "Shut up. You shut up *at once*!"'

Very best love to both

ever your loving
Edith

---

310. *To Quentin Stevenson*[4]

The St Regis
Fifth Avenue and 55th Street
New York

1 March 1955

My dear Quentin,

I have wanted to write to you for ages, to tell you how *deeply* I feel for you in this grief – in these griefs – that you have suffered. Grief when one is old is a dull load, a dull ache. But when one is young, one feels that the walls of one's heart have been crushed in. That nothing will ever be the same again. It *is* not the same. But a new different happiness flowers. One does not – one *never* does – forget those whom one has lost. But I think they send somebody, in time, to help comfort one.

In the first month of the first war, Osbert, then 22, lost *every young friend he had*. (He was in the Grenadiers, and, being the premier regiment, they had to fill up the place whenever the French ran away, which they did continually. Osbert was only not killed himself because he had been gravely ill immediately before the war and had to have a month's training before he could be sent to the front.) In two years from then, Sacheverell, then 18, *lost every young friend he had.* No, I forgot, Osbert still has one friend of his youth left, Lord Alexander (the general).[5] They were at Eton together, and in the regiment together.

So, you see, I have seen grief in youth. . . .

---

311. *To Sacheverell Sitwell*

The St Regis
Fifth Avenue and 55th Street
New York

4 March 1955

My darling Sachie,

I long to see you both. We sail on the 9th of April, on 'The United States', a very fast boat, so should reach London on the 12th or 13th. Do let me know when you can both lunch.

Dear little Lord Fauntleroy is, of course, coming back with us. *He has been away all this time!* I have told O that you know. But *it must have come from Freddie Ashton*[6] – which, of course, it did, actually, in the first place.

Have I any news? None, excepting that that naughty Dylan made a record (whilst reciting at Harvard) of Henry Reed's really brilliant parody of 'Burnt Norton' in *Tom's exact voice!* (Don't tell anyone, as it will 'get round'.) Each line ended with an absolute howl of laughter from the audience, but Dylan, with noble dignity, paid no attention to these interruptions, but continued:

> '*When we get older we do not get younger.*
> *We do not get younger when we get older.*
> *Pray for me under the draughty stair.*'

The record has *not* been published.

Oh to return to little Lord F. Don't mention it to O unless he does to you. I have put my foot in it by saying what I think of the creature.

The murders here have been something unbelievable. I am very cross with the police for shooting poor Mr. Roble,[7] whom I had been *hoping* to contact! Very reliable, and dirt-cheap! Only 250 dollars for 'air-conditioning' someone! I can think of *some-one* who could do with it!

Very best love to both

ever your loving
Edith

---

312. *To Geoffrey Gorer*

Private and Confidential

The St Regis
Fifth Avenue and 55th Street
New York

8 March 1955

Dearest Geoffrey,

. . . I have been, and am, in great distress (as though *every-thing* were not bad enough, anyhow) but now can write more calmly.

O seems to me worse. He has to have his meat cut up, takes ages to dress himself, can hardly pull himself out of his chair, runs when he walks. A creature who owes him *everything*, and on whom he had every right to rely (you have always disliked him), has chosen this moment – or rather, last autumn – to desert him and leave him to the tender mercies of strangers. He went away, first, last July – but I did not know what it was leading to. But as soon as he got here, he simply went off, and has *not been near* O at all, except that he lunched with him once, to talk business. One day when O was being 'difficult' about doing the exercises he has to do for this illness (this was before they came here) he told O he didn't care if O died. To that *desperately* ill man!

Nothing could have brought O's plight home to him more clearly than this base, cruel, heartless, infamous behaviour. He sees himself now, *I know*, though he has not said anything to me, as wearying people by his illness!!!

The creature, of *course*, is coming back to England and will infest the house again. Naturally! It is a beautiful house, and he is able to swank and show off as a connoisseur of the arts to the people he has met through us. . . .

The author and critic Stanley Kauffmann (b. 1916), then editor-in-chief at Ballantine Books, had telephoned ES at the Saint Regis to ask her to write an introduction to a volume of photographs of Marilyn Monroe, whose meeting with ES had been much publicised. Thinking him a journalist, ES denounced this 'abominable nonsense' and hung up. Kauffmann then wrote and explained the true nature of his request. He has described this episode amusingly in 'Album of Marilyn Monroe', American Scholar (Autumn 1991), pp. 565–9.

313. *To Stanley Kauffmann*

The Sesame Club
49 Grosvenor Street
London, W.1

16 April 1955

Dear Mr. Kauffmann,

I thank you for your very courteous letter, which reached me at the exact moment when I was leaving for the ship, so that I had to wait till I arrived to answer.

I am indeed sorry for what was an entire misunderstanding.

Until I received your letter, I was under the impression that I was being rung up by a member of the Press, for about the thousandth time. For two months they have pestered me *unceasingly* on the subject of Miss Monroe. I am an extremely busy woman, am at work on an anthology of 1800 pages, and the reporters think they are at liberty to disturb my work at any moment they choose. Had I known who was speaking, I would certainly have spoken with you.

I have only met Miss Monroe once: she was brought to see me while I was in Hollywood. I thought her a delightful young woman, and told her that if she came to England I hoped she would let me know, as I would like to give a luncheon party for her. People *do* ask each other to luncheon, and it had not struck me that outside a lunatic asylum this would be regarded as a phenomenon in nature.

However, some moron attached to one of the papers got to hear of this – to him – world-shattering event, and saw in it a magnificent opportunity to pester me unceasingly, and to make impertinent intrusions into my private life. Worst of all, to interrupt my work by incessant telephone calls. (They could easily write, and their letters would be dealt with by my secretary.) One of these lower-grade mental defectives rang up and asked me, 'Is Miss Monroe going on the same boat as you, to England?'

The excitement – (this pestering has now lasted for *two months*) – is such that it has reached France, India and Egypt. A Calcutta paper says I live only 'to be a mother to Miss Monroe'. An Egyptian paper says I am going to 'teach her philosophy' (*sic*). The behaviour of these people is intolerable.

I understand from a mutual friend that poor Miss Monroe is allowed no friends by the Press, and that she hardly dares go out for fear of being mobbed. The whole lot of these people ought to be ashamed of themselves.

I was disappointed to learn that Miss Monroe was in New York while I was there, as I should have liked, so much, to see her. If she comes to London, I hope we shall have our long-deferred luncheon party.

With many regrets for this misunderstanding,

I am
Yours sincerely
Edith Sitwell

---

314. *To Benjamin Britten*[8]

As from
Montegufoni

26 April 1955

My dear Ben,

I am so haunted and so alone with that wonderful music and
its wonderful performance that I was incapable of writing before
now. I had no sleep at all on the night of the performance. And
I can think of nothing else. It was certainly one of the greatest
experiences in all my life as an artist.

During the performance, I felt as if I were dead – killed in the
raid – yet with all my powers of feeling still alive. Most terrible
and most moving – the appalling loneliness, for all that it was a
communal experience one was alone, each being was alone,
with space and eternity and the terror of death, and then God.

What a very great composer you are! And what a very great
singer Peter[9] is. I can never begin to thank you for the glory you
have given my poem. . . .

---

315. *To Stephen Spender*

Sesame, Imperial and Pioneer Club

4 May 1955

Dearest Stephen,

It was only on my return here that I received *your* copy of
the wonderful *Collected Poems*, with its most deeply moving

inscription. I say, 'deeply moving' – and I can honestly say *nothing* has *ever* moved me more deeply. I don't know how to express my gratitude, and what it means to me. And I am beyond words proud of that great section dedicated to me.

Of course I had the book before I received your copy, but as I say, only received the latter on my return here.

No poetry of our time is more beautiful, more deep, or more true. It is a pride to me that it should come as a flowering over the desolation, like the rose at Hiroshima of which I wrote. Indeed, the poems are of a quite extraordinary beauty physically (in texture, sound and image) and so deeply experienced. . . .

I think I need not tell you what your and Natasha's friendship has meant to me. It is one of the most important things in my life.

Thank you again, dear Stephen, for everything.

My love to you both, and to the children,

Yours affectionately and gratefully,
Edith

I shall be writing to you shortly about poems for my giant anthology. . . .

Having been instructed in doctrine by the priest and historian Philip Caraman, SJ (b. 1911), ES was received into the Roman Catholic Church on 8 August 1955, with Evelyn Waugh and, in absentia, Roy and Mary Campbell as god-parents. Her biographers have seen her conversion chiefly as an effort to control her rage against David Horner through submission to a higher authority (see Elborn, pp. 220–4, and Glendinning, pp. 314–20). While her struggles with Horner had indeed influenced her decision, her movement towards the Roman church had been gradual, beginning doubtless with the influence of Helen Rootham, who was a Roman Catholic. ES was fascinated by the writings of St. Thomas Aquinas, to whom she alludes directly in her poetry from the early 1940s (see notes to Collected Poems*); he offered her an understanding of the relation between the forms of the* *physical universe and the operations of intellect and grace, which is the main philosophical issue of her later poetry. In this light, her conversion can be seen as the hardly surprising outcome of a long personal and intellectual journey.*

316. *To Philip Caraman, SJ*

Montegufoni

7 May 1955

Dear Father Caraman,

My most grateful – indeed grateful – thanks for your letter, which I found waiting for me on my arrival on Thursday. It gave me great happiness, a feeling of hope.

I believe, and trust with all my heart, that I am on the threshold of a new life. But I shall have to be born again. And I have a whole world to see, as it were for the first time, and to understand as far as my capacities will let me.

Prayer has always been a difficulty for me. By which I mean only that I feel very far away, as if I were speaking into the darkness. But I hope this will be cured. When I *think* of God, I do not feel far away. . . .

---

317. *To Philip Caraman, SJ*

Montegufoni

3 June 1955

Dear Father Caraman,

You told me I might write to you on the subject of the books I have been directed by you to read, and so I do. I only hope the letter will reach you, for I see that the posts are most uncertain owing to the strike.

I cannot express to you my gratitude for having recommended these books to me. The first feeling they give me is one of absolute certainty. They – and especially the wonderful writings of St. Thomas Aquinas, and Father D'Arcy's *The Nature of*

Belief – make one see doubt – perhaps I am not expressing this properly – as a complete failure of intellect. Then again I see that purely intellectual belief is not enough: one must not only *think* one is believing, but *know* one is believing. There has to be a sixth sense in faith.

How wonderful that passage is in *The Nature of Belief* about 'looking through the appearances at reality. Once this is granted the existence of God must be admitted without more ado . . . If there is anything, then there must be something fully real.'[10] And this passage: 'The evil of unbelief is that it must shut its eye to the forms and patterns of truth inscribed in the universe, and retire to the inner sanctuary of the mind, there to rest in uncertainty, in the presence of a fugitive self and the broken idols of its hopes.'[11]

When I was a very small child, I began to see the patterns of the world, the images of wonder. And I asked myself why those patterns should be repeated – the feather and the fern and rose and acorn in the patterns of frost on the window – pattern after pattern repeated again and again. And even then I knew that this was telling us something. I founded my poetry upon it. Did you, I wonder, know Dr. Hubble, of the Expanding Universe – one of the greatest men I ever knew. One day in California, he showed me slides of universes unseen by the naked eye, and millions of light years away. I said to him, 'How terrifying!' 'Only when you are not used to them,' he replied. 'When you *are* used to them, they are comforting. For then you know that there is nothing to worry about – nothing at all!'

That was a few months before he died. And so I suppose now that he knows how truly he spoke. I was most deeply moved by that. I could never cease to be so.

With my deep gratitude,

Yours very sincerely,
Edith Sitwell

This is a most inadequate letter. For some reason I cannot express myself in the slightest at present.

318. *To Edward Sackville-West*[12]

Sesame Imperial and Pioneer Club

4 August 1955

Dear Eddy,

I was deeply moved by your letter – one of the most wonderful letters on any subject that I have ever received, and all the more wonderful because it was on the greatest of all subjects. It gave me great happiness, and I thank you with all my heart.

Today is that on which I shall be received into the Church, and I do, in a way, tremble at the thought. Partly because I am in a deep night, in which there is no sound and no light. I might almost be dead – excepting when I pick up and read St. Thomas Aquinas, when, for some reason – well, an explainable reason – I become violently alive again. But I have had this happen before I had a poem come to me, so perhaps everything will be all right for me.

And what you say about 'the consolation of no longer being in any doubt about life – what to think or do about it' is deeply and abundantly true. And what you say about God not letting those He has called to Him escape is most wonderful.

You say it took twelve years to bring you to your resolution. It must have taken about the same time to bring me to mine. I could not at first. Because Osbert is so ghastly ill, and I felt, so to speak, that I could not leave him. Then one day in New York this winter, he told me that I must become a Catholic. And he said, 'How do you know that I may not become one too.' So I hope he will.

Will you tell me, one day, of that revelation of which you speak? . . .

Yours affectionately
Edith Sitwell

Is Alec Guinness a friend of yours? He is a friend of mine. He, too, is becoming a Catholic.

1956

319. *To Roy Campbell*

Montegufoni
21 January 1956

Dearest Roy,

. . . I am waiting, with trepidation, for John Brinnin's book on Dylan[1] to arrive. I have just written a very short preface for the Bibliography of Dylan to be published by Dent.[2] In the course of this I say that Dylan's death was the signal for an outburst of the most disgusting hysteria, attempts to climb, and hatred that I have ever seen. (I was not, I may say, referring to Brinnin's book, but to other people.) I said that everyone who had ever sat near him once in a pub claimed to be his best friend. And that people who couldn't *begin* to write poetry tried to muscle in on his fame.

I then said that in a recent number of the American *Saturday Review*, devoted to English literature, some person whose name I forget described another person of an equal genius, and his 'Refusal to Mourn the Death of Dylan Thomas'. 'And this, only eighteen months after that tragic death, and while his widow, his mother, and his three children are living.' On that note, I ended.

The life and death of a great artist are equally terrible. In life, poverty, hangers-on, and neglect. Together with the usual tragic temperament – of one kind or another – that goes with genius. Then the death of the Vampire – nailed to the cross-roads, trodden over by filthy feet, dug up and examined to find the cause of the anguish. There it is !

One thing that may amuse you and Mary. I wonder if you know Billy McCann – a wonderful character. Australian, a fervent Catholic, and, looking like a hard thin dust-coloured Spaniard, and speaking Spanish like a Spaniard, he was the head of the anti-spy Spanish section during the war, leading a life like one of Mr. Peter Cheyney's heroes.

Well, he is now in Rio de Janeiro. His office (he is employed by an oil company) looks over the Atlantic. They are in the middle of one of the most terrific heat-waves that Brazil has ever known. Suddenly, looking out of his window, Billy saw an immense black and white procession advancing, in a straight line, over the waves.

As it approached, the city could see it consisted of polar bears, polar seals, walruses, and (or) sea elephants. Poor boys and girls, they had been carried on a current from the North Pole! The journey must have taken them months, and I expect there was a good deal of quarrelling en route. They are now sitting on ice at the Rio de Janeiro zoo, where they received a warm welcome, as the zoo had no specimens of their kinds. Such a sad ending to a lovely outing. . . .

Yours affectionately
Edith

The sad thing is, I honestly believe John Brinnin loved Dylan. Strange! But he cried like a baby at his death.

---

320. *To Beryl de Zoete*

Montegufoni

23 January 1956

Darling Beryl,

It was lovely to hear from you. I had been meaning to write to you for such ages, but have got absolutely *no* letters done, because I am at work on an enormous book about Elizabeth I,[3] so the only letter I have written was one to congratulate dear Arthur on his C.H.,[4] which has made Osbert and me, will have made Sachie, so happy. *When* is he going to be received by the Queen? I long to see you both, and shall be back at the beginning of March, and will ring you up immediately.

I am afraid I am anything but pleased at the idea of this portrait, but *I would like to see a photograph of it,* just to see what has been done to my poor face *now*!

I know it is not meant impertinently, but I think it is taking a very impertinent liberty to paint portraits of me without asking my permission. My face – awful though it may be – is the only one I have got, and is my copyright, as is *Façade*, which anyone who happens to want to, simply takes, without my permission, and wrecks. I have had an awful lot to put up with, from both Face and *Façade* wreckers! . . .

---

321. *To Benjamin Britten*

As from
The Sesame Club

18 February 1956

My dear Ben,

Osbert and I were more than delighted to get your letters. I am writing for both of us – because, you know, his shakiness varies, and at the moment, his hand-writing is very unclear.

We were enthralled to think of your and Peter's last months – the wonders and beauties you must have seen, and also, the very alarming dark side of it. I cannot say that I am attracted by the idea of waiting for Malayan bandits, having no weapons oneself, in the midst of a tropical storm! I don't know, of course, what bandits one would be wise to choose, but I think not Malayan!

The idea of constant danger from nature and man that you speak of in your letter is terrible, and great!

How wonderful it must have been to have seen the mosaics in St. Sophia. Did you know the old American – now dead – who dealt with them? I forget his name now, but we knew him quite well, rather against our will. He was very tiresome in a Bostonian way, but was also a Mahommedan – which made him rather a split personality.

But most of all exciting for you must have been the hearing

of this strange music, new to you. Osbert and I were wildly
thrilled to hear about this – wondering what it will bring to you
(and consequently to us).

I should have written this letter before but have had rather a
trying time. I got influenza twice – or rather it returned to me,
this being a habit of the new kind. And then, just as I had
recovered, and was walking about with legs made of cotton
wool, I crashed onto the stone passage. Why I didn't kill myself,
I can't think. But I bruised, strained, and tore every muscle and
tendon that could be bruised, strained, or torn!

I am beyond anything happy to think that you may be going
to set another poem of mine for the Festival. 'Still Falls the Rain'
is one of the greatest prides of my life. I suggest, if you think it
fitting, 'The Stone-Breakers: A Prison Song' on page 359,
Collected Poems.[5] But for setting, I have made a few alterations,
which I think make it better for the singer, and perhaps more
comprehensible at first hearing. But that of course is for you to
say. I enclose the version that I have made, for your approval.

It is so very kind of you to say I may look at the proof of 'Still
Falls the Rain', to see if I think any additional indications are
needed to show where the lines begin. But I am quite sure no
more *are* needed. The music holds it together so strongly. How
much I long to hear that most wonderful music again. And how
happy I am to think of being at Aldeburgh on the 21st of June. I
wonder when you return. I do pity you both if it is at this cruel
black and white moment. We are 13 degrees below zero here,
and are so cold that not only our bodies but our brains seem
frozen. . . .

Yours ever,
Edith

It is said that the wolves are out in the mountains. I have suggested that the Priest's step-mother, a very fat woman and a
great trial to him and his parishioners, should be exposed, tied
to a tree. This suggestion was greeted with enthusiasm.

322. *To Armando Child*

Private and Confidential

Sesame Imperial and Pioneer Club

20 May 1956

My dear Armando,

Please may I consult you about something exceedingly important that concerns Osbert, very gravely. I am hoping to return to
Renishaw on Friday (I do not know yet if this is possible from
the household point of view). But I could come and see you on
Tuesday at any time, or on Wednesday afternoon or Thursday
afternoon (the latter after the presentation to Osbert by the
Society of Authors at a luncheon party).

I am having, also, to consult Philip Frere, our friend and
solicitor. I have just written to him, and suggested, tentatively,
that if I was to see him on Wednesday or Thursday, we might all
three meet.

Something *has* to be done to protect Osbert.[6] He is being
made much worse by a situation that is horrible, grotesque and
vile. He is too ill, too shocked and too despondent, to do anything himself, so I am going to do it for him. We *cannot* go on
like this.

Love from
Edith

I should think Osbert had better be put into a nursing home
while the situation is being put an end to. It will poison our few
remaining years if it goes on. If I were a man I wouldn't have to
bother you.

323. *To Roy Campbell*

Renishaw Hall

5 September 1956

Dearest Roy,

How long it is since I have wanted to write to you, and to ask for news of you and Mary. But I have been charging about all over the country, more or less from pole to pole, reciting. In Edinburgh, at the Festival, I was televised for five minutes, so was able to pay you tribute.

Dear Roy, I do hope so much that you are better. It is so wretched that you should suffer this pain – brought on you by your nobility and defence of what is good.[7] I am *horrified* to hear what has happened to you because of that uninsured farm hand.[8] It is most wicked, really, that this disaster should have fallen upon you, a most dreadful thing. I feel for you and Mary more than I can say.

How can a great poet be expected to wear out his life and dim his fire by thinking of small practical things? It is quite impossible. The whole of a great poet's life is dedicated to one thing – poetry, and his love for the one being who matters most on this earth.

It is, I may say, one of the great things in my life, this lasting love between you and Mary, in an age of little, fireless unreal would-be emotions, gone in a moment, everything turned to ashes, to know that such greatness and undying love exists, unquenchable. You deserve, and she deserves, your poetry.

I do hope from the bottom of my heart that this tragedy about the farm hand may be – I do not know how – but overcome. I can sympathise with the appalling worry – because – well, you don't know what dear Hollywood has done to me in that direction! Hollywood is my farm hand, so to speak.

I am deeply interested in what you say about Brinnin. I suppose that *is* the reason for it all. Poor Brinnin – (awful as what he has done is). He was born a Catholic, and then lost all his hair because he got religious doubts!!

Caitlin, who was in Italy – may still be there – went to

luncheon with an Englishwoman who lived there, and threw all her furniture out of the window. They knocked each other unconscious, and woke to find themselves in police cells. The English inhabitant of Italy was told to get out of Italy, and stop out! Which I think is unfair!

Kenneth Clark – I don't know if you know who he is: the head of Independent Television, and he was head of the National Gallery – told me when I saw him the other day that the glorious passage from 'The Flowering Rifle' in *Nine*[9] was the most transcendental splendour he had seen since he could remember. He was overcome with enthusiasm. (He and his wife are two of my greatest friends.) I am wondering if you could *possibly* allow me to show him, perhaps give him a copy, of that glorious work, just discovered, the poem to Mary, that you sent me. I ask this, because Kenneth is a tremendous prop of the Arts, and people listen more, almost, to what he says, than to anyone, and it will rouse excitement about the book before it appears.

Osbert and I think and talk of you and Mary ceaselessly.

Our love to you both

Yours affectionately
Edith

I have just given the 'young' 'geniuses' the most frightful beating-up in a lecture. I'll have that part typed, and sent you, because I think it will make you laugh. I have half killed Roy Fuller!

---

324. *To J. B. Priestley*[10]

Montegufoni

12 November 1956

Dear Mr. Priestley,

Your 'Thoughts on Dr. Leavis' have so delighted my brother Osbert and me – indeed have been our sole delight at this terrible time – that in sheer gratitude I am writing on behalf of both of us to thank you.

I think the article may kill him! There has been *nothing* like it yet, nor will there be – although he has had a pretty bad time of it this year! (Incidentally, did you see his interminable whine about the way in which he has been treated, in a letter to *The Listener* a fortnight or three weeks ago?) He is definitely in a very bad state of mind. You are certainly right when you say his goings-on are the result of 'some strange neurosis, as if he had been frightened by a librarian in early childhood'.

I hear, on the best authority, that some time ago, returning from giving a lecture at Downing College, and finding Mrs. Queenie Leavis darning socks in the drawing-room, he, shutting the door behind him, spread his arms across it, as one being crucified, and cried, '*They* nearly got me that time!' We don't know who 'They' were.

Cecil Day Lewis and I tease him horribly. We are in league to do so, though in charge of different departments. He hasn't found out yet who is responsible for the teasing.

I have all the multitudinous letters from lunatics and persons with ordinary bees in their bonnets re-typed by my secretary and sent to him. The persons with bees get letters from me advising them to tell Dr. Leavis *all*, not to be discouraged if he does not answer them, but to write to him once a fortnight for two years. There was, for instance, a gentleman who wrote me a furious letter because I had said, in a broadcast, that The Boy on the Burning Deck was a *fool*! Otherwise, why didn't he get off it? The gentleman said I had cast aspersions on a Very Noble Boy. I had this addressed as to Dr. Leavis, and sent him. Most of the MSS I receive I have sent on to him. And I got him into touch with a lady living in Leamington Spa. She had asked me who gave me permission to take her poems 'The Thrushes', 'Lullabye', and 'The Mouse's Wedding', and publish them as my own? I replied that obviously somebody, somewhere, had behaved disgracefully, but I was not the culprit. 'Write to Dr. Leavis. Tell him *all*. Keep nothing back. He admires you greatly, and has written a long essay on your poetry for *Scrutiny*. Keep on and on!' . . .

325. *To Stephen Spender*

Montegufoni

16 November 1956

Dearest Stephen,

I only received the tragic telegram about Hungary[11] last night, forwarded *in a letter* from Renishaw. Osbert and I are both horribly distressed. As you know, Osbert has this terrible illness, and it would, of course, be utterly impossible for him to go. The danger is, if we applied for a visa, the Russians *might* let us have it, and then the case would be worsened. And with great distress of mind I am forced to say I cannot apply for one either, because I should only be a liability to the rest of the party if we *did* get visas. I shall be seventy on my next birthday, and am now extremely lame. I have arthritis in both knees, acute rheumatism in both feet, and often am only able to walk – and slowly at that – with the aid of a stick. In addition, I get attacks of sciatica in its most acute form. I had it for over a year, and it returns, so that when I travelled back from Aldeburgh Festival, I could not put my feet to the ground when I reached Liverpool Station, and had to be carried out of the train, wheeled along the platform in a truck, and carried into my club. That doesn't altogether prevent ordinary activities; but what would the rest of the expedition do with me in that terrible city? I could not run, if we had to. I could not go down on the ground quickly if the Russians started firing; and I should only risk, probably, other people's lives. And it would, as I say, make matters worse if I applied for a visa, got it, and then didn't go. For Osbert, of course, it is entirely *impossible.*

It would not be possible to exaggerate our wretchedness of mind in saying this isn't possible. You must, of course, make *every* use of my name.

The whole terrible thing is too heart-breaking for words, and one is haunted by the thought of those people, day and night.

I have been wanting to write to you for ages. (That confounded book I am writing about Elizabeth I has practically blotted out my letters for the last year. Thank God it will soon be finished.) How dreadful it is that, now, I should be writing to you on such a subject.

I think the Russians must be mad. Do they think they will *ever* be forgiven?

I do hope Natasha is better. Please give her my best love. I was so sad not to see you and her before I came here. You, of course, were abroad; and she was taken ill the day before she was to have lunched with me.

Osbert's and my best love to you, and to her, and the children.

Yours affectionately,
Edith

James Amos Purdy (b. 1923), American short-story writer, novelist and playwright, had published his books 63: Dream Palace *and* Don't Call Me By My Right Name *with a subsidy publisher in 1956. He sent them to various prominent authors, including ES, who persuaded Gollancz to publish both in a single volume in 1957.*

326. *To James Purdy*

Montegufoni

26 November 1956

Dear Mr. Purdy,

I am most deeply grateful to you for sending me *63: Dream Palace*. It arrived, after an astonishingly quick journey, two days ago, and I have read it twice, already.

What a *wonderful* book! It is a masterpiece from every point of view. There can't be the slightest doubt that you are a really great writer, and I can only say that I am quite overcome.

What anguish, what heart-breaking truth! And what utter simplicity. The knife is turned and turned in one's heart. From the terrible first pages (the first sentence is, in itself, a masterpiece) to the heart-rending last pages, there isn't a single false note, and not a sentence or a word too much, not a sentence or a word too little.

Wonderful as the short stories are – and I have read them many times, and think them – if it were possible to do so – even more wonderful than when I wrote to you before, this book is just as great. Indeed, I am not sure if it isn't even greater. Point after point I go through, and I am inclined to think so.

Have you heard, yet, from Victor Gollancz? Please will you let me know as soon as you do. I will write to him today and tell him of 63: *Dream Palace*. Apart from other reasons for this: he *may* (from a publisher's technical point of view – considering the lending libraries' weekend readers, etc.) want a *larger* book. (It could not be a greater.) And it strikes me that if you were willing, the two books could be bound together. I am inclined to think that if this suited you, it might be a wise move. Naturally – I need hardly say – I am not suggesting this to Victor without your permission.

And now I have several other suggestions to make. For the *English* public, I think it would be wise to put 'Don't Call Me By My Right Name' – the *story*, I mean – later in the book, not at the very beginning. It is a story that English readers who do not know America would not be so quick to grasp as they would with the others.

Then, if I may make the suggestion, I think you ought to have a literary agent in England. Mine (and my brothers') are

Messrs. Pearn, Pollinger and Higham
76 Dean Street
Soho, London W.1

I will write to *David Higham*, who is in charge of the *book* department, and to *Mrs. LeRoy*,[12] who is in charge of the *magazine* department, and will tell them that they may be hearing from you. I strongly advise you to go to them. As the short stories have not appeared yet, in England, it is possible (I think, but am not sure) that some might be placed in magazines in England. But Mrs. LeRoy would know about that.

Stephen Spender's *Encounter* might be a good place for them. Stephen is at present lecturing in America, so has escaped my grasp, temporarily. But perhaps you know, and will be seeing him? In any case, as soon as he returns, I will get on to him about it.

Lincoln Kirstein tells me he has sent *Don't Call Me By My Right Name* to Madame Bradley, the Parisian agent. But it is certain you should have an agent in England, as well.

I shall be here until the end of January, or the beginning of February, and in mid-February I sail for New York, arriving, I think, either on the 25th or the 28th – for an immense recital-tour. I do hope so much that we can meet. I do not know if that will be possible for you, but I do hope so.

When I reach New York, I will set about seeing if the two books can be translated into Portuguese. I have a great friend in London, a young Portuguese, a distinguished poet, and one of the most intelligent and subtle people I have ever known,[13] who I hope will do the translation. He is a close friend of all the most important Portuguese reviewers.

If, by any wretched chance, Victor Gollancz can't take the book, we'll try someone else.

My best wishes to you and the books, and my most profound admiration. You are truly a writer of genius. Lincoln Kirstein in his letter to me, said you are 'quite wonderful'. How right he is!

> Yours very sincerely,
> Edith Sitwell

---

327. *To Quentin Stevenson*

> Castello di Montegufoni

6 December 1956

Dearest Quentin,

Thank you so much for your letter, which I received last night. I should have written to you ages ago; but had a very serious accident. The housemaids *will* wax the floors, and I slipped and crashed on to my face, waking to find myself lying in a pool of blood, with my head on Miss Fraser's[14] knee, she holding towel after towel to my face, and the butler putting ice on my forehead. I cannot think how I escaped breaking my nose and both cheek bones. . . .

My dear, what *can* you mean by The Movement? Is it possible that you are referring to these ridiculous little boys and girls who are bolstered up in the *Spectator*? I suppose that *is* who you mean. But I am not in the least 'appalled' by them. They do not 'direct the traffic' and nobody pays the slightest attention to them excepting themselves and their friends. (They are on the way out, anyhow.) I don't think you have met Mr. Eliot, have you? But you don't suppose that when he comes to see me, we talk about 'The Movement', do you? He would simply laugh. There have always been people like that. When I was young, there were J. C. Squire and *his* gang, Shanks, etc. Where are they now?

But you are entirely wrong in thinking Goodsir Smith and Charles Causley belong to this gang. Who introduced Goodsir Smith to England, and wrote the preface for his poems? Edith Sitwell.[15]

Who did Charles Causley ask to write the introduction to *his* forthcoming book of poems? Edith Sitwell.[16] (I have the proofs of the preface in my cupboard at this moment, waiting to be returned to the publisher.)

I have no news, excepting that there is a great new novelist and short story writer, an American, quite unknown. His name is James Purdy, and I have just introduced his work to Victor Gollancz. There can be no doubt whatever that he is a writer of genius.

I look forward so much, my dear, to seeing you in February; we reach London, I suppose, at the very beginning of the month, en route for America, where I am going on a huge recital tour.

Much love, and delighted congratulations about the splendid news from the Oxford University Press.[17]

from yours affectionately,
Edith Sitwell

328. *To Jack Lindsay*

Durrants Hotel
George Street
Manchester Square
W.1

[LATE 1956?]

My dear Jack,

It will be lovely if you and Ann will lunch with me here on Saturday. Can you be with me at 12.45? I do look forward to seeing you both.

Mr. Anthias[18] means his gift most courteously and kindly; but I really could have *yelled* when I read that part of your letter. I did tell you I was *trying* (in spite of the non-stop interruptions and merciless intrusions on my time and patience from which I suffer) – to write poetry. Also I have a badly strained heart, and I came here without giving anyone but my closest friends my address, because the doctor says I simply have to be quiet. You know that I have the strongest affection for you and Ann, and great respect for your opinion. But nothing is going to make believe that a poem called 'The Song of the Earth' is the sort of poem I would want to read, or is anything but propaganda-poetry.

It is no use sending me poems clotted with incompetent verbiage. Words are just as important to poetry as meaning. And, as I say, the title tells me everything. I have had the identical poem sent me (signed by different authors, but all exactly the same) 7964 times – mainly from Nottingham (it is the Nottingham genre).

I really cannot disturb my work in order to 'make the initial charitable effort' and 'see the original poem under its blur'. I don't like blurs in poetry, *or* 'Songs of the Earth'. How cross this sounds. Of course, I shall write with proper courtesy to thank Mr. Anthias. But next time anyone wishes to send me 'The Song of the Earth', please tell the author – whether from Greece or Nottingham – that I am dead.[19]

My love to you both. I look forward to seeing you on Saturday. I am so happy to hear that the 'Starfish Road' has gone to Dobsons.

Edith

1957

329. *To John Lehmann*

Montegufoni

7 January 1957

My dear John,

I have been wanting to write to you for such ages, to wish you a very happy and triumphant New Year – and should have done, but falling on my face as I did has brought on violent sinus, which causes one of my eyes to pour in a most extraordinary manner. It is most painful, and Jack Lindsay chose this moment to send me a paean of praise of an alleged poet called Ebenezer Jones,[1] whose verses are so utterly horrible that I have really lost my temper. We get lines like

'Ours is the earth – the earth!'

Why *twice*? And it isn't even true. I am, by this post, sending Jack an exceedingly cross letter. He tried before that, to send me a translation of a Czecho-Slovakian 'poem' called 'The Song of the Earth'. This I refused, saying I get exactly the same thing five times a month from Nottingham and Leicester.

This is a household of sufferers. The young cook has influenza and quinsy; her two elder boys have influenza and laryngitis; her sister (who doesn't live in the house but near by) has paratyphoid. Her husband (the young butler) is covered – he says – from head to foot with boils. The head housemaid has influenza; the whole family of her subordinate (they live in the house) have it, but she has not. An old lady who comes in to 'help' has had a stroke.

D.H. is *radiantly* well, and his pretty golden curls are like sunlight in the house and in my heart!!!! . . .

On 10 January 1957 at 6:15 a.m., T. S. Eliot married his secretary Valerie Fletcher at St. Barnabas's Church in Kensington. The wedding plans were kept secret, and it is not clear whether John Hayward, who lived with Eliot, was given notice of it.

330. To John Lehmann

Montegufoni
19 January 1957

My dear John,

. . . Oh! What a *beast* Tom is!!! No, no, what you tell me is really *too* much! You wait! *I'll* take it out of that young woman! I'll frighten her out of her wits before I've done. As for Tom – he will, of course, be punished. He will *never* write anything worth while again. And indeed, hasn't for a very long time now. The *Four Quartets* are, to my mind, infinitely inferior to his earlier work – completely bloodless and spiritless.

It makes me quite sick to think of the pain John has endured – that waking up at 5.30 in the morning or 5.45, to be told that his greatest friend, on whom he depended in his unspeakable physical helplessness and humiliation, had done him this sly, crawling, lethal cruelty. I feel I never want to see T again! But of course I am assuming, when I say that, that T is not going to continue to live with him. Perhaps I am wrong. But certainly that young person will get him out. The friendship is over. . . .

---

331. *To Sacheverell Sitwell*

The St. Regis Hotel
1 East 55th Street
New York City
N.Y.

26 February 1957

My darling Sachie,

We arrived the evening before last, 36 hours late, after what the stewards said was the worst crossing they had ever known. I should have written yesterday, but felt so ill I just lay with my eyes shut.

This is just to tell you the latest news. (I'll write again in a day or two.) As soon as we got on to the boat, O came to my cabin and told me that animal was going off *again* (for the duration) with the same animal as before.[2] O said it was 'a very good thing, *as we need a little holiday*'. I must not refuse to speak to the second animal, as if I did, the other would 'make a scene'! The impudence! The blackmail! The sickening, horrible creature! And they simply aren't house-trained! If you could have seen them on the dock!

Very best love to both

ever your loving
Edith

In addition to my very tiring tour, I now, of course, have all the worry about what is happening to O.

332. *To Georgia Sitwell*

The St Regis
Fifth and 55th Street
New York

2 May 1957

My darling Georgia,

I have been on tour for over a month, and that is why I
haven't written. I've *never* been so tired in my life. I am
absolutely ill with fatigue. We start for England tomorrow, and
should arrive on the 7th or 8th. I *long* to see you both. Please let
me know as soon as you can when you can lunch.

Little Jackal Horner is returning with us. O says he won't
kick him out because he was once a good friend to him. If he
went of his own accord it would be different. He says he thinks
it is because his illness bores Little Jackal that he goes off as he
does – which is a credit to him.

Roy's death has been a dreadful shock to me, and a grief.³ He
was so chivalrous to me, and one of my greatest friends. An oaf
of a reporter told me about his death at a press conference.
When I think that a noble, chivalrous man who was a great
poet is dead – and what we have left!

Very best love to both. Come as soon as you can

ever your loving
Edith

A New York name for someone we know and love is 'A rose-red
pansy half as old as Time'.

---

333. *To Benjamin Britten*

The Sesame Club

28 July 1957

My dearest Ben,

. . . On the 5th (I think) of September I am going to recite some early – very early – and some later religious poems in aid of the restoration of the chapel in Stonor Park, in which chapel the Blessed Edmund Campion[4] said Mass. Some of these poems I am hoping to put together so that they make a pattern, and send them to you. But I'm only just beginning the pattern.

Is there any happy chance of you and Peter being in London, soon, and lunching with me? I shall be here till the 30th.

Beryl de Zoete – about whom I have complained before – is behaving in the strangest manner. She now raises her left hand above her head, and with her right hand twangs at my knee as though it were some archaic musical instrument. It is very painful, and I should like to hit her!

Best love to both from

Edith

I shall be sending you both my English edition of my *Collected Poems*, because it contains some you don't know.

---

334. *To Cyril Connolly*

Sesame Imperial and Pioneer Club

28 July 1957

Dear Mr. Connolly,

I am more deeply grateful to you than I can possibly say, for the magnificent review you have given my poems.[5] It gives me the most *profound* pleasure. You have understood every single thing I have tried to do.

It is very strange that you should have said what you did

about Ravel and *The Sleeping Beauty*; for various works of Ravel were running through my head, continuously, at the time I was writing it. I am particularly happy that you like that poem. How well I remember a time, just after I wrote it. We met you at Granada, and you very kindly asked me to tea and talked about it. That made me very happy, for nobody else seemed to like it at all.

A young gentleman named Mr. Alvarez – whoever he may be – seems rather badly scared, and wrote of me with caution, though he is obviously seething with hatred.[6]

Again, my very deepest gratitude to you.

All best wishes
Yours very sincerely
Edith Sitwell

---

335. *To Sacheverell Sitwell*

Sesame Imperial and Pioneer Club

[6 August 1957]

My darling Sachie,

Your kind sweet letter touched me more than I could ever say. Yes, it was a dreadful shock;[7] so much so that I have been quite numb. One can only say that he was so ill, I doubt if he could ever have painted again, and that would have made life a hell to him.

I think somebody might have told me he was dying. I knew he was very ill, but he had been so since January. If I had known, I should have written to him. But I had influenza very badly, and had waited till I recovered to write, because I do think letters can carry infection.

It has been an awful year. First, dear Roy's death, and now Pavlik's.

The insolence of the papers to me is, I am *convinced*, the work of Grigson, though I cannot prove it. The *Spectator* is frantic because I won't let them have the book to insult. I read a letter of Pope's the other day, in which he said, 'The malice of my calumniators equals their dullness. The first I forgive, the second I pity, and I despise both.' . . .

---

336. *To Hal Lydiard Wilson*

Montegufoni

12 October 1957

Dear Hal Lydiard Wilson,

Thank you so much for your letter, which I have only just got – for you see where I am! I was very happy to hear from you.

Alas, it is sad that I can't open Mr. Whistler's[8] exhibition. I do hope it will be a very great success. It was a pleasure meeting him and Mrs. Whistler after my recital.

How are you and Boodie? I do hope very well, and I hope very much to see you both when I return to England in the early spring.

It has been a terrific year for me. It started off alright. I did a recital tour right across the United States. The tour lasted for six weeks, was a tremendous success, with not a seat to be had; but at the end I really was almost a stretcher case – what with travelling, reciting, reporters, and general badgering.

Then, two of my greatest friends, Roy Campbell and Pavel Tchelitchew, died within three months of each other. *And* the whole of the gutter press rose as one man and insulted me. They have now, however, been put in their place. It really is the lowest profession.

I have just had a very good letter from an old lady, who seems to be in a fury about something, and has written to ask if I *wear a wig*! The letter begins thus: 'You Fool!' and goes on to say that 'in one thousand years, *ten* thousand years, the Common People of the World will unite to call you that!' She then says – which seems rather a non sequitur: 'Time is Space, and Space is Time. But you can get in neither! Nor can you get into Heaven or

Hell. But the Devil will look after his own!' The letter has been returned to her by my secretary, with the simple enquiry: 'Who let you out?'

My love to you and Boodie.

Yours ever
Edith S., D.B.E.

1958

337. *To Anthony Cronin*[1]

Montegufoni

1 January 1958

Dear Mr. Cronin,

My very best wishes to you and Mrs. Cronin for a very happy New Year.

I was particularly happy to get your letter and your *Poems*; delighted to get the poems – of which more in a moment – and happy to have your letter because, early in August, I wrote asking you both to come and see me, and the letter was returned. Immediately after, disaster after disaster fell on me, and I was so wretched that I became completely inert, unable to get anything done or make an effort of any kind.

These poems are full of passionate understanding and living, compassion and truth. 'Surprise' I think particularly fine, with that terrible line 'That knocking sound you hear is just your heart.' 'That knocking sound' made me think of knocking nails into a coffin. Was that in your mind? That and the daily death? (In some ways, I think a poem has two creators, the poet and the reader – although the reader must not take liberties.) The poems transpierce one with their truth – for instance the verse from 'Examination of Conscience' which begins with the line 'I cannot say which murder cleared the air.' You find superb expression for our terrible situation – as in the tragic 'Thief calling to thief from his cross with no Christ in between.' That is *truly* superb. And the suffering, simple truth of 'And the frown of the strong was as false as the smile of the weak', is deeply moving.

I don't know if it will be possible, but I shall try, when Mr. Wright's book appears,[2] to write about both books either for 'Encounter' or 'The Month'. . . .

Elizabeth Salter (1918–81), Australian novelist and biographer, served as secretary to ES from 1957 to 1964. She subsequently wrote The Last Years of a Rebel: A Memoir of Edith Sitwell *(London, 1967), and edited (with Allanah Harper) an anthology of ES's writings,* Fire of the Mind *(London, 1976).*

338. *To Elizabeth Salter*

Renishaw Hall

16 June 1958

Dear Elizabeth,

Osbert asks me to thank you for your congratulations. All my family, I may tell you, are mad about you. I enclose a cheque, in case you have run short.

Here is another chapter, also *additions* to 2 other chapters. Please, my dear, can you add these both to the chapters *you* have, as well as keep a copy for those Jean le Roy has (which we shall have to get back from her presently, before she 'places them with a magazine'). I am having to re-number the later chapters, and will let you have the list as soon as I have compiled it.

You know how I swore I will never speak to Alan Pryce-Jones again![3] I should undoubtedly, if I found him at a cocktail party in London, walk straight out of the room. Well, while I was at Sachie's, the Spenders asked us to lunch (an hour's motor-drive away) at a house they have in the grounds belonging to Mr.

Michael (I think) Astor.[4] When we got there, we found that
without asking us if we wanted to go (and we certainly did *not*)
they had arranged to take us to the Astors' house to luncheon.
Mrs. A., though she knows Sachie and Georgia, had not had
the manners to ring them up and ask us personally. We were
very annoyed. On our way there, Natasha S. told Georgia, 'Alan
Pryce-Jones will be there.' G told her I wouldn't speak to him
unless forced to, and that he could not be allowed to sit next me
at luncheon.

When we arrived he looked *terrified*, [and] said, 'How lovely
to see you', to me. I said, 'How do you do', coldly, and turned
away. At luncheon he stared at me with a glazed and terrified
eye, and afterwards, as we were about to walk back to where the
motor was, said, 'What a *wonderful* poem that was of yours in
The Month. I have just been in New York, and *everyone* there
said how *wonderful* it was' (gushingly). I looked at him coldly
and said, 'I am glad you liked it.' With which I turned my back
and walked away.

In addition to everything else, we were given what I think
must have been originally intended for the dog's dinner. And
our host had, with true old-world courtesy, not troubled to be in
at luncheon. Mrs. A is quite insortable.

Goodness!

I miss you very much.

Much love
Edith

---

339. *To Elizabeth Salter*

Renishaw Hall

30 June 1958

Dear Elizabeth,

Yesterday I felt like a cat that had swallowed the canary –
having read the *Sunday Times*, which really did me proud – what

with Mr. Maurice Wiggins' eulogy on the fearful adventure with
those dreadful little quarter-wits on Wednesday on the Granada
T.V.[5] *and* the printing of my relegation of Mr. Alvarez to his
proper place.[6] The other day, I was told a story of a gentleman
who met a lion in a desert. As there was no way of avoiding the
lion, the gentleman knelt down and prayed. Opening his eyes
presently, he saw that the lion seemed to be praying too. 'How
wonderful,' said the gentleman, 'to see a savage animal praying!'
'Shut your trap!' said the lion. 'I'm saying grace!' I hope Mr. A
realises that *I* am only saying grace, too, and that the meal is to
follow – if he is ever tiresome again. . . .

---

340. *To Quentin Stevenson*

Renishaw Hall

16 July 1958

Dearest Quentin,

I should have written ages ago to thank you for the really
beautiful poems and your letter, but have been ill. I was dragged
against my will to be televised at Manchester, being asked questions by idiot school boys and school girls, and got very tired.
On my return here, I woke at about 1 in the morning, to find
myself lying in an absolute lake of blood from my nose! For
some time afterwards, I was fit for nothing. Then I had to write
an extremely long article about poetry for America.[7] Hence my
silence. . . .

I am being pursued by several fresh lunatics – but alas, *not*
suitable for Dr. Leavis! One is particularly trying. She is the
daughter of a nursery maid we had as children, who left when I
was 11. I am now 70, and have never seen her since. The
daughter absolutely *pesters* me. (I have *never* seen *her*.) I think
she is mad – the others are just semi-mad. When my father died,
she wrote and said she would come and live here, in order 'to be
of use'. 'I'll bring my bike,' she said, 'and run messages.' Where

to? To Heaven? She also said she had been 'engaged to Lieutenant Dick Strong who was recommended for the Victoria Cross, but he never got it, as to my great grief he was killed in action.' *Really*!! She must have been reading *Peg's Own Paper*.

I've started writing poetry again, thank God.

> Much love, dear Quentin
> Yours affectionately
> Edith Sitwell

---

341. *To John Lehmann*

Renishaw Hall

26 July 1958

My dear John,

I am so happy that you are going to take my 'At the Cross-Roads'.[8]

How *very* good the Ted Hughes[9] poem is in this number of the *London Magazine*. One has great hopes of him.

I should like to marry Mr. Wain to Miss Jennings.[10] Their offspring – if any – would be something to wonder at. *Why* do you see good in him? The poor creature can't distinguish between the words 'intelligence' and 'intelligibility'.!! And, to me, his book of so-called criticism varies between the control over the English language of the Baboo, and that of a bus-conductor (on a very slow bus!).*

Much love

Edith

* Also, his coiffure, according to his photographs, is a mistake.

In 'Better Late', a review of Triumph of the Muse *by John Heath-Stubbs in the* Spectator *(8 August 1958), the poet Thom Gunn (b. 1929) had expressed admiration for Heath-Stubbs's poetry but noted negatively that it contained explicit reminders of his allegiance to ES and George Barker.*

342. *To Denys Kilham Roberts*

Renishaw Hall

11 August 1958

Dearest Denys,

As you will see from the enclosed cutting, the *Spectator* is starting its nonsense again. The insignificant little man of a minute talent is annoyed, I suppose, because Mr. Heath-Stubbs said in a poem that the muse likes George and me. No doubt he thinks the muse prefers *him*, but if she does, she has shown no sign of it, for she has not visited him even once!

Can individuals insure themselves against libel? If so, I shall do so, and then go for the whole of the Pipsqueakery, lock, stock, and barrel.

How are you and Betty? I do hope not half-drowned. We are up to our eyebrows in rain water here.

Osbert's and my best love to you both,

Yours affectionately
Edith

P.S. *The Spectator* is such a copy-cat, too. The title of Mr. Gunn's rubbish is obviously inspired by a review I gave Mr. A. Alvarez in the *Sunday Times*, headed, 'Better by and by'.

P.P.S. What great poet has *ever* gone in for 'understatement'? As Ben Jonson – whom I cannot but think is a slightly better poet than Mr. Gunn – said, 'Poetry should speak always above a mortal mouth.' Only poets like Alfred Austin[11] and Mr. Gunn produce under-statements, because they cannot do otherwise. They have no vitality.

343. *To the Editor of the* Daily Mirror

c/o Messrs. Macmillan
St Martin's Street
London, W.C.2

9 September 1958

Sir,

In your issue of today you publish the horrible story of George Chrobruk, of Hadylane, Chesterfield, who poked a cat out of a tree, and allowed his two Alsatian dogs to tear it to pieces – a process which lasted for *seven minutes*. This Monster was – fined £3.

When will it be possible for a proper punishment to be inflicted for cruelty? My own feeling is that a revival of the stocks would be the only way in which to put a stop to this. But of course the person so punished would have to be guarded so that he did not suffer the same fate as the helpless creature he had tortured.

I am, Sir,

Yours faithfully
Edith Sitwell

---

344. *To Sacheverell Sitwell*

Renishaw Hall

20 September 1958

My darling Sachie,

I do hope you and Georgia are having a wonderful time in Japan, and that you will get a very wonderful book out of it. (Of that I am sure.) Will you please thank Georgia so much for her postcard and tell her I am writing to her. I am so terribly sorry her hand is still so bad.

I am *so happy* to have those exquisite new poems. It is the greatest of joys to me that you are writing poetry again – what you were born to do. These poems, like the lovely Rose poems, are full of light, seem made of light, which one sees always, just beyond, even when one is in shadow, as in the poem 'Wild Columbine':

> *'In dark corners of the garden,*
> *Like someone of little fortune,*
> *Or whose purse is thin;'*

How *moving* that is.

Nobody has ever written more wonderfully about the flower world. Every texture of petal, and every scent and all the honey are there.

'Wild Columbine' and . . . 'lady's white petticoats for the stitchwort' are, to me, perhaps the most beautiful of all these latest poems. I read them again and again.

I waited till I got Georgia's card to write because now every letter I send seems to get lost, and I wanted to be sure you had arrived. Then, *of course*, Ted Weeks, who is publishing my giant anthology in America,[12] started making my life hell again! He really is *ruthlessly* inconsiderate. What do you suppose he has done now? He has sent me over, in two detachments, 8000 *sheets for me to sign with my name.* Yes, eight thousand! This isn't a joke, it is true. I have had fearful trouble with the Customs, who naturally think, either that the sheets bear invisible tracings of the latest atomic weapons, or else conceal some new way of smuggling cocaine. However they are now rescued, and my life is one long hell signing them. . . .

---

345. *To Elizabeth Salter*

Montegufoni

[November 1958]

Dear Elizabeth,

This is just the shortest of notes, because I have been very ill indeed, though better today. For three days I couldn't keep any food down, and got no sleep at all. The nights were an absolute nightmare of retching, and a kind of mental horror. This was simply brought on by the Income Tax badgering me to send them details I have not got here, and by poor darling Evelyn's plaints. *Entre nous*, she has *all* my Mother's money (which should have been one third of my income), and because I had been left some money (£3,000) by a great aunt, and owing to Evelyn's sister's incessant whining, I gave her £1,000, Evelyn £100, and both fur coats, and this was found out by an aunt from whom I should have inherited another third of my income, I was cut out of that, and so have been left with 1/3 of what I should have had! Some people might have been rather cross, and I am *beginning* to be a *little* impatient.

She has got nearly all my pictures, and now won't come over to England although I pay for *everything*, because she says she would 'have to get so many things'. She really behaves as if she were Garbo or Monroe. (She had £50 out of my prize last year.) That family is a damned nuisance, and of no interest. Oh dear, I had not meant to go in for this long diatribe, but I was so ill yesterday that I thought I was in for a very serious illness, owing to all that. . . .

There is an appalling scandal here – a sort of Mademoiselle de Maupin one. Savonarola – prepare for a shock – is a *girl*. Not only that. She has killed and eaten nine kittens!!! So *naughty*! She has now been accused of transvestism, incest, child-murder and cannibalism. But I won't hear a word against her. She underwent an anatomical investigation by David H!!!

Best love,
Edith

---

346. *To Katherine Anne Porter*

Montegufoni

22 November 1958

My dear Katherine Anne,

. . . You have been a most wonderful friend to my poetry, and now you are a most wonderful friend to this anthology. It was such an exciting book to do, an endless delight to me because it gave me a splendid excuse to spend my whole time reading poetry (in which occupation I hope to spend Eternity, if I ever get to Heaven). (An awful thought struck me at that moment. If I get sent to Hell, I may be condemned throughout Eternity to reading the works of the nasty bumptious little men and women who are now masquerading as poets in England. They are quite intolerable.)

Osbert *may* be going to America in the spring, and does hope to see you. I only wish I was coming. We think it is high time you came to England. We do miss our American friends. The only ones we have seen for ages and ages are Jock and Betsey Whitney, Minnie and Jim Fosburgh, Monroe (who came to Renishaw, to our joy) and Ted and Fritzi Weeks.

I had, however, an experience with two young gentlemen of the Beat Generation.[13] They were very sweet, but I understand are a trifle 'difficile'. Apparently they have been known to recite completely in the nude!

All my gratitude.

Much love from Osbert
and Edith

1959

347. *To Princess Margaret of Hesse*[1]

Montegufoni

10 January 1959

Madam,

The delightful Christmas card which your Royal Highnesses so kindly sent me, gave me such great pleasure, and I should have written to thank you immediately, but some time ago I strained my eyes correcting the proofs of 14th century poems, and this has given me recurrent agonising migraine.

I apologise for my bad handwriting, but it is so freezing here that I can hardly form the letters on the page. It is *so* cold that it is said the wolves are coming down from the mountains. I want the priest's stepmother – a most tiresome and extremely stout woman, to be bound to a tree at some distance from this house, in order to divert their attention. This suggestion has been repeated in the village, and has been received enthusiastically. But there the matter will end, I am afraid.

We are expecting Willie Maugham tomorrow, and Graham Greene[2] soon. The latter will be visiting us on his way to stay for a couple of months in a *leper* colony in the Belgian Congo. (I suppose there is no accounting for tastes.) On hearing that he was preparing to go there, I told him he had better regard us as moral lepers, and come here first in order to get his hand in.

I have not seen Ben and Peter for many months. I miss them so much when I do not.

There is a really *brilliant* new novel just out – *The Unspeakable Skipton* by Pamela Hansford Johnson.[3] It is at once very tragic, and wildly funny. It is founded on the life of the poor, tragic, terrible creature who called himself Baron Corvo.

With my best wishes to your Royal Highnesses for the New Year,

I am,

Madam,

Your humble and obedient servant

Edith Sitwell

---

348. *To Marianne Moore*

Montegufoni

11 January 1959

Dear Marianne,

Nothing ever gave me greater pleasure than your letter. It gave me so much happiness to know that you like that anthology, to know that what I wrote of you in the *Saturday Evening Post* was right.

I have written of you at much greater length, but, to my fury, it was cut in the anthology, because of its length. I have the entire thing somewhere, but probably at Renishaw. In any case I am going to do it again – and do it better. And when I have done so, I shall send it to you. It will come out in a book of essays on poetry, eventually.

I am *deeply* proud that you should have spoken of me, and written of me, for the Johns Hopkins Lectures.[4] I long to see what you have written.

You see, you are one of the only living poets whom I hold in real reverence. And how wonderfully you write *about* poetry. I was just re-reading a passage from your review of Mr. Wallace Stevens. After quoting him as saying, 'Delight lies in flawed words and stubborn sounds', you continue, 'or, as the metaphoric ox apis might say "bull words", "aphonies".'[5] How wonderful that is.

There are several bad blots on my escutcheon in my anthology. I was pestered into including part of 'English Bards and Scotch Reviewers', which has no place in poetry. At last I gave way out of sheer fatigue. I am really fond of Ted Weeks, a very kind, nice man. But he was trumpetting like a baby rogue elephant that has been deprived of its mother. And this wore me down. . . .

---

349. *To Graham Greene*

Montegufoni

21 January 1959

Dear Graham,

Osbert and I are so sad you will not be able to come to Montegufoni before you go to the Congo. We do *hope* you will be able to come on your way back. We shall be here until about the 12th of March.

All my news consists of travellers' tales. The principal being the adventure of Billy McCann. I wonder if you know him. He is a fervent Catholic, and during the war he was the head of the Iberian section of the Ministry of Information, and led the life of one of Mr. Peter Cheney's spy-heroes. He was then the head of Shell-Mex at Rio de Janeiro (if that is how one spells it). He has a mania for *Birds*. On his way through New York to Janeiro, he paid several visits to a pet-shop, and there a macaw was seized with such a romantic admiration for Billy that every time he went into the shop, the bird would faint dead away and fall off its perch. So Billy thought it would be only kind to buy it. This he did, then realised he would never be allowed to take it on the 'plane. He had it drugged, therefore, and made into a large paper parcel, which he nursed on his knee. Unhappily, the bird came to, half way through the flight, and the woman sitting next him said, '*Must* your parcel wriggle and fidget and poke me in the eye?' There is then a gap in the story, which is only resumed on the arrival of the 'plane, where there was a fearful row at the Customs House, everybody accusing everybody else of this and of that, and the bird staring at Billy and fainting and having to be revived.

It should be a warning to us all – but I don't quite know of what. Bon Voyage. Enjoy yourself with the poor lepers.

Love from Osbert
and Edith.

---

350. *To Marianne Moore*

Montegufoni

22 January 1959

Dear Marianne,

Really you are *endlessly* kind and sweet. I am so very grateful to you for sending me this book, to which I look forward avidly. I shall follow its directions. As I have arthritis as well as these headaches, I feel I shall soon become a new person.

I have a strong belief in folk medicine, in herbs, and so forth. And as, to me, the American doctors are the most wonderful of all – in fact, the only doctors – what with that and the other, I feel I shall soon get rid of everything I have wrong with me. The cure (also that with honey) sounds less like medicine than enjoyment.

I have no news. I am trying to finish a book about Elizabeth I, on which I have lost touch. The moment I start writing it, I seem to lose all vitality! Oh dear!

Thank you *so much* again, dear Marianne.

Osbert's and my love to you

Yours affectionately
Edith

---

351. *To Benjamin Britten*

As from
The Sesame Club

6 March 1959

My dearest Ben,

I was so excited and happy to get your letter last night. I should just think I *will* write that poem. I am enthralled at the thought of doing it, and will start on it the moment I recover from the fatigue of my journey to London where I arrive on Friday the 13th. (I am having to be carried in a wheeled chair to and from the boat, as I am very lame from sciatica.) I think the poem should be extremely triumphant and full of pomp, like one of Christopher Smart's paeans – if that is how one spells it: something like this:

> *Praise with the purple trumpet*
> *Praise with the trumpet flower.*

I don't mean that those lines would come in like that, but something of that kind. I think the poem had better be called 'In Praise of Great Men'. I will recite it.[6]. . .

---

352. *To Rebecca West*[7]

Sesame Imperial and Pioneer Club

10 May 1959

Dear Rebecca,

What *enormous* pleasure your postcard gave me. I can assure you that I deeply reciprocate what you said. It is the rarest thing to be able to feel affection *and* great admiration for someone, as I do for you.

I only got the postcard last night (because it had gone to Renishaw, thence to my secretary, and finally to me) – or I should have answered immediately.

I am going to Renishaw on Saturday, but shall be in London again in June, and do hope you and your husband will be able to lunch with me. I'll write well beforehand, as soon as I know exactly what day I am coming up.

> Love
> Edith

I have got fibrositis in my right arm, so do forgive my appalling handwriting.

---

353. *To Hal Lydiard Wilson*

Renishaw Hall

28 August 1959

My dear Hal Wilson,

I can never possibly express how deeply grateful both Osbert and I are for your ineffable kindness. I should have written to you yesterday, when I got your letter, but had to have two teeth out – not my favourite occupation!

The San Francisco Institute must be working wonders. *If only* my poor Osbert was not so terrified of an operation! But the very thought of anyone doing anything to his head simply frightens him out of his wits. Some fool in America got at him and frightened him,[8] and nothing that any expert can say to him does anything to abolish the fright. I cannot understand why one should listen to a fool who knows nothing about the subject, and not to an expert who does.

I shall, of course, keep on about it. And the fact that he is frightened doesn't diminish his great gratitude. One reason for the fright is, I think, that he is terribly tired. He came back from America much worse, having had a very bad fall the night – or rather early morning – before he left, remaining on the floor from 3.30 A.M. until 7.30 or thereabouts, with nobody to pick him up.

I am *quite distracted*, all the time. I only found out when I got your letter that the new edition of *English Eccentrics* had not been sent off to you!! The household here thinks I have second sight!

What happened was this – and it is a very sad reason. Our dear parlour maid, who, excepting for war service, has been with us since she was 17, has a mother living in the village, so crippled with arthritis for the last twenty-odd years that she cannot even feed herself. She is looked after by another daughter. Some time ago, the mother got gall-stones and was in appalling agony. When this happened, the daughter in charge of her – whose life you can imagine, she looks like a ghost – 'fell' out of a window, but was so unhappy as not to kill herself. Our maid had, of course, to go home to look after the mother (we were not here at the time). Before going she forbade the young woman she left in charge to touch any of my books. When she returned, after some weeks, I suppose she simply forgot to send the *Eccentrics*, indeed, only remembered, yesterday, when I asked her. I am sending them off on Monday. I shall also get the American edition, which is much gayer looking, for you and Boodie.

Apropos of the American edition, I am sending for a number of the *Atlantic Monthly* for you, because it contains, I think, the funniest thing Osbert ever wrote about our impossible father.[9] (What is more, the incidents are *true*.) My father got it into his head just after the first war, that he was being watched by an Income Tax Inspector (dressed in a frock coat, top hat, and spats) from the roof of a house opposite ours in Scotland. This phantom watched him through opera glasses every day for three months. So that at last, terrified by this scrutiny, my father migrated to London. Shortly after this, there was, he alleged, a conspiracy to kidnap him. He received a letter from a man living in Hampstead, who said he was an ex-naval-officer, telling my father that he had a portrait of a bygone Sitwell, and that if my father liked to go and see him, and liked the portrait, he would sell it. Obviously this was a plot, so my father took Osbert's old soldier-servant, armed with a revolver, in the taxi with him, with orders to shoot his way into the house, and shoot my father's host, if the visit lasted for more than half an hour without my father signing to him through the window. However, all went well, and everyone escaped unscathed. The host was, it transpired, an ex-captain in the Navy.

I do hope to be in London at the end of next month, and do look forward so much to seeing you and Boodie.

What *do* you mean about 'referring to me as Miss Sitwell'. My name changes with such lightning rapidity that nobody ever knows what I am called from one moment to another.

I am going to the Edinburgh Festival to give a recital in ten days from now. I must say I dread it, as I am very tired.

My love to you and Boodie, and *such deep* gratitude.

Yours affectionately
Edith

354. *To Hal Lydiard Wilson*

Renishaw Hall

25 September 1959

My dear Hal,

Really, I can *never* say how grateful I am to you. Your kindness is beyond anything. I have terrified the chemists out of their wits by threatening reprisals, and am now getting both your and my own way. (Osbert was once described by the *Observer* as 'Sheffield's powerful neighbour'. And I am Osbert's sister, they realise.) It is the most wonderful tonic, and I simply do *not* know what I would have done without it. Especially as I have been receiving really horrible anonymous letters (added to the fresh attack on me in a theatre[10]).

Oh, *how* I laughed about your phrase 'if people want to do themselves in, good luck to them, I say!' Before poor Osbert was so desperately ill, he was really pestered by amorous females – some known to him, some not. One of the latter was a Miss Rose, who had seen him at a recital, and eventually threatened to commit suicide because of his refusal to marry her, or allow her to come and live here. 'His *Deportment*!' she wrote to me. 'His *Manner*! The look in his eyes! The moment his eyes met mine, I knew it was Love at First Sight for both of us! Will you lead me to him?' I said I wouldn't. She wrote to him twice a day, regularly, and would telephone at all hours. At last, I asked our family lawyer, Philip Frere, to deal with her. The dealings went on and on, but at last the lady rang him up, and said she was going to drown herself, but could not make up her mind if she was going to throw herself into the Thames or the Serpentine. 'That, Madam,' said Philip, 'will be purely a matter of your personal choice – unless a Police Officer happens to be present – in which case, it will be his official duty to prevent you. Otherwise, nobody will interfere!'

Before that, there had been a good deal of trouble, as the lady accused her mother of telling Osbert that she was not a respectable woman, and said that she was coming round to Lincoln's Inn to prove to Philip, in person, that she *was*!

I am coming to the Sesame Club on the 5th, and hope to see you and Boodie as soon as I can capture you both. *What is the best time of day for you?* Lunch, or tea or sherry? Dinner isn't possible, because although luncheon is excellent, dinner might be served by avenging angels in the Cities of the Plains – pillars of salt, Dead Sea fruit – I don't know why.

Long after the time when I hope to see you, I shall give a party to celebrate the appearance of my really gigantic anthology. Only three copies of this will be spread by me – one to you and Boodie, one to the Queen Mother, and one to the most magnificent young pianist I have ever heard – Gordon Watson, an Australian.[11] That poor boy was out in the fog in January, walked off the curb, was knocked down by a motor, had both legs broken in multiple places (thank God, it spared his hands and wrists). He has had (I think) *seven* operations, and will not be out of hospital till next month!!

Osbert's very sweet secretary tells me she has written to you about the prescription you, with *such great* kindness, sent. How grateful we are.

I am sad to miss the opening of Mr. Whistler's exhibition, but shall see it later.

With love to you and Boodie, and my deep gratitude.

Yours
Edith

---

355. *To Georgia Sitwell*

The Sesame Club

17 November 1959

My darling Georgia,

Thank you and Sachie *so* much for your kind, sweet, sympathetic letters.

As Elizabeth Salter hinted to you, I had something beyond the slight flu I had. One *couldn't* telephone about this, because it

is a fact that the lowest part of the press – the evening papers,
etc., *pay the telephone exchange to give them any news.*

For months and months and months, the housekeeper and
the housemaids have *urged* and *urged* and *urged* that my bed –
which is completely broken, roped together (it is divided in
two) by rope, and propped up, as far as the broken mattress is
concerned, by a lot of telephone books, and cushions, *must* be
changed, and I *must* be given another one. This was not done,
as, obviously having been born and brought up in the lowest
slum, I *must* want to sleep on a bed you wouldn't find in a
common lodging house. This belief is an inherited one – a
former housekeeper having said, 'Dame Edith *likes* it.'

At about 1 in the morning on Friday week, I, unable to sleep,
was reaching out to find my lamp (which had been put as far
away from me on the table as possible) in order to read. I must
have got too near the edge of this exquisite bed (which I think
must have been one on which Burke and Hare[12] despatched
their victims, hired specially from Madame Tussaud's for me)
when the whole thing gave way, and I was precipitated with my
face against the iron part of the other bed. By the grace of
heaven, I'd knocked over the telephone, in crashing, and the
night porter rang up and said, 'Are you all right?' I said 'No.'

The next thing I remember was finding myself in bed (I
suppose I was knocked unconscious) with the night porter, a
nurse staying in the Club, the housekeeper, and several other
people bending over me. I had, and still have, a bump the size of
a goose's egg on my right eye, and was black and blue down to
the bottom of my neck. It is not the fault of the Club that I was
not blinded. And a *fearful* row is going on – Mr. Murphy – who
has nothing to do with the bedrooms, being furious beyond any
words.

I *could not* let you and Sachie in, because it would have been
a horrible shock for you. It really would. Also I was suffering
from shock, and the only thing to do was to wait till I was
better. I had, therefore, to ask Armando – who didn't want to
do it, to say I had flu. *The Evening Standard* was, I suppose, told
by the telephone exchange, when the night porter rang up

Armando, and started pestering me. But the housekeeper dealt with them. . . .

---

356. *To Parker Tyler*

Sesame Imperial and Pioneer Club

18 November 1959

Dear Mr. Parker Tyler,

Thank you for your letter – which, alas, owing to the fact that I have just had a very bad accident – nobody can think why I was not blinded, but I *was* knocked unconscious – I have mislaid temporarily.

Of course I remember with great pleasure meeting you at Pavlik's. The most accurate impression I can give you of our friendship is to say that it was the same kind of friendship that existed between Michelangelo and Princess Colonna.

I am feeling too ill, really, to write at this time, and the doctor says I am not to write letters (the accident happened on the 8th), but if I can think of anything to say afterwards, I'll write to you. There are several notes I have made about his art which I will send you.

I dislike discussing my personal life, and never do, and for that reason I never write about my personal friendships – I have had friendships with several great men.

Alas, *I* can't give permission for you to see the letters which passed between Pavlik and me. Not that I would mind. But Pavlik left instructions that he did not wish them to be published until fifty years after the last of us died. But why don't you talk about this with Lincoln, who, I believe, is Pavlik's executor, isn't he? . . .

1960

357. *To Princess Margaret of Hesse*

Montegufoni

27 January 1960

Madam,

I should have written to thank your Royal Highnesses for your most kind Christmas card, and should have sent you my new giant anthology long before, but please forgive me, for I have had two very serious accidents, the second (much the worse) being the result of the first, because I came out here long before I was fit to travel, because I was so afraid of alarming my brother Osbert. He is terribly ill – he has Parkinson's disease.

I have now (that I am once more able to prop myself up again) asked my publishers, Messrs. Gollancz, to send your Royal Highnesses my huge anthology. The first volume really *has* got the most wonderful very early religious and secular poems, and perfectly wonderful *Sidney* (who to me is one of the greatest lyric poets in the English language).

The second volume, alas, was interfered with by my very nice American publisher, with the result that the appalling Amy Lowell and the gentleman who wrote a poem called 'Hurt Hawks'[1] found their way in. Still, there is wonderful Yeats, and the only great poem that Hardy ever wrote, 'The Woman I Met', and a great poem by young Robert Lowell, 'The Ghost'. If the volumes do *not* arrive, will you please ask your secretary to let me know.

My brother Osbert and I have several very bad new lunatics. One lady has just written to tell me that I am going to die very soon (which I think quite likely) but that I am going to be *reborn immediately* as an Indian Untouchable. This threw me into a frenzy of rage. I have the greatest possible sympathy with them. But I like my comforts. On the other hand, it would mean, of course, that bores wouldn't speak to one!

Incidentally, my brother Sacheverell, who is one of the kindest people I have ever known, and *never* realises when he has given somebody a lethal blow, was approached, the other night, at his Club, at 10.17 P.M. by the Club Bore. As the clock struck midnight, the Bore (seeing on Sacheverell's face much the same expression, I imagine, as Robinson Crusoe's face bore seeing a sail disappear into the distance) said, 'I hope I am not boring you.' Sacheverell replied, with a gentle martyred sweetness, '*It doesn't matter!*' . . .

---

358. *To Princess Margaret of Hesse*

Montegufoni

17 February 1960

Madam,

I am most grateful to you both for your letter and the enclosed discoveries. How much the letter made me laugh! I think on the whole the Japanese one is the greatest find, but it is hard to choose. I am returning them to you under separate cover, for they are a real treasure.

It is good to know that if I *do* become an untouchable in the next life, Your Royal Highness will not regard me as such!

I consider that I had a *narrow* escape from becoming one in *this* life, for I have just emerged from the iron *grip* of a Leper's Stepmother. This sounds like an instrument of torture in the Tower of London. But that is not so. The Leper, poor soul, is real, *and* in a Leprosarium in England, and his Stepmother is real, too, alas! (I know he is real – he is English but caught the disease in India – because his Stepmother thoughtfully sent me an envelope of a letter he had written – stamped with the Leprosarium's special stamp in addition to the ordinary one. And as I was dressing at the time the post arrived, the envelope got lost in my room, and had to be hunted, as by blood hounds, for fear of infection.)

It is all, really, Graham Greene's fault that I got involved.

Graham Greene came to luncheon with me two days after his return from a Leper Hospital in Belgian East Africa, where he had spent – I think – two months. So leprosy was much in my thoughts. A few days after this, I got *lumbago*, and the *Evening Standard* (which, I think, hires spies on the telephone exchange) rang me up, *pestering* me, asking what was *really* the matter, and enquiring if one of their young ladies could come and see me. 'Better not,' I replied, 'for I have *everything* infectious excepting leprosy.'

They printed this, and I received a furious letter from the Leper's Stepmother, saying I ought to be ashamed, and leprosy is *not* infectious, and I should have caused great *hurt and humiliation* in the two English Leprosariums. Horrified at this – I didn't even know there were any Lepers in England, I wrote to her.

From then on – this was in March – we never looked back, and she took to *writing* to me, literally *every* day – and sometimes twice a day, with a list of grievances – amongst which are the facts that – apart from her stepson being a Leper, her husband, who is 78, suffers from Lolita-trouble (so that, as the police disapprove of this, he is always being *snatched* away from her and incarcerated either in *jail or in a lunatic asylum*) and that *clergymen fly like the wind when they see her*. I bore this from March till November when having been prevented from working for eight months – as I felt obliged to answer and try to help her – my doctor *wrote* to her and said I was under medical care and not allowed to receive letters.

My *brother Osbert* is busy writing fresh occurrences in my father's life – including that in which he saw the phantom of an *Income* Tax Inspector, dressed in a frock coat, top hat and spats, glaring at him through a telescope from the roof of a house. This haunting lasted for three months. My father used to glare back!

With love,

I am,
Madam,
Your Royal Highness's humble and obedient servant
Edith Sitwell

If my *Anthology* does not arrive, will you please ask my secretary to let me know.

---

359. *To Hilda Doolittle ('H.D.')*

Sesame Imperial and Pioneer Club

Easter Saturday [1960]

My dear Hilda,

I should have written ages ago to thank you for a book which has given and is giving me such great pleasure (and oh such nostalgia, for it brings my youth back to me[2]), but I was suddenly called upon to correct the proofs of my Swinburne collection, which has made my eyes pain – the punctuation is almost invisible – *and* to write an essay of 15,000 words as a preface. And there is nothing to say – is there? beyond the fact that at his best he was an incredibly wonderful poet!![3]

How much your book brings all the sights, sounds, passing moments and flying hours – of the time of which you were writing to life. How extraordinary it is that so few writers nowadays seem to have any pulse, or any blood in their veins!

I am so happy to hear of Perdita's new baby, and do wish the child a very happy life.

I know you are going to Perdita, but am not sure when, so send this to Switzerland, in case you are still there. Please give Perdita and John my love when you do go.

With much love and much appreciation, dear Hilda,

Yours affectionately
Edith

---

360. *To Parker Tyler*

Sesame Imperial and Pioneer Club

2 May 1960

Dear Mr. Parker Tyler,

I was so particularly happy to get your letter and hear you are coming to England. I shall be here until the 29th of this month. So do *please* suggest a day for coming to luncheon with me. I look forward so much to seeing you.

This is the shortest of letters – not out of unfriendliness, but because the publishers of my forthcoming Swinburne selection are bellowing like young hippopotami deprived of their mother, for my Preface, which has to be 15,000 words (and I have done just under 4,000!).

You know, probably, that after the hell-upon-earth row Pavlik made with me (largely because I am a close friend of the Duchess of Windsor – a woman whom I have *never even seen*) he magnanimously forgave me, when I was made a Dame, and the correspondence was resumed. But I will have to find his letters, which are at Renishaw, and which I cannot get at, for the moment.

Oh Dear! I wonder whose were the other letters you found. The Italians were a very bad influence.

All my very best wishes.

I look forward so much to seeing you.

Yours very sincerely
Edith Sitwell

---

361. *To Benjamin Britten*

Sesame Imperial and Pioneer Club

14 October 1960

My dearest Ben,

I was so happy to get your letter yesterday, having been in hospital for *two months* has made me feel as if I am dead and in

Purgatory – far from my friends who are in Heaven.

And I couldn't do any work, in spite of the fact that it was my left wrist that was broken (as the paper slipped about like a fish!). How is *your* hand? I do hope completely recovered.

Of course I'll send a poem. I think I shall send you one which hasn't been seen by anyone but those loyal Catholics who take in *The Month* – a really lethal magazine. It is, with the exception of the poem I wrote for you, the best I have done for a long time.[4]

Alas, dear Ben, it won't be possible for Osbert to send a MS, owing to his dreadful illness. (There are moments when I nearly go raving mad, watching it.)

I was so sorry at missing the *Midsummer Night's Dream* at Aldeburgh. I *do* want to hear what you have made of it. It would be wonderful to go to it with you, when it is done here, and I can walk once more. (I have to be dragged along still, as I am still very lame!! The Great Reaper undoubtedly made a dead set at me, but I intend to resist him!)

There was a fearful scene here the other evening, but I missed it, as I was in my room. The Manager, Mr. Murphy, let the drawing-room to the Archers' Club (bows and arrows) for a meeting, but omitted to tell the housekeeper, Mrs. Hampton. A member of the Sesame turned up, unexpectedly, for one night, and as there was no bedroom vacant, Mrs. Hampton turned the drawing-room into a cosy bedroom for her.

The Archers arrived, and were confronted with the lady's nightgown and washing apparatus. They were *furious*, and stormed at Mr. Murphy. All the housemaids were barricaded into their rooms, and Mrs. Hampton had gone to see a friend, so Mr. Murphy had to remove the lady's belongings personally. The Archers continued to storm, and Mr. Murphy mislaid the lady's nightdress. Presently the lady arrived and asked what a crowd of strange men smoking cigars was doing in her bedroom? Also, where was her nightdress? *She* stormed. At this point, one of the interfering old hags who make this place a replica of Hell went into the Wireless Room (which is next to the drawing-room) and started fiddling with the wireless, with the result that all the lights along that passage went out. The fiddler with the wireless refused to leave the Wireless Room as she said she couldn't see in the dark, and the Archers and the night-dress-less lady stormed at her through the door – as they were fearful of what she would do next.

At last Mr Murphy soothed them all by the light of a single candle stuck into an egg-cup. But he and the housekeeper had a fearful row next day.

I am sending you and Peter copies of my anthology of Swinburne.

Much love to you both

Edith

---

362. *To Parker Tyler*

Sesame Imperial and Pioneer Club
24 October 1960

Dear Mr. Parker Tyler,

Thank you so much for your letter, received by me today. I will of course do as you ask. I am a little – more than a little – grieved to realise that some of Pavlik's most deplorably silly friends will figure cheek by jowl with me in the book, and should not have given permission for my letters to appear had I realised this. But having promised you them I won't let you down, and I am *sure* you will use the utmost tact. (Why the poor dear boy had to know such meaningless pieces of mousseline de soie as were certain of his friends, I shall never know. Loneliness, probably, though I should prefer a desert island, personally.) . . .

---

363. *To the Editor of the* Times Literary Supplement

[published 11 November 1960]

Sir,

In the essay on the late D. H. Lawrence's *Lady Chatterley's Lover* the writer says: 'Among the enemies of love whom Lawrence had encountered elsewhere, however, were the bright intellectuals of his day. Though a conspicuous trio of these, the Sitwells, had their headquarters not far away, in the Dukeries, intellectuals were not, by and large, prominent in coalfield society.'[5]

May I point out that although I and my two brothers are not in the slightest interested in the goings-on to be witnessed (though not, so far, in print) on Monkey-Hill, that does not make us 'enemies of love'.

Sir Osbert and I met Mr. Lawrence but once. Mr. Sacheverell Sitwell, as far as I know, never met him.

Edith Sitwell

---

364. *To Georgia Sitwell*

Sesame Imperial and Pioneer Club

[November 1960]

My darling Georgia,

I am longing to see you both. Let me know when.

Thank you so much for your letter, darling. I should have written ages ago, but have been half-murdered by the physiotherapist, *and* there is an electric drill in the house next door, which is attached to my bedroom wall, and goes on all day from 8.30 to 5.30. It is, of course, impossible to work.

Did you see that the *Times Literary Supplement* is trying to drag our names into the Lady Chatterley case, and to pin the idea of the Baronet, practically, on to Osbert – that poor, desperately ill man? I have written the Editor two letters – one for publication, the other private.

I am going to tell everyone that I was told Enid Blyton was a nom-de-plume of D. H. Lawrence. But that must be incorrect, as she is (officially) alive. Yet I can see how the mistake arose. . . .

1961

365. *To Cyril Connolly*

Sesame Imperial and Pioneer Club

19 June 1961

Dear Mr. Connolly,

I can't tell you how delighted and excited I was to receive your parcel on Saturday. I didn't know that *The Mother* was still in existence. And I would rather *you* had it than *anyone*.

Will you and your wife lunch with me here on Wednesday the 28th at 1 o clock, and I will then give you the book, signed and most carefully preserved. I do look forward to seeing you both, and do hope you can come. (I believe Wednesday is your day for London.) I am so grateful to you, also, for sending me the *London Magazine*. Your 'Break-through in Modern Verse' I find enthralling.

My housemaid has lost Mr. Isherwood's[1] address – why is it that they *will* interfere with one's letters. And I did want to ask him to meet you at luncheon. If you have his address I should be so very grateful if you could send it to me on a postcard.

I have been very gravely ill, with temperatures varying from 103 – and over 105, but am recovering, and am in *no sense infectious*. But I should like to strangle the old trout to whom I owe this. There was one day when it was thought I was dying!!

My best wishes to you both

Yours ever
Edith Sitwell

366. *To David Horner*

Flat 42
Greenhill
Hampstead
N.W.3

[4 September 1961]

Dearest David,

If you are in London, do come to a small party here next Thursday (the 7th) at 5:30. Only a very few people: nice Judge Leon[2] whom you met and liked, and his wife, and one of the Public Prosecutors (also very nice). I simply cannot remember his name. He had to prosecute that dreadful boy who kicked another boy to death through his ears. And I got to know him because I was being badgered by dear good Victor Gollancz to make a scene saying the murderer ought not to be punished. The Public Prosecutor heard this and sent me a message saying if I had heard and seen what *he* had heard and seen for days before the murdered boy died, I would not be distressed. He went completely raving mad from the pain, and shrieked the place down. The murderer's mother told someone 'he was always playful'!!!

Do try and come on Thursday.

Best love
Edith

I have got several very bad new lunatics, most of them religious, and some 'just ordinary housewives, who try to write a little'.

367. *To Bryher (Winifred Ellermann)*

Flat 42
Greenhill
Hampstead
N.W.3

29 September 1961

Dearest Bryher,

I am more distressed and shocked than I could possibly say at this dreadful news.[3] (I only saw it this afternoon, because I didn't see the paper in the morning.)

It was a *horrible* shock, and I can think of nothing but your grief, which must be dreadful, and – too – of the loss to poetry. I never dreamed this would happen. I knew dear Hilda was very ill, but with my usual stupid optimism, said to myself, 'with that great vitality which is a part of her work, it will pass, even though she may never be *quite* strong again.'

I should like to strangle the people in whose hotel she had been, and who suddenly treated all the people who had lived there for years in this heartless manner – for I ascribe this illness of Hilda's to the shock they caused her.[4] Poor girl! I wonder to how many other people they have done a lesser form of this illness to.

I feel terrible when I think of what your grief must be. And I do not know *where* you are. So am sending this to Kenwin. I hope my telegram, sent off as soon as I read *The Times*, reached you.

I still *can't* believe it. It seems to me quite untrue, although I know it *is* true.

Shockingly as Richard Aldington behaved, I still am glad that he *did* see her before the end – painful though the interview must have been. Because with all his ill behaviour, he must have known she was a great woman. And his writing was ridiculous beside hers.

Well, we have lost someone you loved, and who was loved by many, and one of the best poets of our time.

You will be too ill from shock and grief to write to me yet, but as soon as you *can*, I shall hope to get news of you. I think of you all the time.

Best love and deepest sympathy

Your devoted
Edith

---

368. *To Hal Lydiard Wilson*

Flat 42
Greenhill
Hampstead
N.W.3

15 October 1961

My dear Hal,

I was so delighted to get your letter yesterday. I am longing to see you and Boodie, and my silence is due to a long history of disasters – really amazing ones.

I have a feeling that you both go away for week-ends, and am wondering and hoping that *Tuesday the 24th at 5.30* would suit you both to come here. If not, I'll suggest another day.

I have only just moved in here, and haven't got a cook yet, excepting one who wanders in unexpectedly, or I would suggest luncheon.

Life has been absolute Hell! Two days after I saw you last, I went to Renishaw, where I collapsed entirely from fatigue and overwork, and was promptly sent to a nursing home in Sheffield kept by nuns, where life was one long purgatory, as, because I am a Catholic, I was never allowed an instant's peace, with priests coming in and ringing bells and saying I must confess before they could give me Holy Communion, and nuns coming in from other institutions to stare at me.

I was there for a month. As soon as I got out, the very day I emerged, owing to the fact that at Renishaw the maids *will* wax the floors (though I have told them not to), I slipped and broke my left wrist in three places. Another month in the Sheffield Hospital. I was then wrapped in blankets (as I couldn't get a sleeve over my bandages) and, escorted by Osbert's secretary, was motored up to that awful club. (What a blessing that Boodie didn't join. The discomfort and the food are now quite unbearable!) Anyhow, I thought, I shall at least resume ordinary life, work, and see my friends. *No*. The very day after I arrived, Longman's Green, who had bought the house next door, fixed an electric drill on to my bedroom wall, and, as well, hammered in a positively insane manner from 8.30 A.M. to 5.30. P.M. *every* day, to such an extent that the housekeeper told me she thought the walls would collapse, and I had ceaseless excruciating ear-ache. However, I was exceedingly rude to them on the telephone.

No sooner had they stopped this rumpus when poor Sachie had to go into Northampton Hospital for a very painful operation. (I can't remember what it is called, but it is the one that women don't get, but that many men do get at middle age.) He was in great pain, but they were very kind to him. No sooner was he out of hospital than Osbert decided to have the operation that everyone, you in especial, urged him to have, and that he dreaded because he thought that an old American lady who had been trying to marry him some years back, had suggested his having it, and he thought she was trying to kill him because he wouldn't marry her.

I knew nothing of the approaching operation until the day before, and I was being televised at the exact moment when the operation was taking place. He is at the Hospital for Nervous Diseases. The T.V. people gave me a violent cold, so that I didn't dare go near Osbert until two days ago, when I had stopped sneezing. The operation was a success, and he is now able to use his right leg. His right hand is still trembling, but the nurse says that will recover. Is that so? I mean, does it take a few days before one can see the results? Anyhow, he *can* walk a little, thank heavens.

I should like to kill the old lady whose amorous proclivities stopped Osbert from having the operation before. (She used to sit beside him at parties in America, and say, 'Tell me that you love me.' Silence. '*Won't* you tell me that you love me?' 'No. Because I don't!')

With love to you and Boodie, and I do hope you will both be able to come on Tuesday the 24th.

Yours affectionately
Edith

1962

369. *To Lady Snow (Pamela Hansford Johnson)*

Flat 42
Greenhill
Hampstead
N.W.3.

[April 1962]

Dearest Pamela,

I am so *horrified* to hear about poor Charles – horrified and furious. I read about it yesterday morning. What a courageous magnificent being he is. I hope the puny creature who attacked him is now feeling his own size. What he needs is a good thrashing. How wonderful of Charles to keep to his date at St. Andrews – with that long journey before him, and then the prospect of an operation, and a month in hospital.[1]

I cannot think what either you or he are going through, but I *do* think of you both all the time, with affection, great respect, and great anger.

This is a very stupid letter, because it is almost impossible to express myself. A because the workmen outside *do* work so that one cannot think. B because the virtuous kind giggling nurse comes into my room and interrupts me as soon as I begin to write. She always bounds in saying, 'I know you hate it, but *it has* to be done.' I never know what. She then turns the Hoover on, because she says what will People think of Her if she doesn't.

My love and *deepest* sympathy and admiration to you both. I'd like to strangle Leavis.

Yours affectionately,
Edith

---

370. *To Richard Church*

Flat 42
Greenhill
Hampstead
N.W.3

27 August 1962

Dear Richard,

How can I express my deep gratitude to you for one of the most wonderful and heartening letters I have ever received. It came at a moment when I was feeling particularly despondent, contemplating the appalling bosh that is being recklessly encouraged in the weekly papers. Mr. Yeats once said to me – after I had been complaining: 'You pay no attention to what an old man like myself says, but you mind – are distressed by – what the writers in the *New Statesman*, etc. say, although you know that the editors have been at the greatest trouble and expense to find the biggest fools alive – and have found them!'

I have always said that you are one of *the only* critics of poetry: and that is the result of your *own* poetry. You are never deceived, but have an all-seeing eye and comprehension, as for your generosity, it is unending.

The printers of *The Outcasts*,[2] or else the woman who corrected the proofs when I was suffering from eye-trouble, kindly re-wrote 'A Girl's Song in Winter', and, by leaving out two words in line 4, dislocated the rhythm of the whole poem, as well as depriving the line in question of sense. It *should* have run thus:

'Young girl, soon the tracing of Time's bird-feet and the bird-feet of snow'

I do *hope* you will find time to write about the book in *Country Life*. How good you have always been to me! This is my new address. I do hope you will both come and lunch with me here, when you are able. If you could just drop me a line. 'Greenhill' is in Prince Arthur Road.

I have been ill for about a year, and am still in a wheeled chair. I do hope you are well.

My love to you both
Edith

---

371. *To Hal Lydiard Wilson and Boodie Wilson*

Flat 42
Greenhill
Hampstead
N.W.3

1 September 1962

My dear Hal and Boodie,

I am just *beginning* to come alive again, after such a series of happenings, and merciless hard work (finishing a book, proof-correcting, etc.) as would, to quote Swift on the subject of his servant Watts' blunders, 'bear a history'. I was really floored by it all, and could, for the time, do nothing but slave, and hope nothing further would happen.

I wonder if you got my letter, telling you that Osbert *had* had the operation you, Hal, so *very* kindly advised. It was done to the right side of his brain, as I said in my letter, and it has – I hardly dare write this – steadied his right hand, and he walks a little better, although, poor darling, he has still this dreadful tendency to fall. How *grateful* I am to you! *Just* as he had gone to Montegufoni to convalesce, David Horner, who had sat up later than Osbert, turned out the lights on his way up to bed,

and promptly fell on the back of his head down a stone staircase. He was not found until next morning, lying at the bottom
of the flight of stairs in a pool of blood, paralysed down the right
side, and unable to speak. He still, poor boy, doesn't make any
sense. He had split his skull in two places. This was some time
ago. He has now thrown a fit.

Coincident with this – (it is only a minor bother, still it *is* a
bother) – my eyes went wrong, I had to go to the oculist, while
trying to finish my proof corrections) *and* the dentist is capturing
my teeth!

Oh dear!

I am sending you (as soon as I can get it done up,) my gigantic
book on Elizabeth the First.[3] It is the size of the telephone book.
It came out two days ago, is already in a second edition, and will
go into a *third* edition next month! So that isn't so dusty!

Having come to life again – more or less – I am having a very
small party here on *Saturday the 8th* at 5.30, and do *hope* you will
both able to come. I long to see you both. I feel rather like
Lazarus, arisen from the Tomb, and meeting all my old valued
friends as for the first time. Greenhill is in Prince Arthur Road,
Hampstead.

My love to you both

> Yours affectionately
> Edith

P.S. A gentleman called Mr. T. Riley seems to be rather cross
about something. He has written to tell me that he only respects
me because of my age, and that I have senile decay and softening of the brain. (I think he exaggerates.) I tore up his letter,
scribbled across one piece, 'Don't be an ass', and returned the
letter, unsigned (so that he can't sell the thing) addressed to
Miss T. Riley.

P.P.S. Please, Boodie, wear your wonderful gold Elizabethan
ornament, if you can come – I do hope you can – to the party.

372. *To Osbert Sitwell*

Flat 42
Greenhill
Hampstead
N.W.3

[September 1962]

My darling,

Thank you so much for your two letters. I miss you more than I could ever say, and do *hope* you will be in London as soon as possible, although heaven knows it is pretty gloomy here, and wouldn't be much fun for you. You didn't say how you are. I do hope you are getting some peace and quiet, and that it is having a good effect.

The *Sunday Express*, today, puts *The Queens and the Hive* as the top of the best sellers. Of this, more later in the letter.

Why I am so very late in writing to you, darling, is that I got acute fibrositis in my right shoulder, *and* writer's cramp. I should have written to you immediately after getting your letter for my centenary,[4] and your telegram, and that is why I didn't.

Two days ago, a message came through from Elstree, saying that George Cukor had flown over from Hollywood and wanted to see me. So he came yesterday. Having gone, straight on arrival into Heywood Hill's, he bought *The Queens* and on going back to the Savoy, opened it straight on to the dedication. Then dear Mr. Coward either telephoned to him or spoke to him (I couldn't make out which) on the subject, which has apparently given him something to think about.

George is still thinking about the possibility of making *Fanfare for Elizabeth* into a film. *If* Hollywood does, they will have to *pay through the nose* – (it all depends on whether the copyright has reverted to me) *and they* will have to do all the work, as nothing would induce me to go to Hollywood again.

A *4th edition* of *The Queens* is at the printer's. It won't be out for some time, but it isn't so dusty that it is being done, as the book was only published just over a fortnight ago!! . . .

373. *To Sir John Gielgud*[5]

Greenhill

3 October 1962

Dear John,

In spite of your letter, which I only received last night, I refuse to have you call me Dame Edith, or to call you Sir John, and I shall still bow to you if we should happen to come across each other at the railway station, say.

I don't know what you mean by talking about our slight acquaintanceship; I thought we were friends.

My long silence was due to the fact that I have been really very ill indeed, for ages. At one time I had to have three nurses taking it in turns. And I have been so despondent and wretched that I never contacted anyone unless they contacted me first.

I had to go all round the United States in a wheeled chair on a recital tour (having slipped two discs). Half dead from fatigue, what with the tour and the immense work involved in this huge book of mine, I have been ill ever since, had two months in hospital in Sheffield, was given disease of the middle ear as soon as I reached London, by the incessant hammering and the noise of an electric drill fastened to the wall of my room; I am still in a wheeled chair, and cannot stand at all without help. (I have to go in this, and in an ambulance to the Festival Hall.)

I hate all this with such violence that, as I say, I haven't contacted anyone unless they contacted me first, as I loathe for them to see me like this. (They will have to, at the concert, as my energetic young nephew, Francis, is digging me out of my retreat for the occasion, also the television people kidnapped me, to my fury, and got me into a kind of Laocoon-like entanglement. My doctor has now charged them like a mad bull.)

I do hope you can come to the supper party *after the concert*, I have just telegraphed to you on the subject. I nearly did so as soon as the concert was arranged, then didn't, because I thought

the concert might bore you, and that it might add to the non-
stop intrusions on your time that must be your fate.,

My affectionate and deep homage to you,

Yours ever,
Edith

What the reporters are like! They are mad with excitement at
the thought of my approaching demise. Kind Sister Farquhar,[6]
my nurse, spends much of her time in throwing them down-
stairs. But one got in the other day, and asked me if I mind the
fact that I must die.

---

*Francis Sitwell, in association with the Park Lane Group, which promotes
young musicians and the performance of twentieth-century music, organised
a hugely successful concert at the Royal Festival Hall on 9 October 1962 in
honour of ES's seventy-fifth birthday. The programme included ES reading
some of her own works; Peter Pears singing 'Canticle III: Still Falls the
Rain'; and Irene Worth and Sebastian Shaw performing* Façade, *with
William Walton conducting.*

374. *To Francis Sitwell*

Flat 42
Greenhill
Hampstead
N.W.3

[10 October 1962]

Darling Francis,

Last night was a wonderful triumph for *you* as well as for me. I
can *never* be grateful enough to you. Indeed the whole family
owes you the greatest gratitude. You are a superb organiser and a
born impresario. Kenneth Clark says there has been nothing
like it in our time. It was a wonderful experience, and I do
thank you with all my heart, my dear boy.

You must be feeling horribly tired. As for me, I didn't get to sleep till past 6. I was so excited. Even the papers have come to heel!

Am [*sic*] longing to see you after our triumph. Friday evening it will be, won't it?

Please give many messages to Mr. Woolf,[7] to whom I shall be writing. I am very grateful to him.

> Very best love
> Your loving
> Edith

The last seen of Carson McCullers, she was sitting forlorn, on the pavement outside the Hall, attended by two porters, her nurse having fled, and no vehicle being in sight. That was at 1.30 A.M.

---

375. *To Benjamin Britten*

> Flat 42
> Greenhill
> Hampstead
> London N.W.3

11 October 1962

Dearest Ben,

It was such a grievous disappointment to *everybody* that you could not come on Tuesday, and *I* missed you more than I can say. It was so sad that you were prevented from coming by illness. I can't bear to think of you being in pain. I am sure that the incessant hard work you do must have helped to bring on this. But then if you did not work, you would not be living, in the sense that a man like you *does* live.

I was so moved by your wonderful telegram, which I shall always treasure.

Peter was sublime in 'Still Falls the Rain'. He always is. What a great artist! I invariably have to wear black spectacles when I hear that work. I never get over it. My words, and the suffering, seem to have been born with the music.

I have not seen you, or Peter (excepting for our meeting on Tuesday), for so long, and have missed you so much. I have been very ill indeed for ages and ages – due partly to fatigue, and also to the breaking open of some discs split years ago, and wrenched and sprained muscles in my back; also arthritis. I had to have three nurses who took it in shifts, at one time; now I have only one. But I am clamped to a wheeled chair, and on the rare occasions I go out, have to do so in an ambulance. An impressive spectacle! I do not tell you this to bore you, but to explain why I have been uncommunicative. The pain was agonising at moments. . . .

---

376. *To Peter Pears*

Flat 42
Greenhill
Hampstead
N.W.3

11 October 1962

Dearest Peter,

You were sublime on Tuesday. But you always are. I am always in danger of bursting, publicly, into tears when I hear your wonderful rendering of 'Still Falls the Rain'. Only you could make, so terribly and yet so beautifully, the suffering from which it sprang, live again in one's being. What a great artist you are!

I hope you can read this letter. My dear Siamese kittens (or one of them) have played with both of my fountains pens, and crossed the nibs!

Wasn't poor Mr. Shaw *appalling*! I've rarely heard anything to touch it. And he thinks he is going all round the country with this ghastly travesty. At one moment, I and my whole family broke down and had hysterics. I have been practising a life-like imitation of Mr. S.'s opening of 'Four in the Morning' – a grating whisper on his vocal cords, growled through a completely shut mouth. And why on earth was he allowed to recite the 'Waltz'! Such a cart-horse with mud thick on his hooves! . . .

All my deep gratitude to you, dear Peter, and my love to you both.

Yours devotedly
Edith

---

377. *To Bertrand Russell*[8]

Flat 42
Greenhill
Hampstead
N.W.3

16 October 1962

Dear Lord Russell,

Your most kind letter pleased me and made me more proud than I can say. It was very good of you to write, and I shall always treasure the letter.

In a few days' time I am going to honour myself by sending you the book containing my 'Three Poems of the Atomic Age' – *not* for you to *read* – you must be plagued by books sent to you – but because it would give me pride to think of it in your possession.

With gratitude and homage

Yours sincerely
Edith Sitwell

378. *To E. M. Forster*

Flat 42
Greenhill
Hampstead
N.W.3

18 October 1962

Dear Morgan,

How very charming it was of you to write about that concert. I do wish you had been there. I didn't let you know about it, because I would hate to bother you. When you are in London, if you aren't too busy, do ring me up and come and have tea or a glass of sherry.

I do hope you are very well. I have been in a wheeled chair now for months and months with arthritis and slipped discs.

I shall be sending you my new poems tomorrow – what is known as 'a slim volume'.

With affectionate homage

Yours ever
Edith

---

379. *To Cecil Beaton*

Flat 42
Greenhill
Hampstead
N.W.3

21 October 1962

Dearest Cecil,

Your letter did touch me *so* much. And I should have written the moment I received it, but have been having absolute hell with writer's cramp and fibrositis in my right arm, so that I could hardly use my hand. I'm still in a sling.

Oh, how your letter sent me back to some of the only happy

moments in my earlier life! The blue dress you spoke of is now covering a cushion in the Paris flat of poor Helen Rootham's sister.

I was so very glad you were able to come to the concert. . . .

The supper party was sheer terror for me, whatever it was for anybody else. My secretary and I had carefully arranged where everybody sat, but (entre nous: don't let on to her that I know) Georgia got on to the placing, altered everything, and put various people next others with whom they are not on speaking terms! However, I haven't heard of any murders.

I am sending you my new poems tomorrow; and, as soon as it arrives from America, my American edition of *The Queens and the Hive*. I want you to have that, rather than the English one, because the 1st edition of the latter isn't to be got.

Thank you *ever* so much for allowing Francis to use that splendid photograph for the programme. Really, there is nobody who can touch you. Do ring up when you have a moment, and come and have a cocktail.

Much love, dear Cecil, from your aged friend of many years

Edith

---

380. *To Cecil Beaton*

Flat 42
Greenhill
Hampstead
N.W.3

19 November 1962

Dearest Cecil,

I should have written to you immediately after Mr. Andrews' Inquisition[9] – we ought to have been wearing the Sanbenito – but I have been nearly badgered to death, by priests, the B.B.C., thwarted Americans who expect me to devote my life to them, and a Wailing Wall of ex-housemaids who want to devote their lives to me. One priest to whom David Horner had kindly given my telephone number (which isn't allowed to be given to anyone), rang me up in my working time to ask if I would give him one of my 'little poems' for his Parish Magazine, and if I would speak to a mothers' meeting. My temper has been like that of a rhinoceros.

I *am* grateful to you, dear Cecil, for what you said of me during the Inquisition, and for *all* the *great* friendship – most truly valued, and over so many years, you have always and unfailingly shown us. Every time I see you, I feel young again. . . .

---

381. *To Noël Coward*

23 November 1962

Dear Mr. Coward,

I cannot tell you what real pleasure it gave me to see you the other day. I enjoyed our talk so much. Please don't forget you have promised to come see me again after you return on the 6th. Do ring me up any time and say you are coming.

It was so good of you to send me your *Collected Short Stories*. There are no short stories written in England in our time that I admire more. I think 'Aunt Tittie', for instance, a real master-piece. I am not a cry-baby, but it brings tears to my eyes every time I read it – and I have read it over and over again. I can't think what you must have gone through, piercing into the hearts of those two forlorn human beings. The end of the story is almost unbearable; you have done more, so quietly, than most writers do by yelling at the tops of their voices.

All the stories have that extraordinary quality of reality, so that, although the endings are perfect endings, one feels the people go on living after the stories, *qua* stories, are finished, and one wants to know what happened to them, beyond the stories.

I am about half way through the book, and shall write again when I am the whole way through it.

I may say that I had a very bad nightmare last night about 'What Mad Pursuit'. I dreamt that George said that I had to go and stay with some people in Hollywood for a rest. But I was saved in the end, because the maid had hidden all my belongings, so I missed the boat train by two minutes!

I am having rather a harassing time with lunatics, because I was televised the other day. One wrote to say I ought to be ashamed of myself, that I have senile decay and softening of the brain – which, oddly enough, made him respect me. Another has written a very long letter about Einstein, telling me I will never get into Space or Time.

I am sending you my *Notebook* on Shakespeare. The cover is so unspeakably appalling that I nearly faint when I contemplate it. I do not know if it is meant as a portrait of me if I turn blue, or if it is supposed to represent a map.

I am not supposed to show any of my autobiography to anyone at all, but I *can't* resist sending you my portrait of Wyndham Lewis, hoping it will make you laugh. I am afraid it is rather a battered copy, but it is the only typescript I have got. Don't bother to return it.

Please do come and see me again very soon.

All best wishes,
yours ever,
Edith Sitwell

382. *To Cecil Beaton*

Flat 42
Greenhill
Hampstead
N.W.3

30 November 1962

Dearest Cecil,

What a lovely luncheon party that was! I did enjoy every minute of it. Thank you so much for asking me. The Queen Mother has a kind of genius for making everyone feel particularly happy. Do come and see me as soon as ever you can.

I was writing, this morning, full details of the time when you saved my life. 'Yes, yes, I choos *kill* you, you know.'[10]

Though I love working, really, it was sad going back to work after your lunch party.

Much love

Yours affectionately
Edith

---

383. *To Maurice Bowra*

Flat 42
Greenhill
Hampstead
London N.W.3

17 December 1962

My dear Maurice,

. . . We missed you more than I can say at the concert and supper party. *You* missed exactly *nothing*. The man who recited part of *Façade* did so *execrably* – so much so that Osbert and Sachie broke down completely at one moment, and I was left sitting in the ceremonial box trying to keep a stiff upper lip, and feeling like that ass of a Boy on the Burning Deck.

The supper party was *hell*, as darling Georgia started interfering and changing the places at the last moment, so that many people were placed next to persons to whom they had not spoken for ten years. Some people appeared to be in what I can most kindly describe as a 'distressed condition'.

Carson McCullers was there. She was accompanied by her nice, good young nurse whose only raison-d'être at the party was that she should keep an eye on Carson, so Georgia carefully removed her and put her at the other side of the table, so that C was free to do anything that came into her head. Poor girl, she has been terribly ill, and it has affected – between ourselves – don't tell anyone this – her brain to some degree, so that she *will* get up suddenly and kiss people and say 'May I touch you.' I thought that she would respect Father Caraman's cloth, so put her next to him. Not a bit of it! She kept on getting up and asking if she could touch him.

However

> 'Even the weariest river
> Winds somewhere safe to sea.'[11]

And the evening did, at last, come to an end.

I have no more news except that I seem to have quelled the most odious female American gossip-writer.[12] She persecuted me without stopping for over three months, on the score that I can't write English. So at last I wrote to her and said, 'It is very good of a person of your education to teach me how to write English. I do not know how to address you. I cannot call you a goose – as the geese saved the Capitol, and no amount of your imbecile cackling would awaken anybody. I cannot call you an ass, as Balaam's constant companion saw and recognised an angel. I can only gather, therefore, that you are one of the vegetable kingdom and that all this sizzling and squeaking of yours is due to the decaying of a vegetable.'

She has held her peace, at last. I *had* meant to write that to the Drama Critic of the *Observer*, who had been very pert. But I thought it was even more satisfactory to send it to her.

All very best wishes for Christmas and the New Year, dear
Maurice
  from

Yours affectionately
Edith

And I need hardly say, any time you *can* lunch here, let me
know.

---

384. *To Benjamin Britten*

Flat 42
Greenhill
Hampstead
London N.W.3

25 December 1962

My dearest Ben,

I am more proud than I can say to have received, from you,
the greatest work that has emerged from the grief, the horror,
and yet the pride and faith, of our time. What a wonderful work
it is! Not in an age has such a work been engendered and born.

I am most *deeply* grateful to you for sending it to me. It is now
on my book case between my 2nd Folio Shakespeare and the
3rd Folio Shakespeare that was lent me by Bryher, the late Sir
John Ellerman's daughter.

To my rage, I missed the performance at Coventry,[13] because
I was having migraine, and so didn't see it announced. *No fog*
would have kept me from the performance here. Consideration
for you, Peter, and the audience did. For many weeks – indeed
months – I have been so crippled that I am clamped to a wheelchair and have to be taken everywhere in an ambulance, and it
would have disturbed the whole solemn atmosphere if, before
the performance began, I had had to be wheeled in. (At my
birthday celebration, this had to happen; but it was not a
solemn occasion, and if I have not the right to disturb myself,
who has, I should like to know!)

I therefore could only listen on the wireless. I am not a person who ever really *cries*. Tears remain at the back of my eyes. On this occasion, the tears were blood. . . .

1963

Francis Sitwell had driven to Tilbury to see off the S.S. Arcadia, *on which ES, accompanied by Elizabeth Salter, was planning a voyage around the world. She suffered a haemorrhage before completing it and had to be flown back to England from Bermuda.*

385. *To Francis Sitwell*

As from Fernleigh Castle Hotel
Rose Bay
Sydney

30 March 1963

Darling Francis,

I am so unhappy and worried to hear from Osbert that your influenza is still going on and on. Do take care of yourself. You ought *never* to have taken that infernal long drive down here. I am afraid it must have made you much worse. It is a hellish thing to have.

All the staff on the ship have been more than kind to me. And I have been undisturbed excepting by a letter from a gentleman who had discovered I am on a voyage and sent me his masterpieces to read and place with a publisher. He got a human-sized flea in his ear.

I have no news, so this is a fearfully dull letter.

Best love
Your loving
Edith

386. *To Evelyn Wiel*

Flat 42
Greenhill
Hampstead
London N.W.3

12 August 1963

My darling,

Thank you so much for your letter, which I have just got. I am so terribly sorry about these awful worries you have been having. I have written straight off to Mr. Musk,[1] asking him to send you through some money.

I don't know exactly how much it will be (he will tell you) because I am only just come out of hospital. I was picked up unconscious, and rushed to hospital, where the doctors thought I was dying, and told Elizabeth that if I survived the night I had a 50–50 chance of surviving. I had very bad pneumonia, and was delirious.

That is why this letter is so short, as I am still very weak. I know Mr. Musk, who is always kindness itself, will see to everything as soon as he can.

Very best love

ever your loving
Edith

---

387. *To Benjamin Britten*

Flat 42
Greenhill
Hampstead
London N.W.3

23 August 1963

My dearest Ben,

Thank you so much for your letter, which I was so happy to get. How much I have missed seeing you and Peter all this long time. *Do* both come and see me when you are not too busy. (I know how people will pester one when one is both ill and busy – so I swear to you I won't add to the number.) I do hope you are better than you were at this time last year.

I am so furious at having missed your public performance all this long age, as I couldn't put my feet to the ground, *and* had to be lifted in and out of a wheeled chair. If I *do* try to put my feet to the ground, I shriek in a most pitiable manner, and have to be carried back to bed!

What a wonder the 'Requiem' must be. By the way, it was I who prepared the Owen poems for publication – the first edition, before Blunden produced his.

It does excite and enthral me, the idea of doing this work for Aldeburgh with Mr. Williamson.[2] You and Peter haven't got the latest edition of *English Eccentrics*, and I shall send you both copies. The Carlyle ménage ought to give us a lot of fun. Nothing ever seemed to go right!

The book you *have* got contains a chapter about the Carlyles, but the new chapter about them and that about George Eliot are much more amusing, I think. I sympathise with Carlyle, who was much bothered by Harriet Martineau, and who said, 'I wish this dear good Harriet would go and be happy somewhere else.'

I do hope you are not too terribly exhausted. I do look forward to seeing you both in the late Autumn.

How right it is that St. Cecilia's Day should be your birthday. With love, my dear Ben, to you and Peter

Yours affectionately
Edith

388. *To the Editor of the* Times Literary Supplement

[published 28 November 1963]

Sir,

I was delighted to see, in your issue of the 14th instant, the very rightminded review of a novel by a Mr. Burroughs (whoever he may be) published by a Mr. John Calder (whoever he may be).[3]

The public canonisation of that insignificant, dirty little book *Lady Chatterley's Lover* was a signal to persons who wish to unload the filth in their minds on the British public.

As the author of *Gold Coast Customs* I can scarcely be accused of shirking reality, but I do not wish to spend the rest of my life with my nose nailed to other people's lavatories.

I prefer Chanel Number 5.

Edith Sitwell, C.L.

1964

383. *To Bryher (Winifred Ellermann)*

Bryher House[1]
20 Keats Grove
Hampstead
London N.W.3

11 September 1964

Dearest Bryher,

I was, and am, so deeply touched that you should remember my birthday at a time when you must have been feeling so wretched. How good you are to me! There is nobody like you. I asked Sister Farquhar to send you a cable at once, because the post gets worse and worse, and takes ages to get anywhere from anywhere.

I think with your wonderful present I shall get flowering shrubs and bulbs for the garden. And the four cats can sit enthroned among them. I hope they will be less naughty *soon*! Leo behaves with great dignity, rather like a hired butler, but the other three remain out all night, teasing a poor squirrel, chasing him up and down trees all night long, and then turning up here at 7 A.M. in time for their breakfast.

I do hope you are able to read this letter. I am having great trouble with my eyes. When I was a child of 14 or so, I caught Egyptian ophthalmia in Sicily, and now, whenever I am tired or extra unwell, it comes back to me, preventing me from spelling properly, etc. And I am utterly exhausted, having just finished that book I was working at.

I think all the time of what you have been going through! To have to watch that suffering! *Why* should it happen to the good on this earth?

I hope to write again in a few days if the poison in my finger has subsided (I have had it now for exactly a year) and if my eyes will allow me to see anything clearly.

I do long to see you.

All my deepest gratitude

Best love
Edith

390. *To Maurice Bowra*

Bryher House
20 Keats Grove
Hampstead
London, N.W.3

6 October 1964

My dear Maurice,

I daren't imagine what you must think of my ingratitude *and* stupidity in not writing before to thank you for *In General and Particular*,[2] which has kept me alive for so long – including the time when the doctors in hospital thought I was dying. It is a wonderful book, full of not only your learning but all your vitality.

The reason I could not write before is because I have been really fearfully ill. The person in the flat above mine (before I moved here), the son of the local undertaker, could not be bothered to turn off his bath-taps – all the water swamped my flat, and at last I was picked up delirious with pneumonia as a result of his behaviour, and was carted off to hospital. There they drove the pneumonia throughout my whole system, landing it, finally, in both my hands, which they poisoned. I can still only just use my right hand a little. Some people might have been rather cross. I was, and am.

As soon as I was able to hold a book, *In General and Particular* has been [*sic*] an unceasing delight to me. I have been able to feel the beauty of poems, hitherto unknown to me, in other languages. There is no one in the least like you for turning learning into delight. How deeply grateful we must all be to you.

I long to see you. Do *please* ring up any time you are going to be in London. I have moved from that awful flat into this very pretty little house, with a garden for my four cats, who rule the neighbourhood, and tease the squirrels. (It is a great offence when they dare to crack nuts.)

I am still bedridden, and in a fearful temper, as my hands still hurt when I write. Please forgive the marks on this paper, as one of the cats has just trampled on it.

With deepest admiration and gratitude,

Yours affectionately
Edith

---

391. *To the Editor of the* Times Literary Supplement

[published 22 October 1964]

Sir,

I would like to thank the reviewer in your issue of the 15th instant, for quoting from Mr. E. S. Turner's *All Heaven in a Rage*[3] what he most rightly calls the appalling passage about a pony on its way to the slaughter-houses of Belgium, who, after a life-time of service was to have a hoof returned to the family of its owners 'as a memento of its fidelity'. I was made sick with horror and grief by this dreadful story.

I dare not think of the physical fate of that work-worn, trusting body, and that betrayed heart. But, as St. John said, 'my Father's house hath many mansions', and I hope that little creature has found its rest there.

As for its master and his family: I only have one hope for them, and that is that they may never know one moment of sleep again – either in this life or in the eternal Hell that so surely awaits them.

Edith Sitwell

392. *To Osbert Sitwell*

Bryher House
20 Keats Grove
Hampstead
London

5 December 1964

My darling,

I do hope my (and the cats') birthday telegram will have arrived in time for tomorrow. I should have written before, but it wasn't neglect or not thinking of you *all* the time that prevented me from doing so. Dr. Sharto[4] (if that is how one spells his name) was having a furious fight with the universal germ I got in that infernal hospital, and on top of it I had acute inflammation of the sheaths of my leg-tendons. The pain was awful.

A very happy birthday, my darling, and I hope with all my heart that you will have less non-stop worries and wretchedness in this coming year. . . .[5]

ACKNOWLEDGEMENTS

In the course of making this selection of letters, I have benefitted from the generosity of a great many persons and institutions. My greatest debt is, of course, to Francis Sitwell, literary executor and heir of the estate of Edith Sitwell, for his constant encouragement and help, and to Susanna Sitwell, for her kindness and hospitality; likewise, I am deeply grateful to Sir Reresby Sitwell and Lady Sitwell. I am further indebted to the following persons: Quentin Bell; Sarah Bradford; Philip Caraman, SJ; Virginia Spencer Carr; Honor Clerk; C. S. L. Davies; Michael De-la-Noy; John Ehrstine; Valerie Eliot; Philip Gardner; Sir John Gielgud; Victoria Glendinning; Deirdre Greene; Samuel Greene; Sarah Greene; Sir Alec Guinness; Sabrina Hilson; Ted Hughes; Bruce Hunter; Stanley Kauffmann; Peter Levi; William and the late Ann Messenger; Gilles Mongeau, SJ; Gerald Morton; Nigel Nicolson; Mitchell Owens; Derek Parker; Robert S. Phillips; Thomas Rand; Alan Samson; Lady Spender; Quentin Stevenson; Michael Suarez, SJ; Nicholas and Margaret Swarbrick; Mr. and Mrs. Howard Usher; Sir Peter Ustinov; Hugo Vickers; Gore Vidal; Lady Walton; Karina Williamson; and Philip Ziegler. I am grateful to dozens of librarians in Britain, America, and Canada, whose courtesies have been beyond counting.

I have received financial assistance from the Andrew W. Mellon Foundation in order to work at the Harry Ransom Humanities Research Center at the University of Texas at Austin, and from the Connaught Fund of the University of Toronto.

Sources

This selection is drawn chiefly from materials at the Harry Ransom

Humanities Research Center, and I am grateful for access to its manuscript collections. I am also grateful to other owners of letters: Stanley Kauffmann, letter 313; Nigel Nicolson, letter 202; Francis Sitwell, letters 1, 261, 374, 385, and 392; Sir Reresby Sitwell, letters 3, 7, 8, 20, 21, 22, 23, 24, and 25; Lady Spender, letters 204, 224, 226, 307, and 315; The Beinecke Library, Yale University, letters 35, 37, 45, 46, 59, 61, 66, 69, 70, 72, 79, 84, 92, 93, 94, 183, 184, 190, 223, 230, 326, 359, 367, and 389; The Bodleian Library, letters 9, 15, 195, 211, and 225; Boston College, letters 316 and 317; Mugar Memorial Library, Boston University, letters 199, 229, and 386; The British Library, letters 2, 4, 5, 6, 11, 17, 18, 29, 54, 58, 64, 73, 97, 105, 112, 116, 117, 140, 153, 173, 208, 218, 219, 220, 232, 246, 248, 253, 257, 260, 263, 280, and 295; The Britten-Pears Library, letters 314, 321, 333, 351, 361, 375, 376, 384, and 387; Cambridge University Library, letters 83 and 85; Duke University Library, letters 283, 284, and 285; Henry W. and Albert A. Berg Collection, The New York Public Library, Astor, Lenox and Tilden Foundations, letters 235 and 325; King's College, Cambridge, letters 96, 126, 180, 258, 269, 290, and 378; Lilly Library, Indiana University, letters 48, 88, and 127; McFarlin Library, University of Tulsa, letters 242, 266, 289, 334, 352, and 365; McMaster University Library, letter 377; The Rosenbach Museum and Library, letters 288, 348, and 350; Rutgers University Libraries, letter 320; St. John's College, Cambridge, letters 78, 80, 81, 86, 87, 148, 302, 379, 380, and 382; University Libraries, University of Iowa, letters 31, 33, 121, 122, 123, 124, 177, 217, 233, 286, 298, 300, 303, and 337; The University Library, University of Sussex, letters 55, 189, and 318; University of Maryland at College Park Libraries, letters 275, 276, 291, and 346; University of Salford letters 149 and 151; Victoria University Library (Toronto), letter 256; Wadham College, Oxford, letters 214, 383, and 390; Washington State University Libraries, letters 118, 174, 268, 279, 293, 296, 319, 336, 338, 339, 342, 345, 353, 354, 368, and 371; York University Library (Toronto), letters 139, 169, 178, 200, 270, 294, 301, and 312. Letters 206 and 304 are reproduced by courtesy of the Director and University Librarian, John Rylands, University Library of Manchester.

Some letters have been drawn from published sources: *Daily Mail*, letter 89; Osbert Sitwell, *Left Hand, Right Hand!*, vol. 4 (1949), letter

155; John Lehmann and Derek Parker, eds., *Edith Sitwell: Selected Letters*, letters 34, 76, 207, 255, 349, and 373; Elizabeth Salter, *Last Years of a Rebel: A Memoir of Edith Sitwell* (London, 1967), letter 381; *Spectator*, letter 297; Edith Sitwell, *Taken Care Of* (London, 1965), letter 156; *The Times*, letter 181; *Times Literary Supplement*, letters 146, 363, 388, and 391.

ABBREVIATIONS

ES   Edith Sitwell (1887–1964)
OS   Osbert Sitwell (1892–1969)
SS   Sacheverell Sitwell (1897–1988)

Bradford   Sarah Bradford, *Sacheverell Sitwell: Splendours and Miseries* (London, 1993).
Elborn   Geoffrey Elborn, *Edith Sitwell: A Biography* (London, 1981).
Fifoot   Richard Fifoot, *A Bibliography of Edith, Osbert, and Sacheverell Sitwell* (rev. ed., London, 1971).
Glendinning Victoria Glendinning, *Edith Sitwell: A Unicorn Among Lions* (London, 1981).
LHRH   Osbert Sitwell, *Left Hand, Right Hand!* 5 vols (London, 1945–50).
Pearson   John Pearson, *Facades: Edith, Osbert, and Sacheverell Sitwell* (London, 1978).
TCO   Edith Sitwell, *Taken Care Of* (London, 1965).

NOTES

Introduction
1. *The Letters of W. B. Yeats*, ed. Alan Wade (New York, 1955), p.776.
2. 'Poetry for Poetry's Sake and Poetry Beyond Poetry', *Horizon* 13 (April 1946), p. 231.
3. 'Edith Sitwell's Steady Growth to Great Poetic Art', review of ES, *Canticle of the Rose*, *New York Herald Tribune* (18 December 1949).
4. Review of Edith Sitwell, *Collected Poems*, *Sunday Times* (28 July 1957).
5. 'Dame Edith Sitwell', *Four Poets on Poetry*, ed. Don Allen Cameron (Baltimore, 1959), p. 76.
6. Both Levertov and Tate are quoted in the *New York Times* (10 December 1964).
7. Edith Sitwell, *Selected Letters*, ed. John Lehmann and Derek Parker (London, 1970).
8. Derek Parker, letter to Richard Greene, August 1988.
9. P. D. James, preface to *The Letters of Dorothy L. Sayers*, ed. Barbara Reynolds (London, 1995), p. xi.

1903
1. Possibly the Sitwells' nurse, Edith Davis.
2. Presumably OS.

1910
1. L. Cranmer-Byng, trans., *A Lute of Jade: Selections from the Classical Poets of China* (London, 1909).
2. Lafcadio Hearn, a well-known translator and authority on Oriental literature.

1911
1. Lady Hanmer, estranged wife of Sir Edward Hanmer, 4th Baronet, was Harriet Frances, eldest sister of Lady Sitwell. Lady Hanmer died on 17 May 1911, and Lady Sitwell herself died five months later on 2 November.
2. Georgiana Mary Thomas, another sister of Lady Sitwell, was the widow of the Rev. Charles Edward Thomas, great-uncle of the 1st Marquess of Willingdon.

1912

1. Helen Rootham, musician and translator, ES's governess from 1903, and subsequent companion. They lived together in London and, with her sister Evelyn Wiel (d. 1963), in Paris, until Rootham's death from cancer in 1938.
2. This is presumably William King, who had been a friend of OS at Eton.
3. In 1909 Sir George had purchased in the name of OS the Castello di Montegufoni in Tuscany, where he spent most of the latter part of his life engaged in a costly project of restoration.
4. An institution in Camberley where Osbert was preparing for the Sandhurst admission examination.
5. This is evidently a prank played on one of the numerous young clergymen who enjoyed Lady (Louisa) Sitwell's hospitality. In *TCO*, p. 62, ES describes her family as 'Lambeth Palace Lounge-Lizards'.
6. Edda Thomas, daughter of Georgiana Thomas.
7. Marion Fox, a novelist to whom Wake introduced ES.
8. Blanche Rose Sitwell, 1842–1929, the youngest sister of ES's grandfather, Sir Reresby Sitwell.

1914

1. ES and her brothers referred to their father by various names, most referring to the colour of his beard. They eventually settled in their preference for 'Ginger', the title given to him by an abusive taxi-driver.
2. John Masefield, OM, 1878–1967, poet and dramatist. He was appointed Poet Laureate in 1930.
3. Wilfrid Gibson, 1878–1962, poet.
4. Elkin Mathews, 1851–1921, publisher.
5. This refers to chapter 25 of Butler's novel in which a letter of religious exhortation is written by Christina Pontifex and delivered to her son at her death many years later.
6. OS went to France in December 1914 as a lieutenant in the Grenadier Guards.
7. Inez Chandos-Pole (née Arent), d. 1941, of Radbourne Hall, Derbyshire, married to a cousin of the Sitwells.
8. Aunt Georgie. See note 2 (1911).
9. An autobiographical work by August Strindberg.
10. Constance Lane of Nettleden House, Hemel Hempstead. ES sent her drafts of her early poems.

1915

1. Lady Mildred Cooke (née Denison), younger sister of Lady Ida Sitwell. Lady Ida had been released from Holloway Prison.
2. Lady Sybil Codrington (née Denison), Lady Ida's eldest sister.
3. The Countess of Londesborough, née Lady Edith Somerset, mother of Lady Ida, died on 15 May 1915.
4. *The Mother*, ES's first collection of poetry, was published on 14 October

1915. The *TLS* gave the volume two short notices: the first (4 November) remarked on her 'glowing fancy'; and the second (9 December) observed: 'Miss Sitwell does not describe, she lives in her verse. This very little therefore points a long way.'
5. The best known composition of the poet Christopher Smart (1722–71).
6. A collection of Bottomley's verse published in 1907.

1916
1. Probably Constance Sitwell (née Chetwynd-Talbot), who had married Brigadier William Sitwell, a cousin of ES, in 1912. She eventually became a memoirist and was despised by ES.
2. Probably Sir George Sitwell.
3. Major A. B. Brockwell, who had served as Sacheverell's tutor from 1906, became the model for 'Colonel Fantock' in one of ES's best-known poems.
4. Richard Jennings, 1881–1952, literary editor of the *Daily Mirror*, where ES's first published poems appeared in 1913.
5. *Twentieth Century Harlequinade*, a collection of poems by ES and OS, was published on 7 June 1916.

1917
1. *Clowns' Houses* was published by B. H. Blackwell in 1918.
2. The anthology edited by ES, which appeared in six 'Cycles' from 1916 to 1921.
3. Robert Baldwin Ross, 1869–1918, literary executor of Oscar Wilde, and a supporter of younger poets including Sassoon.
4. H. G. Wells had written extensively on war aims during this time, including an article entitled 'A Reasonable Man's Peace', which appeared in the *Daily News & Leader* on 14 August 1917.
5. *Twentieth Century Harlequinade*.
6. Iris Tree, 1897–1968, poet and actress, the daughter of the actor Sir Herbert Tree, and the niece of Max Beerbohm. Some of her writings were published in *Wheels*.

1919
1. Robert Nichols, 1893–1944, soldier, poet and academic.
2. Vachel Lindsay, 1879–1931, American poet who experimented with syncopated rhythms. His best known work is 'The Congo'.
3. Thomas Stearns Eliot, 1888–1965, poet, playwright, critic and publisher. ES had met both Eliot and Nichols in December 1917 at a reading hosted by Lady Colefax.
4. In the election of 1918, OS had been defeated as Liberal candidate in the Scarborough constituency his father had represented as a Conservative from 1885–86 and 1892–95. OS had a far greater interest in politics than did ES or SS, and would later become involved in efforts to settle the General Strike of 1926.
5. Alida Klementaski, a Polish woman who operated the Poetry Bookshop

while its founder, Harold Monro, was at the Front. She and Monro married in 1920.

6. Charlotte Mew, 1869–1928, poet and short story writer. Although her work was highly regarded, she lived in poverty and, following the death of a sister, committed suicide by drinking Lysol.

7. Madeleine Caron Rock, author of two volumes of poetry categorised as 'mystical'.

8. OS's then residence in Chelsea.

9. Nichols's second volume of poems, published in 1917.

10. Susan Owen, mother of the poet Wilfred Owen, who had been killed in action on 4 November 1918.

11. The Fourth Cycle of *Wheels* appeared on 2 November 1919, containing the first substantial publication of poems by Wilfred Owen. ES later collaborated unhappily with Siegfried Sassoon on an edition.

1920

1. William Kean Seymour, 1887–1975, poet, novelist and biographer. A contributor to *Wheels*, he included poems by ES in anthologies he edited in the early 1920s.

1921

1. Leonard Moore, of the firm Christy & Moore, was a literary agent now remembered chiefly for his representation of George Orwell.

2. The Fifth Cycle of *Wheels* had been published by Leonard Parsons in November 1920. The sixth cycle was published by C. W. Daniel in November 1921. Earlier Cycles had been published by B. H. Blackwell.

3. Mary Lillian, wife of the first Viscount Rothermere and daughter of George Wade Share, d. 1937.

1922

1. One of several reciters associated with the Anglo-French Poetry Society.

2. A literary journal set up at Eton by Howard and his friend Harold Acton.

3. Frank Dobson, 1888–1963, painter and sculptor. One of his most admired works is a bust of OS.

4. Harold Acton, 1904–94, author and aesthete, collaborated with Howard on various artistic and literary projects at Eton.

5. Marie Adelaide Belloc Lowndes, 1868–1947, novelist. She was the sister of the author and controversialist, Hilaire Belloc.

6. Bennett read the play *Roasted Angels* by H. Hamar. Although he had not heard of Hamar, he expressed some regard for his skills as a writer, but observed that the play lacked dramatic interest.

7. *Bucolic Comedies* was published on 24 April 1923, bearing a dedication to Bennett.

1923

1. Lady ('Amabel') Williams-Ellis (née Strachey), author and journalist. During 1922–23 she was literary editor of the *Spectator*.

2. Edward Shanks, 1892–1953, poet and critic closely associated with Squire.
3. Alfred Noyes, 1880–1958, poet and critic. He held traditionalist and patriotic views, and generally disapproved of modernism in literature. For an account of this debate, see Elborn, pp. 32–3.
4. Louis Untermeyer, 1885–1977, American poet and anthologist.
5. Jean Starr Untermeyer, 1886–1970, poet.
6. Gerald Cumberland, 1879–1926, poet and critic. He wrote in *Vogue* (July 1923) of a performance of *Façade* at the Aeolian Hall on 12 June: 'To this hour I am by no means certain what some of her poems mean, but if I do not understand their beauty, I divine it, and for that reason am all the more attracted, drawn, seduced.'
7. Edward Marsh, 1872–1953, anthologist, critic and civil servant. From 1912 to 1921 he edited the influential *Georgian Poetry* anthologies.
8. G. K. Chesterton, 1874–1936, poet, novelist and religious writer.
9. David Garnett, 1892–1981, novelist and editor. He was a member of the Bloomsbury circle.
10. Eleanor (Nellie) Wallace, 1870–1948, music-hall actress who specialised in female grotesques. She was enormously popular, and she continued her stage career until 1945.
11. The Three Fratellini were a circus act composed of Gustavo, Alberto and Francesco Fratellini. They toured extensively and were invited to become affiliates of the Comédie-Française in 1922.
12. Conrad Aiken, 1889–1993, American poet and novelist.

1924
1. The passage is quoted from Coleridge's lecture, 'Shakespeare's Judgement Equal to his Genius'.
2. Robert Graves, 1895–1985, poet and novelist. At this time, ES regarded Graves and his first wife Nancy as her close friends.
3. Sydney Schiff, 1868–1944, novelist, translator and patron of the arts. He published under the pseudonym Stephen Hudson.
4. A novel by Schiff published in 1923.
5. Sir Henry Head, 1861–1940, a neurologist who held radical opinions. His work was of considerable interest within the Bloomsbury circle.
6. Violet Schiff (née Beddington), 1876–1962, singer and musician. She married Sydney Schiff in 1911.
7. Virginia Woolf, 1882–1941, novelist. ES had met Woolf in 1918, and the two maintained a close friendship through the 1920s.
8. Weston Hall, near Towcester in Northamptonshire. This house had been obtained by Sir George Sitwell from the estate of his aunt Frederica Thomas (d. 1923). It became the permanent home of SS in 1927. ES sometimes refers to it, incorrectly, as Weston Manor.
9. *Poetic Unreason and Other Studies* was released in February 1925.
10. *The Thirteenth Caesar and Other Poems* was published in October 1924.
11. A 1681 reprint of the fourth edition of Glanvill's *Philosophical Considerations Touching Witches and Witchcraft* (London, 1666).

1925

1. *The Best Poems of 1923*, ed. L. A. G. Strong (London, 1923).
2. George Antheil, 1900–59, American composer. His vigorous piano playing had caused a riot at the Champs-Élysées on 4 October 1923, following which he was celebrated by Pound, Joyce, Yeats, Picasso and others.
3. Ezra Pound, 1885–1972, American poet, critic and translator.
4. Raymond Mortimer, 1895–1980, journalist and author.
5. Duncan Grant, 1885–1978, painter associated with the Bloomsbury circle.
6. 'Sitwell Edith Sitwell', a word portrait subsequently published in *Composition as Explanation* (London, 1926).
7. Richard Wyndham, 1896–1948, landscape and figure painter. He was a close friend of OS and SS.
8. See 'Sweet Tail (Gypsies)', *Geography and Plays* (Boston, 1922).
9. Alice B. Toklas, 1877–1967, author. She lived with Stein for many years as spouse.
10. 'The Work of Gertrude Stein', *Vogue*, 66: 7 (October 1925).
11. Dorothy Todd, editor of British *Vogue* from 1922 to 1926. She commissioned articles from various prominent British writers, including ES and Virginia Woolf.
12. Alice Keppel, d. 1947, sometime mistress of Edward VII, and mother of Violet Trefusis. The Keppels owned a villa outside Florence and were often visited by Mrs Hwfa Williams, who had also been a prominent Edwardian hostess. Mrs Keppel was also the great-grandmother of Mrs Camilla Parker-Bowles.
13. *Who Killed Cock Robin?* was a satire by OS against the 'Squirearchy'. It was published in December 1921.
14. A reference to the family of Liberal politician Cecil Harmsworth, 1868–1948, later 1st Baron Harmsworth.
15. Ruby Mildred Ayres, 1883–1955, author of serial fiction.
16. Henry de Vere Stacpoole, 1863–1951, physician, author and publicist.
17. Judge Llewellyn Archer Atherley-Jones, 1851–1929, politician, judge and author.
18. Allanah Harper (Statlender), b. 1904, author and editor.
19. Nancy Cunard, 1896–1965, poet. Cunard had been involved with the founding of *Wheels*, but ES eventually came to resent her for having won the affection of the painter Alvaro Guevara, with whom she herself had been in love. See Glendinning, pp. 60–1 and 107.

1926

1. 'A Description of the Fifteenth of November', Stein's word portrait of Eliot, was published in the *New Criterion* (January 1926).
2. This party, which introduced Gertrude Stein to writers and artists in London, was described tartly by Virginia Woolf in a letter to Vanessa Bell on 2 June: 'We were at a party at Edith Sitwell's last night, where a good deal of misery was endured. Jews swarmed. It was in honour of Miss

Gertrude Stein who was throned on a broken settee (all Edith's furniture is derelict, to make up for which she is stuck about with jewels like a drowned mer-maiden). This resolute old lady inflicted great damage on all the youth.' See *The Letters of Virginia Woolf*, ed. Nigel Nicolson and J. Trautmann, vol. 3, pp. 269–70.

3. 'Accents in Alsace' had appeared in Stein's *Geography and Plays*. Sitwell's variation on it was given the title 'Jodelling Song', and incorporated into *Façade*.

4. J. R. Ackerley, 1896–1967, author and journalist. He was literary editor of the *Listener* from 1935 to 1959.

5. *Composition as Explanation* had been accepted for publication.

6. Thomas Driberg, later Baron Bradwell, 1905–76, poet, journalist, broadcaster and politician.

7. *Exalt the Eglantine*, a collection of poems by SS, was published in September 1926.

8. Serge Diaghilev (1872–1929), director of the Ballets Russes. Through the autumn of 1926, SS was collaborating with Diaghilev on a ballet, *The Triumph of Neptune*, which was performed on 3 December at the Lyceum in London. The music for the ballet was composed by Gerald [Lord] Berners, 1883–1950, who was also a painter and poet and had a distinguished career as a diplomat.

9. OS had mischievously advised the press that the Sitwells would be reading their poetry on the radio because the stage was in a 'deplorable' state owing to the social pretensions of actors, especially their desire to play golf. For an account of the reactions of various theatrical personalities, see Pearson, pp. 208–10.

10. *All Summer in a Day: An Autobiographical Fantasia* was published on 21 October 1926.

11. Arthur Waley, 1889–1966, translator and orientalist, a close friend of all three Sitwells, but especially of SS.

12. The fourth chapter of the book is a fictionalised description of Miss Emily Lloyd, a Scarborough friend of Lady (Louisa) Sitwell. Miss Lloyd, who had led a colourful and mysterious life, had befriended the Sitwell children and entertained them with her reminiscences.

13. *Dr. Donne and Gargantua, Canto the Third* was published in late 1926.

1927

1. Widgey R. Newman, director of two eight-minute 'phonofilms' of ES reading poems by herself and OS. The films, made at Clapham Studios, are now lost.

2. Madge Garland, later Lady Ashton, 1900–90, fashion writer.

3. Presumably, Baba Beaton, 1912–73, one of the photographer's sisters. It is possible, however, that ES is referring to Lady Alexandra ('Baba') Metcalfe, Lord Curzon's youngest daughter, a close friend of SS and Georgia Sitwell.

4. *Rustic Elegies* was published on 10 March 1927.

5. Arthur Waugh, 1866–1943, biographer, critic and publisher. He was the father of the novelists Alec and Evelyn Waugh.
6. *Rustic Elegies* (London, 1927). The book received a number of anonymous notices and it is not certain which of these may have been written by Waugh.
7. Sir Edmund Gosse, 1845–1928, poet and critic. ES described her friendship with him in *TCO*, pp. 95–8.
8. *The Triumph of Neptune* opened in Paris on 27 June.
9. Sacheverell Reresby Sitwell was born on 15 April 1927.
10. See Edmund Gosse, 'Miss Sitwell's Poems', *Leaves and Fruit* (London, 1927), pp. 255–61. He rejects complaints against her synaesthetic imagery, and remarks, 'She is full of talent and ambition . . . I would have her aim relentlessly at being less funny and more human.'
11. Edward Morgan Forster, 1879–1970, novelist.
12. Lancelot Sieveking, 1896–1972, author, producer and nonsense poet.
13. This corrects Glendinning, p. 113, in which it is suggested that the drawing was intended for a volume of children's verse.

1928

1. Lady Albertina Treowen (née Denison), d. 1929, the half-sister of Lady Ida's father, the first Earl of Londesborough.
2. Edith Powell, OS's beloved housekeeper, is described in *LHRH, passim*. She suffered from breast cancer and died in 1930.
3. Armando Child was one of several physicians regularly consulted by ES and OS.
4. Evidently a reference to the death in mid-February of an elderly friend of Stein's, Mildred Aldrich. Another of her close friends, the painter Juan Gris, had died on 11 May 1927.
5. Emanuel Swedenborg, 1688–1772, Swedish theologian and mystic.
6. Desmond MacCarthy, 1878–1952, biographer and critic.

1929

1. Blanche Rose Sitwell, died 25 February 1929.
2. John Robins.
3. Her estate was valued at £11,000.
4. Schoura Tchelitchew, the painter's sister.
5. *Alexander Pope*, a biography, was published on 7 March 1930.
6. Allen Tanner, pianist, Pavel Tchelitchew's lover.
7. Stephen Tennant, 1906–87, artist and socialite. For a time he was Siegfried Sassoon's lover.
8. Tennant's mother had died the preceding November, and he was himself in poor health.
9. E. G. Twitchett, in a review of *Gold Coast Customs*, *London Mercury*, XX: 116 (June 1929), claimed that 'her poems are still clogged by masses of exhausted perceptions which have been galvanised into unnatural activity.' John Squire, editor of the magazine, published ES's

comments in XX: 118 (August 1929).
10. Possibly the 'paying guest' who lived with Bowen.
11. Sir Gerald Codrington, father of Veronica Gilliat, a cousin of ES, died 3 November 1929.

1930
1. See Glendinning, pp. 135–7, and Elborn, pp. 73–7.
2. Lady Fitzherbert, American wife (divorced 1930) of Sir Hugo Fitzherbert.
3. Gabriel Wells, 1862–1946, prominent bibliophile and book-collector.
4. Thomas Wise, 1859–1937, book collector. In 1934, he was revealed as a forger.
5. ES was attempting to sell on Bowen's behalf the manuscript of one of Ford Madox Ford's novels.
6. See Letter 116.
7. Harriet Cohen, 1895–1967, pianist.
8. Geoffrey Gorer, 1905–85, anthropologist and author. He was a friend of Tchelitchew's from the mid-1920s. Along with his mother, Rée Gorer, and his brother Peter, he became part of ES's intimate circle.
9. Phyllis Vallance (née Reid), wife of Aylmer Vallance, a journalist.
10. Possibly Paul Draper, a singer and friend of Bowen's.
11. Christabel MacLaren (née McNaghten), 1890–1974, memoirist, a close friend of OS. Her husband became 2nd Baron Aberconway in 1934.
12. Edmund Blunden, 1896–1974, poet and critic. In 1930 he was working as literary and assistant editor of the *Nation and Athenaeum*.
13. ES's first *Collected Poems* was first published on 5 June 1930.
14. 'Miss Sitwell's Work', review of *Collected Poems* by Edith Sitwell, *Fortnightly Review*, n.s. 128 (August 1930), 271–2. Blunden warmly praises her 'particularity of genius and workmanship'.
15. Schiff took over the translation of Proust on the death of Scott Moncrieff. *Le Temps Retrouvé* was published in 1931.
16. Bryan Guinness, later 2nd Baron Moyne, 1905–92, barrister and poet; a member of the brewing family. Diana Guinness (née Freeman-Mitford) was his first wife.

1931
1. *The Pleasures of Poetry* was a three volume critical anthology edited by ES. The first volume, in which the misquotation occurred on p. 45 of the Introduction, was published on 1 November 1930. The second volume was published in May 1931, and the third in October 1932.
2. Bruce Richmond, 1871–1964, journalist and lawyer, knighted in 1935. He was a member of *The Times* editorial staff, 1899–1938.
3. Edith Woods, an old retainer of Lady Sitwell, had been a beneficiary under the will of Florence Sitwell, who had died on 30 December 1930.
4. Blanche Sitwell.
5. *Far from my Home*, a collection of stories by SS, was published on 14 May 1931.

6. Henry Ainley, 1879–1945, actor and theatrical manager.
7. Thomas Balston, 1883–1967, ES's editor at Messrs Duckworth.
8. *Bath* was published in May 1932.
9. John Fergusson Roxburgh, 1888–1954, founding headmaster of Stowe School, located a short distance from Weston, across the Buckinghamshire border.
10. Andrew Clark, 1898–1979, soldier, barrister and poet.
11. John Collier, 1901–80, novelist. His first notable success was the satire *His Monkey Wife; or, Married to a Chimp* (London, 1930).
12. Edgar Degas, 1834–1917, Impressionist painter.
13. Paul Cézanne, 1839–1906, Impressionist painter.
14. Henri Rousseau (called Le Douanier), 1844–1910, primitive painter.
15. Georges Rouault, 1871–1958, expressionist painter.
16. Henri Matisse, 1869–1954, French painter, sculptor and graphic artist.
17. A list of successful contemporary writers whom ES considered middle-brow: Sir Hugh Walpole, 1884–1941; W. Somerset Maugham, 1874–1965; Noël Coward, 1899–1973; John Galsworthy, 1867–1933; Clemence Dane (Winifred Ashton), 1891–1965; Victoria (Vita) Sackville-West, 1892–1962.

1932
1. *Canons of Giant Art*, generally regarded as SS's finest volume of poetry, was published on 25 May 1933.
2. Evelyn Wiel, the sister of Helen Rootham. See note 12 below.
3. See *The Scandals and Credulities of John Aubrey*, ed. John Collier (London, 1931).
4. Harold Monro died on 16 March 1932.
5. Presumably Vivienne Eliot, 1888–1947, first wife of T. S. Eliot.
6. Georgie Doble (née Hyde), b. 1875, Nova-Scotian-born wife of the Montreal banker Arthur Doble and mother of Georgia Sitwell.
7. *Nineteenth-Century Poetry* (London, 1932).
8. George William Russell ('A.E.'), 1867–1935, Irish poet, critic and cultural writer.
9. Not listed in Fifoot.
10. Dame Nellie Melba (Helen Porter Anderson), 1861–1931, Australian soprano.
11. A reference to her divorce settlement.
12. ES left her flat at Pembridge Mansions, which had been her home since 1914, in August 1932. She moved to Paris, where she and Rootham lived with Evelyn Wiel. ES moved back to England in September 1939.
13. The house in Long Itchington, Warwickshire, had been occupied by Florence Sitwell. ES had hoped to move there, but was disappointed by the will, which provided for Sister Edith Woods to be the occupant. The house was sold in 1948.

1933
1. *English Eccentrics* was published in May 1933.
2. *Miracle on Sinai* was published in October 1933.
3. D. H. Lawrence, 1885–1930, was believed to have modelled aspects of the character of Clifford Chatterley in *Lady Chatterley's Lover* (1928) on Osbert Sitwell.
4. The Dowager Duchess of Beaufort, d. 1945, widow of the 9th Duke. Lady Ida's maternal grandfather had been the 7th Duke of Beaufort.
5. Duchess of Beaufort, wife of the 10th Duke, elder daughter of the 1st Marquess of Cambridge.
6. Lord Gerald Wellesley, later 7th Duke of Wellington, 1885–1972, diplomat and author. He was married to the poet Dorothy Wellesley, 1889–1956, who was a close friend of Yeats.
7. Violet Gordon Woodhouse (née Gwynne), 1872–1948, harpsichordist, clavichordist and pianist. She was largely responsible for the revival of interest in older keyboard instruments. She was a close friend of SS and Georgia Sitwell.
8. William Henry Davies, 1871–1940, Welsh poet who had lived in America as a tramp.
9. Edward James, b. 1907, poet and art patron. Although a friend of Tchelitchew's, he disliked Ford and his writing intensely. He advised ES that Ford's novel, about which she wanted to be objective, was indecent. She could not comprehend the sexual practices described in it and asked him to explain them to her, but he refused on the grounds that she would be shocked. See Edward James, *Swans Reflecting Elephants* (London, 1982), pp. 169–71.
10. Richard de la Mare, 1901–86, publisher. He was the son of the poet Walter de la Mare, and had become a director at Faber & Faber in 1929.
11. On 24 January 1934 Sir Henry Newbolt presented ES with the Royal Society of Literature's medal for poetry.
12. Artur Rubinstein, 1887–1982, Polish-born pianist.
13. Philip Henderson, b. 1906, critic and biographer.
14. Possibly Margaret Epstein (née Dunlop), d. 1947, wife of the sculptor Jacob Epstein.
15. William Babington Maxwell, d. 1938, novelist and sometime chairman of the Society of Authors. He had been a friend of Lady Ida's parents.
16. Frank Raymond Leavis, 1895–1978, literary critic, Fellow of Downing College, Cambridge, 1936–62, founder and editor of the journal *Scrutiny*. He believed that the Sitwells were chiefly seekers of publicity, rather than significant writers.
17. Geoffrey Grigson, 1905–85, poet, editor and critic. As editor of the 1930s journal *New Verse*, he promoted left-wing poets, especially W. H. Auden. As a reviewer and critic, he was notoriously intemperate. His judgements of ES, her brothers and, later, Dylan Thomas were extremely negative.
18. See 'A Word to the "Poetry Contractors"', *Morning Post* (15 January 1934).

19. Stephen Spender, 1909–95, poet and critic. An admirer of the Sitwells in the 1920s, Spender tended to be critical of them in the 1930s. Later he raised his estimate, especially of ES, with whom he developed a friendship in the 1940s.
20. Sir George Sitwell, see letter 140.
21. 'Her Ladyship', Lady Ida Sitwell.
22. Lascelles Abercrombie, 1881–1938, poet and academic. He had been associated with the Georgian movement.
23. Rée Gorer, d. 1954?, mother of Geoffrey and Peter Gorer.
24. Catherine of Braganza, the wife of Charles II, had been forced to include Lady Castlemaine, one of his mistresses, among her Ladies of the Bedchamber.
25. Edith Olivier, d. 1948, biographer and diarist.

1934
1. Sir Gerald du Maurier, 1873–1934, actor and theatrical manager.
2. *Victoria of England*, a biography, was published on 13 February 1936.
3. Presumably this mocks the expatriates' accent and means 'made mad'.
4. Charles Henri Ford.
5. Jean Cocteau, 1889–1963, French poet, dramatist and novelist. The play ES attended was *La Machine infernale* (1934).
6. Queenie Dorothy Leavis, 1906–81, literary critic.
7. Hannen Swaffer, 1879–1962, journalist and drama critic.
8. Harold Acton was living in Peking in 1934 when OS and David Horner visited the city.
9. Mr Haddock, a manager at Coutts & Co.
10. Presumably Leavis, whom ES regarded as an enemy of art.
11. Mrs Ronnie Greville, d. 1942, a prominent hostess who had often entertained Edward VII. She became a close friend of OS, who referred to her affectionately as 'Aunt Maggie'. She eventually left him £10,000 in her will.

1935
1. Ronald Bottrall, 1906–89, poet, critic and academic. His early work was admired by F. R. Leavis.
2. Stephen Phillips, *Paolo and Francesca* (London, 1900), p. 120.
3. Ronald Bottrall, *Festivals of Fire* (London, 1934).
4. See 'Four New Poets', *London Mercury*, 33 (February 1936), pp. 383–90. In this article ES reviews the work of Bottrall, William Empson, Dylan Thomas and Archibald MacLeish.
5. See Ronald Bottrall, 'XXX Cantos of Ezra Pound', *Scrutiny*, 2: 2 (September 1933), pp. 112–22.
6. Herbert Read, 1893–1968, poet and critic of art and literature.
7. Fifoot does not record the publication of a pamphlet under this title.
8. Walter Greenwood, 1903–74, novelist noted for his portrayal of the life of the working class in the north of England. ES wrote about him in 'Here is a Dickens of Our Time', *Sunday Referee* (24 March 1935).

9. From *Alice's Adventures in Wonderland*.
10. See Correspondence, *Scrutiny* 3: 3 (December 1934), pp. 283–90.
11. Walter James Turner, 1884–1946, Australian poet and critic. In 1925 he had published *Smaragda's Lover*, a clumsy satire on the Sitwells. His work had once been the occasion of a disagreement between the Sitwells and Siegfried Sassoon.
12. From 1933 to 1937, Bottrall taught at Raffles College, Singapore.
13. This correspondent has not been identified. The letter appears in *LHRH*, 4, p. 126, and it is probable that, as in other instances, OS changed the name of an actual person so that she would not be recognisable. It is possible the letter was addressed to Margaret Epstein (see Letter 138). The only person in ES's circle whose name resembled Almer was Mrs. Aylmer Vallance (see Letter 111), but there is not sufficient evidence to judge that either of these women was the recipient.

1936
1. 'Altarwise by owl-light in the half-way house' had appeared together with six sonnets as 'Poems for a Poem', *Life and Letters Today*, 13: 2 (December 1935).
2. See note 4 (1935).
3. Robert Herring, 1903–75, author. From 1935 he was the editor of *Life and Letters Today*.
4. SS was assembling his *Collected Poems*, which was published in November 1936 with an introductory essay by ES.
5. Mrs. Reek, a servant who is supposedly the source of information about the Wadia ('Waddyer') family. It is possible that her name should be transcribed as 'Reeb'.
6. John Beevers, a religious writer, and his wife, Margery.
7. Rubeigh James Minney, 1895–1979, journalist, writer and film producer. He was editor of the *Sunday Referee* from 1935 to 1939.
8. Lady Eleanor Smith, 1902–45, author. Her writings were often concerned with the ballet or with circuses. She was the elder sister of Lord Birkenhead. She was also a close friend of Frances Doble, the sister of Georgia Sitwell.
9. Francis Trajan Sacheverell Sitwell, second son of SS, had been born on 17 September 1935.
10. *Dance of the Quick and the Dead* was published on 1 October 1936.
11. Nancy R. (Ann) Pearn, d. 1950, literary agent. Having been employed by Curtis Brown, she became in July 1935 one of the founding partners of the firm Pearn, Pollinger and Higham.
12. Oliver St John Gogarty, 1878–1957, Irish poet, surgeon and politician.
13. Frederick Robert Higgins, 1896–1941, Irish poet, a close friend of W.B. Yeats.
14. Robert Bridges, 1844–1930, poet and critic. He was appointed Poet Laureate in 1913.
15. In October 1935, Graves had refused Yeats's request for permission to include

some of his work in *The Oxford Book of Modern Verse* (Oxford, 1936), and he refused, also, on behalf of his lover, Laura Riding, whose work Yeats was not seeking to include. Graves's rather grandiose letter to Yeats, for whom he felt personal antipathy, outlined the editorial concessions he and Riding had obtained from Michael Roberts in exchange for permission for him to include their work in his anthology (London, 1936). See Martin Seymour-Smith, *Robert Graves: His Life and Work* (London, 1982), pp. 250–1.

16. ES's only novel, *I Live Under a Black Sun*, published on 27 September 1937, is an allegory in which the life of Jonathan Swift is set within the First World War. The novel provides a disguised account of her relations with Tchelitchew.

17. See Herbert Read, review of *Dance of the Quick and the Dead*, *Spectator*, 20 November 1936 (supplement). Read expresses respect for the writing of SS, but accuses him of 'pre-Raphaelitism' and 'dilettantism'.

18. Robert Nichols's dialogue with Goethe, entitled 'Weimar and Wasteland', appeared in *Time and Tide* (12 December 1936). ES wrote two letters in response, which were published in the issues of 2 January and 23 January 1937.

19. G. M. Young, review of *The Oxford Book of Modern Verse*, ed. W. B. Yeats, *London Mercury*, 35 (December 1936). Young concludes the review praising SS at length: 'On this lugubrious note I must have ended, were it not for one poet of our days, in whose work I do see the promise of a modern verse which shall be verse as well as modern . . . he has written the *Canons of Giant Art*.'

1937

1. See Stephen Spender, 'Admirable Artificiality', review of *Collected Poems* by SS, *New Statesman* (6 February 1937). Spender criticises the unevenness of the poems and their remoteness from ordinary experience, but he also observes that the work can be 'ravishing'.

2. See Review of *Collected Poems* by SS, *TLS*, 23 January 1937. This reviewer complained of 'an excess of sensation over thought', but judged that 'no modern poet has created a richer world of his own out of objects of art'.

3. Magicians, illusionists and plate-spinners.

4. *Present Indicative* (London, 1937).

5. Elsa Maxwell, 1883–1963, flamboyant American hostess and gossip columnist.

6. Henry Moat, described at length in *LHRH*.

7. George Harrap, 1867–1938, publisher, managing director of George G. Harrap & Co.

8. William Webb, d. 1947, an employee of Pearn, Pollinger and Higham from 1935. He was responsible for payments to authors.

9. Humbert Wolfe, 1886–1940, poet, critic and civil servant.

10. John Middleton Murry, 1889–1957, poet, biographer and critic. He was married to Katherine Mansfield, and had been a close friend of D. H. Lawrence.

1938

1. Rootham continued in this desperate condition for almost six months, dying in October 1938.

1939

1. Raymond Marriott, a young journalist who had been employed on the *Era*.
2. Lord Dawson of Penn, 1st Viscount, 1864–1945, Physician-in-Ordinary to the Royal Family. He had earlier performed an appendectomy on SS.
3. Evelyn Wiel.
4. The lecture tour planned for 1940 did not take place. The Colston Leigh Bureau organized the Sitwells' lecture tours to America later on in the decade.
5. A. J. Cronin, 1896–1981, novelist and physician. His works often deal with Catholic concerns.
6. Arthur Quiller-Couch ('Q'), 1863–1944, critic, novelist and poet.
7. Wilfred Meynell, 1852–1948, and his wife, Alice Meynell, 1847–1922, had rescued the poet Francis Thompson, 1859–1907, from a life of addiction and destitution. Wilfred Meynell later edited his works.
8. See Eleanor Smith, *Life's a Circus* (London, 1939), pp. 238–9.
9. See letter 181.
10. E. M. Forster, *Alexandria: A History and Guide* (London, 1922; 2nd ed., 1938).
11. Christian Bérard, 1902–49, artist and theatrical designer, had once been a close associate of Tchelitchew, with whom he had exhibited in 1926.

1940

1. Philip Frere, solicitor. His firm, Frere, Cholmeley and Nicholson, had handled the Sitwell family's legal affairs since the nineteenth century.
2. Possibly one of the many refugees whom Bryher assisted in crossing the Swiss border.
3. Gerald Osborne Slade, 1891–1962, barrister. He was appointed to the King's Bench in 1948.
4. Sir Arthur Colefax (1866–1936), barrister. His wife Sybil, whom OS dubbed 'Old Coalbox', was a literary lion-hunter who had hosted poetry readings in London during the First World War.
5. Patrick Leigh Fermor, b. 1915, travel writer. He was for many years a close friend of SS and Georgia Sitwell.
6. Marsh had, for almost thirty years, served as private secretary to Churchill, whom OS had always regarded as a warmonger.
7. Eden Philpotts, 1862–1960, novelist, poet, and dramatist.
8. Francis Sitwell had been evacuated to Canada on 25 June 1940. He remained there with his mother's relatives until May 1945.

1941

1. Mrs. Addey, presumably a member of the Addey family of Doncaster, who had been friends of the Sitwells.

2. L. P. Hartley, 1895–1972, novelist.
3. Geoffrey Dorling Roberts, 1886–1967, barrister.
4. John Gideon Wilson, 1876–1963, chairman and managing director of John Edward Bumpus, bookseller.
5. Walpole and George Bernard Shaw had testified for the Sitwells in the *Reynolds News* libel case.
6. Leonard Woolf, 1880–1969, writer and publisher. Virginia Woolf had been his wife since 1912.
7. Virginia Woolf drowned herself on 31 March 1941.
8. Vanessa Bell, 1879–1961, painter. She was a sister of Virginia Woolf.
9. Robert Herring, editor of *Life and Letters* and a friend of Bryher's, had rented a house in Eckington near Renishaw.
10. A leading article in *The Times* on 25 March 1941 had argued that leadership in British society following the First World War had fallen to those who had evaded death in the trenches. It further argued that the 'highbrow' art of the 1920s showed contempt for the common man. The article claimed that since the distinction between combatant and civilian had broken down, the current war would not give rise to arts 'unintelligible outside a Bloomsbury drawing-room'. Stephen Spender was among those who wrote letters to the editor challenging this view. Bryher's letter was not published.
11. *Look! The Sun* was published on 29 September 1941.
12. The enclosed letter is from Dorothy Horsman, Director of Victor Gollancz, Ltd., outlining printers' delays with ES's anthology, *Look! The Sun*.
13. Henry Horatio Lovat Dickson, 1902–87, writer and publisher, Director of Macmillan and Co. from 1941 to 1964.
14. *Poems New and Old* was published by Faber on 31 October 1940. Macmillan published ES's next volume of poetry, *Street Songs*, on 20 January 1942.
15. ES had undertaken to write a novel entitled *Spring Torrents*, based on the life of Amalia (Amélie Albertine) Martin (née Sackville-West), the illegitimate daughter of Lionel Sackville-West, later Lord Sackville, the grandfather of Vita Sackville-West, who once referred to Amalia as 'my vinegary spinster aunt'.
16. *Primitive Scenes and Festivals* was published on 19 February 1942.
17. *Street Songs*.
18. Geoffrey Faber, 1889–1961, publisher, barrister and author.

1942
1. Henry Treece, 1912–66, poet of the 'New Apocalypse' movement. He co-edited the journal *Kingdom Come*.
2. Denton Maurice Welch, 1915–48, novelist, short story writer and artist. Having written to him praising his account of a meeting with Walter Sickert that had been published in *Horizon*, ES contributed a foreword to his book *Maiden Voyage*, which was released in May 1943.
3. A cat.

4. Olga Chandos Pole and her husband Bernard Woog, a banker, were later accused by ES, OS and SS of having embezzled Sir George's estate while he was in their care.

1943

1. Sydney Jeannetta Warner, 1890–1979, director of the Dominion and Foreign Relations Department of the British Red Cross.
2. William Arthur Henry Cavendish-Bentinck, Marquis of Titchfield, 1893–1977, MP for Newark Division, Notts. Later in 1943 he succeeded as 7th Duke of Portland.
3. Major General Sir Richard Howard-Vyse, 1883–1962, chairman of the Prisoner of War Department of the British Red Cross.
4. Sir Harold Satow, 1876–1969, diplomat.
5. ES echoes this sentence in the 1946 version of her poem 'Metamorphosis'.
6. Dorothy Wellesley.
7. The situation seems drawn from Firbank's *Vainglory* (London, 1915), but the novel contains no such song.
8. The poem had appeared as 'Bread of Angels', *TLS* (4 April 1942).
9. A visitor at Renishaw.
10. Alec Guinness, b. 1914, actor. He was knighted in 1959.
11. Bryher gave ES this house as a safe place for her to write while London was being bombed. She did not occupy it, but received rent from the Bath Corporation until she sold it in 1949. See Glendinning, pp. 225–6.
12. Hester Thrale Piozzi, 1740–1821, a close friend of Samuel Johnson.
13. The notes to 'Harvest' appear in *Collected Poems* (London, 1957), pp. 427–8.
14. Evelyn Waugh, 1903–66, novelist. His father, Arthur Waugh, died on 26 June 1943.
15. *Splendours and Miseries* was published on 17 December 1943.

1944

1. Cecil Maurice Bowra, 1898–1971, poet and critic. He was Warden of Wadham College, Oxford, 1938–70, and Professor of Poetry at Oxford, 1946–51. He was knighted in 1951.
2. See 'The War Poetry of Edith Sitwell', *A Celebration for Edith Sitwell*, ed. José Garcia Villa (Norfolk, Conn., 1948), pp. 20–32.
3. Bowra eventually wrote a book interpreting the poetry of ES. See *Edith Sitwell* (Paris, 1947).
4. Beryl de Zoete, 1879–1962, an authority on eastern dance and Oriental languages. She became a member of ES's circle through her relationship with Arthur Waley, who was her lover.
5. Lehmann edited *Demetrios Capetanakis: A Greek Poet in England* (London, 1947), which reprinted an essay by ES on Capetanakis that had first appeared in *New Writing and Daylight* (Autumn 1944).
6. *Planet and Glow-worm: A Book for the Sleepless* was published on 31 March 1944.

7. For ten years following the disappointing reception of his *Collected Poems*, SS wrote almost no poetry. He began writing poetry again *c.* 1946, but published little until after the death of ES, when he turned to privately printed pamphlets as an appropriate vehicle to bring his work to a select readership. He eventually published a selection, *An Indian Summer* (London, 1982), but most of the large and distinguished body of his later work remains uncollected.

8. Beryl de Zoete.

9. Robert Herring.

10. Natasha Spender (née Litvin), pianist. She was the second wife of Stephen Spender.

11. London was then subject to sudden attacks from V-1 and V-2 rockets.

12. 'The Song of the Cold'.

13. Norman Ault, 1880–1950, artist and author. He was one of the editors of the Twickenham edition of Alexander Pope. Before writing his book, *New Light on Pope* (London, 1949), Ault consulted with ES, who had written a biography of the poet.

14. John Gay, 1685–1732, poet closely associated with Pope and Swift.

15. Matthew Spender was born in March 1945.

16. The first collected English edition of the *Four Quartets* was published on 31 October 1944.

17. See Letter 150.

18. Rosamond Lehmann, 1901–90, novelist.

19. *Green Song* was published on 15 August 1944.

20. *Street Songs*.

1945

1. H.D.'s *Tribute to the Angels* was released on 11 April 1945.

2. Presumably Wyndham Lewis and Geoffrey Grigson.

3. 'The Age of the Dragon', *The Age of the Dragon: Poems 1930–1951* (London, 1951), pp. 119–21. The poem, in its published form, includes the lines ES objected to.

1946

1. In February 1946 Lehmann's partnership with Leonard Woolf at the Hogarth Press was dissolved. Lehmann then set up his own publishing firm, John Lehmann Limited.

2. See Stephen Spender, 'Poetry for Poetry's Sake and Poetry Beyond Poetry', *Horizon*, 13 (April 1946), pp. 221–38.

3. Elizabeth Kilham Roberts (née Bone), first wife of Denys Kilham Roberts, 1903–76, barrister and author who served for a time as secretary-general of the Society of Authors.

4. Hedli MacNeice (née Anderson), second wife of Louis MacNeice, 1907–63, poet and playwright.

5. Cecil Day Lewis, 1904–72, Irish poet, critic and mystery writer. He later served as Professor of Poetry at Oxford and Poet Laureate.

6. Hayward suffered from muscular dystrophy.
7. Ford edited the journal *View* from 1940 to 1947.
8. David Higham, 1895–1978, literary agent and author. In 1935, he became a founding partner in the firm of Pearn, Pollinger and Higham, now David Higham Associates, which represented ES, OS, and SS. His posthumous memoir, *Literary Gent* (London, 1978), describes his work on behalf of the Sitwells and other writers he represented.
9. Lorenz Oken, 1779–1855, German biologist and philosopher who attempted to establish a correspondence between mathematical structures and nature. ES uses ideas and images drawn from his writings in various poems, especially in 'The Shadow of Cain'.
10. Arthur Schopenhauer, 1788–1860, German philosopher.
11. Lady Cynthia Asquith, d. 1960, novelist, biographer and children's author. She had been secretary to J. M. Barrie from 1918 to 1937.
12. José Garcia Villa, b. 1914, Filipino poet and editor. He did not devote an issue of his periodical, *Viva*, to ES but edited the separately published *Celebration for Edith Sitwell* (London, 1948).
13. On 9 December 1946 Grigson had written to ES suggesting that they should stop commenting publicly on each other's work.

1947
1. Following the agreement they had made in December, Grigson contacted ES again asking for information on her work to be included in an article he was writing for the short-lived periodical *Pavilion*, edited by Myfanwy Piper, the wife of the artist John Piper, 1903–92, who was then illustrating *LHRH*.
2. George Barker, 1913–91, poet, essayist and novelist.
3. In 1947, OS obtained a bursary for Barker. He was also considered for the Society of Authors' 'Travelling Scholarship', which was financed anonymously by Bryher and distributed through a Management Committee dominated by ES. That award went to Dylan Thomas, whose drinking, ES believed, would be curbed by a time abroad. See John Lehmann, *A Nest of Tigers: The Sitwells in their Times* (Boston, 1968), p. 215.
4. Emmanuel ('Manny') Shinwell, later Lord Shinwell, 1884–1986, Labour politician. As Minister of Fuel and Power he nationalised the coal mines in 1946 and was blamed for the fuel crisis in February 1947.
5. *Penguin New Writing* was the subject of numerous disagreements, especially concerning frequency of publication, between the editor, Lehmann, and the publisher, Allen Lane. See John Lehmann, *In My Own Time* (Boston, 1969), pp. 446–50.
6. *The Shadow of Cain* was released in June 1947.
7. Bonamy Dobrée, 1891–1974, writer and academic. He and Read edited *The London Book of English Verse* (London, 1949; rev. ed. 1952).
8. Horace Gregory, 1898–1982, American poet and critic. His main discussion of Baroque elements in the poetry of ES is found in 'The "Vita Nuova" Art in the Recent Poetry of Edith Sitwell', *Poetry*, 66 (June 1945).

9. *Southern Baroque Art* (London, 1924) examines the Baroque in seventeenth- and eighteenth-century Italy and Spain. The success of this book was the high point of SS's early career.

10. ES was unable to find a British publisher for Ford's *Sleep in a Nest of Flames*. It was published in America in 1949 with a preface by ES.

11. Cyril Connolly, 1903–74, author and journalist. From 1939 to 1950 he edited the periodical *Horizon*.

12. Connolly wrote of the Sitwells in *Horizon*, 16 (July 1947), 'during the darkest years of the war they managed not only to produce their best work, to grow enormously in stature, but to find time to be of immense help to others . . . and so this number . . . is wholeheartedly dedicated to them.'

13. The poems would have been read on the 'Book of Verse' programme produced by John Arlott.

14. Gladys Young, 1887–1975, radio and television actress.

15. Catherine Lacey, 1904–79, stage actress.

16. James Laughlin, b. 1914, American poet and publisher. In 1936 he had founded the publishing firm New Directions.

17. The American edition of *Song of the Cold* was released in November 1948. *Green Song* had been released in America in December 1946.

18. Denis Glover, 1912–80, New Zealand writer and publisher. Lehmann had published two of Glover's pieces in *Penguin New Writing*.

19. SS's *Selected Poems*, containing only a few poems written after 1936, was published in October 1948.

20. Diana Reeve, an American poet related to the Roosevelt and Lowell families.

21. Peggy Guggenheim, 1898–1979, art collector. ES and OS were reading *Out of this Century: The Informal Memoirs of Peggy Guggenheim* (New York, 1946).

1948

1. Eliot had received the Order of Merit in the New Year's Honours list.

2. Northrop Frye, 1912–91, literary scholar and critical theorist, professor of English at the University of Toronto, and minister of the United Church of Canada. His best known work is *Fearful Symmetry: A Study of Blake* (Princeton, 1947).

3. A pamphlet published in 1947.

4. An esoteric work by Yeats published in 1925.

5. See Eliphas Lévi, *The History of Magic*, trans. A. E. White (London, 1913; rev. ed. 1964), p. 142.

6. ES abandoned this project.

7. 'Dirge for the New Sunrise' had appeared in *Orion*, IV (1947), pp. 26–7.

8. Lehmann's firm was reprinting ES's novel, which had first appeared in 1937.

9. Richard Church, 1893–1972, poet, novelist and editor. His *Collected Poems* were published in 1948.

10. John Hayward, ed., *Seventeenth Century Poetry: An Anthology* (London, 1948).

11. Jack Lindsay, 1900–90, Australian left-wing author and critic. He also published under the pseudonyms Peter Meadows and Richard Preston.

12. 'The Latest Poems of Edith Sitwell', *A Celebration for Edith Sitwell*, ed. José Garcia Villa (1948) pp. 44–53.

13. 'The Starfish Road, or, The Poet as Revolutionary', a study of modern poetry in relation to the Industrial Revolution, was never published.

14. Alice Pleydell-Bouverie (née Astor), 1910–56, the sister of New York magnate Vincent Astor.

15. David Pleydell-Bouverie, b. 1911, architect. The grandson of the 5th Earl of Radnor, he was Alice Astor's fourth husband.

16. Roy Fuller, 1912–91, poet, novelist and solicitor. Fuller discusses his reviews of Sitwell for *The Listener* in *The Strange and the Good* (London, 1989), pp. 345–7.

17. Julian Symons, b. 1912, poet and critic.

18. In his review of *New Writing and Daylight* (Autumn 1944) in the *Listener* (14 December 1944), p. 665, Fuller had criticised ES's article on Capetanakis for 'overstatement'.

19. Alex Comfort, b. 1920, poet and novelist, now best known as a writer on sexuality.

20. Lady Iris Mountbatten, b. 1920, daughter of the Sitwells' cousin, Irene, Marchioness of Carisbrooke. Mountbatten had moved to New York in 1946, where she worked as a model, song-writer, shop-assistant, and television presenter.

21. Theodore Spencer, 1902–49, poet, author and academic. He was a professor of English at Harvard. In 1948 he married Eloise Worcester.

22. Diana Reeve.

23. Ruth Ford, b. 1920, actress. In June 1949 she appeared as Ophelia in a Danish production of *Hamlet*. She also appeared in other plays later in the year.

1949

1. The grant was possibly from the Society of Authors' Travelling Fund.

2. T. S. Eliot.

3. Denton Welch died on 30 December 1948. He had been partially paralysed and in fragile health since 1935, when his bicycle was struck by a car.

4. Presumably Noël Coward; in 'Musical Events: Cheers for Sitwell-Walton', *New Yorker* (29 January 1949), he is compared unfavourably with the Sitwells.

5. Peter Watson, 1908–56, financial backer of *Horizon*. He had been a friend of Tchelitchew since the 1930s. ES usually referred to him as 'Soapy'.

6. Valentine Achland, 1906–63, poet. She was the companion of Sylvia Townsend Warner.

7. Mary McCarthy, 1912–89, novelist, essayist and memoirist. She had been married to Edmund Wilson from 1938 to 1946.

8. Goddard Lieberson, 1911–77, composer, businessman and author. He was then an executive with Columbia Records.

9. Sylvia (Sapira) Marlowe, 1908–81, American harpsichordist.

10. Zosia Kochanski, widow of the Polish violinist Paul Kochanski.

11. Mary (Minnie) Astor (née Cushing), b. 1906. She was married to Vincent Astor from 1940 to 1952. Shortly after their divorce, she married the painter James Fosburgh. Her sister, Betsey, whose husband Jock Whitney became American ambassador to the Court of St James, was also a close friend of ES.

12. Alice Pleydell-Bouverie.

13. Edgar Wind, 1900–71, German art historian. He was an interpreter and promoter of Tchelitchew's work.

14. For a description of ES's encounters with Cocteau and Igor Stravinsky, see Elborn, pp. 190–1.

15. Monroe Wheeler, 1900–88, publisher and book designer.

16. *The American Genius* was published on 26 July 1951.

17. Robert Lowell, 1917–1977, American poet. His second collection, *Lord Weary's Castle*, had been published in 1946.

18. Lincoln Kirstein, 1907–96, promoter of the arts, Director of the New York City Ballet. He was a close friend of Tchelitchew.

19. Leonor Fini, 1908–96, Italian painter and set designer associated with the surrealist movement. ES believed that the erotically inclined Fini had usurped her place in Tchelitchew's affections.

20. ES dedicated 'The Stone-Breakers: A Prison Song' to Kochanski.

21. Presumably, Dorothy Marshall, 1900–94, social and economic historian specialising in the eighteenth century.

22. ES's anthology *A Book of Flowers* was published on 5 September 1952.

23. The persons referred to in this letter are SS, Georgia Sitwell, OS and David Horner.

24. William Maxwell Aitken, 1st Baron Beaverbrook, 1879–1964, newspaper proprietor and politician.

25. Daniel George (pseudonym of D. G. Bunting), 1890–1967, author and critic.

26. William Plomer, 1903–73, South African poet, novelist and librettist.

27. Evelyn Wiel.

28. The writer Lillian Bowes-Lyon, whom Plomer had once wished to marry, died in July 1949 following a long series of amputations because of gangrene. Plomer had written extensively to ES describing his own feelings as Bowes-Lyon deteriorated. See Peter Alexander, *William Plomer: A Biography* (Oxford and New York, 1989), p. 254.

29. Presumably Geoffrey Gorer.

30. In 'Moo! Moo! Or Ye Olde New Awarenesse', review of *Poetry of the Present*, edited by Geoffrey Grigson, *Poetry Review* (August/September 1949), Campbell had attacked the poets of the 1930s and characterised Grigson's own relation to the muses as that of 'of a cuckold at his own key-hole'.

31. Cecil Day Lewis, one of the prominent poets of the 1930s.

32. Lehmann had a romantic connection with Day Lewis, which ended in 1950.
33. Alice Hunt, a wealthy widow who wished to marry OS. ES referred to her variously as 'La Chasseur', 'La Chasseuse' and 'La Chasseresse'.
34. Edwin Muir, 1887–1959, poet. ES's failure to consider Muir's work is hard to explain. He was, from the 1920s, one of the most consistently favourable and penetrating reviewers of the poetry of ES and SS. None the less, ES referred to Muir as 'Goosey-gander'.
35. Kathleen Raine, b 1908, poet and critic.

1950
1. Katherine Anne Porter, 1890–1980, American short story writer and novelist.
2. See 'Edith Sitwell's Steady Growth to Great Poetic Art', review of *Canticle of the Rose*, *New York Herald Tribune* (18 December 1949). A passage from the review is quoted in the introduction to this book; see p. vii above.
3. 'Pale Horse, Pale Rider', title-piece of a volume of Porter's stories published in 1939, describes a love affair set in the midst of an influenza epidemic during the First World War.
4. Edward Weeks, 1898–1989, editor of the *Atlantic Monthly* from 1938 to 1966. He wanted that organisation to become ES's American publisher, but her contractual obligations to Macmillan had not yet been released.
5. Armitage Watkins, ES's agent in America.
6. Astor's new-born niece.
7. The American edition of *A Poet's Notebook* was published on 26 October 1950.
8. C. W. (Billy) McCann, a former British intelligence officer and an executive with the Royal Dutch/Shell Group. He had lived in Moscow Road as a child and afterwards maintained a friendship with all the Sitwells.
9. 'You, The Young Rainbow'.
10. Moore wrote in the *Spectator* (24 March 1950) that no British poets excited Americans as Auden and Spender had in the 1930s. ES responded in the following issue (31 March) that 10,000 people had been turned away from a reading given by herself and OS during their recent tour. Letters on the subject appeared in five subsequent issues and in the *Daily Telegraph*. The letter which ES asked Lehmann to write was eventually provided by Beryl de Zoete.
11. Edmund Wilson, *Axel's Castle: A Study in the Imaginative Literature of 1870–1930* (London, 1931), a highly regarded literary history.
12. Maurice Bowra, *The Heritage of Symbolism* (London, 1943).
13. *Edith Sitwell* (Paris, 1947).
14. Carson McCullers, 1917–67, American novelist.

1951
1. Negotiations had just been completed for the sale of screen-rights to McCullers's novel *The Member of the Wedding*. See Virginia Spencer Carr,

The Lonely Hunter: A Biography of Carson McCullers (New York, 1975), esp. pp. 364–9.

2. Tennessee Williams (Thomas Lanier), 1911–83, American playwright, poet and novelist. Williams held the party on 31 October 1950 at which ES met McCullers.

3. McCullers had recently been advised that a partial paralysis from which she suffered was irreversible.

4. Presumably David Bulwer Lutyens, poet. He was related to the architect Sir Edwin Lutyens, who had undertaken various projects for Sir George Sitwell in the early years of the century.

5. Richard Austin ('Rab') Butler, later Baron Butler of Saffron Walden, 1902–82, prominent Conservative politician. See Letter 181.

6. Ann Lindsay, b. 1914?, Jack Lindsay's wife.

7. Elizabeth Winifred ('Jane') Clark (née Martin), d. 1976, wife of the art historian Kenneth Clark, later Lord Clark.

8. Josephine Crane (née Boardman), 1873–1972, widow of Senator W. Murray Crane. She was co-founder of the Museum of Modern Art. Her 'literary evenings' attracted many prominent writers.

1952

1. Marianne Moore, 1887–1972, American poet.

2. Presumably Moore's *Collected Poems* (London and New York, 1951), which won a Pulitzer Prize.

3. F. R. Leavis's essay, 'The Progress of Poesy', in *The Common Pursuit* (London, 1952), pp. 240–7, attacked, in scatter-gun fashion, various targets, including Auden, ES and OS. Cyril Connolly, John Hayward and Maurice Bowra were criticised as well for having praised the Sitwells.

4. In 'Mr. Eliot, Mr Wyndham Lewis, and Lawrence', *ibid.*, pp. 240–7, Leavis observes that there is too much 'formal religion' in Eliot's *After Strange Gods*.

5. John Heath-Stubbs, b. 1918, poet. He was then editing with David Wright *The Faber Book of Twentieth-Century Verse* (London, 1953). ES eventually permitted the inclusion of six of her poems in the anthology.

6. A new edition of this anthology appeared in 1951, supplemented with poems chosen by Anne Ridler, who took over the project upon the death of Michael Roberts.

7. *Selected Poems* had been published by Penguin on 21 March 1952.

8. Hal Lydiard Wilson, a physician, and Boodie, his wife. He had apparently been known to ES as early as 1931, when she recommended a Dr. L. Wilson to Siegfried Sassoon. *English Eccentrics* (1933) is dedicated to the Wilsons.

1953

1. Aldous Huxley, 1894–1963, novelist, short-story writer and poet, and his wife, Maria (née Nys), d. 1955, had been close friends of ES in the early 1920s.

2. Edwin Powell Hubble, 1889–1953, American astronomer. From 1919 to 1953 he was a member of the staff of the Mount Wilson and Palomar observatories.

3. The lines are taken from Coleridge's 'To a Young Lady On her Recovering from a Fever'.

4. *Gardeners and Astronomers* did not appear until 20 November 1953.

5. Lehmann had been editor of *New Soundings* (BBC *Third Programme*) through 1952. He was replaced in 1953 with the poet John Wain (1925–94).

6. Lehmann's spaniel, Carlotta. OS and David Horner had observed that when opera records were played the dog 'sang' in tune.

7. Honor Tracy, b. 1913, novelist and journalist, had reviewed Rosamond Lehmann's novel *The Echoing Grove* in the *New Statesman* (11 April 1953). She claimed that readers 'may feel as if they were making their way through a sea of toasted marshmallow.'

8. Benjamin Ifor Evans, 1899–1982, critic. In a review of *Collected Stories* in *Truth* (April 10, 1953), he had accused OS of heartlessness, 'especially where old ladies are concerned'.

9. This journal appears not to have existed.

10. Humphrey Searle, 1915–82, composer, and his first wife, Gillen, d. 1957. Searle, who had composed a setting for *Gold Coast Customs* and later wrote scores for 'The Shadow of Cain' and 'The Canticle of the Rose', had asked Lehmann and other friends of ES to provide financial guarantees for a concert of his music. These transactions resulted in ES absorbing the losses relating to the concert.

11. Dylan Thomas died in New York of alcohol poisoning on 9 November 1953.

12. Natasha Wilson (?), a member of Astor's circle.

13. Peter Ustinov, b. 1921, actor, dramatist and writer. He was knighted in 1990. His play, *No Sign of the Dove*, was thought to be a satire on ES and OS.

1954

1. The review appeared in the issue of 22 January 1954. Correspondence pertaining to the review continued to be published until the issue of 26 February 1954.

2. Kingsley Amis, 1922–95, novelist and poet. He was knighted in 1990. His now best-known work, *Lucky Jim*, had been published in January 1954.

3. ES had been the subject of a mildly satiric portrait as 'Queen Edith' in the *New Statesman* (23 January 1954). The next three issues printed letters to the editor approving or disapproving of the piece. ES's response was published on 13 February.

4. Kingsley Martin, 1897–1969, editor of the *New Statesman* from 1932 to 1962.

5. Alan Pryce-Jones, b. 1908, critic and journalist. He was editor of the *TLS* from 1948 to 1959.

6. Presumably Percy Wyndham Lewis.
7. Joining in the controversy over the Hartley review, Amis had contributed a whimsical letter to the *Spectator* (29 January 1954) under the name of 'Little Mr. Tomkins'. He claimed 'the sap of a tree is more like Double Diamond than peridots and beryls . . .' ES, in a letter (published 19 February) observed that she and the reviewer, Hartley, could agree on the merits of *Lucky Jim*. In the following issue (26 February), Amis confessed to having written the Tomkins letter and thanked ES for her praise.
8. ES presumably means Garson Kanin and Ruth Gordon, who often worked on the scripts of Cukor's movies. The script of *A Star is Born* was actually written by Moss Hart.
9. In The Queen's Birthday Honours of 1954, ES had been made a Dame Commander of the Order of the British Empire.
10. Maurice Carpenter, b. 1911, poet and critic. ES had become godmother to his son John Sebastian in 1947.
11. Alberto de Lacerda, Portuguese poet and translator. ES appears to have been trying to find work for him as a reviewer.
12. British farmers were artificially spreading myxomatosis, 'the rabbit plague', to eliminate the animal from their fields. The practice was the cause of widespread controversy in 1954.
13. A volume of Cocteau's poems published in 1954.
14. Spender dedicated to ES the 'Later Poems' section of his *Collected Poems 1928–53*.
15. In late 1954, both Stephen and Natasha Spender toured Australia, he lecturing and she playing concertos with The Sydney Symphony Orchestra and conducting recitals.
16. Probably Robert Richman, who ran a series of readings at the Corcoran Gallery in Washington, D.C.
17. Tchelitchew's exhibition at the Hanover Gallery opened on 26 October.

1955
1. Daniel Maloney, an Irish painter who had served in the United States Navy. For an account of his relations with OS, see Pearson, pp. 418–19.
2. Possibly Anthony Powell, b. 1905, novelist. He had been a friend of the Sitwells since the 1920s, when he had been an editor at Duckworth's.
3. George Copeland, *c.* 1882–1971, American pianist who was partly responsible for introducing Debussy's works to American audiences.
4. Quentin Stevenson, a young Catholic poet whom ES adopted as a protégé and whose work she praised highly. He subsequently became an actor and playwright.
5. Harold Rupert Leofric George Alexander, 1st Earl Alexander of Tunis, 1891–1969, field-marshal. He had actually studied at Harrow and then served in the First World War with the Irish Guards.
6. Frederick Ashton, 1904–88, choreographer. He was knighted in 1962.
7. August Roble, described by the *New York Times* (21 February 1955) as a 'squint-eyed killer', had been shot to death in a siege of his apartment, fol-

lowing a running gun battle with police and a three-day man-hunt.

8. Benjamin Britten, later Baron Britten of Aldeburgh, 1913–76, composer. His 'Canticle III: Still Falls the Rain', op. 55 (1954) had its first public performances in early 1955.

9. Peter Pears, 1910–86, tenor. Pears, who was Britten's companion from 1937, was the first performer of many of the composer's works, including 'Canticle III'. He was knighted in 1978.

10. Martin D'Arcy, SJ, *The Nature of Belief* (London, 1931), p. 261.

11. *Ibid.*, p. 34.

12. Hon. Edward Sackville-West, later 5th Baron Sackville, 1901–65, author, translator and broadcaster. He had been received into the Roman Catholic Church in 1949.

1956

1. John Malcolm Brinnin, b. 1916, New York poet and a friend of both ES and Thomas. ES was concerned that his book, *Dylan Thomas in America: An Intimate Journal* (Boston, 1955), would vulgarise Thomas's memory.

2. See ES, 'The Young Dylan Thomas', preface to J. Alexander Rolph, *Dylan Thomas: A Bibliography* (London and New York, 1956), pp. xiii–xv.

3. *The Queens and the Hive* was published in August 1962.

4. Arthur Waley was appointed Companion of Honour in the New Year's Honours of 1956.

5. *Collected Poems* had been published in America in December 1954. The English edition was published in July 1957.

6. ES believed that David Horner's conduct was worsening OS's illness.

7. During service in the Second World War, Campbell had injured a hip already weakened by complications of sciatica.

8. In early 1955, an uninsured labourer employed by the Campbells in Portugal had fallen from a ladder and become disabled. According to Portuguese law, the Campbells were financially responsible for him for the rest of his life.

9. 'Vision of Our Lady Over Toledo', *Nine*, 4: 2 (April 1956), pp. 11–14. Dedicated to ES, this is the Finale to Book V of the revised 'Flowering Rifle', Campbell's long poem on the Spanish Civil War.

10. J. B. Priestley, 1894–1984, novelist, playwright and essayist. His 'Thoughts on Dr. Leavis' appeared in the *New Statesman* (10 November 1956).

11. Spender had invited ES to join a group of western writers to go to Hungary and show solidarity with the uprising against the Soviets.

12. Jean LeRoy, literary agent. She represented ES in her dealings with English magazines.

13. Alberto de Lacerda.

14. Miss Fraser, ES's secretary until August 1957. In other accounts of this accident, ES refers to OS's secretary, Lorna Andrade, and not to Fraser.

15. See ES, preface, Sydney Goodsir Smith, *So Late into the Night: Fifty Lyrics 1944–1948* (London, 1952), pp. 7–8.

16. See ES, preface, Charles Causley, *Union Street* (London, 1957), pp. 8–10.

17. The Oxford University Press had accepted a volume of Stevenson's poems for publication.
18. Tefcros Anthias (pseudonym of Andreas Paulou), Cypriot poet. He had, evidently, offered to send ES *The Song of Earth*, trans. P. L. Nicolaides (London, 1952).
19. Lindsay's habit of sending books and manuscripts to ES, whose eyes were failing, led, several years later, to an outburst from ES that ended their friendship.

1957
1. Ebenezer Jones, 1820–60, English poet whose verses contain an element of social protest.
2. David Horner was again keeping the company of the painter Brian Connelly.
3. Roy Campbell died in a car crash in Portugal on 23 April 1957.
4. Edmund Campion, *c*. 1540–81, English Jesuit martyr.
5. Review of *Collected Poems* by ES, *Sunday Times* (28 July 1957). For a quotation from this review, see above, p. vii.
6. See A. Alvarez, review of *Collected Poems* by ES, *Observer* (28 July 1957).
7. Pavel Tchelitchew died in Rome on 31 July 1957.
8. Laurence Whistler, b. 1912, engraver on glass.

1958
1. Anthony Cronin, b. 1926, Irish poet, novelist and biographer. *Poems*, his first collection of verse, was published in 1957.
2. David Wright, 1920–94, poet, journalist and editor. His *Monologue of a Deaf Man* was published in 1958.
3. The *TLS* had run a short but highly favourable notice of *Collected Poems* on 20 September 1957. Although the book was described as 'outstanding', ES believed that Pryce-Jones, the editor, had subtly belittled her work by not running a longer and more prominent piece.
4. Hon. Michael Astor, 1916–80, soldier and patron of the arts. From 1942 to 1961 he was married to Barbara Astor (née McNeill).
5. ES had been asked questions by school-children in a television programme from Manchester. One boy asked whether she thought her poetry would last, and in her answer ES used the word 'impertinent'. This led to a discussion in various newspapers about whether she should apologise to the children.
6. See 'Better Bye and Bye', review of *The Shaping Spirit* by A. Alvarez, *Sunday Times* (29 June 1958).
7. Presumably 'The Poet's Vision', *Saturday Evening Post* (15 November 1958).
8. 'At the Cross-Roads' appeared in the *London Magazine*, 6: 3 (March 1959).
9. Ted Hughes, b. 1930, poet. He was appointed Poet Laureate in 1984. His poems 'Groom's Dream' and 'Constancy' appeared in the *London*

Magazine, 5: 8 (August 1958). Lehmann reports that among poets who achieved prominence in the 1950s, ES admired only Hughes and Causley. See *Nest of Tigers*, p. 262.

10. Elizabeth Jennings, b. 1926, poet, translator and anthologist.

11. Alfred Austin, 1835–1913, Poet Laureate, whose verses are judged to have been thoroughly incompetent.

12. *The Atlantic Book of British and American Poetry* was published on 12 November 1958.

13. The Beat Poets, Allen Ginsberg, b. 1926, and Gregory Corso, b. 1930, had visited ES at the Sesame Club. ES, who particularly admired Ginsberg's *Howl*, was one of the few leading British writers then in sympathy with these poets. It was incorrectly reported that they had smoked marijuana in her presence.

1959

1. Princess Margaret, the Scottish-born wife of Prince Ludwig of Hesse and the Rhine (1908–68). Prince Ludwig, a patron of the arts, was a friend and supporter of Benjamin Britten.

2. Graham Greene, 1903–91, novelist. ES had been acquainted with Greene since the early 1920s.

3. Pamela Hansford Johnson (Lady Snow), 1912–81, novelist. She was married to Charles Percy Snow, 1905–80, physicist and author, who had been created Baron Snow of the City of Leicester in 1954.

4. Moore had lectured on Sitwell at the Johns Hopkins Poetry Festival in November 1958. The lecture was published as 'Dame Edith Sitwell' in *Four Poets on Poetry*, ed. Don Allen Cameron (Baltimore, 1959). A quotation from the lecture appears on p. vii above.

5. Marianne Moore, 'There is a War that Never Ends', review of *Parts of a World* and *Notes Toward a Supreme Fiction* by Wallace Stevens, *Kenyon Review* (winter 1943); reprinted in *Predilections* (New York, 1955).

6. ES read 'Praise We Great Men' at the Royal Festival Hall on 10 June 1959. A long-delayed setting for this poem was the last important musical project of Britten's life, but he died before completing it.

7. Dame Rebecca West (Cicely Fairfield), 1892–1983, author.

8. Apparently Alice Hunt.

9. 'The Door-Knocker: Further Notes on my Father', *Atlantic Monthly*, 200: 5 (November 1957).

10. A reading by ES at the Edinburgh Festival had been disrupted by complaints from the audience that she was inaudible; however, she bluntly refused to speak louder. The sound was eventually improved by a replacement microphone. The incident was widely publicised.

11. Gordon Watson, an Australian pianist, had been introduced to ES by the composer Humphrey Searle. He was a close friend of Elizabeth Salter.

12. William Burke and William Hare, mass murderers. They smothered at least 15 people in the 1820s and sold their bodies to a surgeon.

1960

1. Robinson Jeffers.
2. *Bid me to Live (A Madrigal)* (New York, 1960), a novel written by H.D. in 1939 but set in the time of the First World War.
3. *Swinburne: A Selection* was published on 16 September 1960.
4. Presumably, 'His Blood Colours my Cheek', which had appeared in *The Month* (May 1958).
5. 'A Man in his Senses', *TLS* (4 November 1960).

1961

1. Christopher Isherwood, 1904–86, novelist and playwright.
2. Henry Cecil Leon, 1902–76, judge and author. Some of his writings were published under the pseudonyms Henry Cecil and Clifford Maxwell. He and his wife Barbara (née Blackmore) became close friends of ES in the last years of her life.
3. H.D. died on 27 September 1961 in Switzerland.
4. In the spring of 1961, H.D. had been evicted from a sanatorium near Zurich which had been her home since 1946.

1962

1. On 28 February 1962 F. R. Leavis had given a lecture, which was published in the *Spectator* (9 March 1962), attacking C. P. Snow's ideas on the separation of literary and scientific cultures. Leavis criticised the 'Two Cultures' argument as vulgar, and characterised Snow himself: 'Not only is he not a genius; he is intellectually as undistinguished as it is possible to be.' This provoked widespread debate, in which ES took some part on the side of Snow. In April, Snow's retina was discovered to be detached. He first gave an address as Rector of St Andrew's University, wearing an eye-patch and a large handkerchief to keep it in place, before undergoing surgery.
2. *The Outcasts*, a collection of poems, was published on 30 August 1962.
3. *The Queens and the Hive*.
4. ES referred to her seventy-fifth birthday (7 September 1962) as her centenary.
5. Sir John Gielgud, b. 1904, actor.
6. Sister Doris Farquhar, an Irish nurse who cared for ES through the last years of her life.
7. John Woolf, violinist. He was director of the Park Lane Group.
8. Bertrand Russell, 3rd Earl Russell, 1872–1970, philosopher and social reformer.
9. On 22 October 1962 ES was the subject of Eamonn Andrews's *This is Your Life*. Beaton appeared on the programme and recounted the history of his friendship with ES.
10. ES maintained that Beaton had once interrupted a wild outburst by Tchelitchew, in which he pushed ES in a chair across his studio, hurled canvases, and threatened to kill her. Beaton's arrival diverted the painter's attention to tea. See *TCO*, pp. 163–4.

11. From Algernon Swinburne's 'The Garden of Proserpine'.
12. Hedda Hopper, with whom ES had conducted a long-standing feud.
13. Britten's 'War Requiem', incorporating poetry by Wilfred Owen, had been composed for the reconsecration of Coventry Cathedral in 1962.

1963

1. Charles Musk, a director of Coutts Bank. He and his wife Kathleen had become friends of ES.
2. Malcolm Williamson, b. 1931, composer. He had been commissioned by Britten to write an opera for the Aldeburgh Festival based on *English Eccentrics*.
3. See 'Ugh', review of *The Naked Lunch*, *The Soft Machine*, *The Ticket That Exploded* and *Dead Fingers Talk* by William Burroughs, *TLS* (14 November 1963). The reviewer compares reading Burroughs to 'wading upstream in the drains of a big city'.

1964

1. In June 1964, ES moved to a house in Keats Grove, Hampstead, which she named after Bryher, as a sign of gratitude for her many years of friendship and support.
2. *In General and Particular*, a volume of Bowra's essays and lectures published in 1964.
3. Turner's book is a history of cruelty to animals.
4. A reference to Dr Czarto, a Hungarian.
5. ES died of a cerebral haemorrhage at St Thomas's Hospital on 9 December 1964.

SELECT BIBLIOGRAPHY

⁓

BOOKS WRITTEN BY EDITH SITWELL

The Mother (Oxford: Blackwell, 1915)
Twentieth Century Harlequinade (with OS; Oxford: Blackwell, 1916)
Clowns' Houses (Oxford: Blackwell, 1918)
Children's Tales from the Russian Ballet (London: Leonard Parsons, 1920)
Façade (London: Favil Press, 1922)
Bucolic Comedies (London: Duckworth, 1923)
The Sleeping Beauty (London: Duckworth, 1924; New York: Alfred A. Knopf, 1924)
Troy Park (London: Duckworth, 1925; New York: Alfred A. Knopf, 1925)
Poor Young People (with OS and SS; London: Fleuron, 1925)
Poetry and Criticism (London: Hogarth Press, 1925; New York: Henry Holt, 1925)
Augustan Books of Modern Poetry (London: Ernest Benn, 1926)
Elegy on Dead Fashion (London: Duckworth, 1926)
Poem for a Christmas Card (London: Fleuron, 1926)
Rustic Elegies (London: Duckworth, 1927; New York: Alfred A. Knopf, 1927)
Popular Song (London: Faber and Gwyer, 1928)
Five Poems (London: Duckworth, 1928)
Gold Coast Customs (London: Duckworth, 1929; Boston and New York: Houghton Mifflin, 1929)
Alexander Pope (London: Faber & Faber, 1930; New York: Cosmopolitan Book Corporation, 1930)
Collected Poems (London: Duckworth, 1930; Boston: Houghton Mifflin, 1930)
In Spring (London: p.p., 1931)
Jane Barston (London: Faber & Faber, 1931)
Epithalamium (London: Duckworth, 1931)
Bath (London: Faber & Faber, 1932)
The English Eccentrics (London: Faber & Faber, 1933; Boston and New York: Houghton Mifflin, 1933. Revised edition published New York: Vanguard Press, 1957; London: Dennis Dobson, 1958)
Five Variations on a Theme (London: Duckworth, 1933)
Aspects of Modern Poetry (London: Duckworth, 1934)

Victoria of England (London: Faber & Faber, 1936; Boston: Houghton Mifflin, 1936)

Selected Poems (London: Duckworth, 1936; Boston: Houghton Mifflin, 1937)

I Live Under a Black Sun (London: Gollancz, 1937; Garden City, N.Y.: Doubleday, 1938)

Trio (with OS and SS; London: Macmillan, 1938)

Poems New and Old (London: Faber & Faber, 1940)

Street Songs (London: Macmillan, 1942)

English Women (London: Collins, 1942)

A Poet's Notebook (London: Macmillan, 1943)

Green Song (London: Macmillan, 1944; New York: Vanguard Press, 1946)

The Weeping Babe (London: Schott, 1945)

The Song of the Cold (London: Macmillan, 1945; New York: Vanguard Press, 1948)

Fanfare for Elizabeth (New York: Macmillan, 1946; London: Macmillan, 1946)

The Shadow of Cain (London: John Lehmann, 1947)

A Notebook on William Shakespeare (London: Macmillan, 1948)

The Canticle of the Rose (London: Macmillan, 1948; New York: Vanguard Press, 1949)

Poor Men's Music (London: Fore Publications, 1950; Denver: Alan Swallow, 1950)

Façade and Other Poems (London: Duckworth, 1950)

A Poet's Notebook (Boston: Little, Brown, 1950)

Selected Poems (Harmondsworth: Penguin, 1952)

Gardeners and Astronomers (London: Macmillan, 1953; New York: Vanguard Press, 1953)

Collected Poems (New York: Vanguard Press, 1954; London: Macmillan, 1957)

The Pocket Poets: Edith Sitwell (London: Vista Books, 1960)

The Outcasts (London: Macmillan, 1962. Issued in America as *Music and Ceremonies*; New York: Vanguard Press, 1962)

The Queens and the Hive (London: Macmillan, 1962; Boston: Little, Brown, 1962)

Taken Care Of (London: Hutchinson, 1965; New York: Atheneum, 1965)

Selected Poems (ed. John Lehmann; London: Macmillan, 1965)

Selected Letters (ed. John Lehmann and Derek Parker; London: Macmillan, 1970)

The Early Unpublished Poems of Edith Sitwell (ed. Gerald W. Morton and Karen P. Helgeson; New York: Peter Lang, 1994)

WORKS EDITED BY EDITH SITWELL

Wheels: First Cycle (Oxford: Blackwell, 1916)

Wheels: Second Cycle (Oxford: Blackwell, 1917)

New Paths 1917–18 (London: C. W. Beaumont, 1918)

Wheels: Third Cycle (Oxford: Blackwell, 1919)

Wheels: Fourth Cycle (Oxford: Blackwell, 1919)

Wheels: Fifth Cycle (London: Leonard Parsons, 1920)

Wheels: Sixth Cycle (London: C. W. Daniel, 1921)

The Pleasures of Poetry (3 vols. London: Duckworth, 1930–32; New York: W. W. Norton, 1934)

Edith Sitwell's Anthology (London: Gollancz, 1940)

Look! The Sun (London: Gollancz, 1941)

Planet and Glow-worm (London: Macmillan, 1944)

A Book of the Winter (London: Macmillan, 1950; New York: Vanguard Press, 1951)

The American Genius (London: John Lehmann, 1951)

A Book of Flowers (London: Macmillan, 1952)

The Atlantic Book of British and American Poetry (Boston: Little, Brown, 1958; London: Gollancz, 1959)

Swinburne: A Selection (London: Weidenfeld & Nicolson, 1960; New York: Harcourt Brace, 1960)

INDEX

9 781844 085088